THE FAMILY
AND SOCIAL CHANGE

A STUDY OF FAMILY AND KINSHIP
IN A SOUTH WALES TOWN

by

COLIN ROSSER

and

CHRISTOPHER HARRIS

With a Foreword by

R. HUWS JONES
Director, National Institute for Social Work Training

LONDON
ROUTLEDGE & KEGAN PAUL
NEW YORK: THE HUMANITIES PRESS

First published in 1965
by Routledge and Kegan Paul Ltd.
Broadway House, 68–74 Carter Lane
London, E.C.4

Printed in Great Britain
by Cox and Wyman, Ltd.
London, Fakenham and Reading

FOREWORD

IN 1957 the Institute of Community Studies published their first findings about kinship and family in east London; these challenged accepted views about the family in urban society: they disturbed current sociological cliches and they questioned basic assumptions in contemporary social policy. Michael Young and his colleagues generalized no wider than their evidence and this, for the most part, came from Bethnal Green, one square mile of east London, somewhat special in character and in recent history. No wonder that many asked: this may be true of Bethnal Green, but is it true, for instance, of Rotherham or West Kensington?

There was obvious need for a study, parallel to the ones in Bethnal Green, in a different part of the country. After reviewing other possibilities, Swansea seemed both convenient and almost dauntingly different. Bethnal Green is remarkably homogeneous in social composition; Swansea is not. The population of Bethnal Green is small and compact; the population of Swansea is three time larger and occupies an area thirty times as great. The districts differ widely in occupation, history, tradition, topography, climate and to some extent in language.

The idea of a comparative study was first discussed with Mr. Lewis Waddilove, Director of the Joseph Rowntree Memorial Trust, who fostered the proposal; Sir John Fulton, then Principal of the University College of Swansea, was also encouraging. In consequence, and with characteristically liberal support from the Joseph Rowntree Memorial Trust, the study started in 1959 when two fortunate research appointments were made, Dr. Colin Rosser, a social anthropologist, South Welsh in origin but Nepalese and Indian in his professional speciality, and Mr. Chris Harris, a sociologist with particular interest in social conditions and the social services in Britain. As they acknowledge, these researchers have had ready help from a host of people and institutions and particularly from the citizens of Swansea who met them more than half-way.

The results of some four years' work are presented in this volume, much of which is written with racy directness, recording a multitude of revealing incidents and phrases as well as conclusions that are thoughtful, bracing and sometimes startling. Those who know 'this sea town', as Dylan Thomas called it, will recognize the authentic accent, idiom and irony and may agree that its voice and spirit have rarely been recorded so faithfully.

In those aspects we were most concerned to compare, it is tempting to say that family and kinship in Swansea are just like Bethnal Green —only more so. The frequency of face to face contacts, for all the difference in the areas, is almost identical. The 'mam', typically the wife's mother, holds the family together, 'the dominant centre of the web of kinship'. There is a powerful tendency for a married daughter to live with her mother or to get a home close to her. As in east London the pattern of reciprocal support reveals itself in myriad ways, mostly similar to those in Bethnal Green. The Swansea findings prompt the authors to ask whether, in these respects, we have a regularity of behaviour which is a common feature of urban kinship in Britain. But the differences between Swansea and Bethnal Green are also important and sometimes piquant.

It was intended from the first that the survey should pay particular attention to old people and their social situation. This part of the study started with the rare advantage of a random sample of old people and it included a medical survey of those old people who were willing to co-operate.[1] Old people, like other people, illustrate the resilience of family support, which moves in with impressive reliability when care is necessary, declining when it is not; this appears as *the* function of the extended family: mutual comfort and support, effective and astonishingly steady, reflecting the strong emotional ties between members.

The authors have devised some bold methods of analysis in their various 'jigging and tooling' exercises; they have been equally courageous in advancing novel hypotheses which they know—and hope—will be fiercely debated.

It is my privilege to thank them, and those who made their work possible, for this valuable addition to the small stock of significant local studies of family and community life in contemporary Britain.

R. HUWS JONES

National Institute for Social Work Training,
December, 1965.

---

[1] The results of the medical survey have not been published but may be found in 'The Health of Swansea's Old Folk', Dr. P. L. Parsons; M. D. Thesis, Cardiff 1962. This work can be consulted through the Library of the Welsh School of Medicine, Cardiff.

CONTENTS

Contents

TABLES

ix

Tables

MAPS

ACKNOWLEDGEMENTS

WE have been helped in many ways by many people. Foremost we must thank the Trustees of the Joseph Rowntree Memorial Trust for the generous grant which made this research possible; and in particular Mr Lloyd Owen one of the Trustees, and the Director, Mr Lewis Waddilove, who both took a personal and continued interest in the progress of the work. They were both members of the Advisory Committee which guided our efforts, and with the other members— Professor Roger Wilson, Dr Michael Young, Mr Robin Huws Jones, and latterly Mr Andrew Lochhead—made many helpful suggestions for which we are grateful. The study was originally conceived in the fertile, energetic mind of Mr Robin Huws Jones, then Director of the Social Science Courses at the University College of Swansea, and now Director of the National Institute for the Training of Social Workers. We are indebted to him for his constant encouragement and for the Foreword which he has kindly contributed at our request. He has thus seen the study through from beginning to end (so far at least as this publication is concerned).

We thank also Dr Michael Young, and Mr Peter Willmott of the Institute of Community Studies for much painstaking help with the statistical techniques of research, following their own experience in Bethnal Green and Woodford—and for challenging discussion in the early stages. We have differed, sharply at times, in our views but fully recognize our debt to them both for their lively books on the family and for their stimulating and sympathetic criticism of our approach. We learnt much from them regarding the study of our own contemporary society.

The list of people who have helped us in Swansea is vast, and included not only the two thousand or so persons who kindly and patiently answered our questions, but also many colleagues at the University College, especially those in the Department of Social Administration and in particular Mr Bob Leaper who read the text and gave us the advantage of his criticism; the twenty-one interviewers who worked for us for varying periods, many officials at the Guild-hall, and a host of friendly Church and Chapel Ministers, doctors and social workers, newspaper editors, secretaries of clubs, and others. We cannot name them all but thank them now. This book, with the other publications which will ensue from this research, is theirs as much as ours—though no doubt any one of them would have written it very differently! We are only too aware that we have produced what must in their view seem an inadequate picture of this most friendly and hospitable town which is so clearly a good place to live in.

We owe special and particular thanks to the following: Robert John Williams, a remarkably educated—though he left school at fourteen—octogenarian of Morriston who told us of the exclusive world of the chapels and of Welsh culture of which he is such a splendid representative; the General Manager, Mr J. B. Southall, of the B.P. Oil Refinery at near-by Llandarcy for permitting us un-restricted use of the Powers-Samas punching and sorting installation there, and in particular to Mr Ray Tarrant, then in charge of this installation, for invaluable technical advice and for many long hours of his time in the evenings and at week-ends; Cam Gears Ltd., Resolven, for allowing us to use their punch card installation for a short period; Mrs J. Davies who produced the maps, Mr Arthur Marsh and Mr Donald Rosser who tidied the diagrams, Miss D. Leyland and Mrs E. Gratrix who did the typing so efficiently and helped with a great deal of the analysis of the replies to the various questionnaires.

Our debt to our teachers and colleagues in the field of Social Anthropology and Sociology is of course profound. It will be well recognized, if poorly discharged, in the following pages.

The publication of this report was delayed, and the latter half written under some difficulty, because one of us had to return to India to become immersed in sociological problems a good deal more familiar to him than those described in this book. In these unexpected circumstances, we must thank the Trustees of the Joseph Rowntree Memorial Trust for their tolerance in allowing us to extend the time-table originally agreed.

I

FAMILIES IN A MOBILE SOCIETY

THIS book is the outcome of about two years of investigation in
Swansea by the small social research section which we formed within
the Social Science Department at the University College of Swansea.
During these two years we collected information in varying degrees of
detail about some two thousand families of all shapes and sizes
within this large County Borough splendidly sited on the coast of the
Bristol Channel in South-west Wales. Our main purpose was to
examine the immediate kin relationships of these randomly selected
families, to determine the patterns and regularities in this field of
social behaviour, and to consider their social importance.

In many respects, a major Welsh town seems an excellent place for
a study of this kind. Anyone with any experience of Welsh households
must be well aware of the passionate interest that families, and
particularly the women, have in details of marriages and relationships. And this interest, and indeed delight in remembering and
disentangling the facts and nuances of relationship, is by no means
confined to themselves and their own kin. We heard someone say
that 'Swansea is really a string of villages tied together with gossip',
and a good deal of this gossip is concerned with kinship information.
This interest is extended with zest to cover the family networks of
neighbours, friends, acquaintances, new arrivals in the district, and
any public personality living or dead, particularly royalty, film stars,
and local characters who for one reason or another 'get into the
papers'—or into the gossip streams. Both Rosser and Harris (or
Harries, with the same pronunciation) are local Welsh surnames,
particularly the former. It was a normal experience to be asked at
once such questions as 'Are you one of the Llansamlet Rossers?' or
'My grandmother on my mother's side was a Harris. She came from
Fforestfach. Have you got any relatives from around there?', and so
on. We also became quickly familiar with the inevitable lengthy

1

digressions, often highly entertaining and tremendously difficult to recapture later, as each new name cropped up in the conversation while the individual concerned was 'fixed' in terms of what the people present could glean from the recesses of their formidable memories about marriages and relationships, and they decided whether this person was related to them or not. This was particularly true with older informants. The torrent of information and anecdote, rich with comment on the social history of Swansea since the turn of the century, which we came to expect from our informants concerning kinship relationships is ample testimony to the continuing vitality of these wider familial ties in an urban environment—and not least to the kindness with which we were received in the homes we visited.

Our two thousand families covered the full range of the social and cultural complexity of this Welsh regional metropolis—the whole social spectrum from 'the professions' to unskilled manual occupations, from affluence to poverty, from high Anglican to Pentecostal (with a proportion of Roman Catholics, and a handful of 'others'), from zealous to nominal Christians, from the fluent bilinguals in Welsh and English to the monoglot English. House-owners and tenants, the long-marrieds and the newly-weds, large composite three- or four-generation households and households of persons living alone, families with numerous relatives living close at hand and families whose kin were thin on the ground and widely scattered beyond the borders of the Borough, families long resident in the same neighbourhood and those recently arrived in Swansea from the outside world. Consider the following list of occupations of some of the persons we interviewed (or of the husbands in the case of the wives we saw) taken at random from our survey sample—in this case, we give just the occupations of the first and last, taking the next where necessary to avoid duplication, on our lists for each of the fifteen Wards of the Borough:

> Wireman, Dustman, Baker, Chapel Minister, Steel Erector, Furnace Hand, Fireman, Chartered Accountant, Park Groundsman, Motor Mechanic, Farmer, Dock Labourer, Watchmaker, Florist, Insurance Agent, Centrifugal Pump Driver, Ticket Collector, Coach Painter, Schoolteacher, Merchant Seaman, Driving Examiner, Collier, Tobacconist, Plasterer, Doctor, Banana Ripener, Postman, Solicitor, Steelworker, Shop Assistant, Boxer.

A very mixed bag of ordinary families living in all kinds of housing from the large, detached and very desirable residences with spacious tree-lined lawns in the drives and avenues and crescents of Swansea's residential west to the two-up, two-down, step-in-off-the-street cottages in the rows and terraces and places of the industrial east. Even this brief list of breadwinners reflects the social diversity of the population typical of any large urban centre, and about which we will have a good deal to say in later chapters. But these families have at least one thing in common in that they were all resident in the County Borough of Swansea at the time of our study.

It hardly needs to be emphasized, however, that in vital respects, and certainly from its own point of view, each of these families is essentially singular and unique, an individual permutation of distinct human personalities (not including 'the old dog and two budgies' which one old lady insisted on having entered as members of her household), biological incidents and accidents, and social and historical events. It would take a lengthy volume, and the pen and insight of the novelist, to bring any one of them to life in the pages of a book —a sort of 'Jones Saga' or 'The Chronicles of the Llewellyns of Balaclava Row' or, in the modern idiom, an endless serial such as 'The Arthurs', or 'Mrs Davies's Diary', or 'Corporation Street'. There can be little doubt, moreover, that it is a good deal easier to create a fictional family than to record an actual family in all its intimate and often boring and repetitive detail. Any attempt to do the latter comes at once up against what Margery Spring Rice has called the 'Monroe doctrine for the family' which safeguards its essential privacy.

> There is hardly a garden in England which is not surrounded by a wall or hedge or railing, the obscurer the better. . . . There is hardly a window in any family house which is not curtained effectively to obscure the view of the inquisitive passer-by. And as a consequence there is no play or book or film so successful as that which deals with the intimacies of family life which, except in *one* family,—his or her own—are a complete mystery to the ordinary man or woman![1]

There is a certain exaggeration here, of course, but there can be no question that this characteristic and 'natural' concern with privacy is one of the major difficulties the sociologist encounters in the normal fieldwork situation. He succeeds to the extent that he is the embodiment of tact and discretion, that his assurances of confidence are accepted,[2] and in the end to the degree that his informants

---

[1] Margery Spring Rice, *Working-Class Wives*, 1939, p. 16.

[2] The cases cited in this book all refer of course to actual individuals and families but we have, following the assurances given, altered names and various details (such as inventing street names or moving street names from one part of the Borough to another) to ensure privacy and to prevent identification.

understand his fundamental approach—which is the search for general patterns in the apparently unique behaviour of individuals. Having said this, we must also add that we were continually surprised by, and indeed grateful for, the freedom and frankness with which the individuals we met in Swansea were willing to talk about themselves and their families in response to the curiosity of the social investigator.

Indeed our inquiry in Swansea began in just this way with an encounter in Morriston in the north-east of the Borough which occurred during our preliminary reconnaissances. We can conveniently begin our discussion with this selected case-history, chosen not because it is 'typical' but because it raises in concrete form some of the themes and questions about family and kinship behaviour that we will be concerned with in this study. Here then is an example of the raw material of our research taken from the compact and cohesive community of Morriston, a stronghold of traditional Welsh working-class 'chapel' culture, characteristic of the Swansea Valley which extends south into the Borough at this point.

THE HUGHES FAMILY, MORRISTON: PAST AND PRESENT

We met Mr Griffith Hughes by chance in the bar of the Red Lion in Morriston. This was a week or so after our arrival in Swansea to begin the study of family relationships here described. There were a dozen or so in the bar, some in working clothes having apparently just come off shift in the steelworks near-by in this old industrial community, all men, mainly Welsh-speaking and all well known to each other judging by the flow of conversation along the bar and across the crib tables. A typical working-class 'local' in a close-knit community, and one in which a stranger stood out at once. We joined an elderly pair on a bench in the corner and we were soon drawn, not of course unwillingly, into a probing conversation to establish who we were and what we were doing in Morriston.

Half an hour later, Griffith Hughes and his friend, Evan Rees, had us 'placed'. They had discovered that we had just arrived in Swansea from London to join the University College, that one of us had been born and bred locally in South Wales and that the other was a Londoner on his first visit to the Principality, that we were married ('A Welsh girl? Good lad!') and single, that one of us had rented a house on the other side of Morriston ('Ah, so it's you who's moved into Dyffryn Villa in Morfydd Street. Morgan the Milk was telling me that strangers had moved in. Yes, mun, I know the old place well —it's had some ups and downs I can tell you . . . I remember when I was a boy . . .'), and that we were working on a survey of family life

4

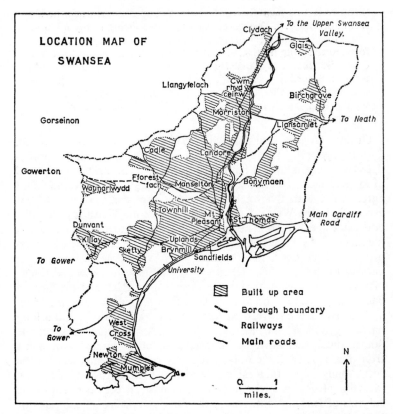

LOCATION MAP OF
SWANSEA

in Swansea ('Come to the right place you have then—Morriston's a
real tin of worms, at least it used to be years ago. They say "Kick one
in Morriston and they all limp"'.)

For our part we had learnt that they were both retired tin-workers,
boyhood friends and life-long workmates at the Dyffryn Works—
'We did close on a hundred years there between us. How's that for
some man-hours now!' Griffith Hughes—white haired, chapel suit,
stiff white collar, gold watch-chain, laced black boots, cloth cap,
pipe—was 74 and Evan Rees 69. They were both Morriston born.
'I've lived in only three streets since I was born,' said Mr. Rees, 'and
next time I move it will be feet first.' 'I can beat you there, Evan—
I've been fifty-seven years in the same house.' Both were regulars at
the pub—and at the chapel round the corner. 'If you want to have a
chat about Morriston, come round to the house any afternoon. I'll
soon put you on the right road,' said Mr Hughes.

5

'I can go farther back than Evan here. But don't come when there's racing on the T.V. I've never been to horse-racing in my life and never took any interest in it somehow, but funny thing I do look forward to seeing it on T.V. in the afternoon. Hardly ever watch it otherwise, except of course for the Internationals. And don't come up on a Saturday because it's bedlam then what with our grand-children all over the place. The children come over most Saturdays regular bringing their kids along to see the Mam. Visiting time at the zoo, I call it.'

Griffith Hughes and his wife Rachel live in Chemical Road, Cwmrhydyceirw, an extension of Morriston on the north. 'Cwmrhy-dyceirw—do you know what that means now? The Valley of the Ford of the Red Deer. Doesn't seem much like it if you look around you, I agree, what with the works and everything—but it sounds lovely, especially in the Welsh. I like the warmth of the Welsh myself—pity you can't speak it, but never mind.' Their small terraced house is identical with all the rest in the street—door opening off the pave-ment, well-scrubbed step, a dark passage leading past the silent parlour to the cheerful kitchen with its shining, black-leaded range, blazing coal fire ('I always say the missus ought to have been a furnace hand') and gleaming brass hobstand: then a small scullery with sink and gas stove, a backyard with coal-house and lavatory, and a long narrow garden leading to the back lane. An essentially respectable home, snug, well-worn but immaculate, old-fashioned but, apart from the T.V. in the corner, culturally consistent and secure. We spent many hours there at the fireside with Mr Hughes discussing everything from his boyhood in Morriston before the Boer War to the subjects of current controversy, the Sunday opening of the pubs or the present composition of the Welsh Rugby Team. Here are some brief extracts concerning the family relationships of this elderly couple. They need of course to be read with a strong Welsh accent:

'Three sons and two daughters—all married and only one without children so far. Good children they are too, they'd carry you any-where. Do anything for the Mam and me, I will say that. Mind you, I don't say we don't have our squabbles from time to time, but nothing serious. The boys come to see their mother when the fit takes them, sometimes three days in a row, and the girls are always in and out. Sometimes every day, but never less than once a week. They all live somewhere in Swansea—the oldest boy in the next street here, and one of the daughters about ten minutes' walk away.

'Now let me see now—Dai's the oldest, he's 42, then comes Ifor, Gwyn, Peggy, and Mair—she's 34. Dai's a foreman bricklayer over at the Margam Steelworks, Ifor's an electrician in the

Aluminium Works in St Thomas, Gwyn's a schoolmaster in the
new Grammar School at Penlan—he's the bright one of the family
—B.A. at the University down there. He was an officer in the
Army during the war. Peggy was a typist in an office in Morriston
before she was married. Her husband's the manager of a shoe shop
down in the centre of Swansea. And Mair is a State-Registered
Nurse. She only got married last year—Haydn, that's her husband,
he's a clerk in the Guildhall, Rates Department I think it is. His
family are very well off—they run a garage selling cars and vans
over in Fforestfach.

'Who did the others marry? Well now there's change from the
old days, I can tell you. I was only thinking the other day that I
was one of sixteen in a Sunday School class at the Chapel. I think
there was about ten of them married girls from in the Chapel. I
did myself. I could name them—Tommy Jenkins, Tom Jenkins,
Jenkin Thomas, Roger Thomas, Johnnie Williams, Ben Jones,
William Lewis, Rees Williams—they all married girls in the
Chapel. Nowadays you just don't know who they are going to
hitch up with.

'Our Dai married in the Chapel—Lilian, I've known her family
all my life. Her father, Charlie Edwards, is a deacon in the Chapel
with my brother, Sam. Ifor now—his wife, Glenys, comes from
St Thomas down in the Docks. They live down there now with her
mother—she's an invalid more or less, had a stroke three or four
years ago, and Glenys is looking after her. And then there's Gwyn
he was teaching up in London for about ten years. His wife,
Margaret, is a London girl. We used to go up there regularly every
year like the clock for a week's holiday, and they came back here
in the summer to us. Gwyn and Margaret and the three children
moved down here about two year ago when her mother died.
They'd always wanted to get back down to Wales, at least Gwyn,
did, and he managed to get in to the new Grammar School here.
They've just bought a new house over in Sketty—we rounded up
the whole family practically to go over and help him get the
garden started. Margaret is just like a daughter to the Mam, always
gets her to go with her when she's buying something new for the
house. But then she's lost her own mother, and hasn't anyone of
her own down here. Peggy married a boy from Neath—I think
they met originally at a dance in Swansea. They started off with us
here while they waited for a house. The twins were born here, and
my wife brought them up while Peggy went on working. Then they
got a Corporation house up on the Clase Estate, just about ten
minutes away. And as I say, Mair's husband came from Fforestfach. She's living with his mother for the time being while they
get a house. She tells me they are thinking of buying one of the new
bungalows they're putting up in Cockett, just near to Fforestfach
there. Mair is a Sister in Morriston Hospital just behind us here,

7

and calls in to see the Mam every day on her way to and from work, except for her day off.

'It's just a matter of luck who they marry, and how long they stay put in one place. Mine are all round about in Swansea for the time being, but Gwyn has only just come back this way and Mair and Haydn are talking about emigrating to Australia. Haydn seems quite set on it and it's upsetting the Mam no end. It's got that she can't bring herself to speak to him. Children seem so restless somehow nowadays, always on the move. It didn't use to be like this—the wife and I have been here in Morriston all our lives, and the same with my family and hers—well Morriston and Landore anyway. People didn't use to wander off, you know. Now you know how it is, the boys usually follow their wives off to wherever they come from. A girl doesn't want to be far from her mother, not unless the husband has a very good job of course and they have to follow the job. We must count ourselves lucky I suppose that ours are all near enough to call in regularly. But I don't know how long it's going to stay like that.

'Grandchildren? Well, yes, there of course is the real tie. You like to have your grandchildren around you and see them grow up and get on. Nine we've got so far. Dai's two girls are always in and out from the next street—the youngest, Susan, does practically all Mam's shopping for us. Dai's eldest boy, David, has just gone to London University, London School of Economics. He's nineteen now and a red-hot Socialist: it's funny to hear him talk, remembering the old days in Morriston here. It's hard for him even to imagine what it was like. But good luck to him—he's going a long way, that boy. And Peggy of course is always over with the twins. Gwyn and Margaret bring their three over most Saturdays in the car—and I go over there about once a week to baby-sit for them while they go out for the evening. Gwyn comes over to fetch me in the car. We hardly see anything of Ifor's boy Des. He's eighteen now and motor-bike mad, so I've heard. He's the only child and they can't seem to do much with him, in and out of jobs, can't stick to anything. Last I heard he was going in for a motor mechanic, but I haven't seen anything of him for well over a year now. Mind you, Ifor's a funny boy too. Very quick-tempered is our Ifor. He doesn't seem to have much to do with the rest of the family, hasn't been up here to see the Mam for months, though I have heard that he's been up to Morriston several times drinking with his mates. The Mam would be very upset if she heard that, and him not even calling to see her—she's upset about him enough already. She knows Glenys is tied with her mother but there's no reason why Ifor couldn't come up to see her.

'My own family? Well, my father was a Carmarthen man, came from a farming family in a village near Llandeilo. His parents died there, never left the land. My father could hardly speak a word of English when he first came into Swansea round about 1870. I still have cousins back in Carmarthen but I haven't been there since I was a boy—to funerals and that sort of thing with my father. We seem to be cut off completely from them nowadays. It's a different world altogether back there in Carmarthen. My father started off on the roads, digging ditches and road-making. He landed up in Llangyfelach, up on the hill there above Morriston. That's where he met my mother, she came from a big Welsh family near the Church—all colliers they were. Then my father got a job in the new steelworks that had just opened in Landore. There were new works opening all over the Swansea Valley at that time, and there must have been thousands like my father coming in from all over the place to get work. They lived in Landore for a time, and so did two of his brothers and their families. Then the Dad moved up here to Morriston when he got into the Beaufort Works. Some of the Mam's family were in the Beaufort too, and in Dyffryn and the Upper Forest and Worcester Steel and Tinplate. They lived in Tir-Penry Street there—that's where we were all born —until we moved over here to this house in 1902, just after the war.

'Five brothers I had and three sisters—I was the last but one, and we were all in steel and tinplate here in Morriston, sisters' husbands and all. And we all lived close, and went to the same Chapel—Seion Baptist near the Cross there. There are only three of us still alive now—Sam, who's just turned 80—he still lives in the old house in Tir-Penry Street, a widower now with one of his married girls looking after him. He's well away, and very active—deacon in the Chapel, a big noise in the Old Comrades' Club in Morriston, doesn't touch the beer—used to, mind you, but not since he was made a Chapel Elder. I see him every Sunday at the Chapel, and when I go, which isn't very often, at the Old People's Club on a Friday night. My youngest sister, Sarah, is a widow. She lives on her own in Cwmbath Road (about five minutes away). Suffers badly with asthma but manages to get about a bit. Don't see much of her except when I meet her in the street. She and the wife took different sides a few years ago over a squabble in the Chapel, something to do with cutting the bread for a Whitsun Tea, and they've gone their own ways ever since. Her children are scattered all over the place, one of them's up in London I think, but she still has a daughter a few doors away to give her a hand when she needs it. But very independent is our Sarah.

'We buried my father soon after we came to this house. £130 I think it was that we paid for it, a tremendous sum for a working man in those days, but the Mam was determined to have her own house and with all the boys working she just managed it. But we no sooner got there than the Dad went down with his chest. He must have been off work for well over a year before he passed on in 1906—only 59 he was, and of course he didn't get a penny while he was off. The Mam was left then, of course, and all the boys were married except for me and Sarah the youngest. I was earning good money in the Works so I kept the home going. I was 23 when the Dad was buried. I didn't get married until I was 32. Rachel moved in here with us, and it worked out all right so Sarah was able to marry her boy and move out. The wife looked after my mother like a daughter until she passed on in 1926, the year of the strike—she was 77 then and nearly paralysed for many years after a stroke. Rachel had to do everything for her, and bring up a family herself. She's earned her place in Heaven I can tell you.

'Just two sisters and a brother my wife had. Both the sisters still alive and both widows for many years. The brother was killed out in France in 1915, soon after the war started. He was one of the first to go. Their mother died when they were all young. I think Rachel—who's in the middle—was about six at the time. Their father, he was a collier, married again and moved up to Clydach (two miles away) where his second wife came from. The wife's step-mother is still alive, gone 90 I believe, but her father has gone these many years and the wife is out of touch with the step-mother and with sons and daughters up there, half-brothers and sisters I suppose they are. They have always kept completely separate somehow. The wife and her sisters were brought up by an aunt, a sister of the mother, here in Morriston. She's gone now of course and her husband, Uncle Tom. He was in the tinplate at the beginning but he had a bad accident at the Works, no "compo" then, of course, and he had to give up altogether. He became the Chapel caretaker then, and was right up till he died.

'The wife's sisters had just one son each and both the boys have done very well for themselves—both got letters after their names, one's an engineer up in Birmingham with a chemical firm, and the other's a schoolmaster in Essex, near London there. They always call in to see us when they are down this way. The wife's two sisters linked up after the second husband died, cancer it was, and they are now in the youngest sister's house up there on Pentrepoeth Road, just up on the hill there. My wife goes up once a week regular, and of course they sit together in the Chapel—they all go to the Sisterhood, and very strong it is, on a Tuesday night.

'Yes that was the thing about us—we all lived close, perhaps too close I sometimes say when you think of the animosities and so on that cropped up now and then. But in those days you just had to help one another—there was no Welfare State then. When all the men were out at the Works there'd be no money coming in from anywhere. That's when you needed your family and good neighbours. We were all in the same boat together. All the men of the family, uncles and cousins and all, would go picking coal together up on the tips, or hunting rabbits and getting blackberries up on the mountain. If you went to the Parish you had to go through that damned Means Test. I remember them coming to my house and making me sell my piano before I could get a penny from them. And when you did work you had to pay back to the Parish every shilling they'd given you. The lists were sent to the Masters at the Works and they knocked it off each week. Everybody's business was public knowledge and everybody hated it. Shameful it was. We just had to stick together and fight, and help each other out if we could. There are hundreds of stories I could tell you of my own family let alone all the others round here. We knew our duty and we did it. You could count on your relatives—you didn't have to ask. But then we were all in the Chapel, you see—not necessarily the same one, but we all went *somewhere*—and Welsh was the language for everybody. You *knew* everybody. It's different altogether nowadays. Mind you, I'm not saying anything against the children—good children they are too. But it's a different atmosphere altogether now.

'Take ours now. Only Dai and Lilian and their children belong to the Chapel and still keep up the Welsh. It's a treat to hear the children talking. But Gwyn's wife, Margaret, comes from London, she's English through and through and doesn't know a word of Welsh—she's Church of England and the three children have followed her. They couldn't speak a word of Welsh when they came here two years ago—the Mam blames Gwyn for that—they learnt a bit of Welsh now in the school down here. It really hurts the Mam to have to talk to them in English when they come over here on a Saturday. It's the same with the others—I don't think Ifor and Glenys go anywhere at all now, and she certainly hasn't any Welsh. Peggy is still a member at the Chapel but Dick isn't—though, fair play, he does speak a bit of Welsh. And as for Mair's husband, Haydn—a lovely boy, mind you—well his family are more English than Welsh even though they have been all their lives in Swansea—they come from over Newport way originally I think. It's the same with other families around here . . . No wonder the Chapels are half empty. Take Tabernacle up there in Woodfield Street. Largest Chapel in Wales it is, room for 1,500 at least. It was common to see people standing in the aisles on a Sunday because they couldn't get a seat. Now they've only got about 300 members all told, I think it is, and the Chapel isn't a quarter full. And half of those that go can't speak Welsh properly.

'Mind you, the Chapels here in Morriston are still pretty strong but it's the women that keep them going—Sisterhoods mainly. It's not so much a *family* affair as it used to be. I was still going to Sunday School regular right up to the time I was married—I went occasionally afterwards but not so regular—to the men's class that is—there was a separate class for the women. Some women now, they were great on the Bible. Whole families,

11

all together—that's how it was. And what families they were—real characters, mun. There was Joseph Powell's family, Aubrey Rees's family, Price Price's family, John Jenkins's family (though I didn't think much of him), William Owen's family, Thomas Jenkins's family—I could name them all—and all linked in the Chapel. If one of the boys was absent from the family pew—well, the Minister would be round the house on the Monday morning to know why. Then there were the choirs, and Whitsun Teas and Outings, and the annual eisteddfod, and the Prayer Meetings, and the Band of Hope. It still goes on, mind you—but it's not the same as it was. It's not so clannish as it used to be. And there's not so much *respect* as there used to be—in the Chapel or in the family.

'A different atmosphere altogether, I tell you. The children are all over the place now, and you never know where they are going next. The Mam holds them altogether somehow, but I don't know what it's going to be like when she's gone. You want to see them get on, of course—the Mam is always saying that she doesn't want to stand in their way—but we've lost something from the old days, I can tell you. They don't *cling* as we did. Once they're married, they're off. I sometimes wonder just what we've gained, taking things all round. Not that I want to put the clock back—I remember it all too well for that—the misery and the pinching and the poverty. And when I say "poverty" I don't just mean poor. I mean *real* poverty—and no messing about. I don't want to go back to that, but I do think we've lost a lot too when I look at the way the children seem to live, hardly ever seeing one another except when they meet here at their Mam's and hardly knowing who their neighbour is. Tell you the truth I wouldn't like to live with any one of them. We lived all together in the old days in Morriston—now they all seem to live in worlds of their own.'

It is difficult to capture the exact phrases of this elderly Welshman describing his kinship universe and his cultural roots. The inflexions of the voice, the continuous gestures and changing facial expressions, the moments of passionate emphasis and declamation, the careful pauses for the right word, the acting out of incidents recollected with intensity rather than in tranquillity: these form a descant of meaning interwoven with the spoken words. They can be remembered, not reproduced. And we give of course only a fragment, edited from various conversations and stripped, reluctantly, of the welter of details about his own relatives, of asides and digressions on the kinship and cultural behaviour of neighbouring families in Morriston, of staccato and irrelevant reminiscences, and repetitive comment. Like most Welshmen, never using one word where ten will do, Mr Hughes will go on talking all day, and with enthusiasm, once he has properly warmed up and so long as he has a provocative and sympathetic audience—to the pleasure, one must add, of the anthropologist, who is essentially a professional *listener*.

Though necessarily brief, these are representative extracts giving the heart of the matter, if little of its form. The words of an old man, thoroughly embedded in his own traditional Welsh working-class culture built around the chapel and the neighbourhood. They set the scene for the inquiry into family relationships which we conducted in Swansea. Directly expressed, and covertly in the undertones, are some of the main themes of our discussion. We are confronted at once with a wide variety of kinship situations, even in this single case, with a number of different forms of household composition, and with a number of separate households linked together through kinship ties in a complex web of contact and of reciprocal help and support in need or crisis, particularly as regards the care of the elderly. Clearly in the lives of Mr Hughes's own generation, if apparently to a lesser degree in the lives of the younger, these ties of kinship had, and still have a basic significance—both emotional and practical. 'We knew our duty, and we did it', he says; 'you could count on your relatives, and you didn't have to ask.'

We do not propose to analyse this case at length—this would require a good deal more evidence of actual kinship behaviour than is given in these extracts—but simply to note the lines of inquiry that it indicates. The basic themes emerge with considerable clarity, and require little emphasis on our part. We can summarize them briefly now since they will, with others not directly involved here, form the subject matter of later chapters in this study.

Foremost as regards the structure of relationships, we can see at once the dominant position of the mother at the centre of this web of kinship—the pivot around which the extended family revolves, managing the family affairs, criticizing or approving behaviour, exacting affection and loyalty and demanding family cohesion, 'holding the family together', with her home serving as a nodal point and junction-box for relationships. The mother is the key figure in Mr Hughes's account: 'the Mam', a term used significantly by him both for his own mother and for his wife and the mother of his children. The Mam is dead, long live the Mam. Further, throughout the whole kinship network which emerges in outline form at least in these verbatim extracts, the stress appears to be on the links through women and on the roles of women. Women appear to have specific roles in maintaining contact with kin, in determining residence after marriage ('the boys usually follow the girls off to where they come from. A girl doesn't want to be far from her mother . . .'), in providing the actual domestic care for an aged or infirm parent or parent-in-law, in

13

bringing up the children of a deceased relative, or in helping to look after a daughter's children whilst she continues working. The relationships through women seem, to an important extent, to form the basic pattern into which the men concerned are fitted, called upon to provide economic support and authority as husbands and fathers; loyalty and affection, and help where needed as sons and grandfathers. And it is mainly through these men, as workers and providers, that the world of the family is linked externally to the total social and economic system.

But if the evidence of this single case suggests a stress on the roles of women within the wider family, it equally indicates that the kinship structure is essentially bilateral, equal prominence being given so far as recognition of relationship is concerned to both sides of the family, to relations through the father equally with those through the mother. This of course is a fact well known from common experience, though its precise significance and implications in terms of actual behaviour remains to be examined. Looking downwards from the point of view of this elderly informant, no distinction is made between a son's children and a daughter's children: they are both equally grandchildren, and are treated alike. Within this bilateral framework, the emphasis on the grandparent – grandchild relationship ('Well there of course is the real tie. You like to have your grandchildren about you and see them grow up and get on') is particularly important. In terms both of mutual affection and of frequent interaction, if not of co-residence, the effective family covers three generations, with links extending laterally from this basic grouping to collateral relatives— uncles, aunts, cousins, nieces and nephews, and so forth. In relation to the kinship structure in this particular case, this central three-generation descent group stands out quite clearly as being of major importance.

Prominent among the other basic themes running through this case are the importance of physical proximity in the effective maintenance of relationship, the effect of the geographical range of marriage on the family cohesion, the use of alternative kin and in-laws to fill up gaps in close relationships caused by death or distance, and the considerable degree of individual variation and personal choice, depending among other things on personality factors, in the relations between kin.

It is, however, when we come to consider Mr Hughes's remarks and attitudes about the effects of social change on family behaviour that we begin to grasp the significance of what he is saying. And here he is quite specific. The social and cultural change of the last seventy years or so, spanning his life experience from his childhood in late nineteenth-century Morriston to his retirement in the middle of the twentieth century, has clearly had profound and pervasive effects on family behaviour. He is talking of two radically different worlds, and describing in effect two distinct patterns of family behaviour. The first is that of his earlier years and is based fundamentally on the close clustering of kin in a limited locality, with a high degree of social and economic homogeneity and with close and complex ties of mutual co-operation between kin and neighbours. The second is that of his present family, a modified version of the former, continuing much of the older patterns but altogether looser in structure with a much wider scatter of relatives, and markedly heterogeneous in occupation and income and in social and cultural values. The contrast is striking and he is well aware of it. His use of words is significant: *formerly* they 'stuck together', 'didn't wander off', 'used to cling', 'had to help one another', 'all lived close', 'were all in the same boat'; *nowadays* 'the Mam holds them together somehow', 'all over the place now', 'always on the move', 'once they're married, they're off', 'don't cling like we did', 'seem to live in worlds of their own'. There is over half a century of rapid social and cultural change between these two sets of statements.

It is necessary to be precise about what is being said here. It is of fundamental importance in understanding contemporary family and kinship behaviour (and we will be discussing it in detail later). The contrast is not between the extended family on the one hand and on the isolated elementary family on the other. It is essentially between two types of extended family. If we examine the contemporary situation in Mr Hughes's family, we can see in the frequencies of contact he mentions and in the many instances he gives, casually but significantly, of interdependence and mutual support between his household and those of his married children, that the wider or extended family in his case is still very much alive. But its structural form is basically different from that of the earlier family system which he describes with a good deal of pride and nostalgia.

Formerly there was a local cluster of kin linked by continuous interaction and multiple social relationships from home to home, in the chapel, at work, in common adversity, at play. In a handful of sentences in these extracts from our long conversations with him on this subject, Mr Hughes gives a vivid picture of the Morriston of his youth—a picture of what might be termed, in contrast to the Mobile Society, the Cohesive Society: small in scale, limited and narrow in its social horizons, homogeneous in social composition, familiar and familistic, with a strong community consciousness generated by common residence and common necessity. It was clearly much more than a community of residence. A community also of work with the men engaged in identical or similar occupations, a community of worship in the chapels, a community of basic cultural uniformities in language, in housing and material possessions, and in moral values. An exaggerated picture perhaps, seen in retrospect over half a century, with the conflicts and internal tensions omitted (though there are fleeting references to these also in the remarks of this informant: animosities and conflicts are of course also social relationships) but with a sure basis in reality.

The Morriston which emerges in these statements—and it certainly still survives in physical form if less in social 'atmosphere'—is in many respects typical of the traditional working-class communities described, sensitively or sentimentally, in numerous works of fiction, in the accounts of sociologists and social historians, and in social commentaries of one form or another. Its cultural virtues have been the subject of frequent comment, pervaded often by a picturesque and nostalgic romanticism born of contemporary dissatisfactions. These strengths appear, however, to be basically related to its economic homogeneities and congested housing and to its common privations and adversities. Richard Hoggart is well aware of this basic fact—as indeed is Mr Hughes—when he writes,[3] describing 'the strengths which working-class life can especially show':

> I mean, for example, the capacity for self-respect and self-sacrifice under adverse conditions, the sense of common need which makes individualistic ambition often suspect, the respect for the interdependence of different generations within a family and a neighbourhood.

The family structure which matches this traditional close-knit community structure is indicated with clarity in the case we have been describing. It is based on the close cohabitation of a multiplicity of kin and in-laws, covering the successive contemporaneous generations, and bound together in a network of many-sided social contacts, with each family home a centre of intersecting relationships. The cohesive family in the cohesive society—'and what families they were!' says Mr Hughes, reciting the names, familiar in his mouth as household words. 'We *knew* everybody,' he says proudly, and with the sadness of an epitaph marking the passing of a distinctive way of life.

'It's a different atmosphere altogether now, I tell you'. The tide of social change has been running strongly against this community

[3] Richard Hoggart, 'Challenge of the Working-Class Scholar', *The Observer*, 11 February, 1962.

cohesion and this particular family structure, and undermining its foundations. Our informant's married children, though all at present in Swansea, are scattered over a number of different and separate neighbourhoods, are sharply differentiated by education and income and occupation, occupy different positions in terms of class and status, have married wives or husbands from a variety of social and economic backgrounds, have reacted variously to the retention or abandonment of former cultural traditions particularly as regards Welsh-speaking and chapel-going. They have little in common, besides their elderly parents. In the place of the former essential homogeneity there is now heterogeneity: a fundamental internal diversification within the extended family, which is the product of a variety of factors of social and economic change. And the contemporary family structure in this particular case is basically modified, an adaptation of the older form to the realities of the current situation. The extended family is clearly still very much in existence and still has a considerable practical and emotional importance for its members. But now the relationships by and large radiate outwards over considerable distances and over disparate neighbourhoods from a single centre, the parental home presided over by 'the Mam'. In his own words, the married children 'hardly ever see one another except when they meet here at their Mam's. . . .' 'They all seem to live in worlds of their own. . . .' 'I don't know what it's going to be like when she's gone.' There can be little doubt, reading his later remarks, that Mr Hughes views this contemporary family structure with a good deal of uneasiness, recognizing its difference and its inherent instability, regretting the loss of family solidarity and disliking the emergence of individualistic and self-centred attitudes as opposed to the co-operative and group-centred attitudes of the former cohesive family system which he remembers so well from his youth. The form is still there to a considerable extent, but little of the older spirit. The break-up of the natal home through the death of the mother will lead, he seems to suggest, to a disintegration of this loosely organized wider family, a disruption of what little cohesion it still possesses, and a fragmentation into isolated elementary families with few effective links to one another—though, we must add, each of these may well grow with the cycle of the generations into a separate extended family. The social and cultural changes he is conscious of can be elaborated at length: essentially they add up to a new way of life.

There is a rich field of discussion here. Every informant is a window opening on to the social world we are examining. But to get an accurate perspective we need to identify the angle of vision. The detailed study of a single case can be extremely useful in opening up lines of thought and inquiry, in raising the questions that need to be asked rather than in providing the answers—the most difficult problem of all research being to discover the right questions rather than the right answers. This case has raised, in terms of actual behaviour, a number of central issues for the understanding of family and kinship behaviour in present-day Swansea. It is, however, an individual case, given by a particular informant of a particular economic and cultural background and in particular social circumstances.

We need to ask how representative it is of all those in similar circumstances, and whether the behavioural patterns and attitudes which we discern in it vary significantly when we consider other cases which differ basically by social class and culture and economic condition. We need in short to examine a succession of cases, of as varied circumstances as possible, in order to decide what is common and general and what is special and idiosyncratic. The viewpoint of the old, as here, gives us one perspective of kinship behaviour: those of the young and middle-aged give others. The task of the sociologist in this field, as ever, is to relate these perspectives to one another and to set them within the framework of the social system of the society he is investigating. With the help of this elderly Welshman from Morriston, we have at least begun this task so far as our inquiry in Swansea is concerned.

We leave the consideration of the Hughes Family Morriston at this point to consider in a more general manner the major theme which has emerged, and which underlies everything we have to say about family behaviour in this book—the effects of social and cultural change on the structure of the extended family.

THE EXTENDED FAMILY AND MODERN URBAN SOCIETY

In recent years a widespread and somewhat confused argument appears to have been developing about the characteristics of family behaviour in a modern urban environment. Not surprisingly for sociological discussions, some of the obvious confusion can be traced to vagueness or to simple disagreements, not always readily apparent, about the meaning and usage of terms. There is little difficulty so far as the term *elementary family* is concerned, though it has a bewildering number of aliases in the literature. Whatever it be called, there are few difficulties of definition or identification with this basic 'biological' group of spouses and offspring—husband, wife and their children. Every individual (except in certain rare and exceptional circumstances such as those of foundlings, for example) becomes

18

automatically the member of an elementary family by virtue of birth. And every married individual belongs to a further elementary family, founded by the marriage, this time as husband, or wife, and parent. These two linked elementary families to which a married person belongs as child in one and parent in the other have been termed the 'family of orientation' and 'the family of procreation' respectively. Young and Willmott[4] refer more directly to the 'family of origin' into which a person is born, and the 'family of marriage' formed by the act and issue of the union. There are no points of fact or theory involved in this change of terms as applied to the study of Western society; the Young and Willmott terms are, however, simpler and less easily confused, and we use them in this present study. So far as the elementary family is concerned, there is indeed a possible source of confusion, as Lorraine Lancaster has pointed out in a most useful and thoughtful article,[5] arising out of the 'emphasis on the family as a residential unit and the family as a socially recognized entity'. We are rightly warned by Lancaster that it is necessary for the accuracy and clarity of analysis to avoid mixing these two concepts—the 'household' on the one hand and 'the family'—as a set of continuing relationships—on the other. Movement from a particular household clearly does not mean cessation of membership of a particular elementary family. This is a simple but important point and we preserve this distinction when we come to consider the composition of households in Swansea in a later chapter. It is these continuing relationships between elementary families—three such families being involved in every marriage, the family of marriage founded by the marriage itself, and the families of origin of the husband and wife—which form the basis for the extensive ramification of kinship ties and for kinship and familial groupings wider than the individual elementary family.

It is with the nature of these wider familial groupings, and particularly with the usage of the term *extended family*, that we enter the familiar jungle of terminological confusion and apparent contradiction. An examination of the literature quickly produces a welter of contradictory statements and assumptions about the external relationships of elementary families in urban areas. We do not propose to undertake a lengthy critical examination of this profuse sociological literature or to engage in debate on the usage of terms. However, if we are to make a contribution to this general and important

[4] Michael Young and Peter Willmott, *Family and Kinship in East London*, 1957.

[5] Lorraine Lancaster, 'Some Conceptual Problems in the Study of Family and Kin Ties in the British Isles,' *British Journal of Sociology*, Vol. XII, No. 4, 1961, p. 329.

discussion about the characteristics of the urban family in a modern industrial society it is obviously necessary both to discern the trends of argument and to make clear our own usage of terms.

At one extreme there are those sociologists, mainly but certainly not exclusively American, who appear to take for granted the isolation of elementary families—seen as primary *domestic* groups—in towns and cities. They either ignore or dismiss kin ties beyond this primary unit as being of little or, at best, marginal importance. They appear to assume that urban living by its very nature leads to a shrinkage of the wider family and to an atrophy, through loss of function, of extra-familial relationships and to the separation of the elementary family *qua* household from its traditional kinship context, comparing town life with that of 'traditional' rural areas. This view, explicitly or implicitly, is extremely common, particularly in the American sociological literature. Ruth Benedict,[6] for example, in a characteristic survey of 'the American family' which makes no reference whatsoever to wider kin ties, writes of 'our atomistic American families' and of 'our great cities where each family is strange to all others', echoing Margaret Mead's[7] extreme case of 'the tiny biological family of the modern three-room-apartment dwellers who have no kin within a thousand miles'. Ralph Linton in a famous essay on the family, discusses the breakdown of kin ties in the city: 'The average city dweller recognizes his extended ties of relationship only in the sending of Christmas cards and in the occasional practice of hospitality of visiting kin'.[8] Nels Anderson, in 'a world perspective' of 'the urban community' devotes a chapter[9] to reviewing and summarizing the evidence from a variety of countries on the relationships between urbanism and the family. The generalized picture that emerges is of the stripping away of extra-familial ties, the progressive loss of former extended family functions, the diminution of wider relationships, the decline of family size, the virtual isolation of the elementary family as 'the final familial unit' in the urban environment. 'The economic and other influences that have affected family life (in the city) have tended to keep down the size of the extended family, leaving only the nuclear family of parents and children, with occasional other relatives.' Anderson, discussing the problem of

[6] Ruth Benedict, 'The Family: Genus Americanum' in *The Family, its Function and Destiny*, ed. Ruth Nanda Anshen, 1959, pp. 59 and 63.

[7] Margaret Mead, 'The Contemporary American Family as an Anthropologist sees it' in *Social Perspectives on Behavior*, ed. Stein and Cloward, 1958, p. 20.

[8] Ralph Linton, 'The Natural History of the Family' in Ruth Anshen, loc. cit., 1959, p. 46.

[9] Nels Anderson, *The Urban Community*, 1960, Chapter 1, *passim*

ageing parents 'confronted with a future of loneliness', concludes that 'with a variety of exceptions, which help to confirm the generalization, the modern family is a one-generation arrangement. It waxes up to and through the adolescence of children and declines as the children marry and move.'[10] He contrasts this modern arrangement with what he calls 'the normal form in family history . . . the extended family: grandparents, their married children and grandchildren, even great grandchildren; perhaps also cousins, uncles and aunts'.

There can be little doubt that this is a view of the urban family which has passed into general acceptance through constant reiteration and, it must be added, through constant reinforcement both from particular sociological studies and from widespread personal experience. The break-up of the wider family in the city is a familiar theme of discourse. Indeed it has become so much of a commonplace that, until the recent revival of critical interest in this proposition, few sociological studies of urban families—usually of course of 'problem families'—for one reason or another have paid any attention whatsoever to kinship ties or groupings wider than the elementary family seen as a separate household.

Some sociologists, notably Ralph Linton and Talcott Parsons, examining this proposition with greater theoretical rigour than is usually apparent, have argued that this disruption and isolation must *necessarily* occur in contemporary urban societies because the extended family system is in fundamental conflict with a modern industrial economy. Ralph Linton, in the essay we have already mentioned, relates this disruption of wider kin groupings directly to the predominant characteristics of the total economic system:

> The family of the future will be a direct outgrowth of present familial conditions and trends, and in order to predict its possible form it is necessary to have an understanding of the current situation. The outstanding feature of this situation is the almost complete breakdown of the consanguine family as a functional unit. Although the Western European consanguine grouping has never dominated the conjugal one, its potentialities for function and its claims on the individual were much stronger even a hundred years ago than they are today. This breakdown seems to be directly correlated with the increased opportunities for both spatial and social mobility which have been created by the current technological revolution. A strong consanguine family organization provides its members with a high degree of economic security, but it also imposes many obligations. When the value of this security becomes less than the handicap imposed on the individual

[10] Note here the confusion of 'household' and 'family' to which Lancaster has drawn attention.

by the associated obligations, he is willing to sacrifice the former in order to avoid the latter. Colloquially speaking, when a man can do better without relatives than with them, he will tend to ignore the ties of kinship. The unparalleled expansion of Western Europe and American economy in the past century, with the wealth of individual opportunity which it has produced, has struck at the very roots of consanguine family organization.[11]

Talcott Parsons,[12] describing in precise and careful theoretical terms the kinship system of the contemporary United States but from the point of view of general middle-class experience rather than as the result of field investigation, points to the structural isolation of the elementary family in relation to external kin ties 'as the most distinctive feature of the American kinship system' which 'underlies most of its peculiar functional and dynamic problems'. He goes on to argue that, because of stress on *individual* mobility, which is an inherent feature of the occupational and status systems of the total society, the isolated elementary family is the only family type which is functional in such a society. He stresses that 'this type of occupational system and its structural correlates in the society places severe limitations on the kind of kinship structure which is compatible with such a system' and that wider family groupings of the extended family form must disintegrate or fail to evolve because they are basically incompatible with the social system as a whole. This is an important argument with a clearly enunciated hypothesis, to which we will return presently.

The counter-arguments to these points of view about the disintegration of the extended family and the consequent isolation of the elementary family in contemporary urban society appear to be three-fold—those which state that this disruption does indeed occur but that it is merely a temporary phenomenon caused by a particular phase of social change and by particular population movement and re-distribution, the extended family reconstructing itself as it adapts to these changes; those which appear to deny altogether that urbanization necessarily causes family disruption and isolation, pointing to the vigour and vitality, and indeed social necessity, of the extended family in these areas; and finally those which accept the incompatibility of a particular and 'classical' form of the extended family but

[11] Ralph Linton, op. cit., p. 45. Linton makes in this essay his well-known distinction between the *conjugal family* as spouses and offspring, and the consanguine family as a diffuse and almost unorganized group of blood relatives.

[12] Talcott Parsons, 'The Social Structure of the Family' in Ruth Anshen, loc cit., pp. 262–3.

which argue that a modified form has emerged as an adaptation to these changed circumstances.

The first of these arguments has a growing number of adherents judging by the frequency with which it is beginning to appear in a variety of contexts. It has been ably expressed by Raymond Williams, a shrewd social spectator who sees most of the game:

> We think of the new housing estates, the new suburbs and the new towns as characteristic of the new Britain, and on the whole it is in these areas that Labour hopes are now most regularly disappointed. This is the living space of that other popular figure of contemporary analysis, the 'semi-detached proletariat'. But in fact people of many different kinds live in these places, which also between themselves have important differences. Attention has been concentrated on the break-up of old community patterns, by such physical removal, but this needs discriminating description. There is social variation, all the way from the estate still mainly serving a single works to the new town wholly mixed in origins and centres of work. There is also historical variation, from the first-generation estate in which social relations are still at the level of casual neighbourly contact, to the second-generation estate on which people have been born, grown up and married. The disruption of extended families noted in some removals is in itself a temporary phenomenon: all first-generation estates will become second- and third-generation, though not necessarily with exactly the same family patterns. We cannot be sure what will happen, but it would be rash to assume that all former patterns are permanently gone. The old working-class communities grew, over a century, from a situation of removal and exposure fully comparable to the present phase. When the temporary and artificial nature of the newest communities has been allowed for, and when we have overcome the simple determinism of supposing that things (whether houses or washing machines) shape men, we shall perhaps be more cautious in assuming that there are wholly new permanent patterns and in particular that we know what these are.[13]

There is clearly a great deal of truth in this argument which urges that current events be seen in a wider historical perspective and which emphasizes the importance of time- and generation-depth in the formation of family and community behaviour patterns. We shall be examining the growth of Swansea from this point of view, and we can of course recall the case of Mr Hughes of Morriston which brings out this point quite clearly. Mr Hughes contrasts the clustering of kin in the Morriston of his youth, and the high degree of community integration and neighbourliness, with the contemporary dispersion

[13] Raymond Williams, *The Long Revolution*, 1961, pp. 331–2.

of the younger generation in communities with a low level of social and cultural cohesion. But if we go back one step to his parental generation we are at once in the turmoil of the Industrial Revolution in South Wales. His grandparents were agricultural workers in rural Carmarthenshire: his father was one of the thousands drawn off the land and into the growing industrial communities by the magnet of iron and steel. Trace the genealogy of any elderly informant from the old industrial areas on the east side of Swansea famed a few decades ago for its concentration of thriving metallurgical industries, and in one or two generations you are back in the countryside amongst a rural peasantry. Morriston and its neighbouring communities grew over more than half a century of rapid industrialization and urbani-zation. The new communities of a 'semi-detached' (and in the next generation, completely detached) proletariat clustered under the walls of the works, or in the shadows of the pit-wheels. And as the memories of the removals and upheavals faded and a new residential stability emerged the familiar family patterns and wider kin groups were re-constructed in the new environment. But it took time, more than a single generation. Is this not what is happening now, it may be asked. Are we not simply in another phase of social upheaval, a later stage of the 'long revolution'? If we answer 'yes' to these questions and agree with the basic argument, we have also to recognize certain fundamental differences in the present situation, differences which are critical to the renaissance of the family in its older structural form. We have emphasized some of these in our discussion of the Hughes Family earlier in this chapter, and we will be examining them in greater detail and with an accumulation of evidence from a variety of social circumstances in later chapters. In many vital respects the social structure of the old industrial communities like Morriston was similar to that of the traditional rural areas from which the original migrants had come. The urban village was constructed on the model of the rural village. There were fundamental identities in the two social situations, notably geographical concentration and propinquity of kin, continuous homogeneity of occupation and of economic con-dition, a restricted range of marriage, cultural uniformities in religion and language and education, restricted opportunities of social advancement and physical mobility. As Mr Hughes is well aware, the present situation differs fundamentally in its heterogeneities and diversifications *within* the family, and the essential basis would appear to have been lost for the reconstruction of family patterns according to the former model, even given an adequate framework of time and generation depth. The analysis of Talcott Parsons and his central hypothesis of the incompatibility of the extended family with the contemporary economic system is obviously of basic relevance here.

The second challenge to the proposition asserting the isolation of the elementary family as the result of urbanization and industrialization has also a growing audience as the reports of recent sociological field studies, mainly in Britain, have become available. It is being strongly led by the Institute of Community Studies, founded and directed by Dr Michael Young, whose publications have attracted wide attention both among sociologists and among those concerned with social planning and with the formulation and implications of social policy, particularly in relation to housing and to the social and economic condition of elderly people. This is particularly true of the trilogy[14] on family life in Bethnal Green in the East End of London, published in 1957 and 1958. The first study examined kinship, both in Bethnal Green and in a new housing estate on the outskirts of London to which many Bethnal Green families had been moved; the second study was concerned specifically with the family relationships of old people in the same area of East London; and the third with the special family problems and relationships of widows.

Edward Shils, in a review of one of the publications of this Institute, has summarized the results of its field investigations of family behaviour: 'The Institute of Community Studies has denied one of the most respected of the clichés of contemporary sociology which asserts that urbanization isolates and decomposes the kinship group',[15] and by the latter it is clear from the context that he is referring to the extended family. In a similar vein, Richard Titmuss introduces the first of the studies of Bethnal Green:

> It is hoped that these studies will make some small contribution to correcting the present unbalanced views about 'the British family'. Much of the nonsense that is written on the subject today does require challenging. For it is indeed compounded of a curious mixture: theoretical treatise from the United States, by no means of universal application, combined with a pathological series of British studies of 'abnormal' and 'problem' families all heavily loaded with moralistic judgements which reached their eminence in the recent Report of the Royal Commission on Marriage and Divorce.[16]

[14] Michael Young and Peter Willmott, *Family and Kinship in East London*, 1957.
Peter Townsend, *Family Life of Old People*, 1957.
Peter Marris, *Widows and their Families*, 1958.
[15] Edward Shils, *New Statesman*, 23 February 1952 reviewing *Family and Social Change in an African City* by Peter Marris.
[16] Richard Titmuss, 'Foreword' to Michael Young and Peter Willmott, op. cit., p. xi.

Young and Willmott say they began their study in Bethnal Green expecting, from their reading of social science on family life in modern cities, to find small isolated households, containing mainly husbands, wives and their dependent children, separated from their kin, 'the wider family of the past having, according to many sociologists, shrunk in modern times to a smaller body'. But, to their surprise and interest, the actual situation in this ancient working-class borough in the East End was very different:

> Thus prepared, we were surprised to discover that the wider family, far from having disappeared, was still very much alive in the middle of London. This finding seemed to us of much more interest than anything we had been led to expect, all the more so when it transpired that the absence of relatives seemed to be as significant on the estate as their presence in the borough. We therefore decided, although we hit on it more or less accidentally, to make our main subject the wider family.[17]

The reports of these studies, vividly and colourfully presented, describe the functioning of the extended family in Bethnal Green, a 'pocket' of traditional working-class culture, stress the family system of care in old age, identify the mother–married daughter tie as the key relationship, note the sense of isolation and loneliness, particularly of the wives, of the families who have moved away to the housing estate from the warm friendly kinship atmosphere of the hustling East End, and conclude that for reasons of family ties and reciprocal familial obligations 'very few people wish to leave the East End'[18] though in fact the population of Bethnal Green had declined dramatically from 108,000 in 1931 to 54,000 in 1955 with the removal of some 11,000 families mainly, it seems, through war devastation and public re-housing policy.[19] Essentially these studies direct attention to the important part extended family relationships play in the daily lives of the people of Bethnal Green: 'grandmothers look after grandchildren while the mothers are at work, the old and infirm are cared for by their children, social life centres on the family gatherings, and the family circle provides a reliable source of help with all manner of problems'. The emphasis is on the necessity of the extended family in its supportive role for the individual elementary families, and therefore on the destructive and deleterious effects on family organization of migration produced by public policies of urban de-congestion, slum clearance and re-housing on distant estates. Since one of our main purposes in this present study in Swansea is to compare our findings on these matters with those of the Bethnal Green studies, we shall be considering these conclusions in detail in later chapters. For

[17] Young and Willmott, op. cit., p. xvi.   [18] ibid., p. 155.   [19] ibid., p. 99.

the moment we must note that in relation to the general sociological discussion about the characteristics of the urban family, the Bethnal Green studies, operating a simple contrast between the extended family (Bethnal Green type) on the one hand and the isolated elementary family (Greenleigh housing estate type) on the other, present a strong case for the continuation in urban areas, of a particular sociological character, of the extended family—though the evidence from their comparative investigation on the housing estate would appear to confirm the proposition that mobility leads to a decomposition of the kinship group.

Finally the general proposition about the disruption of the extended family in modern democratic industrial society and, in particular, Talcott Parsons's hypothesis that only the isolated elementary family is functionally consistent with such a social and economic system have been challenged recently by Eugene Litwak in two splendid companion articles in the *American Sociological Review*.[20] Litwak points out that 'Parsons assumes only one kind of extended family relational pattern, the "classical" type exemplified in the Polish and Irish peasant families, marked by geographical propinquity, occupational integration, strict authority of extended family over nuclear family, and stress on extended rather than nuclear family relations'. He maintains that the Parsonian hypothesis tends to be valid only during periods of emerging industrialization. Litwak, presenting the evidence from a survey of 920 wives in the Buffalo urban area, argues that 'in a mature industrial economy' *a modified* form of this classical extended family can be maintained in the face of physical and social mobility because of improvements in communications which overcome the disruptive effects of spatial separation, because in these conditions the members of the extended family have come to accept a greater freedom of movement as normal and natural, because the aid which is given between members is mainly concerned with such things as housing, illness, old age, companionship and so forth and is not concerned with the occupational system (nepotism, for example, being generally condemned). He carefully argues that extended family relationships with significant reciprocal aid and support can be maintained without geographical proximity and without a single authoritarian family head—the classical *paterfamilias*—exercising strict control over the extended family group covering three generations and a number of component elementary families. Thus Litwak accepts Parsons's analysis that the classical extended family is

[20] Eugene Litwak, 'Occupational Mobility and Extended Family Cohesion' and 'Geographic Mobility and Extended Family Cohesion' in *American Sociological Review*, Vol. 25, 1960, Numbers 1 and 3.

incompatible with contemporary industrial society, but 'rejects his view that the isolated nuclear family is the only theoretically meaningful alternative'. Litwak sums up his own position as follows:

> The modified extended family differs from past extended families in that it does not require geographical propinquity, occupational nepotism, or integration, and there are no strict authority relations but equalitarian ones. Family relations differ from those of the isolated nuclear family in that significant aid is provided to nuclear families, although the aid has to do with standard of living (housing, illness, leisure pursuits) rather than occupational appointments or promotions.[21]

We have given this summary of the various arguments that have been advanced about the present-day urban family because, even though the cursory nature of our account does scant justice to authors quoted as representative of schools of thought, it is necessary and useful to see the picture as a whole before we concentrate our attentions on the characteristics of family life in Swansea. This is the universe of discourse against which we must interpret our own findings. Whichever point of view has been expressed, there is no dearth of evidence in its support—though, it must be added, the evidence in favour of alternative arguments appears rarely to be considered, the final instance above being a notable exception. It is impossible to examine the literature and evidence in any detail without recognizing the necessity for an orderly synthesis of these apparently contradictory arguments. There can be few sociologists, familiar with the evidence, who would agree with Shils that the Institute of Community Studies had in fact successfully 'denied' the assertion that the extended family is 'decomposed' by urbanization (and thus to have disposed of Parsons's hypotheses, for example). But there can equally be few who would not agree that the Institute has made a spectacular and important contribution to this discussion, *qualifying* the general proposition about the urban family in modern society.

Two points of major importance for our present study emerge from this brief canvass of the varying points of view that have been expressed. First, towns differ, and industrialism has a variety of characteristics—a simple point which is as important as it is obvious. The argument adopted depends essentially on the particular social and cultural conditions being considered. There is considerable variation of social system from one urban area to another (this variation, as we see with Bethnal Green and will be seeing with Swansea, possibly occurring to a marked degree even within a single

[21] Eugene Litwak, op. cit., *American Sociological Review*, Vol. 25, No. 3.

urban area). We cannot assess the wider applicability of the conclusions of a particular study until we have a full and detailed picture of the particular social environment in which the study was undertaken, the family structure dealt with being an integral part of the total social structure of that society. As the total social system changes so we would expect to find concomitant change a family behaviour. With this in mind, we devote the two chapters which follow to a description of Swansea and to an examination of social class and cultural distinctions and to the trends of social change in Swansea, before turning to discuss family behaviour in this environment.

Secondly, the force and implications of the views presented depend fundamentally on the meaning given to the term 'extended family', variations in definition and usage accounting for a good deal of the apparent conflict of opinion. The problems of description and comparative statement would be much easier if sociologists could agree on the meaning and usage of terms. This is of course unlikely. Take the following four usages of 'extended family':

> A group may be described as a *joint family* when two or more lineally related kinsfolk of the same sex, their spouses and offspring, occupy a single homestead and are jointly subject to the same authority or single head. The term *extended family* should be used for the dispersed form corresponding to a joint family.[22]

> Extended family is used to refer to any groupings, related by descent, marriage, or adoption, that is broader than the nuclear family. [23]

> The extended family may be said to consist of a group of relatives, comprising more than the immediate family, who live in one, two or more households, usually in a single locality, and *who see each other every day, or nearly every day.* [24]

> Sometimes a family (that is parents and children) is living in the same household or dwelling with other related people. . . . We call such a grouping of related people an 'extended family'. A family may also, although not occupying the same household with relatives, share so much of their daily lives that they and their relatives *do in effect constitute one domestic unit.* . . . We use the term extended family to apply as much to a family and relatives living together in this way as we do to a family and relatives who are occupying the same household all the time. [25]

[22] *Notes and Queries on Anthropology* (Sixth Edition), 1951, p. 72.
[23] Norman W. Bell and Ezra F. Vogel, 'Toward a Framework for Functional Analysis of Family Behaviour,' in *A Modern Introduction to the Family*, ed. Bell and Vogel, 1960, p. 1.
[24] Peter Townsend, *Family Life of Old People*, p. 108.
[25] Michael Young and Peter Willmott, op. cit., pp. 201–2. (Our italics.)

The first definition is that normally used by anthropologists in their accounts of tribal and peasant societies in Africa and Asia and so forth. It is of course freely used in descriptions of the traditional family organization found among European peasantries—and indeed in discussions of 'pre-industrial' towns and cities. The emphasis is on a cluster of related elementary families, normally but not necessarily living together as a co-residential group, and essentially all *under a single family head* with authority in law. This is a familiar form of family organization in contemporary and ancient tribal and peasant societies. It is clearly the family form that Parsons had in mind in his analysis of the incompatibility of the extended family with a modern industrial system.

The third definition is an adaptation of this orthodox anthropological usage to meet the situation encountered by Townsend in Bethnal Green. He retains with modification the criterion of common residence, adds with emphasis an apparently precise measure of contact as a new defining feature, and omits without mention the basic characteristic of authority. The fourth definition similarly omits reference to authority, retains the criterion of residence but adds a new condition: the sharing of domestic functions. It is clear both from these definitions and from their vivid descriptions that the authors of these Bethnal Green studies are already dealing with a modified form of the 'classical' extended family. They have not discovered in Bethnal Green 'the wider family of the past', if by this is meant the traditional peasant family type covered by the anthropological definition: they have in fact discovered a modified version of it, an adaptation to a changed environment. They do not discuss whether there are any other modified forms of the *extended family* because their elaborate definition, as it were, already precludes these. They are left in effect with only the concept of the isolated elementary family to oppose to their Bethnal Green-type extended family as this is (variously) defined.

If we recall for a moment the case of the Hughes Family of Morriston described earlier, it will be remembered that we detected in Mr Hughes's account two forms of 'extended family'—that of his youth in Morriston based on a close clustering of kin sharing certain basic social and cultural homogeneities; and that of his contemporary situation based on a dispersion of his married children and their families, with marked internal social and cultural heterogeneities within this family grouping, though with a retention of much of the older patterns of reciprocal help and support.

If we use Townsend's definition to apply to this case, we are faced with a curious paradox. On the one hand we can say that each of these family forms is an extended family for different reasons based on the same definition—in the former case on grounds of clustering and common residence, in the latter on grounds of frequency of contact *to the parental home*—thus obscuring a fundamental variation in family structure, of which Mr Hughes at least is well aware. And on the other hand, both the Bethnal Green definitions forbid us to use the term for the *whole* of his present 'family' (whatever be the actual situation in his childhood family of which we know very little) because only his two married daughters and the two daughters of his son in the next street are seen 'every day or nearly every day', or are near enough to participate in each others' household arrangements. The frequent visiting between households that this involves presumably means that Mr Hughes is, according to these definitions, a member of an extended family which only includes some of the children with which he is in regular contact. The elementary family in Sketty on the other side of Swansea is only seen on Saturdays, and the other married son and his family down in the docks have not been seen for some months. Then the children of this elderly couple, brothers and sisters and their spouses, are widely separated and meet irregularly and only at the parental house—and thus, by these definitions, the extended family from the point of view of any one of them cannot include their siblings. Again whilst the second son and his wife and three children were away in London for ten years, they ceased to belong to the extended family—even though Mr Hughes and his wife went up there 'like the clock' for annual holidays and they came back to the parental home regularly for holidays themselves. Now that they have returned to Swansea they could at least rejoin the extended family if only they could manage to step up their frequency of visiting to the prescribed daily or near-daily amount, or move close enough to share each others' household functions.

The absurdities here are obvious and they illustrate the difficulties arising from apparent precision of definition. We need in fact to approach this problem differently, to use terms precisely where this precision is *significant* and yet with sufficient flexibility to reflect accurately the social reality we are describing.

The second definition quoted above, apparently vague at first sight, seems to us to be precisely what is needed here: it concentrates attention on the extended family *as a social entity*, and yet leaves its actual form under varying conditions to be determined by analysis. In this sense it does not prejudice the analysis by giving a false and predetermined precision, and thus does not beg the questions that have to be answered by research. It does not involve confusing the two quite separate concepts of household and family. It directs attention to the complicated interplay of a variety of factors in family structure rather than on the emphasis in advance on certain factors at the expense of others. It enables us to observe in analysis modifications of extended family organization emerging under different social conditions, in the manner illustrated by Eugene Litwak in the Buffalo study to which we have referred.

We therefore intend adopting this definition of the extended family in this inquiry with a slight but important modification from that given by Bell and Vogel. They say 'any grouping . . . broader than the nuclear family'. We feel that the definition should obviously exclude such temporary groupings of relatives as assemble at weddings and funerals, for example, and have therefore re-phrased the definition as follows: *the term 'extended family' will refer to any persistent kinship grouping of persons related by descent, marriage, or adoption, which is wider than the elementary family, in that it characteristically spans three generations from grandparents to grandchildren.*

Discussions of terminology can be extremely boring if they dwell on trivialities, and immensely irritating if they turn into arid pedantry. We hope to have avoided these dangers in this particular discussion. If we are not to add to the existing confusion and to 'the nonsense that is written about the subject today', in Titmuss's phrase, it is essential that we use terms in a clear and meaningful way. This we seek to do.

RESEARCH PLAN AND METHODS

This journey to South Wales was for one of us a return to his native heath, and to his own numerous kin, after some years of anthropological research in Asia—a return from the exotic to the familiar. For the other, a Londoner by birth and upbringing, this was his first visit to Wales and an initial acquaintance with its distinctive manners and customs. Native and stranger, we formed at least a balanced team for this first reconnaissance of the family life of the urban Welsh. Neither of us had any previous experience of social research in a modern industrial society of the scale and economic complexity of Swansea. In recent years there have been a number of fascinating studies of Welsh rural communities, but no previous examination of family behaviour in a major Welsh town[26].

[26] There is a fragment on the Mid-Rhondda in the Nuffield Foundation report of a Survey Committee, under the chairmanship of Seebohm Rowntree, on the problems of ageing and the care of old people, published as *Old People* in 1947, but, interestingly enough, in the light of what we have been saying

This is therefore something of an experimental study in a number of senses, and particularly from the point of view of an anthropologist familiar with the study of small-scale systems—and for both of us an initiation into the particular techniques and peculiar difficulties of research in the social conditions of our own complicated contemporary society.

In its original conception in the Social Science Department of the University College of Swansea, this study was seen as a direct extension, to a distant and different part of Britain, of the work of the Institute of Community Studies in the East End of London. It was felt that the publications of this Institute offered an important challenge to current views on family life which, if confirmed, would influence social theory and point to the need for profound changes in social policy. The need for comparative investigation in a different part of the country from Bethnal Green, with different traditions, different industries and a different social history was obvious if the conclusions of these Bethnal Green studies were to be seen in a wider perspective and their adequacy and degree of universality assessed. Swansea was chosen, because of the interest of the Social Science Department there in this question and because this interest was supported by a most generous grant from the Joseph Rowntree Memorial Trust, as being a suitably contrasting urban area for this comparative investigation.

We began this study therefore with the problem of comparing our findings with those of the Bethnal Green studies as one of our given terms of reference (though of course we were not limited solely to this comparison). It was originally envisaged that a considerable part of the study would be concerned with the social problem of old age. In the event we were unable to include all the results of our inquiries into this problem in the present work, and it is hoped that these will form the subject of another publication. We received initially from the Institute of Community Studies most valuable help, based on their experience, with planning our inquiries and with the technical details of statistical sampling, schedule construction, the use of punched cards for the sorting and analysis of data, and so forth. This advice, and the prescription of comparison (a central necessity for all sociological investigation) with the Bethnal Green inquiries, heavily influenced the research design we eventually adopted and the field-work methods we used. The responsibility for this, and for the

---

earlier in this chapter, this valuable report makes little reference to the family relationships of the old—only ten brief paragraphs out of 280 numbered paragraphs being devoted to this subject and then exclusively in terms of household composition.

outcome, rested of course entirely with us, and not in any sense with the Institute of Community Studies which was concerned only in a most helpful consultative role.

The methods used in any study depend of course on the problems chosen for examination, on the aims of the inquiry, on the development of thought and concept as the research proceeds, and essentially on the kind of environment in which the research is being conducted. However advantageous it may be for comparative purpose, the simple translation of methods from Bethnal Green to Swansea presents serious difficulties. Swansea and Bethnal Green as two theatres for research are radically different, and this indeed was why Swansea was selected for this study. First in scale—Swansea is three times larger in population than Bethnal Green (166,000 compared with Bethnal Green's 53,000), and perhaps more importantly in relation to fieldwork methods, more than twenty-five times the area (41 square miles compared with the $1\frac{1}{2}$ square miles of Bethnal Green). Swansea in area if not in population is indeed one of the largest County Boroughs in Britain. Secondly in social composition—Bethnal Green is a characteristically compact and almost exclusively working-class enclave in the heart of London's East End; Swansea is a large regional metropolis, geographically distinct, divided internally into a series of topographically well-defined localities which are strikingly heterogeneous, comparing one with another, by the factors of age and of settlement, social class, composition by age, Welsh-speaking, religion, and economic condition. It is impossible by the simple act of living there to develop the same total familiarity with Swansea as a whole as it would be to do this in Bethnal Green. Indeed we were constantly surprised to discover how little Swansea people knew of localities, other than their own, which were some distance away and markedly different in social character.

The study of kinship and of varying forms of family organization has become 'the perennial theme', as Raymond Firth has described it, of the social anthropologist, certainly in his familiar role as student and interpreter of primitive societies. It was our intention in Swansea to use, so far as was practicable, anthropological techniques of inquiry in our study of family behaviour. There are, however, considerable difficulties in the adaptation to the conditions of modern society of these techniques which have mainly been evolved, as Nadel puts it, 'on small islands in the Pacific and in the study of small groups and cultures infinitely simpler than our own historical civilizations'. Basically they are field techniques based on the village as the normal fieldwork situation: the vast majority of anthropological studies, as we have come to expect and understand them, have been undertaken in villages of one kind or another, whether the resulting monograph be about the village alone or about a people or a tribe or a wider community. And we have become familiar by now—usually by inference from published studies rather than by detailed expositions of method—with the fieldwork methods normally used: continuous observation by the anthropologist living for a lengthy period with the community under study and speaking its language, genealogies, house lists and village censuses, records of disputes, case histories, descriptions of ceremonies and economic activities, and so forth. More often than not these studies, though rich in descriptive detail, make little use of statistics (except of the most elementary kind) and rarely have resort to sampling techniques, coded schedules, punched cards, or any of the other trappings and paraphernalia of quantification. Very often the need is expressed for an increased use of techniques of quantification even in these traditional fieldwork situations, and there have of course been notable attempts in this direction, as with Meyer Fortes's work on the composition of Ashanti households, or in Raymond Smith's study of family structure among the Bush Negro of British Guiana. But by and large the groups studied have either been too small in size, or have apparently too small a degree of homogeneity, to make an extensive use of sampling techniques either necessary or desirable. Broadly speaking, the traditional anthropologist is a kind of notebook-and-pencil man, working alone, living in the community he studies, with a sort of highly skilled and holistic 'I-am-a-Camera' approach[27] which, as the evidence of the results obtained and the theoretical advances made has shown, has proved strikingly successful.

The anthropologist's first reaction confronted with a town of the scale and complexity of Swansea is to search for a particular community or neighbourhood or locality (call it what you will), small in scale, well defined, of particular interest from the point of view of his general research problem—and then to live in it, observe behaviour, get to know as many people there as possible, use all six senses—in short, to dig a deep hole with a small circumference. There were indeed many times when, struggling with unfamiliar, and often unsatisfactory, statistical techniques, we could have wished that we had done exactly this. Our fieldwork problem in Swansea was, however, very different from that of traditional social anthropology. It was in fact not unlike that which Nadel faced with the Nupe: 'The West African society dealt with in this book is half a million strong. It is far from "simple" or "primitive". Its social and economic complexity

---

[27] For a discussion of this approach see P. J. Bohannan, *Justice and Judgement among the Tiv*, O.U.P. 1955.

is comparable only with the civilizations of Imperial Rome, of Byzantium, of Medieval Europe.'[28] Nadel points out the inadequacy of anthropological fieldwork techniques in the accepted sense for dealing with such a society, discusses the existence of sharp social and cultural differences within the tribe and of the high degree of variation on a common pattern, and continues, 'the investigation thus became perforce a comparative study within the framework of one tribe and one culture'. The field technique he used was based on a kind of sampling of communities throughout the territory of the Nupe, each selected community being subjected to intensive investigation. This is essentially the method we have used in Swansea, with modifications to meet the particular local conditions, and the limitations of time, within which we worked.

We shall be discussing in a later chapter certain specific problems of method—as, for example, the use of genealogies for determining the range of kinship recognition. In general terms, we followed the methods adopted in the Bethnal Green studies—extensive surveying using random samples drawn from the Borough as a whole, supplemented by detailed case histories taken from within these random samples and also, in our case, from informants like Mr Hughes, who has figured prominently in this opening chapter, whom we met by chance or to whom we were introduced by friends and acquaintances. We of course lived in Swansea throughout the period of the study—initially for six months or so in Morriston and Llansamlet respectively in the industrial East, and for the remainder in Sketty and Uplands respectively in the residential West. So far as was possible, we used the familiar method of 'participant observation', attending church and chapel services all over the Borough, visiting a wide selection of Swansea's 246 pubs and the 57 Old People's Clubs, enjoying the performances of many choirs, joining as members a number of different social clubs and cultural groups, voting in elections, lecturing to a variety of Guilds and Institute and Adult Education Classes. In short, we saw Swansea from the inside as citizens, if for a brief period, of this friendly and hospitable town. We also learnt a great deal from the fact that we were both involved in personal kinship networks. One of us had many relatives and a natal home close at hand, and the other married a Swansea girl during the course of this study (surely an excellent example of 'participant observation').

Whilst these activities and involvements provided valuable contributions to the task of understanding social behaviour in Swansea, our main sources of information were undoubtedly the surveys which we conducted within the Borough.

[28] S. F. Nadel, *A Black Byzantium*, 1942, p. viii.

Families in a Mobile Society

Our main survey was that which we completed in May and June 1960, some seven months after we arrived in Swansea. Using a random starting-point we took every fiftieth name from the complete Electoral Register covering all 15 Wards of the Borough. With the aid of 21 temporary interviewers, selected and trained by us, we set about the task of interviewing the 2,272 persons thus randomly selected; 1,962 interviews were completed (87 per cent), 195 persons could not be contacted, mainly through removals and deaths, and 115 or 8·6 per cent refused—the refusal rate being substantially higher in the middle-class residential areas than in the working-class districts.

The schedule of questions used, which is reproduced in Appendix II, is essentially similar to that used in the Bethnal Green inquiries in that it was constructed around the two basic measurements of proximity of residence of kin and frequency of contact. It differed from the Bethnal Green schedule as used by Young and Willmott[29] in certain important respects. Firstly, it included additional questions on extra genealogical categories, notably on relationships through marriage (which we judged from our preliminary inquiries to be of particular importance to the understanding of family behaviour), on the grandparent generation to give a greater generation depth, and on father's siblings and mother's siblings to give a wider range of kinship than was covered by the Bethnal Green schedule. Secondly, it included an extra table on the arrangement of marriage (proximity of the homes of bride and groom at marriage, and both area of residence and type of household immediately after marriage). This in the outcome provided us with information on 1,730 marriages and enabled us to analyse trends in the geography of marriage and to examine the importance of this question in relation to changes in family and kinship structure. Thirdly, our schedule contained extra questions on religion, social class, Welsh-speaking and various cultural attitudes which we thought to be relevant to the study of kinship in Swansea, and which we wanted to explore in our analysis. Finally, we used throughout the concept of neighbourhood and locality variation in behaviour within Swansea with the aim of making our analysis internally comparative by locality, after the manner of Nadel in the Nupe study to which we have referred.

In many respects this schedule was unsatisfactory, seen in retrospect and with the benefit of our subsequent experience of analysing the information it produced. It omitted questions that we ought to have included, and it included questions that we ought to have omitted. But, allowing for these normal dissatisfactions, the yield of information on certain aspects of family behaviour was very considerable and

[29] Young and Willmott, op. cit., Appendix 2, p. 178.

37

we will be presenting much of it in this report. The effect of this increase of scope in the schedule compared with its Bethnal Green counterpart was to make it a good deal longer—though this fact appears to have had little effect on the response rate—equally to increase both the product of information and complexity of the subsequent analysis. It was in many ways the measure of our in-experience with the techniques of coded schedules and mechanical sorting with the use of punch-card machines that we failed to ap-preciate just how laborious and time-consuming a process this is, often with a gain in knowledge and understanding surprisingly incommensurate with the effort and time expended.

We followed up this main survey a year later with a supplementary survey, using a specially prepared schedule, of the 435 subjects from the main sample who were over pensionable age (that is, 60 and over for women and 65 and over for men). This survey of a random sample of the elderly within Swansea enabled us to concentrate our attention on the social condition of elderly people and in particular on the family relationships of the old. In relation to this particular interest in the elderly, we conducted also a survey of the 57 Old People's Clubs in Swansea. We use the results of the survey and of the detailed interviewing to draw comparisons between the situation of the elderly in Swansea as regards family relationships and that of the elderly in Bethnal Green as described by Peter Townsend in his Bethnal Green study.

The same random sample of the elderly was used for a separate, but related, medical study, conducted by Dr Peter Parsons, covering the medical condition and, since Parsons is a psychiatrist, in particular the mental states of the elderly in Swansea. Though in many vital respects this medical inquiry has been undertaken in close and continuous collaboration with our own study, it is a separate inquiry.

Basically then our research design consisted of detailed case studies to examine the interplay of a variety of factors, in particular family structures and kinship behaviour, coupled with extensive surveying using random and representative samples from the Borough as a whole to determine the degree of typicality of these cases, to establish the statistical regularities in this field of family organization, and to identify for explanation significant variations on the basic patterns, by neighbourhood, by social class and by cultural distinc-tions. We assembled and collated, in addition, a variety of informa-tion on the Borough as a whole and on its component communities: from our personal observations, from knowledgeable informants, from the census reports, from the reports of various Corporation Departments and of a variety of local organizations, and, not least, from the three excellent local newspapers which circulate in Swansea. We planned originally to carry our studies a stage farther with intensive anthropological 'community studies' in five selected localities within the Borough, chosen to represent in sum a cross-section of Swansea's internal heterogeneity. For this, we selected Morriston as an old industrial community representative of traditional Welsh chapel culture, Sandfields as an old 'anglicized' working-class district in the Town Centre, Sketty as a middle-class residential area, Townhill as a second-generation housing estate, and West Cross as a recently established post-war estate. Through intensive studies in these chosen localities, we hoped to extend our understanding of the relationships between family organization and community structure in Swansea.

In practice, we made far less progress with these community studies than we would have liked to have done. We maintained our special interest in these five localities throughout the period of our fieldwork but really succeeded in making satisfactory progress with only two of them—Morriston and Sketty. We learnt a good deal from focusing our interests in this way within the scope of our general research design, but we are aware that we did little more than skim the surface in this respect, identifying lines of inquiry and problems for analysis in future research rather than exploring these selected communities with any substantial degree of penetration. It is one thing to locate what appear to be significant problems, and quite another to have the resources of time and staff to pursue them in a particular study.

What we have undertaken here is more in the nature of a large-scale reconnaissance of this most interesting field of study rather than a full-scale investigation commensurate with its scale and complexity. We did not explore every avenue in Swansea, and there are of course still many stones that need a careful turning over in future research. We did, however, survey the field as a whole and reach the conclusions which we present in this essay.

II

PROSPECT OF SWANSEA

CONTEMPORARY LANDSCAPE

SWANSEA is a town with a view. Its Welsh name is Abertawe: not Aberdarcy, though the traveller's tales of Kingsley Amis, following his explorations of 'The Evans Country', may well have succeeded in confusing some of its great majority of English monoglots whose knowledge of Welsh extends little beyond an ability to pronounce the tongue-twisting place-names of the town and hinterland. As its Welsh name indicates, Swansea stands at the mouth of the River Tawe. The town swarms over the narrow coastal plain to the cliffs of the Mumbles headland, up the river valley, and over the hills overlooking the valley and the splendid bay. Its hilly site beside the sea has great natural beauty. It is a town of sudden hills, of humpback, switchback streets, of tier upon tier of terraces clinging to the slopes, of panoramic views of the Bristol Channel from bedroom windows, of bird's-eye views from numerous vantage-points of the town below. At night the view from the yacht clubs at Mumbles is spectacular. A necklace of yellow street lamps encircles the black sea for some fifteen miles to the distant promenade at Aberavon and the flaring furnaces of the steelworks at Port Talbot and Margam. Above the centre of this great arc the hills of Swansea sparkle with the lights of homes and streets. And in the bay there are the lights of ships riding at anchor or moving past the sweeping Mumbles Light to the docks.

'This sea town was my world,' wrote Dylan Thomas, born in Cwmdonkin Drive,

> an ugly, lovely town, or so it was and is to me; crawling, sprawling by a long and splendid-curving shore where truant boys and Sandfield boys and old men from nowhere, beach-combed, idled and paddled, watched the dock-bound ships or the ships steaming away into wonder and India, magic and China . . . outside, a

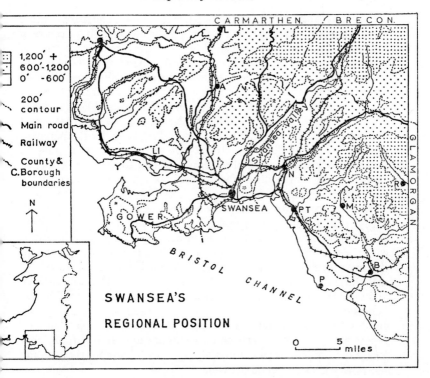

SWANSEA'S

REGIONAL POSITION

0 ___ 5 miles

strange Wales, coal-pitted, mountained, river run, full so far as I
knew of choirs and football teams and sheep and story-books, tall
black hats and red flannel petticoats, moved about its business
which was none of mine.

This 'strange Wales' of mountain farms and industrial valleys
begins in the north of the Borough where the Swansea Valley stretches
away towards the mountains of Brecon. Swansea itself, the old town
clustered around the harbour and the fragment of the Norman castle
that still remains, has always been English, or Anglo-Welsh at most.
Yet it is the centre and commercial capital of a large surrounding
region of South-west Wales which is predominantly and characteristically Welsh.

From the ancient Town and Franchise of just under two thousand
acres between the hills and the sea, the Borough boundary has been
extended (in 1832, 1889, and very substantially in 1918) to its present
shape. We include three maps in this chapter to summarize and
illustrate the main facts of Swansea's regional position, internal

topography, and historical growth (pp. 41, 55, 70–1). The maps indicate that Swansea has not so much grown outwards from a single centre of habitation as grown together. The historical pattern is one of nineteenth-century Morriston in the north expanding and linking up with other industrial settlements down the Tawe Valley towards 'Old Swansea', and at the same time the expansion of new areas of habitation to the west and north-west to engulf long-established village communities like Sketty, Fforestfach, Cockett, Mumbles and Waunarlwydd. Many still retain their distinctive local character, although some of them now form part of the continuous built-up area. History and topography have combined to produce a sort of cellular pattern of distinct and well-recognized communities within the modern administrative area.

The County Borough today, the area of this study, is not a 'natural' entity. It is a town with a multiple personality (displaying at times considerable psychological confusion because of this) which cannot easily be summed up in a single phrase—ancient and affluent Borough, the main ocean port in the Bristol Channel, famed centre of the metallurgical industries marred by historic industrial ruins, holiday and seaside resort with its own coastline and the bays of the Gower[1] Peninsula on its doorstep, regional shopping centre attracting vast crowds from the hinterland to its chain stores and supermarkets, provincial centre of the arts and communications and of traditional Welsh culture, embryonic university town with its rapidly expanding University College beside the bay.

This regional metropolis now spreads over 24,000 acres, covered mainly by extensive residential districts. Some 1,300 acres are reserved for industrial uses, including a vast and bleak lunar landscape in the Tawe Valley of abandoned tips and derelict factories weathered into gaunt and grotesque shapes: a blasted heath covered with the debris of Victorian capitalists, litter louts on the grand scale, astride the main railway line from London to shock each trainload of visitors and to confirm their worst fears of industrial South Wales. It is said to be the worst area of industrial blight in Britain. It gives in fact a

---

[1] We must not omit to mention that Gower has recently been designated the first Area of Outstanding Natural Beauty in Britain. One of the largest, and certainly one of the most vocal, societies in Swansea is the Gower Society. Gower *is* of course an area of outstanding natural beauty (with or without the capitals). Nowadays it has a certificate to prove it to the great satisfaction of the Gower Society—which, by the way, publishes an excellent footpath map of the Gower Peninsula under the heading 'Officially approved by the Gower Society'. The word 'officially' is a significant indication of the *de facto* influence of this private local pressure group which does much hard work in preserving Gower from the alien encroachment of the twentieth century.

quite false first impression of Swansea, but one which few visitors can forget. The docks, to the south of this area, cover 690 acres and handle more cargo annually than any other South Wales port. The central business and shopping district, the Town Centre, covers about 150 acres. It has been twice ravaged in the last two decades—once temporarily on three successive nights in February 1941 through the attention of the *Luftwaffe*, and more permanently through the now antiquated intentions of the subsequent town planners. The Borough includes also 635 acres of parks and recreation grounds, 7,300 acres of farmland (divided amongst 172 farms) slowly being encroached by public and private building, large areas of woodland, open common, lowland marsh and upland waste, and 2,641 acres of sandy foreshore. It includes within its boundary some ten miles of lovely coast-line—extending in fact from Caswell Bay on the west around the great curve of Swansea Bay to Crymlyn Bog on the east.

'The significant fact,' says the *Swansea Industrial Handbook*, 'is that this is twice the area of, for instance, Nottingham, which has 100,000 greater population, and only one-fifth less than Edinburgh which has two and a half times Swansea's population. So Swansea's people are well supplied with breathing space.' This ample internal space has had important effects on the social character of the town—in preserving to an important extent the physical identity and separation of its component communities, in determining the size and location of the fifteen Corporation housing estates, in providing room for overspill building and expansion within the Borough without the extensive clearance of existing properties, in enabling what amounts in effect to the building of a new town alongside the ruins and dilapidations of the old.

The main facts of the physical environment can be most succinctly expressed in the form of the various maps included both in this and subsequent chapters. Certain details of the physical layout and social composition of the Borough, which are of importance in understanding patterns of family behaviour, will be emphasized as our discusssion gathers way and where the description appears most relevant. However, before we come to the first of our chapters dealing specifically with family composition and relationships, certain basic themes need special attention. We deal briefly in this chapter with the data on population and housing in Swansea, with the division of the Borough into distinct communities, and with the dramatic changes which have occurred within the last few decades in local industry and employment. Our main aim here is to give as briskly as possible a clear picture of the social background. In the chapter which follows we examine the facts on social class and cultural divisions in

43

contemporary Swansea both to extend this picture and to explain our methods of analysis.

Like so many other towns in Britain, modern Swansea is a product of the Industrial Revolution. For 800 years up to 1700 it was little more than a handful of houses grouped around the harbour, with a population of under 2,000. 'Then, quite suddenly,' as Mansel Thomas puts it,

> Swansea emerges as a town with a future. Industry, mainly copper – and lead – smelting, was spreading rapidly up-river, and the harbour itself was growing into a busy port. Vigorous attempts were made from time to time to open up the sea-front on fashionable lines, with a park, assembly rooms, a museum, a new town hall: today some of the most elegant buildings of the town are to be seen unexpectedly in the business area near the harbour. A by-law was even passed prohibiting all industry within the ancient Town and Franchise. But fate had other plans for the town. As industry grew, new docks had to be built, the railways opened up the area—and before long Swansea became the greatest metallurgical centre of the Victorian era.[2]

The eighteenth century saw the establishment in the broad Tawe Valley of the copper industry (the first copper works being set up at Landore *circa* 1717) using ores from the mines of Cornwall brought in through the port, and coal for smelting from the vast coalfield to the north of the Borough. 'It is no exaggeration to say that the growth of Swansea as a metallurgical centre is founded upon copper. The multiplicity of smelting industries of various kinds—lead, tin, zinc, gold, arsenic, sulphur, etc.—is a natural outcome from the basic smelting of copper ores.'[3] By 1800 the population of the old town (apart from the growing industrial communities in Tawe Valley area) had jumped to close on 10,000 and was expanding rapidly.

The nineteenth century was one of spectacular industrial growth in the Tawe Valley on Swansea's East Side, and throughout the South-west Wales region within a radius of some fifteen miles of the docks at Swansea. The lower valley between Clydach and the sea became tightly packed with great iron works, steel works, and tinplate

[2] J. Mansel Thomas, '800 Years a Town' in *Picture Press*, the Journal of the Pressed Steel Company Ltd., Vol. 1, No. 2, 1962—which includes a special series of articles on Swansea, edited by Huw Wheldon.

[3] D. Trevor Williams, *The Economic Development of Swansea and of the Swansea District*, 1940, p. 70.

and sheet works, crowded side by side with the existing smelting industries.[4] Just a hundred years ago George Borrow, on his celebrated perambulation through Wales. trudged down the valley to the old town. 'As I proceeded,' he wrote, 'I sometimes passed pleasant groves and hedgerows, sometimes huge works; in this valley there was a singular mixture of nature and art, of the voices of birds and the clanking of chains, of the mists of heaven and the smoke of furnaces.' By the end of the century there was little left of nature.

With the growth of heavy industry and the opening of dozens of blast furnaces and rolling mills and coke ovens, a flood of immigrants arrived—from the neighbouring Welsh counties (like Mr Hughes's father in the case described in our first chapter), from Ireland, from all over England but particularly from the Midlands and from Gloucester and Devon and Cornwall and Somerset just across the Bristol Channel. 'As long ago as 1823 there were steam-packets sailing regularly three times a week between Swansea and Bristol and twice weekly between Swansea and Ilfracombe.'[5]

As each decade passed there were huge increases of population. By 1901, the number had reached 94,000—more than nine times the figure for a corresponding area, a century earlier. Comparisons between one census and another are complicated in some cases by intercensal changes in area. The general pattern of the population history of the town and district can, however, be seen quite clearly. In the last forty years since 1921 the area of the Borough has remained constant. During this period the population rose from 157,000 to 165,000 between 1921 and 1931, and then declined slightly, with unemployment and migration during the thirties, to 161,000 in 1939. After a sharp drop during the abnormal conditions of the war years, the population figure had recovered to its 1939 level by 1951. In the last ten years up to the census of 1961, it has again increased to above 167,000—an increase over the ten-year period of 3·9 per cent (compared with an increase of 5·3 per cent in the population of England and Wales as a whole, or with an increase of 2·1 per cent in the South Wales census region: Bethnal Green incidentally declined dramatically by 19·4 per cent in the same period—an important difference between Swansea and Bethnal Green which must be borne in mind in any comparison of family relationships in the two areas).

[4] There are, fortunately, a number of excellent studies of the recent social and economic history of the South-west Wales region—particularly, D. Trevor Williams, op. cit; T. Brennan, E. W. Cooney and H. Pollins, *Social Change in South West Wales*, 1954; and W. E. Minchinton, *The British Tinplate Industry*, 1957.

[5] D. Trevor Williams, op. cit., p. 169.

Whilst the details of Swansea's earlier economic and population history are of considerable background interest, the period which concerns us particularly in this study is the eighty years since 1881, approximately the life-span of the most elderly people still alive in Swansea. The changes which interest us most are those which have occurred during the lifetimes of our elderly informants. There is no doubt whatsoever that the information yielded by the decennial censuses during the period is extremely important to our study of family composition and relationships. The detailed analysis of census data is a specialist task beyond our competence. However, certain conclusions, relevant to our study, emerge clearly and without complicated analysis—notably of course the decline of family size and of household size, and the changes in population structure. We will be discussing these changes in later chapters. The evidence on population movements from the various census reports is much more difficult to assess briefly and simply—the complexities in the analysis of migration are a familiar theme of the writings of demographers. This evidence is, however, of particular interest to us as it gives a most useful indication of the geographical spread of family relationships.

A picture of migration into the Borough during the last eighty years can be obtained by examining the data given in the decennial censuses on the birthplace of the people living in the town at the time of the particular census. Table 2.1 below gives the composition of the population by birthplace at four points of time covering this period.

Table 2.1: Birthplace of Swansea's population: 1881—1961

Place of Birth	1881		1901		1921		1951		1961	
	Nos.	%	Nos.	%	Nos.	%	Nos.	%	Nos.	%
Swansea ⎫ Glamorgan ⎬	42,090	64	69,509	74	Not available		130,582	81	Not available	
Other Wales	8,643	13	9,760	10			9,537	6		
Wales—Total	50,733	77	79,269	84	133,965	85	140,119	87	144,611	86
England	11,770	18	12,063	13	18,516	12	15,507	9	16,781	10
Scotland	396	1	461	—	767	—	986	1	1,134	1
Ireland	1,824	3	1,174	1	1,558	1	1,246	1	1,311	1
Abroad and ⎫ Not stated ⎬	874	1	1,570	2	2,748	2	3,130	2	3,232	2
Total Population	65,597	100	94,537	100	157,554	100	160,988	100	167,069	100

The figures for those actually born in Swansea itself at these various census dates would have been interesting, but the census reports give only the total figure of those born in Swansea and in the surrounding county of Glamorgan (and not even this for 1921 and 1961). Still the figures given do show that, throughout the period, immigrants have formed a substantial proportion of Swansea's population. In 1881 more than a third of the population had been born outside Swansea and Glamorgan, just under a quarter outside Wales altogether. By 1951, with increasing population stability, the proportion of immigrants had declined to a fifth of the total population of the town. But the actual numbers of immigrants were still very considerable, totalling over 30,000, the great majority of these (13 per cent of the Borough total) having come from beyond the borders of Wales—with probably, if not inevitably, family and kin connections extending back to their places of origin.

In our sample survey of the total population in 1960, we did not include a question on place of birth. We did, however, ask several questions about the residential history and movements of the adults we interviewed. Asked where they had been brought up (that is, where they had spent the period of their schooldays) the replies were as follows:

Table 2.2: Main Sample—Area Brought Up

Reply	Numbers	%	%
Locality of Swansea in which now living	663	33	⎫ 74
Other locality within Swansea	807	41	⎭
Region around up to 12 miles	116	6	⎫
Elsewhere in Wales	130	7	⎬ 26
Elsewhere	246	13	⎭
Totals	1,962	100	100

This table gives some indication both of movements within the Borough to which we will be referring presently—and also of the influx of immigrants. The figures are of course not strictly comparable with those from the census but they emphasize the conclusions about the importance of immigration in the composition of the population. About a quarter of those we interviewed in 1960 had spent their schooldays outside the Borough, 13 per cent outside Wales. The replies to the next question—where have you spent most of your life? given in Table 2.3 on page 48—provide an interesting comparison with the figures on place of upbringing.

The degree of absorption of immigrants depends on many factors, particularly on the length of time they have been living in Swansea. Though they may well have been born and brought up elsewhere, it is

Table 2.3: Main Sample—Area Spent Most of Life

Reply	Numbers	%	%
Locality of Swansea in which now living	1,051	54	84
Other locality within Swansea	606	30	
Region around up to 12 miles	74	4	16
Elsewhere in Wales	72	4	
Elsewhere	159	8	
Totals	1,962	100	100

at least likely that if they have lived for a long enough time within the Borough they will have come to see Swansea as their only 'home' and to have developed a local cluster of family relationships. By the test of where they have spent most of their lives, only 12 per cent of the population are true 'outsiders' as far as Swansea and its immediate environs is concerned, as compared with 20 per cent brought up outside this local region and at least 18 per cent born outside it according to the 1951 census (we say 'at least' because the census figure of locally-born is that for the whole of Glamorgan and not that for Swansea and the surrounding twelve miles to which the figures from our survey refer).

Even a cursory glance at the names listed in the Electoral Register or in the telephone directory is enough to confirm the diversity in the origin of the town's population which has had such a marked effect on its social and cultural evolution into this modern and complex urban community—the second largest town in Wales—here in Wales' 'Middle West'. Interspersed with the great parade of familiar Welsh names—the legions of Jones, Evans, Williams, Davies, Morgans, Lewis, Llewellyns, Owens, Thomas, Rees, and so on—there are hosts of typical English names and sizeable contingents of Irish and Scots. Not only have Swansea's connections with the sea lent an aura of romance to the unromantic—'the old dock' in Mansel Thomas's description 'once bustling with blue-water men, Cape Horners and their theatrical four-masters'—but generations of sailors have settled in the town and produced families with exotic names like Mohammed, Schleswich, Zanetti, Beaujean, Cutajar or Ullah. Names like these together with others borne by descendants of those who in the nineteenth and early twentieth centuries were drawn not only from the fields of rural Wales but from all parts of the British Isles—particularly from Devon and Cornwall and Somerset or from Ireland across the water—to seek a share in the industrial prosperity of

Swansea, provide a continual reminder of the cosmopolitan character of the town.

Whilst from the censuses and from our survey it is possible to assess numerically and, for those in our sample, to identify immigrants into the Borough (we consider the family relationships of immigrants in a later chapter), there is little that can be said about migrants from Swansea to outside areas. Our survey covered only those families resident in the Borough in 1960. In all urban populations there is a continuous circulation of population—individuals and often whole households pack up and move out to other areas in Britain or even overseas, whilst others move in from the outside world beyond the borders of the town. It is impossible from the various census reports to discover the exact numbers who have either moved out or moved in within the previous decade: the reports give only the net gain or loss by migration after the intercensal population change has been examined in the light of the natural increase or decrease through births and deaths. Should there be an exact correspondence in the numbers moving in and those moving out, the net change through migration shown in the census would be nil—even though the actual movement might have been substantial. It is of course possible to get some idea of this actual movement through the figures of birthplace but, apart from the fact that it is an exceptionally laborious task to scrutinize the numerous county reports to discover where migrants from Swansea have settled, these figures give only a very general picture with many important details obscured.

So far as the figures for the net gain or loss by migration are concerned, the various census reports show that throughout the period of vigorous industrial growth of the nineteenth century Swansea had a very favourable balance of imports in terms of people. In the last decade only, from 1891 to 1901 (well within the memories of our older informants), did the picture change dramatically with a net loss through emigration of over 11,000 people—the effect of a decade of economic depression and contraction in the tinplate industry and the closure of many tinplate works in the Swansea area.[6] By 1911 the industry had recovered and Swansea was again showing a large net gain through immigration with a balance of over 12,000 people coming in to recover the losses of the previous decade—many of these, as our family histories show, returning home after a period

[6] W. E. Minchinton, op. cit., p. 72, describes the gloom in the industry at this time as a result of the McKinley tariff, frequently referred to by elderly people we interviewed who well remember this severe slump and the wave of emigration it provoked.

away. From 1921 onwards the picture has changed profoundly. The prolonged economic depression of the inter-war years clearly had its effect on Swansea as on the whole of industrial Wales.[7] Between 1921 and 1931, the population continued to increase, through the excess of births over deaths, even though there was a net loss of 4·4 per cent (some 7,000 persons) through migration. Between 1931 and 1939, with a declining birth rate, the population fell and the loss through migration increased to 5 per cent. In the twenty years from 1931 to 1951, including the war years, the net loss through migration was just under 10 per cent of the 1931 population. The population balance sheet showed that in these years some 16,000 more persons moved out of the Borough than moved in. In the last ten years, however, the amount of movement in and out of the Borough as measured by the net migration figures has been small, and the direction of the movement reversed. During these years Swansea has made a net gain of population through migration amounting to just over half of 1 per cent.

The constant circulation of population in this regional centre in the recent past, the ebb and flow under the influence of changing economic conditions, is only vaguely outlined by these bare figures. The picture is clear enough, however, to indicate that we are not dealing with a remote and inaccessible area, relatively self-contained and isolated so far as its population is concerned. On the contrary it is immediately clear from these census reports that the geographical spread of family relationships resulting from substantial population movements must form a basic theme of our analysis. Swansea may be near the end of the line but throughout the last eighty years or so large numbers of people have got on or off the train. There are relatively few families now living in Swansea who have been unaffected by this movement of individuals into or out of the Borough. We asked each of the subjects in our main survey a series of questions concerning the whereabouts of their existing relatives—these questions did not cover the whole range of kinship, but were confined to those categories of relatives normally included in the phrase 'close relatives'.[8] If from the replies given we classify these families by the

[7] J. Parry Lewis, 'Population' in *The Welsh Economy*, edited by Brinley Thomas, 1962, p. 179. 'Between 1921 and 1931 there was a sharp reaction; the Welsh population actually fell by 2 per cent, while that of England rose by 6 per cent . . . In the years 1931–51 Wales lost 6·7 per cent of its population through migration, which was almost equal to the natural increase of 6·9 per cent . . . the incidence of migration had been heaviest among men born between 1905 and 1925.

[8] The actual categories can be seen from the schedule itself which is given in Appendix II.

farthest-living relative mentioned in each case, we get the following picture of the maximum spread of family relationships:

Table 2.4: Maximum Geographical Range of Family Relationships

Families in Category				Numbers	%
1. All kin and in-laws mentioned reside in Swansea				291	15
2. Farthest-living relative in region around				135	7
3. ,, ,, ,, in S. Wales				145 ⎫ 158	8
,, ,, ,, in N. Wales				13 ⎭	
4. ,, ,, ,, in Midlands				185	9
5. ,, ,, ,, in London				197	10
6. ,, ,, ,, in other part of Britain				598	31
7. ,, ,, ,, Overseas				398	20
			Total Number of Families	1,962	100

This is an unsatisfactory table from a number of points of view: we have included it because it does give a rough indication of the effect of recent migration on the geography of family relationships. In fact, only 15 per cent of our total sample of families had all their close kin living within the Borough of Swansea. Indeed the proportion is still less than a quarter if those families with no kin outside the surrounding region, up to twelve miles from the Borough boundary, be included. Under a third of our subjects had all the relatives mentioned on our schedules living within Wales. For the remainder (70 per cent of our sample), their kinship networks extended beyond Wales to various parts of Britain—and one family in five had at least one of its close relatives living overseas. There have been no previous surveys in Swansea with which we could compare these figures, and no previous study in Britain has considered the geographical distribution of family relationships in this way. It is impossible therefore to assess precisely the extent to which the situation in Swansea has changed over recent generations, or to discuss the extent to which Swansea follows or diverges from the pattern in urban areas generally. The brief evidence on migration which we have given above, particularly Table 2.1 giving the birthplace of Swansea's population at five points over the last eighty years, seems to suggest that there has been no great or sudden change in this picture of the geographical scatter of relatives during the lifetime of elderly people still alive in Swansea. The proportion of the population born locally has increased substantially over this period (from 64 per cent to 81 per cent) but equally there has been a considerable increase in emigration (in the thirty years between 1921 and 1951). In stressing the continual movement of population in the past eighty years and the consequent scattering of kin we do not wish necessarily to imply that the geographical clustering of close relatives of the people of Swansea was thereby destroyed. One of the reasons why Table 2.4 is in some ways unsatisfactory is that many people surrounded by large numbers of relatives fall into the overseas category simply because they have a brother who has emigrated to Patagonia, or Australia. In the nineteenth century Swansea was gaining population and in these conditions once a family had moved to the town they were likely to remain and establish a stable family pattern in the new environment. When, between the wars, Swansea began to lose population the migration this involved acted on the family rather as a plague or a famine might have done, not radically altering the geographical structure of the familial group, or destroying the residential stability of the neighbourhood, but creating gaps in both structures. For the majority of the population who remained life went on very much as before even if the ranks of both family and community had been somewhat thinned. We shall be discussing, in Chapter VI and elsewhere, the effect of physical separation on the maintenance of relationships: for the moment we merely wish to emphasize, from a brief glance at the census data and some details from our own survey, the importance of this problem in our study.

THE WESTWARD DRIFT

The large-scale movements of people from area to area within the Borough that have taken place within living memory are of equal importance and, in a sense, more immediately relevant to our study. Though the wider picture of the spread of family connections far beyond the borders of the Borough as a result of external migration does not appear to have changed very much over the last eighty years or so—the gains from the swings being more or less matched by the losses from the roundabouts, there have been major and striking changes during this period in the distribution of population within Swansea itself.

Within little more than a single generation the town has altered dramatically. Contemporary Swansea is a radically different place from the Swansea of the first two decades of this century. And nowhere is this change more immediately apparent than in the building of houses and the creation almost overnight of new residential areas. Indeed in the short space of the last two years or so that we have spent in Swansea, we have seen tremendous changes in the town's landscape: great new blocks of flats tower over the open spaces of Sketty Park and over the shells of council houses in various stages of completion as a large new housing estate takes shape; in the old, tightly packed, working-class districts of Dyfatty and Greenhill just north of the town centre a wholesale transformation is taking place as narrow streets and rows of small terrace houses are bulldozed into oblivion to make room for the giant twelve-and fourteen-story blocks of flats that already have their first Corporation tenants. Throughout Swansea the scene of change and transformation is repeated as new roads are laid and new housing estates and projects, created by private builders' speculation or by Corporation contract, alter the landscape.

In the last forty years alone, the number of houses has increased by 71 per cent—from 28,920 in 1921 to 49,392 in 1961—whilst the area of the Borough has remained unchanged and the population has grown by only 6·2 per cent. Since 1921, vast new housing estates have covered the windy hills and sprawled over large areas of farmland and open common; 8,000 new homes have been completed in the last ten years alone and the number of dwellings shows a net increase of 7,500—an increase of 18 per cent in dwellings, compared with a population growth of only 3·9 per cent. With public and private building proceeding at such a rate, the town continues to expand rapidly, particularly to the west and north-west. The booming prosperity of post-war Swansea is nowhere more visible than in this surge of building.

The most notable feature of this expansion has been the growth of Corporation and private housing estates. In 1921, the Corporation had built 126 houses for municipal tenants: today, forty years later, the figure of Corporation houses has passed the 14,000 mark. Over a quarter of all the private dwellings in Swansea are now owned by the Corporation—lived in, as our survey revealed, by 29 per cent of the total adult population of the Borough. By 1939, Swansea Corporation had completed the immense Townhill and Mayhill estate on the hills immediately above the town centre, and seven smaller estates, mainly on the east side of the town. These have by now just reached the stage of becoming 'second-generation' estates as the children born on the estates to the earliest tenants are beginning to marry and take over tenancies. The remaining eight large estates scattered over the Borough, but mainly in the north-west, are all products of the immediate post-war emphasis on public building.

Only in the last five or six years has private building really got under way again—with an annually increasing momentum to meet the urgent and apparently insatiable demand for privately owned houses;[9] a sure sign of affluence. In the last few years at least seventeen new private housing estates have been completed or nearly completed (3,025 houses were built by private enterprise between

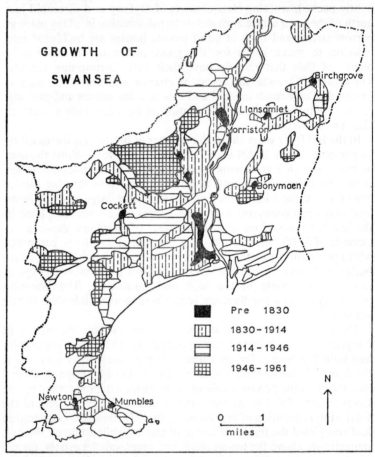

GROWTH OF SWANSEA

	Pre 1830
	1830 – 1914
	1914 – 1946
	1946 – 1961

[9] Swansea is already notable for its high incidence of house-ownership and its above-average percentage of Corporation-owned houses. Of our total sample of 1,962 households, 48 per cent were owner-occupiers, 29 per cent Council tenants, and 23 per cent other tenants. Compare this with a recently-published national survey in England which showed that in the category—'Other Urban, pop. 20,000 or more'—to which Swansea belongs, the breakdown of tenure was 40 per cent owner-occupiers, 19 per cent Council tenants, and 40 per cent other tenants. *Housing Since the Rent Act*, Occasional papers on Social Administration, No. 3, by D. V. Donnison, Christine Cockburn, and T. Corlett, 1961, p. 14.

1954 and 1961), and many others have begun and are well under way.

This rapid development has had profound effects on the sociological character of the town. The centre of gravity of the town, the psychological focus as it were, has noticeably shifted west as the modern, anglicized, 'middle-class' areas on the residential west have expanded, and equally as the old industrial 'working-class' areas on the east have declined. With the housing development a general population shift of considerable dimensions has occurred. If we divide the Borough into four geographical areas, we can observe that of just over 24,000 new homes built in Swansea (or in process of being completed) between 1919 and 1962, only 1,500 or so have been built in the old neighbourhoods of the Central area of the town, and only 3,500 in the whole bleak Tawe Valley area on the east. The major expansions, as can be seen from the map on p. 55, have been to the west of these older areas: 7,000 new houses have appeared on the scene in West Swansea and more than 12,000 on the wide open spaces to the north-west.

We can illustrate the movements of population and the differential expansion on the east and west by comparing the statistics given by the censuses of 1921 and 1951 for the two parliamentary constituencies into which Swansea is divided—Swansea East and Swansea West. In area, Swansea East (with 12,247 acres) is considerably larger than Swansea West (with 9,353 acres). The dividing line between the two constituencies runs more or less north-west to south-east across the middle of the Borough. It divides the Borough politically—and, approximately, socially and culturally, as we shall see when we examine this basic dichotomy in the chapter which follows.

The following table shows the substantial changes which have occurred in population distribution and housing during the short space of thirty years.

Table 2.5: Distribution of Population and Houses, 1921 and 1951, by Swansea's two Parliamentary Constituencies

Constituency	1921	1951	Net change	% change
	Population			
Swansea East	91,302	77,404	− 13,898	− 15
Swansea West	66,252	83,584	+ 17,332	+ 26
Total Population	157,554	160,988	+ 3,434	+ 2

Table 2.5 continued

Constituency	1921	1951	Net change	% change
	Houses			
Swansea East	16,738	20,271	+ 3,533	+ 21
Swansea West	12,182	21,667	+ 9,485	+ 78
Total Houses	28,920	41,938	+ 13,018	+ 46

Between 1921 and 1951 thousands of people moved west within Swansea—out of the old industrial communities and into the new residential areas. In 1921, Swansea East outnumbered Swansea West by more than 25,000 in population and by 4,500 in dwellings. By 1951, the situation had been reversed in both respects. The table above shows quite clearly the major westward population drift within the last generation.

The above figures give the net loss or gain in people and homes for the two constituencies respectively. A detailed examination of the census data for each of the eighteen wards[10] provides a fuller picture of the actual trends of growth and internal movement. The greatest population decline took place in the wards covering the old industrial communities in the Tawe Valley—Morriston, Landore, Llansamlet, and St John's—and in the wards covering the old working-class neighbourhoods in and around the Town Centre and the docks—Alexandra, Castle, St Helen's, Victoria and St Thomas. These wards are mainly, but not entirely, in Swansea East constituency. The greatest population growth occurred in the predominantly middle-class communities on the west. Sketty, for example, doubled its population and almost trebled its number of houses in this thirty years, and so did the Ffynone ward which borders Sketty. The two old villages of Cockett, just to the west of Townhill and Oystermouth, at the extreme west of the bay, doubled their number of houses and had thousands of new residents. Penderry in the north-west, formerly a ward of bare hills and open common, almost trebled both in population and homes with the development of the large housing estates within its perimeter. Every single ward of the Borough showed a profound change in both population and housing during this

---

[10] In 1952 the ward boundaries were changed, and the number of wards reduced to fifteen, as a result of these substantial population changes. For this reason it is not possible to compare the 1961 figures with earlier information. At the time of the two censuses we are concerned with here, those of 1921 and 1951, the boundaries and areas of the eighteen wards were identical.

period. The whole of Swansea it seemed was on the move westwards, and the process still continues, though the contemporary situation is now more complicated.

The 1961 census figures show that the population of West Swansea has remained stationary during the last ten years while the population of East Swansea has grown. Paradoxically this is a result of the westward drift. As the western part of the borough becomes more crowded and prices rise a movement even farther west over the Borough boundary has begun, while those who do not wish to move so far or cannot afford the higher costs in the near west remain where they are. At the same time the advantages of building on the *extreme* east of the borough are beginning to be realized. This area is predominantly rural, away from the industrial Swansea Valley, has the advantage of being—at the moment—inexpensive and lies nearer the coastal plain on which are sited many of the industries to which a considerable proportion of Swansea's industrial labour force travels. The extreme eastern fringe of the borough also merges at some points with the more select residential districts of the neighbouring borough of Neath.

The dominant theme of the nineteenth century and the first twenty years or so of the twentieth century was the rapid growth of compact industrial communities clustered around the great works and thriving industry of the Tawe Valley. Strongholds of Welsh-speaking and nonconformity, with crowded chapels and a multiplicity of splendid choirs and working-men's clubs and rugby teams, they displayed a vigorous working-class culture and a deep-rooted community cohesion affected by the periodic waves of economic adversity, religious revival, and political radicalism. We have seen something of the Morriston of his youth through the eyes of Mr Hughes in our first chapter: the same could be said, by elderly people born and raised in these valley communities, for the others—Landore, Llansamlet, Bonymaen, Treboeth, Hafod, Clydach in the extreme north, or St Thomas around the docks. The dominant theme of the last forty years or so, and particularly of the last fifteen years since the war, has been the decline of these old communities, as the younger generation has moved away, and the rise of new communities on the hills to the west. Today, as the focus of the town has shifted west, an air of decline and decay hangs over the Tawe Valley, exaggerated by the scene of derelict, silent works and abandoned tips scarring the landscape. Thousands of families have moved away to the new housing estates, turning their backs, psychologically as well as physically, on this 'old-fashioned' working-class environment and culture. Thousands more would like to move.[11] The drift away of population is associated with a striking change in cultural attitude and social aspiration. It is not simply a case of packing up and moving away to a new house in another district: at the destination there is not only a new home but a new way of life. It is this prospect which attracts the young and deters the old, accentuating the gulf between the generations so clearly visible in the account of Mr Hughes as he compares the situation and attitudes of his married children, widely dispersed over many different neighbourhoods in contemporary Swansea, and those of his own generation clustered in Morriston and the adjoining industrial communities in the valley.

We noticed with family after family in our survey the effects of this internal population movement of the last generation or so on the pattern of family relationships. As we shall be discussing in our next chapter (and as emerges quite clearly from the lengthy account of Mr Hughes) it is not just a question of physical separation but of the profound change in behaviour and attitude which is associated in so many cases with this movement of residence. In Swansea as elsewhere social and physical mobility are closely linked.

In Table 2.2, page 47, we gave the results of the question we asked about where the persons we interviewed had been brought up. 74 per cent of our subjects had spent their schooldays in Swansea, but only 33 per cent in the localities in which they are now living. A further examination of these replies shows the effects of the west-ward movement of population during the last few decades. Of 470 subjects in our survey who had been brought up in Swansea and are now living on the west, 215 (that is 46 per cent) had spent their childhoods in the old industrial communities on the east side of the town.

The strong attraction of the west—of the modern anglicized, middle-class' residential areas near the sea and the bays of Gower and of the new housing estates with the fine schools and modern community facilities on the hills west of the valley—is clearly shown in the preferences expressed by those in our survey who said that they would like to move from their present homes if they had the chance. Altogether of our total of 1,962 subjects, 710 (36 per cent) said that they would like to move. We asked where they would like to live and the replies, grouped into three broad areas according to where the informants were living at the time of our survey, were as follows:

[11] Thirty-six per cent of our subjects wanted to move—36 per cent of the total number of households in the Borough is approximately 18,000.

Table 2.6: Preference of those subjects wishing to move: Main Sample 1960

Subject now living in:	Western Area	Central Area	Eastern Area
% *Would like to move to:*			
Western Area	80	68	61
Central Area	8	12	11
Eastern Area	6	17	23
'Anywhere' Outside Borough	6	3	5
Total %	100	100	100
Numbers of movers	51	249	410
Potential movers as percentage of sample in area	14	43	40
Sample numbers in area	367	474	1,021

The more favourable conditions of life in the west are reflected by its relatively low percentage of potential movers—approximately three times as many people living in and around the Town Centre or in the communities of the Tawe Valley would like to change their present places of residence. Of those wishing to move in the western area of the town, the vast majority would like to continue living within the area—whereas some two-thirds of the potential movers of the central and eastern areas would prefer to move out of these areas altogether and live on the west of the town.

With the co-operation of the Borough Housing Department, we undertook a special analysis of the housing list which, even after the large-scale rehousing that has taken place already in the period since the war, still contained over 6,000 applicants for council houses in 1962.[12] We selected 600 of these at random and examined various

[12] Such lists often include a large number of outdated applications. We sampled Swansea's housing list within a year of its revision. It has been revised on several occasions since and now contains approximately 4,000 names.

information given on the application forms—in particular the preference for one or other of the fifteen Corporation estates. The great majority (87 per cent) of these applicants lived in the older neighbourhoods of the east and central areas of the town. Their preferences for particular estates markedly followed the pattern revealed by our own survey of potential movers. The West Cross estate overlooking the bay on the far west of Swansea headed the list by a very considerable margin, followed by the Townhill and Mayhill estates (favoured because of their proximity to the main shopping centre) and the Portmead, Gendros, Penlan and Blaenymaes estates on the northwest. The least-preferred estates were those on the eastern side of the Tawe Valley. At a recent meeting of the Housing Committee, the plans were considered for the extension of the existing estates on the north-east of the valley by a further 600 houses: this was opposed by the Housing Manager who alleged that he would have considerable difficulty letting council houses in this unfavoured area.

One of the major conclusions of the Bethnal Green study of family relationships was that the people there did not wish to leave the East End and were in fact forced out by public rehousing policy.[13] Young and Willmott discuss this at length and recommend the planned reconstruction of Bethnal Green with the emphasis on the provision of houses within this ancient borough to preserve its traditional culture and close-knit family life. This no doubt would be equally the view of many old people in Swansea bewildered and confused by the social revolution of the last generation or so, and filled with nostalgia for the friendly, familiar, stable, familial atmosphere of the past in these old communities of the Tawe Valley. But the young seem less sentimental. The evidence from our survey and from our analysis of housing applicants confirms, on the contrary, a marked willingness on their part to move out of these areas, and a strong desire to give their children an opportunity to grow up in the modern social and cultural conditions of the affluent west of Swansea rather than in the grim and drab industrial east (for all its old-fashioned cultural strengths and virtues). Time and again we noticed in our analysis of housing applicants—and in our detailed interviewing—how young married couples preferred relatively distant housing estates, public or private, on the west to near-by estates close to their work and to their elderly relatives. The Clase estate is on the hill just above Morriston, a few minutes' walk or a short bus-ride away. But it was noticeable how few Morristonian applicants for council houses gave the Clase estate as their first choice—preferring obviously to get right away to a new social environment and a new way of life altogether. The same could

[13] Michael Young and Peter Willmott, op. cit., Chapter XII, *passim.*

be said of the other estates on the east on the doorstep of the other old valley communities. The journey out of the valley to a home in the west may be only a few miles (it is about eight miles from Morriston to the West Cross Estate) but the cultural distance is great. It is for many a journey out of the past, and out of the traditional working class. The profound disturbances of the older patterns of family and neighbourhood relationships which ensue, and which form the theme of this present study, are part of the price paid. 'Nowadays' said one old man living alone in a small terrace house under the wall of the old, and now disused, tinplate works in Landore in which he spent most of his working life 'they get up on the hills above the valley here and see West Swansea like Moses looking at the Promised Land —and if they get the chance they're off before you know it.' Perhaps only the old generation, left behind in the old neighbourhoods, are fully aware of the cost. It is the relatively small-scale contemporary movement which has been described in this section, we shall be arguing, that has had a more important effect on the *structure* of the extended family than the migrations (over much larger distances) of yesterday.

THE SEARCH FOR A HOME

We have stressed the changes that have taken place in recent years in the distribution of population and in the rapid growth of housing because the effects of these changes, in terms of the behaviour of individual families, are going to form a recurring theme in our discussions in later chapters. There is one further aspect of the housing situation that needs emphasis. As the census data shows, Swansea has been expanding faster geographically in the last thirty or forty years, but particularly since the war, than it has been growing in terms of population. There are now many more houses to go round, relative to the size of the population, than there were for example in 1921. The average number of persons per dwelling has declined sharply from 5·2 in 1921 to 3·4 in 1961. In the thirty years—1921 to 1951—the proportion of households sharing dwellings had fallen by a third, from 31 to 21 per cent. And in the last ten years, this proportion of shared dwellings has been halved again. The 1961 census shows that then only 6·4 per cent of Swansea's households were sharing a dwelling with other households.[14] The number of private dwellings

[14] In the Bethnal Green sample in 1955, 39 per cent of the people interviewed lived in shared dwellings. Fourteen per cent of all the households in Great Britain shared a dwelling at the time of the 1951 census. Young and Willmott, op. cit., p. 211.

in Swansea (49,392) almost equalled the number of recorded private households (51,119)—a household being defined as a group of persons in a private house who normally live together and eat together. The impression one gets reading these figures is that, with the rapid increase in the number of houses available, the people of Swansea in general are now better housed than ever before. These figures can, however, be very misleading if interpreted to mean that there is now no great housing shortage in Swansea. On the contrary, the pressure of housing paradoxically remains intense—as can be readily inferred from the fact that in 1962 there were still over 6,000 families on the Borough's housing list waiting for a Corporation house or flat.

In fact a large number of the 'private households' recorded in the census contain what Ruth Glass in her Middlesborough survey[15] called 'concealed households'—that is, married couples and their children living with relatives, usually one or other set of parents, because they are unable to find a home of their own. We shall be examining the incidence and composition of these composite households, produced by 'doubling-up' or, in the Swansea idiom 'living through and through' (rather than sharing a dwelling with separate households), when we discuss household composition in detail in Chapter IV. We know that the proportion of shared dwellings in Swansea has decreased sharply with the improvement in housing, but it is impossible from the census data to calculate whether the proportion of composite households has altered over the last generation or so. Eighteen per cent of all married persons in our sample were either sharing a dwelling with another household (7 per cent) or living in a composite household that included another married couple (11 per cent). If all these married persons wanted a home of their own, and it is reasonable to assume that most if not all of them would, Swansea would need at once a further 4,000 houses.[16] This is 29 per cent of the existing number of Corporation houses and at the rate of 800 a year at which houses have been built by both private builders and the Corporation over the last ten years would take five years to build. This rough estimate does not allow for many other factors affecting housing pressure—single people wanting a home of their own, slum

[15] *The Social Background of a Plan: A Study of Middlesborough*, edited by Ruth Glass, 1948, p. 225.

[16] Eighteen per cent of married adult persons in the Borough is 15,700. The number of couples doubling up is therefore 7,850. The number of houses required would be half this—enough to enable one family from each dwelling to move out or 3,925. This is 8 per cent of the existing total of just under 50,000 houses. We have assumed that there are two households only per shared dwelling. In so far as there are cases of more than two households in a dwelling this figure is an underestimate.

clearance, population growth either through migration or natural increase, increased longevity, reduced family size or earlier age at marriage. It deals only with one aspect of present overcrowding, and is thus a *minimum* estimate of the current housing shortage in Swansea.

At first glance it seems a curious fact that this situation of shortage should exist. Since 1921 there has been a spectacular increase in the number of houses in Swansea which has well out-paced the actual population growth in that time. This is a fact which clearly perplexes many people who are astonished to see the Corporation housing list still containing such large members of applicant families, and showing no signs of reduction, even after the provision of thousands of new houses in the post-war years and the feverish expansion of Corporation estates. If this is the position in 1961 with 49,392 houses and a population of 167,322 one wonders how people managed for example in 1921 when there were only 28,920 houses for a population of 157,554.

Indeed many elderly people comment, from personal observation and experience, that things have got worse rather than better. 'House to Let' signs have now completely disappeared from the scene though they were not uncommon before the war, and a frequent phenomenon in the years before the First World War. 'Well, there were plenty of houses to be had in those days—if you could pay the rent,' said an elderly widow in Plasmarl describing how she and her brothers and sisters had all found homes after marriage within a few minutes' walk of their parental home, 'there was a street by Plasmarl school—well, they called it Death Row. The people who were living there were all old and they died off one by one. I remember the whole row empty— about ten houses. The street gradually filled up again as new families moved in. But there was no rush at all—some stood empty for months and months.' Nowadays a single advertisement in *The South Wales Evening Post* for a house to let produces an immediate torrent of letters and phone-calls—and most families in the Borough seem to operate a sort of bush-telegraph service on behalf of house-hunting relatives (particularly for young newly-weds) with manned listening posts, in as many districts as possible, watching and waiting for signs of movement.

It is difficult to establish the precise facts to compare the past with the present, but it is probably true to say in respect of the availability of houses that the position has in fact worsened rather than improved. The reasons for this somewhat paradoxical situation are many and complex, and are concerned both with changes in Swansea's vital statistics and with changes in the housing standards that people, in a more affluent era, are willing to accept. The basic fact is the decline in family size and consequently in household size.[17] A population divided into smaller families and households needs more houses. The decline in the age at marriage over the same period means a higher proportion of married couples and consequently an increased demand for housing.[18] The fact that old people tend to live longer means, on the other hand, that fewer houses become vacant through deaths. Finally with the general improvement in economic conditions, there is the widespread and obvious demand for better housing and the general reluctance to share dwellings with other families. Houses no longer stand vacant because people cannot afford the rents asked (even the high blocks of council flats in Sketty Park and Dyfatty with 'high-rise' rents of over four pounds a week will undoubtedly find their Corporation tenants when they are completed even though many families will have to skip their turns on the housing list because they cannot afford these rents). Formerly the poorest section of the population were forced through their poverty to share a dwelling for most of their lives or to find room with relatives. The poor are still with us, though their numbers are smaller. The extent to which people and families are forced—and are willing—to live on top of one another has substantially decreased.

Like most towns in Britain, particularly industrial towns, Swansea has the usual legacy from the past of acres and acres of miserable, sub-standard housing in narrow, crowded streets—the Victorian 'barracks for the proletariat' within a stone's-throw of the factories. The large areas of buildings more than a hundred years old can be seen on Map 3, page 55, showing the growth of Swansea. It has, however, surprisingly few real slums—the majority of those in the Old Town were cleared with the expansion of the commercial and business centre of the town before, and immediately after, the First World War. The Chief Public Health Inspector earmarked a further 2,747 houses (including 850 temporary, prefabricated dwellings) for clearance as potential slums. Large numbers of these, and of old, substandard property generally, are lived in by old-age pensioners confined to these conditions both by habit and sentiment

[17] The average size of the completed families of women married 1900–9 was 3·4 according to the Report of the Royal Commission on Population, p. 25. The size of families of women aged 45–49 at the 1951 census was 2.

[18] The percentage formed by married persons is an index of changes both in family size and age at marriage. This percentage has risen from 38 per cent in 1921 to 50 per cent in 1951. If there had been the 1921 percentage of married persons in the 1951 population the number of married couples would have fallen by 10,000. If Swansea today had the same proportion of married people as in 1921 its population would be 213,000.

and dislike of upheaval, and also by their inability to pay higher rents.

Little Gam Street and Hoskins Place, for example, a corner of the Sandfields area in the Town Centre—and a neighbourhood in the full sense of this term—consists of seventeen houses scheduled for clearance as 'unfit for human habitation' because of internal damp, insufficient lighting and ventilation and lack of rear access. These two adjoining streets are short and narrow, and most of the cottages have just one room downstairs and one up; none have bathrooms, indoor lavatories, or gardens. The families living there objected strongly, at the public inquiry into the clearance order, to their homes being called 'slums'—inside they are 'little palaces': indeed the Public Health Inspector at the inquiry said 'In forty years' experience of housing I have never come across an area with better tenants than those at Little Gam Street and Hoskins Place. The cleanliness and decoration in these homes is indeed fantastic and full credit must be paid to the tenants.'[19] We did our own survey of these two streets following this public inquiry (which produced a unanimous protest by the residents against their homes being pulled down, the streets 'rubbed off the map of Swansea', and the families compelled to move away to council houses elsewhere in the Borough). We discovered that of the seventeen houses, twelve were occupied by old-age pensioners, paying rents of between twelve and eighteen shillings a week. The average age of householders in these two streets was 64 years—two being over 80 and six over 70. Six of the tenants had lived in these houses for over fifty years, and a further four for over forty years— the average length of residence for the two streets as a whole being forty-two years. This is not an uncommon situation in the older neighbourhoods of the town, with the old clinging to their antiquated, if spick-and-span, homes and the young moving out in search of higher standards of housing.

The type and availability of housing are fundamental factors in family behaviour. The sharp improvement in housing over the last generation in Swansea, with the decline both in the number of persons per house and in the number of families sharing dwellings, is a very important fact to bear in mind in considering the changes that have taken place in family behaviour. There is in fact more room in houses nowadays for people to take in relatives should they so desire, either briefly for holidays or for lengthier periods to provide them

[19] Reported in the *South Wales Evening Post*, 15 May 1962, under the heading 'An Order Threatens the Life of a Community'. We shall refer again to the people of Little Gam Street and Hoskins Place in Chapter VIII when we examine the social conditions of elderly people in Swansea.

with a home. As we stressed, a severe shortage of houses continues and affects people in two ways relevant to our study of family behaviour.

First, families are more or less compelled to accept a house where-ever they can find one and regardless of their preferences for partic-ular neighbourhoods or proximity to kin (this is particularly true of Corporation housing, with the vast waiting list, even though the Housing Department, as we shall see later, does do as much as possible to take account of these preferences). For a family to manage to stick together with several related households close to one another is more a matter of luck than of choice. The dispersal of families is the result of many factors: the availability of houses is of major importance and the current housing shortage favours dispersal rather than clustering.

Secondly, this shortage tends to produce composite households— 'doubling-up'—of a particular and temporary type in that it forces young married couples to live for a period with one or other of their parents. Newly-weds cannot put their names down on the housing list until they are married, and must then expect to wait about ten years for a Corporation house. As we shall be seeing in Chapter V when we consider the situation of young couples immediately after marriage, the proportion of newly-weds starting off their married lives by sharing a home—usually 'living through and through'—with relatives has substantially increased over the last two generations or so. The improvement in housing, by providing more room, has actually made this more likely to happen nowadays than was formerly the case in Swansea. We shall be discussing the implications of this important change in family behaviour.

SWANSEA'S URBAN VILLAGES

The facts that we have given so far about this extensive County Borough—its varied topography and internal diversity of land use, its recent history of physical expansion and population growth, the complex origins of its inhabitants, the contrast in the population histories of the old and new communities, the recent internal move-ments of people—all emphasize the point made earlier that Swansea is not a natural sociological entity. Except in a very general sense of external geographical reference, and in a few internal contexts con-nected with municipal administration and sport particularly, indi-vidual families do not live *in* Swansea but rather in one of the many neighbourhoods or local communities *within* Swansea. It is doubtful whether more than one man in a hundred could say with reasonable precision just where the Borough boundary runs—and it is a matter of little importance that they should be able to do so. The term 'Swansea' is used mainly, and much as one would expect, for the Town Centre; people in the outlying communities within the Borough (in Llansamlet or Killay for example) talk about travelling 'into Swansea' to shop or to work. In Morriston indeed, proud of its Welsh tradition and conscious of being an old industrial township in its own right, many older inhabitants speak jocularly and with sturdy independence of 'Swansea, *near* Morriston'. The important and effective sociological unit is the local community rather than the Borough as a whole.

As must be clear from our account of its growth, and from the maps given in this chapter, Swansea is in fact a town of striking social and cultural contrasts, a loose federation of topographically distinct and dispersed communities ranging from Morriston to Mumbles, from Portmead to Port Tennant. Even a brief tour of the town is enough to indicate that these 'urban villages' vary drastically in their physical appearances and in their main cultural and sociological features. This heterogeneity of community is, as we pointed out in our section on research methods in Chapter I, one of the major features distinguishing Swansea from such places as Bethnal Green or Bermondsey in which previous studies of urban kinship have been undertaken.

In recent sociological writings, there have been numerous and elaborate discussions of the terms 'neighbourhood' and 'community'. We do not propose in this book to enter this familiar debate over definitions. For our purposes it is enough to say that we have divided the town into its twenty-three natural and named localities (using this word advisedly to emphasize that these are primarily geographical areas, most of them 'given' and defined by the nature of the land-scape). Broadly speaking, they are the names one sees on the fronts of the bus services operating within the town. Together they represent the physical and social image of the town that the people who live here carry about in their heads. In popular usage, they are 'communities', though they vary strikingly from one to another in their degree of community consciousness and in the psychological response of individuals to the physical fact of common residence. All contain neighbourhoods within them, and the Chinese puzzle of neighbour-hoods within neighbourhoods down to a single street, or side or end of a street, or turning or cul-de-sac, or whatever. Some—Morriston, for example, or St Thomas or Sketty or Townhill—are so large as to contain within their borders minor geographical sub-divisions of importance and general recognition to the people who live within these areas. We have ignored these further internal distinctions in our statistical analyses, though we took account of them where they seemed relevant in our detailed interviewing and case studies of particular families.

This division of the town into localities is for us a research method —in which we have followed as closely as possible the general picture of the Borough as seen by its inhabitants. It is not intended as a detailed contribution to the social geography of Swansea or to the sociological problems of neighbourhood analysis. That would be a different study altogether from the one we have undertaken here: it may indeed be taken up as a future development of our research in Swansea. Our problem may be stated as follows: Are there noticeable variations in the patterns of family behaviour from area to area within Swansea, and, if so, can these variations be correlated with differences in the social structures and cultural characteristics of these areas? In an effort to answer these questions we have taken the twenty-three localities that emerge readily from the topography of the town (and in popular opinion), grouped these into four broad geographical areas (bearing in mind the obvious social and cultural contrasts that we have referred to in this chapter, and which we will be examining more closely in the chapter which follows), and ensured that our sample survey covered each locality in proportion to its population.

The map on pp. 70–1 shows the geographical distribution of these localities over the Borough, and Table 2.7 (p. 69) gives a picture of the variations in the size of these localities and of the distribution of population over the four districts into which these are grouped. The population figures given are estimates obtained by multiplying the number of electors in each locality, given on the Electoral Register, by the fraction that the general population in the Borough formed of people over 21 at the time of the most recent figures given by the Registrar-General. Table 2.7 shows also the distribution over these localities of the persons we interviewed during our main random-sample survey in 1960.

Whilst they vary internally in the sizes of the component localities, three of the four districts are approximately equal in population; the fourth, the Town Centre, is substantially smaller. Though the table does not show this, the four districts differ substantially in their densities of population and of housing. West Swansea has a general population density of about 30 persons per acre—though the density of its two localities of large bay-windowed terrace houses, Brynmill and Mount Pleasant bordering the centre of the town, is well above this, in the region of 60 persons per acre. The average density in the Tawe Valley is closer to 75 to the acre, whilst that in the North-West,

Table 2.7: Estimated Locality Populations, 1960

District	Locality	No. in our Sample Survey	Estimated Population	Total for District
West Swansea	1. Mumbles (and Newton)	87	7,300	
	2. West Cross	66	5,500	
	3. Killay	21	1,800	
	4. Sketty	136	11,300	44,900
	5. Uplands	44	3,700	
	6. Brynmill	108	9,000	
	7. Mt Pleasant	75	6,300	
Town Centre	8. Sandfields	79	6,600	
	9. Castle	45	3,800	29,100
	11. Hafod	80	6,700	
	10. St Thomas	144	12,000	
Tawe Valley	12. Brynhyfryd (and Manselton)	161	13,400	
	13. Landore and Plasmarl	77	6,400	
	14. Morriston (and Cwmrhydyceirw)	167	13,900	
	15. Glais	9	800	46,200
	16. Birchgrove	23	2,000	
	17. Llansamlet	69	5,800	
	18. Bonymaen	47	3,900	
North West	19. Townhill (and Mayhill)	187	15,600	
	20. Penlan (and Gendros)	134	11,200	
	21. Clase	34	2,900	43,700
	22. Fforestfach (and Portmead)	155	12,900	
	23. Waunarlwydd	13	1,100	
	Totals	1,962	163,900	

the area of the new housing estates predominantly, is about 45 to the acre. The most crowded of all the four districts is the Town Centre with an average density of over 100 persons per acre, reaching well above the 120 mark in pockets of congested housing in all four of its neighbourhoods. These figures give the approximate net densities for the built-up areas only in these localities, and are taken from the Survey Map prepared by the Town Planning Department: the gross density for the Borough as a whole, taking the total area, is 7 per acre. 'Broadly speaking the residential areas of the County Borough do not reflect the high density of population common to most large industrial towns of England and Wales'.[20] The internal variations in

[20] County Borough of Swansea: Development Plan, 1955, p. 34.

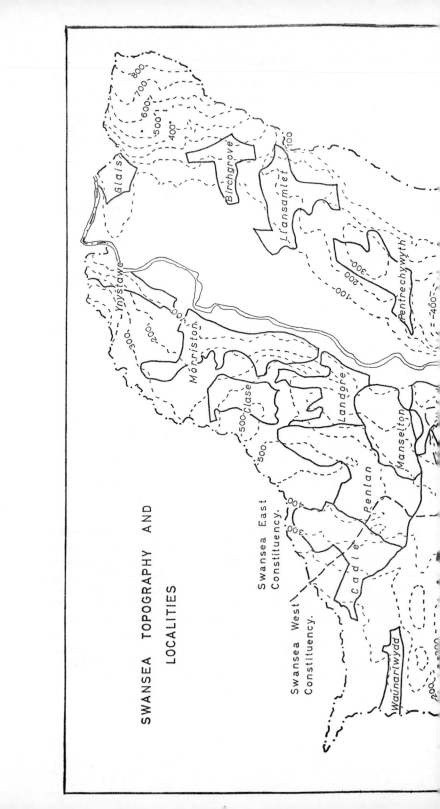

SWANSEA TOPOGRAPHY AND
LOCALITIES

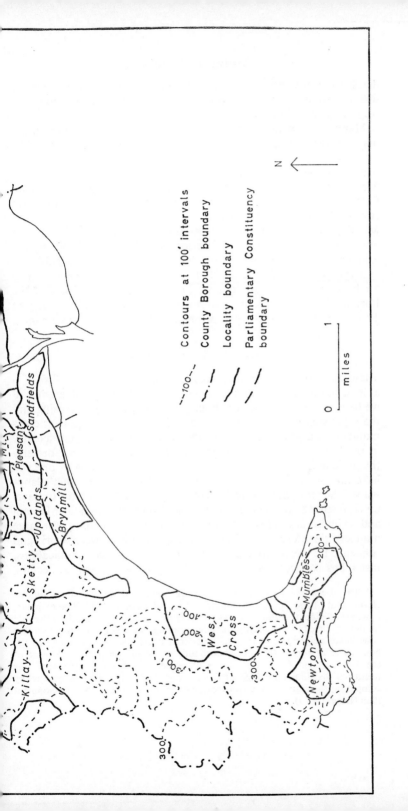

Contours at 100' intervals

County Borough boundary

Locality boundary

Parliamentary Constituency boundary

N

0   1
miles

density, however, are indicative of the contrasts that exist between the distinct localities, and between the four geographical areas into which we have grouped them.

Many of the names of the localities given in the table and on the map are also the names of electoral wards within the Borough. The ward is, however, an arbitrary administrative unit bearing little relation to the territorial division of the Borough into communities—Morriston, for example, is cut in half by ward boundaries, and so are Sketty and Sandfields; sometimes several distinct localities are covered by a single ward (as is the case with the Llansamlet and Mumbles Wards). To avoid confusion, we must emphasize that in our extensive references to these localities in this and subsequent chapters, we mean in every case the localities as given in Table 2.7 and as depicted in Map 4, pp. 70–1.[21] Except in a few instances, where we have tried to be explicit, we have ignored the division of the Borough into fifteen electoral wards (in fact, of our localities, only St Thomas coincides exactly with the electoral ward of the same name).

WORK FOR A LIVING

These local communities are places of residence, not places of work—at least not for the great majority of their inhabitants. Underlying all we have said in this chapter about population changes, housing and the expansion or decline respectively of Swansea's component communities, is a series of fundamental economic changes, particularly in the last few decades. The great metallurgical factories, formerly the pride of Swansea, in the Tawe Valley have closed one by one and have now almost completely disappeared from the Borough's landscape. The thousands of workers in heavy industry now have to travel much farther afield to the new steel and tinplate works at Margam and Velindre and Trostre beyond the Borough boundary: for large numbers the close link which formerly existed between work and residence has been broken. Greatly improved road communications, faster bus services and the tremendous increases in car ownership,

[21] The division into localities which we have used in this study follows closely that of the Town Development Plan published in 1955. The planners, however, divide the Borough into twenty-six 'residential neighbourhoods': we have reduced this to twenty-three by grouping Morriston with three smaller and similar neighbourhoods to its immediate north. We have also altered the boundaries of some other neighbourhoods where we disagreed with those of the Development Plan. For those interested, the differences between our territorial divisions and those of the Swansea town planners can be seen by comparing the map we give and that given in the Report of the Development Plan (Diagram M).

has made it no longer necessary for workers to live under the factory walls. Gone also is the preoccupation with heavy industry within the Borough: new light industries have been, and are continually being, established providing both a much greater industrial diversification and also increased employment for women. The town has expanded rapidly as a business and marketing centre with many more jobs (and a greater variety) for both men and women in the town centre. Wages have improved dramatically, the working day is shorter, and unemployment is no longer a perpetual fear. The emphasis has shifted from 'the clanking chains and smoking furnaces of the Tawe Valley' to the business and commercial heart of the town which, certainly in the years of expansion and reconstruction since the war, has exhibited all the signs of a bounding affluence and prosperity with its new office blocks, its traffic-packed dual carriageways, its new department stores and show-rooms and supermarkets. 'It's a different atmosphere altogether nowadays.' We could say that again.

The census figures showing the kinds of work done by the people

Table 2.8: Employment of Males in Swansea—Censuses of 1911, 1921, and 1951

Category	1911		1921		1951	
	Numbers	%	Numbers	%	Numbers	%
Heavy Industry	10,907	27	7,362	14	4,991	9
Transport	8,528	22	8,552	16	7,994	16
Retail Distribution	3,276	8	4,623	9	4,653	9
Building	3,013	8	2,726	5	5,302	10
Light Industry	2,899	7	8,496	16	8,919	17
Agriculture	271	1	1,055	2	722	1
Mining	1,343	4	3,976	7	979	2
Domestic and Personal Service	818	2	865	2	1,147	2
Professional, Financial and Administrative	4,551	12	5,375	10	6,840	13
Armed Forces	28	–	94	–	933	2
Other[22]	3,334	9	9,505	18	9,368	18
Totals	38,968	100	52,629	100	51,848	100

[22] This residual category includes a variety of unskilled labourers not specified in any other category, and such occupations as 'warehousemen, packer, and stationary engine driver' (the latter has nothing to do with British Railways, in spite of evidence to the contrary, but with such things as mechanical cranes and pumps).

The Occupational Tables of the 1961 census were not available at the time of publication.

of Swansea in 1911, 1921, and 1951 reveal the profound changes that have taken place well within living memory. The figures for men are given in Table 2.8 (p. 73)—with the necessary adjustments made to take account of inter-censal changes in industrial classification by the Registrar-General so that accurate comparisons can be made.

The major extension of the Borough in 1918 is the explanation for the increase of some 14,000 in the total number of men employed in 1921 as compared with 1911. The effects of this extension can be seen in the figures for agriculture and mining particularly, as rural and mining villages became incorporated within the Borough. The slight decrease in the totals from 1921 to 1951 (with the area of the Borough remaining constant) is due mainly to two factors—alterations in the population age structure giving an increasingly 'ageing' population with more men past retirement age, and educational changes with more boys remaining longer at school and college and starting work later.

In 1911, heavy industry (mainly iron and steel and tinplate) and transport (mainly railways and docks) together accounted for half the total employment of men. By 1951 these two together provided work for only a quarter. Since 1921, the numbers employed in mining and agriculture have declined noticeably, particularly mining with the constant closure of collieries: up to the First World War there were ten collieries *within* the present Borough boundary, and dozens in the region around—now there is none in the Borough and large numbers have closed in the surrounding region. On the other hand, the numbers employed in building have doubled since 1921, and those in light industry have trebled since 1911.

The most important change has been the relative decline of heavy industry.[23] In the area of the Tawe Valley between Morriston and

[23] In spite of the development of oil refining—the large oil refinery at Llandarcy just outside the Borough on the east was originally built in 1920, and has since been modernized and extended. It now employs some 2,500 workers, just over 700 of whom live within the County Borough of Swansea. The changes in basic industries for South Wales as a whole, and for the Swansea and West Wales area in particular, are discussed briefly and clearly in an admirable recent article by W. E. Minchinton; '"New" South Wales', *The National Provincial Bank Review*, May, 1961. Minchinton shows that the pattern for South Wales in general is much the same as that we have been describing for Swansea. He writes 'the changed structure of industry and the generally much higher level of employment have materially affected the occupational pattern in South Wales. If a comparison is made between 1923, a year of fairly high employment before most of the changes got under way, and 1958 the picture becomes clear as the following table demonstrates:

the sea there were 40 major factories in the years immediately before the First World War, including 15 iron and steel and tinplate works, 10 chemical plants, 5 large spelter works producing zinc, and 9 smelting industries producing copper, gold, silver, lead and nickel. By 1934, 14 of these great works had closed, and today only 4 are left in this whole area, the rest stand silent and in ruins. The effect of these changes on the neighbouring industrial communities which grew up with and around these works has been profound. Morriston alone had eight large metal and chemical works as recently as 1934: today not a single major works is left in Morriston—some have been demolished completely, the gaunt chimney stacks of the others, so long a symbol of Morriston's industrial prosperity, stand cold and smokeless.

The most recent census figures available are those for 1951, but it is certain that those for 1961 when available will show even more striking changes within the last ten years as more and more of the older works have petered out and their workers absorbed into the new light industries established in or near the Borough or into the modern tinplate works at Velindre and Trostre or into the great steelworks at Port Talbot and Margam fourteen miles or so away around the curve of Swansea Bay. Today more than 2,000 steelworkers from Swansea make this daily journey to the Margam steelworks and a further 1,000 travel out to Trostre and Velindre (mainly from the Morriston area). A 'Journey-to-Work' survey, conducted in 1960 by the Glamorgan County Planning Office, of industrial firms in the Swansea area of West Glamorgan showed that 6,688 workers (or 32 per cent of the total labour force engaged in productive industry) travel daily out of the Borough to their places of work.[24] Our own survey showed that of the 797 male workers in our sample (covering all forms of employment and not just productive industry) only 27 per cent are employed in the same neighbourhood of Swansea in which they live; 51 per cent work in other parts of the Borough and 22 per cent travel out daily to the surrounding region (over half of these latter travelling outwards more than twelve miles). Several

[24] This survey of the relationship between workplace and residence is as yet unpublished. We are grateful to the Glamorgan County Planning Officer for making the results available to us.

Percentage of total employment by sectors		
	1923	1958
Basic industries	65	28
Other manufactures	13	33
Service industries	22	39
	100%	100%

thousand workers, mainly women working in shops and offices, travel in to Swansea to work, but as Graham Humphrys has pointed out from a study of the census figures, Swansea is unusual for towns of its size in Britain in exporting daily more labour than it imports.[25]

This daily movement of workers over considerable distances was a continual subject of comment by our elderly informants particularly on the east side of Swansea. They constantly contrasted the present situation of diverse and scattered employment with that of their earlier days in which crowds of men thronged the streets as they walked to and from the neighbouring factories and foundries, in which fathers and sons and uncles and brothers and a variety of in-laws worked side by side in the same works or were in similar employment in near-by works or pits, in which workmates lived together as neighbours in the same street or near-by streets and, with their wives and children, worshipped together in the same chapels, or were members together of the same works' clubs. These solidarities of work and living were an integral part both of the strong community consciousness and of the cohesion of family life. Only Morriston with its continuing preoccupation with tinplate and steel (though the works themselves are now miles away), and St Thomas with its emphasis on employment in the neighbouring docks, preserve, if faintly now, this former and familiar working-class tradition.

Nowadays the older Valley communities, and certainly the new housing estates, have increasingly become dormitories for men travelling in a variety of directions to a variety of jobs. In contrast with the former pattern, the same street will contain wide differences in the distances men travel to work, in the jobs they do, in the type of industry in which they are employed, and in the pay they bring home. Neighbours are rarely workmates, and the chances of son following father into the same works, or even into the same employment, have decreased strikingly within living memory. The old pattern of family homogeneity of employment and income has given way in the face of major industrial change and greater educational opportunity. With full employment and no scarcity of jobs the value of parental influence and the need for the help of relatives in finding work in the same factory has greatly declined. As we saw with the case of Mr Hughes in Chapter I—which is a typical illustration of the changes that have occurred and of the attitude of the old to the collapse of a familiar traditional way of life—this increasing heterogeneity of jobs and

[25] Graham Humphrys, 'The Economic Importance of Commuters to their Area of Residence, with a Case Study of the South Wales Coalfield', *Journal of Town Planning Institute*, March 1962. Swansea is 'One of the few large towns in Britain having a net outflow of commuters.'

status and income within families and immediate neighbourhoods has had a profound effect on the character of family life and on the cohesion of the extended family—and of the communities over which it is scattered. We shall see more of the effects of these changes on family relationships when we examine later the current patterns of family interaction.

The development of a variety of light industries (clothing, toys, brushes, zip-fasteners, tensional steel trapping, potato crisps, furniture-making, dental appliances, mineral waters, and so forth, on the post-war Trading Estate at Fforestfach and at Waunarlwydd, and refrigerators, brewing, machine repairs, foam rubber sponges, and various consumer goods in St Thomas and Sandfields, and scattered over the east side of the town)—these industries have not only provided men with more varied opportunities for employment, but have also considerably increased the numbers and types of jobs available for women. The development of the town as a commercial and business and administrative centre, with the great increase of jobs in shops and offices, in professional and white-collar occupations generally, has also provided a greater number and greater variety of jobs for both sexes, but particularly for women.

The table below gives the comparisons between the three censuses of 1911, 1921, and 1951 of the employment of women in four categories which together cover over 90 per cent of the total occupations of women:

Table 2.9: Employment of Females in Swansea at the Censuses of 1911, 1921, and 1951

Category	1911		1921		1951		% increase or decrease on 1921 figs.
	Numbers	%	*Numbers*	%	*Numbers*	%	
Professional and Commercial	1,332	13	2,984	19	5,200	30	+ 74
Domestic and Personal Service	3,977	37	5,525	39	4,178	24	− 26
Light Industry	2,285	21	2,768	19	3,718	21	+ 34
Retail and Distribution	2,179	20	2,675	19	3,338	19	+ 24

Both in 1911 and in 1921, 24 per cent of the total female population of Swansea were working; by 1951 this figure had increased to 27 per cent but still remained well below the national average of 35 per cent for women in employment in England and Wales as a whole. With its past predominance of heavy industry, Swansea has always had relatively fewer jobs for women. As the table shows the changes in the kinds of work done by women have been considerable, particularly in the increase of three-quarters since 1921 of the numbers in office jobs and of a quarter in the numbers working in shops and of a third in the numbers in factories of one kind or another. At the same time there has been a sharp decline of the numbers of women employed as domestic servants or as waitresses and barmaids and chambermaids in hotels, and so forth—though a quarter of the total number of women in work are still employed in this way. With the rebuilding of the Town Centre over the last ten years or so, and the arrival of large department and chain stores, the numbers of women employed in shops have undoubtedly increased. The Ministry of Labour and National Service figures for June 1959 show over 5,000 women employed in wholesale and retail distribution within the Borough, and the numbers are continually increasing as the Town Centre continues to expand.

Of the 996 women on the Electoral Register, and therefore aged over 21, that we visited on our main survey in 1960, 18 per cent were working full-time (that is, thirty hours or more a week), 7 per cent part-time, and 75 per cent did not go out to work. As one would expect, the percentages of women working varied by marital state, by age, by whether they had children under 15 at home (particularly very young children), by where they lived within the Borough and therefore the accessibility of work, and by social class (we comment on this latter factor in the chapter which follows). Fourteen per cent of the total number of married women were working full-time, but only 7 per cent of married women with children under 15. It is clearly becoming increasingly common, indeed commonplace nowadays—in contrast to the general experience of the elderly—for many wives to remain at work after marriage, to delay where possible the arrival of the first child so that the wife may continue to supplement her husband's income during the phase of home-making, and then to return to work if possible after the children have all passed the early school years. If the young couple live with one or other of their parents, and if the wife's mother or husband's mother is available to help look after young children, the chances of the wife going out to work increase. And with the present flood of consumer goods easily obtained on hire purchase and the intense pressure of mass-advertising encouraging an acquisitive society, it is hardly surprising that, with more and more jobs available, the numbers of married women at work should be continually increasing. There have been a number

78

of recent sociological studies of women at work, particularly of working wives and mothers, and evidence and conclusions are available about the effects of this on the elementary family and on individual households. Little is known, however, of the effects of this increased employment for women, particularly married women with families, on wider familial relationships. We will be examining the results obtained from our own survey in this respect in Chapter V.

Like most places in Britain, Swansea has been the scene of rapid and major social changes during the last few decades. For the old, the First World War marked the great watershed between the past and the present, between the confident if chaotic industrial growth of Victorian capitalism and its post-war aftermath of industrial recessions and contraction, between a familiar and relatively stable social world and one of continuous and bewildering change. For the younger generation, the Second World War was a major break with the social and economic patterns of the twenties and thirties, and marked another watershed between the past and the modern Swansea of today. The basic and recurrent theme of this chapter has been that of rapid social change, illustrated for certain selected subjects from the data provided by the various decennial censuses and by data from our own surveys. There are of course numerous other figures (for the increase of car ownership, for example, or in the provision of educational facilities, or the development in standards of living) which would extend this picture of change. Not only have there been major alterations in the industrial structure of Swansea, but there has clearly also been a redistribution of employees between the manual and non-manual grades of employment. We do not have the information available to consider this subject specifically for Swansea (though we do consider later the incidence of occupational mobility) but there is no reason to believe that Swansea differs in any important respect from the picture of national shifts in employment given by Dr Abrams.[26] Indeed the decline of heavy industry in Swansea, and the replacement of many small firms in this industry by a few large ones means that such shifts are likely to have been greater in Swansea than elsewhere. Dr Abrams writes:

[26] Dr Mark Abrams, 'Social Trends and Electoral Behaviour'. Paper delivered to the British Sociological Association Conference, March 1962, and reprinted in extracts in *Socialist Commentary*, May 1962, p. 10.

The data from our survey indicated that the proportion of our subjects falling in the Registrar General's socio-economic class V was 9 per cent lower than in 1951 (see Appendix III, p. 326). We do not quote this data in the text since part of this difference may be due to a fault in the sample. It seems unlikely, however, that the whole of the difference between the figures can be explained in this way.

Between 1950 and 1960 the total number of workers in the whole of British manufacturing industry increased by slightly under one million; but of these additional employees only one-third were manual workers and the remaining two-thirds were white-collar workers, i.e. those with clerical, administrative or technical jobs. Within industry there are still many more manual workers than white-collar workers, but the balance between them is changing steadily. Ten years ago the manpower of an average factory was made up of one white-collar worker for every six manual workers on its pay-roll; but today it apparently needs one white-collar worker for every four manual workers in the factory.

But this is not the whole picture. There are many millions of workers who are employed outside the scope of manufacturing industry. . . . Today the number of people working in these five groups of non-factory occupations (distributive trades, banking, insurance and finance, public administration, professional and scientific services, and miscellaneous service trades) is larger than the number of workers—both manual and white-collar—in the whole of manufacturing industry. And, what is more important, over the past ten years two out of every three people added to the nation's total working population have been absorbed by these five non-industrial occupations. . . .

These employment changes are slowly, but persistently and fundamentally, affecting our non-working lives. For example, they largely account for the much greater concern today with higher education and particularly with technical and professional training. Again, as more people work at jobs which are not physically exhausting, home-life and family-life have taken on a new importance and vitality. Compared with a generation ago, people today show a greater interest in their homes, in house-ownership, in moving to the suburbs, and in the family 'doing things together'.

This quotation, and its implications so far as Swansea is concerned, raises precisely and clearly the whole difficult problem of social class and culture, to which we now turn in the chapter which follows.

III

CLASS AND THE WELSH

'THIS town, as we used to say in our Sardonic Twenties' writes Swansea-born Wynford Vaughan Thomas, 'has got as many layers as an onion and each one can reduce you to tears.' With rapid social change, the layers which can most quickly reduce the social observer to the verge of lachrymation are those concerned with social class. Add in Swansea the layer formed by Welsh culture, where the champions and partisans fight desperate rearguard actions, and it is clearly difficult to avoid the natural consequences of peeling the onion.

This complex and troublesome subject could more than fill a book on its own. In many ways, this is the central sociological problem of any modern urban society which underlies and pervades all social research whatever the actual topic selected. In our case, though we must deal with this subject much more cursorily than we would have liked, there can be no question of its major relevance to the main themes of our study. Following their study of Woodford, Young and Willmott concluded that 'social class is one of the decisive influences upon family life'.[1] We have tried to discover whether this statement is correct for Swansea, and under what circumstances. Does the recognition of differences in class or status or culture between relatives lead to avoidance of contact, to the severance or minimization of relationships, and to the failure to meet obligations that would otherwise be met? Does concern with social class vary significantly for men and women? Are there important differences in the patterns of family behaviour from one social class to another, or do these patterns vary for the Welsh as compared with the non-Welsh elements of the population? We shall be considering these questions at various points in this book and presenting the conclusions we have reached. Questions of this type raise at once the methodological problems of definition and approach and procedure in

[1] Willmott and Young, *Family and Class in a London Suburb*, 1960, p. 86.

81

analysis. What do we mean by social class? How many social classes in Swansea do we think it useful to distinguish for the purpose of analysing family behaviour? What indices of class or cultural groupings appears most useful in the classification of the two thousand or so families that we visited in Swansea? We deal with these latter questions in this present chapter, and explain as briefly as possible our methods of analysis. We must emphasize that we are not here concerned specifically with an analysis of social stratification in Swansea but with the methods of using social class and cultural divisions as variables in the study of family behaviour.

WHAT SOCIAL CLASS DO YOU THINK YOU BELONG TO?

A consideration of the opinions and attitudes about class and cultural distinctions held by the people who live here is informative but, being fraught with complications, a good deal less useful than might be supposed at first sight. Take the following series of comments made by the people we interviewed: they indicate the range of opinion and attitude, and the complexity of self-assessments:

> Mrs Roberts (29, daughter of a Landore plumber, wife of a quantity surveyor, recently moved to a new house on a private estate at Killay): 'We're working class, I suppose—at least that's where we came from. Perhaps we should say "middle" now, though I'm no lady. It's very difficult to say what we are. I have started going to the hairdresser's once a week if that means anything.'

> Mr Maddocks (68, retired railway ticket clerk): 'I'd say we are all the same round here in Manselton, particularly up this end. Lower middle class, but not too lower, if you know what I mean. Things have changed a bit since the war but Manselton definitely used to be considered a cut above Landore or Cwmbwrla—and I'd say it still is. This is a very respectable area, whatever the people do for a living.'

> Mr Bevan (47, crane driver in the docks, born and bred in St Thomas): 'I've always been an ordinary working man myself like the people I see on the bus in the morning or the chaps I work with. I'm very poor at this class business—I just can't see them myself. People are people to me. Some are better off than others but we're all exactly the same in the sight of God. I don't discriminate. I think it's the women who are responsible for all this bloody snobbery —they're always pushing to appear better off than they are. And if one of their kids gets into the Grammar School there's no holding them. You can't make a silk purse out of a sow's ear—that's what I say.'

Class and the Welsh

Mrs Peterson (51, wife of office manager at a chemical factory, both born of 'routine white-collar' parents in Mumbles): 'Oh quite definitely middle class. I belong to the Conservative Women's Association and both my husband and myself are members of the Gower Society. You can't quite say "upper" can you? We moved here to this house in Sketty two years ago—and that should put us a step up, in my opinion anyway—though I don't want to appear snobbish. This is a very select area. I don't know what it's going to be like though when all those Council houses and flats are finished behind us here. My husband says that we'll have to turn this house into a fish-and-chip shop.'

Mrs Davies (55, wife of a bricklayer, living in the small terrace house in Sandfields where she was born): 'We are all working class in Swansea—it's Sketty you find a different type of people, business people and doctors from the hospital. We don't mix with them of course. The dentist I work for, scrubbing and cleaning in the mornings before the surgery opens, lives over in West Cross and his wife thinks she's Lady Muck—though her father had a milk-round down in the town somewhere. You get her sort all over, trying to make you feel inferior. The teachers at the school along the road here think themselves superior to the dinner ladies. I don't take no notice myself. I don't care if they're dripping with diamonds —we're all right and that's the main thing. I put by the money I get cleaning and my husband and I go abroad for a holiday every August. Last year we went to Austria, and this year we're going on a coach tour of Spain. I really live for that now that the children have all married and left home. Let's enjoy ourselves while we can, I say.'

Mr Bartholomew (36, Personnel Officer, living in West Cross): 'I don't know what to call myself—my father was a collier in the Swansea Valley and yet I went to Cambridge. I don't believe in class at all. I find I can mix easily with my neighbours round here—executives and professional people mainly—and also at home in Ystalyfera, and with the neighbours there, in very different conditions. With this home and car and telephone and so on, I suppose I could be pigeon-holed with the middle class, but I think the "educated" class would be more accurate. It's education and speech and general style of living that counts nowadays—not just money or family background.'

Mr Williams (41, male nurse, lives in Corporation house on the Penlan estate): 'Swansea has the usual three classes—working, middle and kidding themselves. I'd say we were all working class here but there's plenty of showing off—you know the sort of thing, beautiful curtains on the windows but nothing on the bed. If anybody does a bit of decorating or buys something new, they leave the lights on with the curtains open to make sure the neighbours get a good look. And the palaver with the dustbins when they are put out on the pavements for collection on a Tuesday morning is quite a sight—all the best tins, or bits of expensive vegetables or chicken bones or whatever, stuck prominently on the top where the neighbours can see how well off the family is, or pretends to be. And then every Monday, though nobody admits it of course, we have the Battle of the Washing Lines. I tell my wife she buys all this fancy nylon underwear just to stick out on the line to give the neighbours something to think about. If one of them has something new, particularly something for the kids, the others are matching it on the line by the following Monday.'

Mrs Hopkins (73, widow of tin shearer, has lived all her life in Morriston): 'With all this moving going on, it's difficult to know who's who around here. But things haven't changed very much even if the people have. Pentrepoeth and Clasemont were always the better-class areas of Morriston, and the poor areas were around the Globe and Wychtree and some of the streets in Cwmbath. Apart from the shopkeepers and doctors and chemists and ministers, the rest of us were all very much the same, all the men were in the works. But there were differences. The women who worked in the tinplate works were either in the pickling section or in the section opening plates. They were totally different. The women who worked in the pickling section were really from the lowest class in Morriston. No girl from a respectable family would do this sort of work—the girls who did work there were well known for their loose living and bad language. If a respectable family in Morriston heard that one of its boys had an attachment for a girl who worked in the pickling section, they would be very worried indeed. On the other hand, the girls working on the plate-opening came from ordinary working-class families of course—but Chapel-going respectable families and certainly there was nothing against them. I don't take much notice about what's going on nowadays—things have changed so much since my day—but I expect you'd find the same differences now if you looked for them.'

Mrs Roderick (28, daughter of a storeman, wife of lorry driver, living in Corporation house on Townhill estate): 'I never wanted to be anything else but what I am, even though I went to the High School and could have gone in for teaching or something. I found a lot of snobbery in the School. I didn't like it there at all. You were snubbed if you said you came from Townhill or Mayhill. I had an inferiority complex while I was there. There were doctors' daughters and rectors' daughters and moneyed girls from round Sketty— very nice girls, but always so sure of themselves and I was not in those days. They could always talk themselves out of anything and

I fancy the teachers put up with more from them than they did from us.'

Mr Turner (24, unmarried, motor mechanic, of Birchgrove): 'Social class? If you get under £18 a week you are working class, more than that and you're middle class. That's all there is to it—it's just a matter of money.'

Mrs Griffiths (33, wife of a local government clerk, both Welsh-speaking and born in Morriston of fathers working in the steel-works, now living in a Corporation house on West Cross estate with six-year-old daughter, Sandra): 'We've changed a lot since we moved here from Morriston. We seem to live differently altogether from our parents—and it causes some trouble at times, I can tell you. . . . We hardly ever speak Welsh now, and Sandra doesn't at all, and I'm not keen for her to learn either. It isn't much use over here, is it? I wouldn't like her to grow up speaking with a very Welsh accent like they do in Morriston. I like to hear her speaking English properly. Some of the little girls down the road (in the private houses off the estate) speak beautifully. I think it makes all the difference if you can speak properly.'[2]

Mr Martin (69, retired railway shunter of Bonymaen): 'There's only two classes—the employers and the employed. You can guess which one I belong to. At least that's how it used to be anyway. Nowadays I don't know what to make of it. Years ago class distinctions were much more rigid—you knew your place and that was it. Now it's a case of "I'm as good as you are". I think it's all this education that's made the difference. Young people nowadays have very different ideas from what we used to have. It's made a big difference inside families. My brother's grand-daughter is a B.A. and her family have gone up with her. I wasn't invited to the wedding, although I'm her grandfather's only surviving brother. I expect they thought I would let her down.'

These testimonials to the general awareness of social inequalities, and the existence of distinct class sub-cultures within Swansea could easily be multiplied by the score—as they could indeed for any community in these class-afflicted islands. Varied, informative, contradictory, they reveal the complications of class judgements in individual cases. Some see class primarily in economic terms stressing what have been called 'the objective factors' (occupation, education, place of residence, family background) others are prompted to react mainly

[2] Dylan Thomas was scathing about this repudiation of the Welsh accent, and of social climbers, 'corseting their voices so that no lilt or inflection of Welsh enthusiasm may exult or pop out'. 'I know a Welsh hairdresser in London who has striven so vehemently to abolish his accent that he sounds like a man speaking with the Elgin Marbles in his mouth.'

in psychological terms, emphasising 'the subjective factors' concerned with prestige and status and class-consciousness (notably prejudice, snobbery, aspiration, concern with status-giving possessions, awareness of speech and dress differences, sense of belonging, hostility, cultural taste, and so forth). The list of ingredients seems endless: individual judgements of class differences and of personal position within the social scale are compounded variously of a mixture of these objective and subjective factors. It is particularly noticeable how the names of localities within Swansea tend to be used as symbols and 'verbal banners' (in Centers' phrase) of class distinctions—the names of the neighbourhoods on the west of Swansea (Sketty, particularly, but also Uplands, West Cross and Langland) convey at once the connotation of social superiority: those on the east and of the public housing estates carry the inference of a lower social class—regardless of the internal complexities of these local communities. Equally noticeable is the apparent tendency to think in class terms of a simple two-fold division into middle and working class, a tendency reinforced by the basic geographical dichotomy of Swansea into east and west in the popular image of the town.

We noticed this apparent stress on a two-fold division in the replies to the question we asked of the 1,962 subjects in our main survey about what social class they considered they belonged to. In the context of a comparatively long interview covering a wide range of topics, our informants were restricted by the nature of the interview to a brief answer to this question. We tried not to prompt or guide the informants in any way, but simply to record whatever reply was given to the question on the interview schedule. The responses, with those for men and women shown separately, were as follows:

Table 3.1: Self-estimates of Social Class—Main Sample

Reply	Men		Women		Sample Total	
	Numbers	*%*	*Numbers*	*%*	*Numbers*	*%*
'Upper Class' ⎫	16	2	18	2	4	·2
'Upper Middle' ⎬					30	1·5
'Middle Class' ⎱	288	30	340	34	600	30·5
'Lower Middle' ⎰					28	1·4
'Upper Working'⎱	599	62	563	57	11	·5
'Working Class' ⎰					1,151	59·0
Other	35	4	52	5	87	4·4
Don't know	14	1	14	1	28	1·4
Refuse	12	1	11	1	23	1·2
Totals	964	100%	998	100%	1,962	100%

Class and the Welsh

Nine out of every ten persons said either 'middle class' or 'working class'. Of the tenth of our sample who gave some other reply to this open question on self-estimation of class membership, by far the largest number are included in the category we have called 'other'; these gave a variety of responses such as 'Conservative' or 'Labour' or 'ratepayer' or 'the exploited' (or 'educated,' or 'employed') class or simply 'the poor' or 'Pensioner'. A considerable number said things like 'I'm half and half' or 'I don't think there are any classes nowadays'. Under 4 per cent of our total sample placed themselves in the social scale by using class terms other than simply middle or working class, and this figure was the same for both men and women. A slightly higher percentage of women, however, placed themselves in the middle class with a correspondingly lower percentage in the working class. This latter difference between men and women corresponds with the general impression we formed during our research in Swansea of a somewhat greater emphasis on class and a greater competitiveness over status on the part of women generally—though we must add that the statistical difference shown in the table does not reach the level of significance.

On the evidence of these individual estimates it could be said that, verbally at least, our informants appear to operate in the main with a two-fold model of the class system consisting of the middle class on the one hand and the working class on the other—approximately one-third and two-thirds respectively of the Swansea population. But is this in fact the meaning of these replies? To have confidence in this conclusion we would need to be reasonably satisfied that the term 'middle class' (or 'working class') had much the same content of meaning for each of those who gave this reply. Our sample included persons of very wide differences in occupation and education and income describing themselves as 'middle class'—for example, a solicitor as compared with a policeman or with a foreman in a tinplate works; both a company director with a large house in Langland, a Jaguar and yacht, and shop assistant living in a Corporation[3] house with a bicycle. Equally, there were wide variations in these factors of occupation and wealth and so forth amongst those who replied 'working class'—our sample included amongst those using this term some university lecturers, some chapel ministers, some well-to-do garage proprietors as well as dockers and dustmen (as examples of the contrasts). Our sample of course, being a random cross-section of the population, varied also by age, sex, marital status. Assuming that

[3] Altogether 102 Corporation tenants in our sample described themselves as 'middle class'—that is, 19 per cent of the total number of Corporation tenants.

87

these replies are honest attempts by the individuals concerned to place themselves within the class structure as they see it (and we cannot know their motives or the criteria used in individual cases) it seems rash to conclude that the two commonest terms used—middle and working class—have respectively sufficient identity of meaning for the variety of people who use them to infer that people generally conceive of class in two-fold terms. It may well be simply that in response to a question of this type they do not know what else to say.

Given the difficulty of understanding precisely what is meant or implied by the reply in a particular case, it is doubtful whether this collection of responses sheds much light on the class structure of Swansea in general. It is well-nigh impossible to live in Swansea, as of course in any other town in Britain, without being aware of major differences and contrasts and inequalities between various sections of the population, or from one neighbourhood to another, in general economic condition or in social attitudes or in styles of living. It is, however, a curious fact, which we noticed continually in discussions with people throughout the Borough, that though individuals are clearly conscious of these differences and distinctions, they are in general exceptionally inarticulate and hesitant about them, and indeed embarrassed by this subject of social class. They obviously find it difficult to know what terms to use to express the social reality they perceive, and retreat quickly into the common and obvious middle-class/working-class dichotomy. They equally have difficulty in knowing what criteria to use in placing themselves, even more so when they feel that their behaviour is contradictory in respect of their stereotype of this popular two-fold social division. As Raymond Williams has pointed out in a particularly sensitive discussion of current social attitudes:

> 'Working class', for very many people, is simply a memory of poverty, bad housing and exposure, while 'middle class' is a name for money to spend, better housing, and a more furnished and controllable life. Since the styles of living of the whole society are in any case changing this contrast very easily becomes one between the past and the present: 'working class' is the old style, that people are steadily moving away from: 'middle class' is the new 'contemporary' style. It is easy to point out that by this time these terms have lost any relevant meaning, as descriptions of actual social organization, but their emotional charge is no less powerful for that.[4]

There is no doubt that in Swansea these terms are used to express attitudes to social changes in this manner and that the movement

[4] Raymond Williams, *The Long Revolution*, 1961, p. 334.

west of the population out of the old industrial areas—to which we referred in our previous chapter—is closely associated with these attitudes and with the way people feel about these class labels in the Swansea of the nineteen-sixties.

These limitations and ambiguities of language in popular usage and the confusion over criteria tend to favour this simplified version of the class system, even though from their hesitations and difficulties of decision a large number of people clearly find it a crude and inadequate picture of the actual situation as they understand it. It is rather like being asked to vote in an election contested by just two political parties. Many will vote for one or the other without much thought or hesitation, if for a wide variety of personal reasons; others will have much more difficulty in reaching a decision with only this choice, and end perhaps either by abstaining or by voting against the party they most dislike rather than for the one they feel they can positively support. The result of the vote will tell us something about the broad patterns of political divisions given only this twofold choice, without revealing much of the subtleties of political allegiance or about the range and variation of political opinion or about the factors in voting decisions. The results of our own survey in Swansea so far as these individual judgements of class are concerned are similar in many respects. They do not tell us how many classes there are in fact but only that people feel that the choice is between 'the middle class' and 'the working class' whatever they mean by these terms, and opt for one or the other for reasons known only to themselves. The 'floating voter' in class terms is obscured by the final result.

The use of these self-estimates alone in classifying a particular population is obviously a hazardous undertaking from the point of view of clarity and precision in analysis. But, treated as clues to the general social and cultural attitudes of individuals, they cannot easily be ignored by the sociologist seeking to understand the structure of the society he is investigating. However they have been arrived at, these self-estimates are an indication of the individual's subjective view of his own social position. This personal assessment provides an important piece of information about the basic cultural allegiance and social orientation of the individual concerned—and, as we shall be showing presently, we have used it as such in our own particular method of social classification.

BY THEIR WORKS SHALL THEY BE JUDGED

Though there appear to be as many views of social class and as many ingenious methods of classification as there are sociologists, it does appear to be generally agreed among sociologists that the most useful piece of information to have about a man to place him in a social context is to know what sort of a job he does. This method of placing people is of course not confined to sociologists; one hears it widely and generally used in ordinary conversation, in anecdotes, in gossip, in introductions; one sees it used on countless forms and applications, in newspaper reports, in election literature. If you know a man's occupation, it is possible with reasonable accuracy and safety to infer many other facts about him—what sort of education he has had, what his income is likely to be, what type of house he is likely to have, what kind of district he is likely to live in, what sort of 'status possessions' he is likely to own—all facts generally accepted as 'involved' in social class. It has the further advantage of being a piece of information which can be obtained relatively easily and precisely. There are of course a vast multiplicity of occupations, as anyone who has perused the Registrar-General's *Classification of Occupations* for census purpose will be aware, and there are many difficulties and likely inaccuracies in grading them and reducing them to the necessarily small number of categories needed for any method of occupational classification. For this, however, the sociologist has readily available a number of different classifications to choose between, and, as Hall and Jones have reported, there is 'a fair degree of correlation between different systems of social grading designed on any reasonable common basis, such as the codes used by the Registrar-General, the Population Investigation Committee and the Social Survey'.[5] Most commonly the elaboration of class categories, a large number being possible with this method, is restricted to five or six. There may be disagreements over the details of occupational grading but, these apart, the method clearly has the great advantage of universality (within Britain and within reason at least) and therefore ease of comparison.

In recent studies in Britain the complex problem of social class has been dealt with in this direct and simple manner, with indeed the occupational classification often being reduced to two categories— non-manual and manual—and these equated with the middle class and the working class respectively. This was the method used by Young and Willmott[6] in their study of family behaviour and social class in Woodford, by Jackson and Marsden[7] in their examination of

[5] J. Hall and D. Caradog Jones, 'Social Grading of Occupations,' in *The British Journal of Sociology*, I, No. 1, (March 1950), p. 49.

[6] Michael Young and Peter Willmott, op. cit., p. xi.

[7] Brian Jackson and Dennis Marsden, *Education and the Working Class*, 1962, p. 10.

the effects of grammar school education on 'working-class' boys, by Brennan, Cooney and Pollins[8] in their study of social change in South-west Wales, and by Bendix and Lipset,[9] in extensive comparisons of social mobility, who maintain that 'the break between manual and non-manual occupations as an indicator of low and high occupational status is justified whenever a dichotomous division of males in urban occupations is used'. Bendix and Lipset do not, we must emphasize, equate occupational status with social class but the other studies most certainly do.

The main, and perhaps the only, advantages of this method would appear to be its simplicity and facility in application. Its disadvantages are manifold—it neglects altogether the subjective aspects of class, it ignores the problem of social mobility and of the different social origins and family backgrounds of the individuals it classifies, it ignores the change in social attitudes to the distinction between manual and non-manual occupations, it classifies in a single category too wide a range of the social scale (both a clerk and a doctor are ranked together in the non-manual 'middle class', and so are a Chief Constable and a policeman, for example), it places too much weight on a single arbitrary occupational division, it assumes a twofold classification as an accurate reflection of correct social reality, and as sufficient to reveal such differences of behaviour and attitude as actually exist.

For the study of family relationships and social class specifically in Woodford, Young and Willmott justify on two grounds the use of this method of using the 'break' between manual and non-manual occupations as an indicator of social class:

> There were two arguments for making the simple twofold division. One was that in occupation Woodford is almost entirely without what many people would think of as an 'upper' or 'upper' middle class. . . .
> The second—and more telling—argument was that in dividing our informants into two social classes we were doing what our informants themselves did. We tried to find out what classes people thought (or perhaps 'felt' would be the better word) existed in Woodford, and the commonest view was that there were two, usually described as 'middle' or 'working' or 'lower'.[10]

We have seen that much the same could be said about Swansea. But, as Carlsson has pointed out in a penetrating discussion of the

[8] T. Brennan, E. W. Cooney, and H. Pollins, *Social Change in South-West Wales*, 1954, p. 62.
[9] R. Bendix and S. M. Lipset, *Social Mobility in Industrial Society*, 1959, p. 17.
[10] Michael Young and Peter Willmott, op. cit., p. xii.

semantics of 'social class', whilst the sociologist must obviously be concerned not to differ altogether from everyday usage, 'he has also to consider the need for clear thinking, analysis, and the way of conceptualization which in the long run promotes our knowledge and helps us to build a comprehensive theory'[11] (Carlsson's own study of social mobility in Sweden is an excellent demonstration of this.) The people of Woodford and of Swansea may appear to think of class in simple twofold terms (though this interpretation of popular usage is arguable, to say the least), but even so they clearly do not, as Young and Willmott and others do in social research, identify the two classes with the division between non-manual and manual labour. Indeed as Young and Willmott themselves show (for Woodford)[12] 'nearly half (48 per cent) of the 335 manual workers in the general sample considered themselves middle class'. How can one reconcile this with their statement that 'in dividing our informants into two social classes (by the non-manual/manual division of occupation) we were doing what our informants did'? Of those in non-manual occupations in our Swansea sample who assessed themselves by social class, 68 per cent said they were middle class, and 32 per cent that they were working class. Of the manual workers, 23 per cent said that they were middle class, and 77 per cent working class. Whatever is actually meant by these self-estimates, and whether or not they do indicate a twofold class structure in popular opinion, it is clear that in Swansea almost a third of the non-manual or white-collar workers and almost a quarter of the manual workers do not accept the division between manual and non-manual occupations as being meaningful in social class terms. The sociologists who use this method are encouraged by this apparent contradiction to talk of manual workers 'putting themselves into the middle class', or 'working class people becoming middle class', of 'the bourgeoisification of the workers' and so forth. This conforms with current popular opinions of class mobility —and the method used apparently confirms it. They generally omit, however, to discuss the other part of the evidence—the problem of the third (in Swansea) of non-manual workers putting themselves in the working class. Is this evidence of the 'proletarianization' of the middle class?

In our view this method produces a gross over-simplification of the complexities of social class to the extent of reducing its operational value in analysis to near vanishing-point so far as the study of family behaviour is concerned. It seems so crude in application and to diverge so far from the social reality we seek to describe that it is

[11] Gosta Carlsson, *Social Mobility and Class Structure*, 1958, p. 18.
[12] Op. cit., p. 114.

well-nigh impossible to understand the significance of any differences in family behaviour that may emerge, besides serious doubts as to whether or not other differences, perhaps more significant, are being concealed by the sheer crudity of this method. We do not use it in this study.

THE PEOPLE IN BETWEEN

It is a misleading and virtually meaningless question to ask: What social classes actually exist in Swansea? Not only does this depend on the definition of 'social class' adopted (and there are a bewildering variety of definitions to choose from) but it implies a far greater degree both of common consensus in terminology and of precision in the determination of accepted social distinctions than is apparent in general experience. The scales of social inequalities—a vague enough concept in itself—are *continua* of infinite and subtle gradua-tions, and it is an essentially arbitrary question where one draws the line or lines to mark off 'social classes'. The correct question for the sociologist here is: *What invented system of classification is it most useful to impose on the empirical data to further understanding and to facilitate fruitful analysis?* It is clear that whatever system is used, 'some modicum of semantic validity is desirable' (in Carlsson's phrase) but its prime purpose is not to reflect popular opinion but to reveal the nature of the social structure and the characteristics of social behaviour. It is a working model we make to help us to under-stand social reality. It is *not* a mirror in which the community under study can recognize its face. (To try to create one would be an impossible task because there are almost as many versions of this 'face' as there are people.)

Our rejection of the distinction between non-manual and manual labour as the indicator of social class does not of course mean that we do not agree that occupation is a most useful and valuable index of class status. There are indeed several serious difficulties in the use of a man's present occupation alone in assigning him to one class or another, and we discuss these below and show how we have tried to deal with them in our own method of classification. We have argued, however, that a twofold scheme based on the manual/non-manual occupational distinction is an inadequate model of the contemporary class structure. The division into middle and working class may be a popular stereotype, but in practice there are too many socially-mobile people in between to make this a useful analytic device. In *The Road to Wigan Pier*, George Orwell made the same point a quarter of a century ago (and in a language which seems curiously out-dated in the nineteen-sixties, as the Labour Party has discovered to its cost):

Class and the Welsh

In order to symbolize the class war, there has been set up the more or less mythical figure of a 'proletarian', a muscular but downtrodden man in greasy overalls, in contradistinction to a 'capitalist', a fat, wicked man in a top-hat and fur coat. *It is tacitly assumed that there is no one in between: the truth being, of course, that in a country like England about a quarter of the population is in between.* If you are going to harp on the 'dictatorship of the proletariat', it is an elementary precaution to start by explaining who the proletariat *are*. But because of the Socialist tendency to idealize the manual workers as such, this has never been made sufficiently clear. How many of the wretched shivering army of clerks and shopwalkers, who in some ways are actually worse off than a miner or a dockhand, think of themselves as proletarians? A proletarian —so they have been taught to think—means a man without a collar. So that when you try to move them by talking about 'class war', you only succeed in scaring them; they forget their incomes and remember their accents, and fly to the defence of the class that is exploiting them.[13]

The tremendous social and political changes since the thirties may well have rendered Orwell's interpretation of class alignments out of date, but they have not altered the accuracy of his observations that between the traditional middle class and the traditional working class there is a substantial intermediate class of routine white-collar workers, often socially-mobile individuals with social origins in the class above or the class below. With the profound industrial change that we described for Swansea in our last chapter, and with the ubiquitous shift in employment described in the quotation we gave from the article by Mark Abrams, this intermediate class has grown in size. Many now in this half-way house clearly find it difficult to describe themselves in terms of the traditional middle class/working class stereotype. They often display considerable embarrassment and hesitation in assigning themselves, and many take refuge in denials of the existence of social classes nowadays, or in assertions that things have changed so much that the familiar class terms are inapplicable or meaningless. Like the long-suffering men of the famous Duke of York, when they are only half-way up, they are neither up nor down. Our own estimate, based on our own method of classification, suggests that 36 per cent of the population of Swansea are currently in this vague interstitial area between the two traditional social classes. These people 'in between' form an important element in the contemporary class structure, blurring the distinction between the middle and working classes by closing and bridging the gap that formerly

[13] George Orwell, *The Road to Wigan Pier*, Penguin Edition, 1962, p. 199. (The first italics are ours.)

94

was more evident in popular experience than it is today. This intermediate class is vitally related to the dynamics of the class system—to status-seeking and social climbing, to social ambition and aspiration, to the upward or downward circulation of individuals or families over the generations—in short to the whole problem of social mobility, an inherent characteristic of social stratification in an 'open' society.

The incidence of occupational mobility presents a formidable difficulty in the use of present occupation alone as an index of social class. Movement upwards or downwards in class terms certainly involves a good deal more than simply a change of job. It involves also profound changes in attitude and behaviour. A social class is more than one of a series of economic strata, though this aspect is obviously fundamental. We think primarily of social classes in effect as broad economic divisions composed of individuals who recognize one another as peers; but they are also cultural groupings marked by distinctive standards and styles of living, and by characteristic values and social attitudes. The social origins and family backgrounds of the individuals concerned are both an important element in their social acceptance as status equals within a particular social class and also in their degree of assimilation to the distinctive values and way of living characteristic of that social class. Economic status may qualify an individual for interaction on terms of social equality with people of a particular social class but his social origins may impede his cultural acceptance of, or familiarity with, the manners and customs involved. Numerous studies have indicated that the socially-mobile person tends to be less confident and secure and less culturally well-integrated than those born into the social class to which he has moved. Considering the situation of socially-mobile individuals, Blau emphasizes the importance of what he calls 'the pattern of acculturation' and continues:

> they do not have sufficient opportunity for complete acculturation to the values and style of life of the one group, nor do they continue to experience the full impact of the social constraints of the other. But both groups exert some influence over mobile individuals, since they have, or have had, social contacts with members of both, being placed by economic circumstances amidst the one, while having been socialized among the other. Hence their behaviour is expected to be intermediate between that of the two non-mobile classes.[14]

[14] Peter M. Blau, 'Social Mobility and Interpersonal Relations', in *American Sociological Review*, 21, 1956, p. 291.

Generations of social experience confirm the accuracy of this observation.

Occupational as opposed to social mobility can be relatively quick and dramatic, and we found numerous instances in Swansea of sharp contrasts between the occupational status of sons and of fathers. The following table gives the incidence of occupational mobility in Swansea for the occupied males within our sample, comparing the occupations of our subjects with those of their fathers. The division into six occupational classes follows that used by the Registrar-General in census classifications, being briefly Class I—professional and higher managerial; Class II—intermediate professional and managerial occupations; Class III—skilled manual and lower non-manual; Class IV—partly skilled manual; and Class V—unskilled manual occupations. The Registrar-General with his Class III does not separate non-manual occupations from skilled manual. In the following table we have divided this Class into two, following the classification distinguishing manual from non-manual occupations within this Class III adopted by Young and Willmott in their Woodford study.[15]

Table 3.2: Occupational Mobility in Swansea. Six-fold Classification, Main Sample—Occupied Males Only

Registrar General's Occupational Grades	Father's Occupational Class					
			non-manual	manual		
	I	II	III	III	IV	V
				Percentages		
I	31	12	—	2	5	2
II	31	38	33	12	12	8
Subject's (i.e. son's) occupational class III n.m.	15	8	17	10	10	9
III m.	23	29	22	49	48	51
IV	—	8	11	14	12	7
V	—	5	17	13	13	23
Total %	100%	100%	100%	100%	100%	100%
Numbers	26	110	36	358	59	121

It is not necessary to make detailed comments on this table: the figures show that there has been extensive occupational mobility when we compare the sons' occupations with those of their fathers.

[15] See the explanation given by Young and Willmott in Appendix 3, op. cit., p. 159.

In no single case do the present occupational classes have more than half of their members belonging to the same occupational grade as their fathers; the maximum figure (in the boxes showing the percentages of subjects belonging to the occupational class of their fathers) is 49 per cent for skilled manual workers, only two other percentages (for the top two classes) are in the region of a third, the remainder below a quarter.[16] This is the detailed picture; if we summarize the data by the distinction between non-manual and manual occupations, the following emerges:

Table 3.3: Occupational Mobility in Swansea by the distinction between manual and non-manual occupations.
Occupied Males only

Father's Occupation Class Subject's (or subject's husband's) Occupational Class ↓	White-Collar	Manual
White-Collar	59 %	23 %
Manual	41 %	77 %
Total %	100 %	100 %
Numbers	172	538

Notwithstanding the extremely wide range of occupations covered by these two categories, 41 per cent of the sons of men in white-collar occupations have 'descended' into manual work, and 23 per cent of the sons of manual workers have 'risen' into the white-collar grades. The amount of inter-generational mobility of all occupied males is 27 per cent. It is impossible to accept this as an accurate picture of the changes in *social class*, in terms of the middle class/working class dichotomy, which have occurred between the sons' generation and that of their fathers, even though it is of course an important piece of evidence that must be borne in mind in discerning the contemporary class structure.

The extensive occupational mobility which has occurred over a single generation presents a serious difficulty to the use of a man's present occupation to assign him to a social class without regard for his social background. It is even more difficult for women. In classifying a married woman it is usually assumed that her husband's occupational status is a sufficient and accurate guide to her own

[16] At the 1 per cent level of confidence the population proportion for III manual might be as high as 56 per cent.

position in the social scale. There would be no great difficulty here if it could be shown that the occupational classes discerned were strongly endogamous—that marriage tended in the great majority of cases to be limited to men and women of the same occupational grade (judging by their fathers' occupational status—that is by the grading of the two families of origin at the time of the marriage). The evidence, however, of the wide range of marriage in terms of this occupational status indicates that this assumption is unwarranted by the facts. If we divide the occupational scale into three grades for the purposes of examining the range of marriage—the three grades being Managerial (the Registrar-General's Class I and II together), Routine Non-manual (the lower white-collar occupations), and Manual—and then relate the position of the two families of origin at the time of the marriage of the 746 married *women* in our sample in Swansea, we can reach the following conclusions about the degree of endogamy by these three occupational classes:

(a) Of the daughters of those in the managerial and professional grades, only 30 per cent married the sons of men belonging to the same occupational category, 16 per cent married the sons of men in lower non-manual grades, and 54 per cent married the sons of manual workers.

(b) Of the daughters of those in routine white-collar jobs, only 12 per cent married the sons of men of similar status, 11 per cent married the sons of men from the higher managerial and professional grades, and 77 per cent married the sons of manual workers.

(c) Of the daughters of manual workers, 78 per cent married the sons of manual workers, 13 per cent married the sons of men in the higher managerial and professional class, and 9 per cent married the sons of routine non-manual workers.[17]

The same analysis of the marriages of the married *men* in our sample produced, much as one would expect since this is the other side of the same coin, an almost identical picture of a wide marriage range and a low correlation between the occupational ranking of the two 'families of origin' of the brides and grooms. Of the three occupational classes by social origin into which we divided the married men and women we interviewed, only the manual-worker class has a relatively high degree of endogamy and even here something like a quarter of all the men and women married outside the manual category. The other two categories are very much more unstable in this respect—over a half of all the men and women with family

[17] Only the difference between the proportions of the manual group and the other two groups marrying sons of men in the same group is significant.

backgrounds in the higher managerial and professional classes, and over three-quarters of those originating in the lower white-collar category, found their husbands or wives in the homes of manual workers. Much of the differences between these three categories is due to their relative sizes—the manual workers category forming 72 per cent of the total, and the managerial and lower white-collar 17 per cent and 11 per cent respectively—the larger the size the greater the chance of a marriage within the category due to the availability of potential spouses. But even allowing for this variation by occupational class, the total extent of this mobility through marriage is considerable—we have calculated that 37 per cent of married men and women in our sample as a whole found their marriage partners in an occupational class other than that in which they themselves were born and raised (for the two higher occupational classes the figures are 67 per cent and 88 per cent respectively).

The obvious conclusion is that there are a very large number of homes in Swansea in which the husbands and wives come from different social backgrounds as a result of 'mixed marriages'—from the viewpoint of occupational class. It is an extremely difficult matter to assess the full implications of this mobility through marriage on the structure of the families concerned. This is an aspect of our analysis to which we have given a good deal of thought, and we will be discussing the conclusions that we have been able to reach in a later chapter. Our main point here, since our present task is to discover a satisfactory method of revealing what differences exist in Swansea in the patterns of family behaviour by the factor of social class, is that it would be absurd to ignore this evidence both of occupational mobility and of mobility through marriage. In our view to take the information about a man's present job *alone* (or of her husband's job in the case of a married woman) to construct a system of classification *by social class* produces too great a distortion of the data and too great a divergence from the perception of the existing social order afforded by ordinary common sense to be acceptable in this study.

OUR METHOD OF CLASSIFICATION

Because our need to devise a method of classification derives from a desire to compare the family behaviour of different social classes we were concerned less with the economic or status aspects of class than with the different styles of life associated with economic and status groups. The rapid occupational mobility and the considerable degree of occupational exogamy which we have noted makes the task of isolating groups which exhibit class related cultural differences extremely difficult.

'It is evident that movement up the social ladder is slower than movement up the occupational ladder' write Bendix and Lipset,[18] and there can be little doubt that this is correct. If we use facts on occupation as a main indicator of social class, and this we clearly must do, we need to find some method of braking the speed of occupational movements up or down the scale to take account of this discrepancy. This can be done in two ways—first by taking a dynamic two-generation view and thus using the evidence of the social origins of the men and women concerned to weight their allocation to one social class or another on the basis of their present jobs, and secondly by using also the evidence of their subjective assessments of their class orientations to correct the picture produced by occupation alone.

This briefly is the method we have followed in this study in producing a working model of the class structure for use in the statistical analysis of the data we have assembled from our survey on family composition and extra-familial relationships. For ease of exposition, the analysis we have used in constructing the classification can be divided into three steps:

I

Taking the Registrar-General's classification of occupations sorted into eleven occupational grades, we grouped these into three status categories as follows:

Status Category	Grade	Examples	Registrar-General's Classes
Managerial and Professional	1	Judges, Doctors, Bank Managers, Company Directors, Clergymen, Surveyors and Architects, Civil Service Administrative Officers, University Teachers.	I
	2	Farmers, Industrial Managers, Auctioneers, Chemists, Chief Constables and Superintendents, Teachers, Executive Officers, Librarians.	II
	3	Proprietors and Managers of Retail Businesses, Moneylenders Agents, Hotel-keepers, Buyers.	II
	4	Bank Clerks, Cashiers, Costing and Estimating and Accounting Clerks, Book-keepers.	II

[18] Bendix and Lipset, op. cit., p. 275.

Status Category	Grade	Examples	Registrar-General's Classes
Clerical	5	Insurance Agents, Bookmakers, Salesmen, Shop Assistants, Commercial Travellers.	III
	6	Clerks, Typists, Office Workers generally.	
	7	Telephone Operators, Laboratory Technicians, Policemen, Driving Instructors, Nurses, Lower Local Government Officials.	
	8	Foremen, Overlookers, Supervisors, Inspectors and Testers.	
Artisan	9	Skilled Manual Workers—Furnacemen, Fitters and Mechanics, Bus Drivers, Plumbers, Railway Drivers, Carpenters, Chefs, Painters.	IV
	10	Semi-skilled—Gardeners, Miners, Asphalters, Bus Conductors, Roundsmen, Postmen, Coalmen, Window Cleaners.	
	11	Unskilled—Labourers, Porters, Dock Labourers, Messengers, Lift Attendants, Watchmen, Dustmen, Newspaper-sellers.	V

The division of this scale into three status categories is of course arbitrary but it does make use of two well-accepted and comparatively 'natural breaks' between manual occupations and routine-white-collar on the one hand and between the latter and the higher-managerial and professional occupations on the other. This we would argue is more reasonable and useful than the twofold division into manual and non-manual occupations. It enables us to distinguish the middle category—'the clerical' in our terms—as intermediary and transitional between the extremes formed by the two others. For those unfamiliar with the occupational grading used by the Registrar-General we have given examples of occupations in the various grades so that the general validity of the ranking can be considered.

II

We then sorted all the subjects in our survey sample into one or other of these three status categories according to their own occupations (or the husbands' occupations in the case of married women). If this grouping is then matched with that produced by grouping in the same way the fathers' occupations (representing the family backgrounds and social origins) of these same individuals the following arrangement of nine groups is obtained:

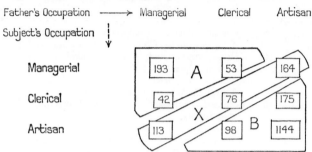

The numbers in the boxes show the distribution of the persons in our sample when their own occupations are compared with those of their fathers (in a handful of cases we did not know the fathers' occupations and the people concerned have been included on the basis of their own occupation alone—in four cases we did not have any information on the subject's own occupation; these have been left out altogether in this analysis). As shown in the diagram, we then 'polarized' these nine groups into two extremes—the triangles marked A and B, and one intermediary category marked X. We did this on the argument that the occupational shift (comparing son with father) between the managerial category and the clerical is slight in effect, and so is that between the clerical and artisan. This grouping produces the following three occupational classes:

		(Father Managerial)	(Father Clerical)		
A	*Managerial* =	(Son Managerial)	(Son Managerial)	288	14%
		(Father Managerial)			
		(Son Clerical)			
		(Father Clerical)	(Father Managerial)		
X	*Intermediate* =	(Son Clerical)	(Son Artisan)	353	18%
		(Father Artisan)			
		(Son Managerial)			
		(Father Artisan)	(Father Clerical)		
B	*Artisan* =	(Son Artisan)	(Son Artisan)	1,317	68%
		(Father Artisan)			
		(Son Clerical)			
			Totals	1,958	100%

Two of these three occupational classes (A and B) are relatively stable in occupational terms, and one (X) relatively mobile. Those individuals who have moved in one generation from the managerial status category to the artisan or vice versa, have been put in Class X, the intermediate category of people 'in between'. Hence the Managerial Class contains no individuals whose fathers were artisans, and the Artisan Class contains none whose fathers were of the higher-managerial or professional grades.

III

Using this occupational 'control' as it were, we then took account of how these persons ranked themselves by social class (see Table 3.1, page 86) adding those who said 'upper' or 'upper middle' or 'lower middle' to the 'middle class'; and those who said 'upper working' to the 'working class'. Correlating these replies with the three occupational classes constructed above, the following arrangement emerges:

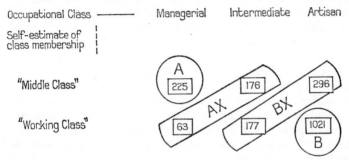

The 7 per cent of our sample who gave some other reply when asked to assess themselves by social class, or who refused or who said 'don't know', have been distributed over this classification according to their occupational class alone—they represent a minute and insignificant proportion of any one category but, since our sample was comparatively small in size, we did not want to leave them out of our later family analyses.

The diagram above shows at one corner 225 persons of the Managerial Class who classified themselves as 'middle class', and at the other diagonal extreme 1,021 persons of the Artisan Class who call themselves 'working class'. We have accepted these 'consistent' replies as designating respectively the people in our sample who belong to the traditional (and relatively stable) middle and working classes respectively (they are marked A and B in the diagram). The remainder of the sample between these two extremes consists of persons whose self-assessments are apparently inconsistent with their occupational status (i.e. persons who appear mobile in class attitudes for some reason) and also those of the intermediate occupational class who are divided exactly in half in their 'class orientation'. We have grouped this remainder into two classes, AX and BX, in the manner shown in the diagram, giving priority to occupation over self-estimates, to produce two intermediary 'fringe' classes of a mobile, transitional character, the one bordering the middle class and the other bordering the working class.

It may seem that after our discussion of the problems involved in interpreting our respondents' own estimates of their class membership, we are inconsistent in including 'self estimates' of class in our classification at all. They have been included because, although there can be little consistency in their application by individuals occupying different positions in the total occupational range, this is not to say that they have no meaning. We believed, moreover, that self ascription was related, *within each occupational strata*, to an awareness by the individual of his social position and that claims to class membership, when consistent with his occupational class, represented an assertion of his cultural solidarity with his social peers. To put it more simply: we have assumed only that individuals who have been in white-collar occupations for two or more generations use the term middle class in a consistent way, that people in manual occupations are similarly consistent in the use of the term working class, and that these usages have a certain semantic validity in that they approximate to the usage expected on the grounds of what is usually accepted as being involved in class membership. What inconsistent class ascription means we do not pretend to know and cases where such inconsistency was present have accordingly been excluded from the two polar groups of our classification. The purpose of the classification it must be reiterated is to isolate two homogeneous *cultural* groups at either extreme of the 'class' continuum.

The steps in this analysis are quite simple, though they may appear complicated in explanation. Together they produce the classification system by social class which we have used in this study. The final result is a fourfold class system grouping our total sample from Swansea in the following proportions (and with the following terminology):[19]

[19] We have retained this traditional terminology simply because there is no satisfactory alternative. We, however, entirely share Peter Laslett's view, in his broadcast talk on 'The Solid Middle Class' (*The Listener*, 4 Jan. 1962) that it is a nuisance 'that we all find ourselves using a terminology from which one term is permanently missing. . . . Still, the cry for a new set of terms is too often the way to sterility in this sort of discussion. Perhaps all that can reasonably be hoped is that we shall use those we have with critical awareness.'

	A Middle Class	AX Lower Middle Class	XB Upper Working Class	B Working Class	Total
Numbers	225	239	473	1,021	1,958
Percentage of total	11%	12%	24%	53%	100%

We must add that in our preliminary analyses we tried out a number of other possible systems of classification. This one gave the 'best' results when tested out as a variable in the analysis of other data in that it revealed the largest statistical differences between the four social classes depicted, and particularly between the middle class at one extreme and the working class at the other. This is a good enough reason for using it. If there are differences by social class in the patterns of family behaviour this method should reveal them and enable us to consider their explanation. We do not pretend that this classification portrays social classes which 'actually exist' in Swansea (though it does conform pretty closely to the picture we have formed in our own minds of the class structure) nor that it solves all the difficulties of classification of which we are aware. We do say that this method is successful in doing what we wanted, which was to isolate two homogeneous cultural groups, that this is the most satisfactory method we have been able to devise to meet some of the major objections to other methods previously used, and that we have found it useful in the statistical analysis of our survey results. This is what we propose to make social class mean in this study.

As Carlsson has pointed out in describing the classification system which he used in his study of social mobility in Sweden:

> the application of the system means that many mistakes will be made in individual cases. Still, the rough and imperfect rules may give us groups that differ, statistically, from each other in important respects. No more of this is expected of the system as a whole, or any part of it. Not only individual cases, but certain occupations as a whole may have been referred to the wrong category. Again we may hope that this will not invalidate the whole system, or a particular distinction. The use of the system when analysing other data will help us to decide on its value.[20]

CLASS DIFFERENCES IN SWANSEA

We have thus sorted into four piles the interview schedules representing the sample of just under two thousand Swansea families that we visited in our survey. We know how these four classes differ by

[20] Gosta Carlsson, op. cit., p. 57.

105

occupation and self-ascription by class because we used these factors in their construction. But what about education, income, housing, distribution by neighbourhood, and so forth—all factors commonly accepted as 'involved' in social class? Does this method of classification bring out the differences that one would expect from general experience to exist between the various social classes? In short, does this method work? In answering this question we can also present more information about the nature of these four social classes, and therefore about the people of Swansea at the time of our study.

The following table shows the variations by social class for a series of topics. The percentages shown (all calculated of the class totals shown in the table heading) should be read across the table, comparing one class with another. In some cases, the percentages given for a particular topic—house-type, for example—add downwards to a hundred because we have included all the categories into which we divided the replies for this topic:

Table 3.4: *Class Differences in Swansea. Main Sample—Percentages only*

Topic	Replies by Category	Middle Class Number=225	Lower Middle Class =239	Upper Working Class =473	Working Class =1,021
		%	%	%	%
Education	Left school at 14 or 15 (or less)	31	67	85	95
	Left school at 16+	69	33	15	5
	Went to fee-paying school	37	12	9	4
	Went to University or College	26	10	4	1
Income	Under £6 per week	1	4	10	13
	£6–£15 per week	30	58	74	80
	Over £15 per week	69	38	16	7
	Total	100	100	100	100
	Refused to state income	25	20	11	8
House Ownership or Tenancy	House-owners	75	64	53	36
	Corporation Tenants	5	15	26	39
	Tenants of other Landlords	20	21	21	25

Table 3.4 (*continued*): *Class Difference in Swansea. Main Sample—Percentages only*

Topic	Replies by Category	Middle Class Number=225	Lower Middle Class =239	Upper Working Class =473	Working Class =1,021
		%	%	%	%
House Type	Small-Terrace House	20	33	42	58
	Large-Terrace House	13	11	12	8
	Flat/Apartment/ Other	11	13	8	7
	Semi-detached	40	35	33	25
	Detached	16	8	5	2
	Total	100	100	100	100
Rateable Value of House	Under £30 p.a.	38	63	81	93
	Over £30 p.a.	62	37	19	7
Prestige Possessions	Households with car	59	44	30	18
	,, ,, telephone	55	31	13	4
	,, ,, piano	44	38	33	24
Holidays	Went away on holiday last year	72	66	50	36
	Stayed with relatives	27	33	21	18
	Relatives came to stay	56	47	35	30
Football	Self (or husband) follows Rugby	32	23	19	14
	Self (or husband) follows Soccer	18	26	35	35
Movements	Subject would like to move from present locality	28	29	38	39
	Subject brought up outside Wales	25	16	11	10
	Subject has spent most of life outside Wales	18	14	7	5
Clubs	Subject belongs to at least one club or society in Swansea	45	38	33	29
Sunday Opening of Pubs	Approve	56	45	40	40
	Disapprove	35	47	52	51
	Don't know	9	8	8	9

Even a fairly brief glance at this table presenting the analysis by social class of the information provided by our interview schedules on eleven selected topics is enough to establish that substantial differences exist in their characteristic behaviour and attitudes between the four social classes that we have constructed. The middle and working classes are shown as the two extremes—whatever category of reply is being considered—with the two socially-mobile classes (lower middle and upper working) in between displaying the intermediate behaviour postulated by Blau's hypothesis quoted earlier, and expected from common experience. Detailed comments on this table are unnecessary: the figures can speak for themselves. Three-quarters of our middle class, for example, own their own houses, the percentage diminishing down the class scale to just over a third with the working class. Ninety-three per cent of the working class earn under £15 per week as compared with 31 per cent of the middle class earning under this amount. Over half of our middle-class families have cars and telephones, but less than one in five of working-class families have cars, and less than one in twenty have telephones. Three-quarters of the middle class went away from Swansea for a holiday in the twelve months before our survey, but only just over a third of the working class. In each case, taking these examples, the percentages for the two intermediate classes fell between these two extremes—with the lower middle class being nearer to the behaviour patterns of the middle class, and the upper working class nearer to those of the working class. That this happens is not in the least surprising of course—it merely shows that our method of classification is satisfactory. When tested against these other data, it does in fact work, showing up the differences, in areas where we would expect to find them, in a clear and useful manner.

The figures given for education need a brief word of explanation. The ages of 14 or 15 are the minimum statutory school-leaving ages (depending on the age of the informant: we have included in this category those elderly subjects who said they left school below these ages): those who left school at 16 or more can be inferred to have completed a grammar or technical school education. The percentages show that over two-thirds of the middle class fell into this latter category, while only one in twenty of the working class. We must emphasize (and this equally applies to the percentages given of those of each class who went to a University or College) that this does *not* mean that only 5 per cent of working-class children receive a grammar or technical school education in Swansea—or at least, leave school at 16 years or more. It means rather that this percentage of those *now in the working class* by our method of classification received this education. The son or daughter of a miner or steelworker for example who passed the eleven-plus and went on to become a schoolteacher (and there are many cases of this in Wales) would be classified by us in the Intermediate Occupational Class and then in either the lower middle or upper working class according to his or her subjective assessment of class membership. We have thus siphoned-off from the 'working class' the upwardly-mobile individuals. The 5 per cent of the present working class who were educated to 16 or more, and the 4 per cent who went to a university or college, have *remained* working class by their subsequent occupations (manual or routine-white-collar) and by their expressed class attitudes. Education and occupation are of course closely linked. Though we have used a dynamic two-generational picture to construct our classification, the method in application must obviously give a current, static picture of the present allocation by social class of the people we interviewed. We stress this point to avoid a possible misinterpretation of these figures on education.

Given then this static picture of contemporary class membership, the figures for education do show the *effects* of education on the class structure. More than nine out of ten of the present working class left school at the minimum school-leaving age, this proportion decreasing through the intermediary classes to three out of ten for the middle class. Only one in a hundred of the present working class received any higher education, whereas twenty-six out of a hundred in the middle class did so. We do not give the figures for males and females separately though there are of course well-known differences in the expectations about the education of boys and girls (though these differences have diminished sharply over the past generation or so). For all four social classes, the proportions of males who stayed on at school beyond the minimum age, and of those who went on to colleges or universities, were substantially higher than that of females. On the other hand, again for all the social classes, the proportion of females going to fee-paying schools was higher than that for males. Swansea has eleven independent fee-paying schools, only one of which is a 'preparatory' school for boys (between the ages of 8 and 13); the remainder are described as 'mixed' though in fact the numbers of girls attending are far and away in excess of the numbers of boys. These voluntary schools include two taking children between 4 and 11 only, and four 'senior mixed' schools—emphasizing commercial and business subjects in the curriculum—for which the minimum age of entry is 11 or 12 (the critical years of the notorious eleven-plus examination for grammar and technical school entry).[21]

---

[21] Swansea Education Committee have now (1963) announced their intention of 'abolishing' this examination.

Swansea's middle classes, like those in the rest of Wales, appear to have little interest in packing their sons off to the public schools which play such an important part in bolstering the English class system— particularly in the class-ridden South. Though a small proportion of boys do go to boarding schools, mainly to those outside Wales (and equally a handful of young ladies do reach Cheltenham), the dominant local educational tradition in the upper reaches of the social scale, as of course in the lower, is to make use of the local grammar schools. There are many subtle differences between class distinctions in England and those in Wales, though it is an exceptionally difficult task (and thankfully one outside the scope of this book) to put one's finger on the exact points of regional difference and to demonstrate them in a statistical analysis. As with so much of the hazy, if very real, world of social class one's views depend heavily on personal impressions and insight, and vary from individual to individual with individual experience and the sensitivity of personal class-antennae. We simply record our own impression that these differences exist, that they are mainly concerned with what Peter Laslett has called[22] 'the shape of society'—'the social height' contained in the class pyramid—and that the comparative absence of public school education for the sons of Swansea's middle classes and the consequent class mixing that takes place in the ordinary grammar schools has a good deal to do with this.

Indeed the deliberate mixing up of boys from different social backgrounds appears to be part of the educational policy of the Corporation of Swansea so far as its three boys' grammar schools are concerned. One of these—Bishop Gore founded in 1682 by Hugh Gore, Bishop of Waterford 'for the Education of the sons of the poorer sort of Burgesses in Virtue and good Literature'—is in Sketty in a middle-class residential area. Attended generation after generation by the sons of Swansea families, it was until recently the only public grammar school in the town; it is indeed still referred to as 'The Grammar School'; until it was moved west to Sketty after the war it was sited, in ancient buildings, in the Town Centre. Its place in the Town Centre has been taken by a comparatively new grammar school—Dynevor County Secondary—providing a similar education. The third—Penlan Multilateral School—is way out on the Penlan post-war housing estate: a new school in modern buildings—on a bleak site—with a 'grammar' stream, but not quite a traditional grammar school as the other two are. The annual problem in Swansea causing many heartbreaks among parents and doubtless many head-

[22] Peter Laslett, 'The Social Revolution of our Time', *The Listener*, 11 January, 1962.

aches in the Education Department, is how to allocate by school the successful candidates at the eleven-plus examination. In the parents' order of preference there can be little doubt that the rank order is Bishop Gore—Dynevor—Penlan, and there is clearly a sizeable ingredient of social snobbery in these parental preferences. Given the spatial sorting of the Borough by social class with marked social and cultural differences between east and west, if a physical 'zoning' principle were followed in this annual allocation, Bishop Gore would have a predominantly middle-class entry annually and sharp social differences would undoubtedly emerge between the three schools. The Labour-controlled Corporation has recognized this probability and set its face sternly against this method of allocation. To preserve the equality of the three schools it follows a 'secret' method based on a ballot of the successful candidates, with account taken of parental preferences where possible after the sorting by ballot has been completed. Of the 380 boys who passed the eleven-plus in 1961, only six gave Penlan as their first choice; 185 opted for the 150 vacant places at Bishop Gore and 199 for the 150 places at Dynevor (the greater preference for the latter being accounted for, partly at least, by the popular opinion that 'everybody wants to go to Bishop Gore' and hence that one has a better chance of getting into Dynevor— rather than missing the boat at Bishop Gore and being sent out to Penlan). The annual spate of letters of complaint over this system by parents who have failed to get their sons into the school of their choice are a familiar feature of the local newspapers. 'In Swansea,' says one irate parent 'there are two hurdles to overcome—one the eleven-plus, the other the educational bureaucracy in the Guildhall— in getting a boy into the Grammar School'. The Guildhall policy with this recurrent difficulty does not eradicate entirely the status distinctions between these three schools but it acts in this direction and probably does prevent existing class differences in Swansea from becoming inextricably associated with the schools providing grammar school education. To this extent it is a democratic policy: its wide- spread unpopularity among middle-class parents, while partly a result of a natural desire for their children to have as short a jorney to school as possible, is also an interesting reflection of their class- consciousness.

We pointed out earlier that the proportions of girls going to fee- paying schools was higher for all four social classes than that for boys. It must be added that the only significant difference by social class in this respect occurred with the upper working class where the proportion of girls (13 per cent) who went to a fee-paying school was over three times the proportion for boys (4 per cent)—a much wider difference than for the other three classes. At this point in the social scale, socially-mobile individuals are it seems particularly concerned with giving their daughters—those who do not pass the eleven-plus into the girls' grammar schools—the social benefits in the way of 'proper speech' and manners conferred by convent-type 'finishing' schools, as well as the access to clerical and commercial occupations provided by the commercial schools. Underlying this interest is probably the recognition that this private, and relatively inexpensive, education facilitates the upward mobility of daughters through marriage, to which we have referred earlier in this chapter. In this respect, it is a good investment for this upwardly-mobile social class.

The differences between the four social classes demonstrated in Table 3.4, covering the wide and varied range of topics encompassed by our interview schedule, are sharp and clear. They are given as examples of the class differences which emerge readily in a statistical description of contemporary Swansea society. There are many other differences between these social classes which are equally capable of expression in this simple statistical form, comparing the percentages obtained for a particular dimension of social and cultural behaviour from one social class to another. Some of these differences—notably those in family size, in age at marriage, in the employment of women—are fundamentally related (as are some of those already given in Table 3.4) to the patterns of family relationships that we are particularly concerned with in this study: we will be examining them in later chapters. We have devised this fourfold classification precisely for this purpose: so that we can use it as a research tool to identify the differences or similarities that exist in these patterns of family interaction. It is a practical classification of the two thousand or so Swansea families that composed our random sample of the town in 1960. We have tried to make it reflect as realistically and as accurately as possible (given the nature and limitations of a statistical description) our perception that social classes in Swansea, as in any community in Britain, are not simply a series of arbitrary economic strata—with built-in, if somewhat rickety, economic ladders bridging the gaps and enabling individuals from one level to clamber up into another, or slither down, as their personal economic circumstances change. This is a common but essentially inaccurate view of the class structure. Economic factors are certainly vitally involved, but we have thought rather of our social classes primarily as broad *cultural groupings*—using the term 'culture' in the anthropologist's sense of a total style and manner of living, a way of life.

We emphasize this aspect of the cultural differences between social classes, but recognize of course that considerations of *status* are inextricably involved with this whole business of class differentiation. Notions of social superiority or inferiority are the most obvious characteristic of any class system. They congregate readily around different items of cultural behaviour (particularly with speech mannerisms, food habits or leisure activities) but in practice a good deal of *physical* segregation occurs, a sort of general cultural 'apartheid', which reduces the social impact of these notions of status. The social classes not only live differently: to a large extent they live separately (a fact which is related to the disorganizing effect of social mobility within particular families). Status differences tend to be 'accommodated' by this physical separation, the different social classes in effect keeping out of one another's way, accepting that the other lot behave differently, and letting them get on with it. 'We're all right, Jack'! We will be seeing something later of the effects of this status accommodation when we look at the behaviour within families fragmented by internal social mobility. By seeing class primarily in cultural terms, we do not wish to minimize these status differences (though we do think that there has been much exaggeration of the importance of 'status-seeking' and 'status symbols' in recent sociology)—and we certainly do not wish to take the sting out of class.

Our impression, following our brief examination of social class in Swansea, is that the major feature distinguishing the contemporary class system from that two generations ago (say just before the First World War) is that in the former system economic factors were the clear and dominant social differentiators whereas now it is cultural differences which mainly differentiate the classes from one another (in a much more subtle and complex manner). Cultural differences have existed but formerly these were much more subordinate to dominant economic factors than they are today. The hierarchical aspects of class tend to be closely related to these economic differences—the wider the economic gap, the more pronounced the sense of hierarchy. Status and economic position go hand in hand. With the closure of the economic gap between the classes much of the former recognition and acceptance of a definite hierarchy of classes has disappeared, or faded noticeably in the current egalitarian atmosphere. Status derived from differences of wealth and income and housing and possessions is of course still there but much less pronounced than formerly—certainly in provincial Swansea. And with the lack of clarity and precision in the economic aspects of class, a good deal of social confusion has arisen, and there is a growing emphasis on cultural behaviour as a means of social differentiation. The contrasts are noticeable. For example, consider the following rough cultural dichotomy:

Working Classes	Middle Classes
Bingo	Premium Bonds
Football Pools	Unit Trusts/Shares
Holiday Camps	'Private' holidays
Coach Tours	Motoring—Home and Abroad
Hire Purchase	Budget Accounts
Weekly Payments	Bankers' Orders
'Pop' Music	'Good' Music
'Pop' Art	Impressionists/Abstracts
(Tretchikoff, etc.)	
Beauty Queen Contests	Horse Shows
I.T.V.	B.B.C.
Shore fishing	Sailing
Dance Halls	Dinner-Dances
Bowls	Golf
Motor-bikes	Scooters
Mild	Bitter
Daily Mirror[23]	*Daily Mail*, etc.

There would of course need to be a separate list of this kind for each age group. But even so, taking the above examples, it is generally true to say that most people fall, by and large, one side or the other of this great cultural divide in contemporary Swansea, as elsewhere in Britain. And the more consistently they do so, the easier it is to 'place' them in social class terms, regardless of economic factors. Economic differences are clearly involved in these various ways of behaving but seem less significant nowadays, with general affluence, in class distinctions than are these cultural attitudes and distinct styles of living.

Within a single broad cultural uniformity—that of the characteristic way of life of a modern urban society—the class structure in effect is composed of a series of sub-cultures, shading one into another and having a great deal in common so that it is exceptionally difficult in practice to say with any clarity where one begins and the other ends. But they are sufficiently contrasted and distinct at the extremes for the differences to be commonly recognized and accepted. Our conversations and discussions with informants throughout Swansea constantly echoed this theme, and our interview reports were packed with the comments people made, directly or indirectly, on these social differences by class. Anyone whose work takes him in and out of a

[23] The Senior Common Room at the University took almost all the national dailies but not the *Mirror*—the largest morning newspaper in Swansea as elsewhere in Britain. It decided in 1963 to take the *Mirror* for the first time.

wide variety of Swansea homes—say, a family doctor, or a priest, or a plumber, or newspaper reporter, or a reader of gas or electricity meters—will have no difficulty in recognizing with the sociologist the full force of the truism that the middle classes live very differently from the working classes. Any normally observant person in Swansea will detect without difficulty the continual sorting by social class that takes place in restaurants and cafés in the Town Centre, in the various bars of hotels and pubs (and from one pub to another), in shops of various types, in the membership of clubs and societies, in the audiences at various cultural events (from symphony concerts to bingo), in the crowds at various sporting events, in the holiday crushes on the beaches and bays of Gower (and from one bay to another), in the newspapers and magazines that people read, in the clothes they wear, in what they have to say and how they say it—and so on throughout the whole fabric of social living. Class is everywhere, pervasive, intangible, recognizable, but hard to define, with its importance variously exaggerated or belittled according to the personal opinion—and often the personal social standing—of the particular individual observer. Were there time and space enough, we would at this point describe these cultural differences, as we have observed them in Swansea, at some length (and the anthropologist's temptation to have a shot at this cultural description in a familiar modern society rather than in his more normal tribal haunts is very strong) but we must get on. Accepting that these social classes differ culturally, our sole interest here is whether variations in family behaviour form part of these cultural differences. We will be using the technical classification explained in this chapter to discover whether or not this is so.

We leave the subject of social class for the moment (we will be returning to it briefly later in this chapter when we comment on the geographical distribution of these four classes within the Borough) to turn to another form of 'layering' within Swansea society—the vertical cultural division of this population into Welsh on the one hand and non-Welsh on the other. The question of whether there are variations in family behaviour by the horizontal layering of social class forms one aspect of a more general comparative problem which can be stated as follows: are there *regional* differences in family behaviour in Britain associated with local and distinctive cultural traditions? Swansea is a Welsh town—at least to the extent that it is located in Wales. Are there discernable family differences which can be attributed to, and need explanation in terms of, this particular fact?

One relatively simple way of tackling this problem would be to compare the results obtained from our inquiry in Swansea as a whole with the conclusions of other studies elsewhere in Britain—say those for Bethnal Green or Woodford or Bermondsey for the London area, or those for Oxford or Banbury or Liverpool. At various points in this book we do in fact draw these comparisons where possible and they are, in our view, interesting and illuminating. But such comparisons are fraught with complications arising not only out of differences from study to study in methods and definitions but also from differences from one area to another in factors of scale, population density, topographical lay-out, class structure and so forth. The general differences between Swansea and Bethnal Green for example are immense, and straightforward comparisons in family behaviour which do not take account of these general physical and social differences are clearly unsatisfactory. And what of the range of variation within Swansea (concealed by the total figures for the Borough as a whole)? Bethnal Green, as a working-class 'pocket' in East London, may well be reasonably homogeneous but, as we have tried to show in this and earlier chapters, this certainly cannot be said of Swansea. Certain rough and general conclusions, usually on similarities rather than differences, do emerge from these gross comparisons between one urban area and another in Britain. It is equally clear, however, that we will make more progress and achieve a more precise understanding of family behaviour (as of other sociological problems) if we can make regional comparisons which are more strictly controlled, if more limited in scope.

The internal heterogeneity of social and cultural composition within Swansea gives us an opportunity to make this kind of limited comparison within the confines of a single study. Not only can we compare the behaviour of one social class with another but, recognizing the diversity in the social origins of Swansea's inhabitants which we described in our previous chapter, we can also compare the behaviour of the Welsh element as a group on the one hand with that of the remainder of the population on the other and ask whether this cultural difference is associated with a significant difference in family composition and in the interaction between relatives living apart. In order to do this we must first overcome another difficult problem of definition; who indeed are the Welsh within Swansea, and how can we identify this section of the population within the random sample which formed the subject of our survey? Social class is a difficult enough subject to have to grapple with but this, the identification of the Welsh, in the prevailing atmosphere of emotionalism and ultra-sensitivity, is enough to daunt the strongest spirit. There seems little doubt that whatever we have to say about this tricky subject we are likely to bring the roof down on top of our heads. As the *Voice* (which claims 'the largest circulation of any weekly newspaper in Swansea and the valleys') recently commented in its editorial column: 'as readers of this newspaper may have gleaned from the correspondence on our letters page, the feud between Welsh-speaking and non-Welsh-speaking residents of this area has been conducted with undertones of bitterness and racial prejudice which are almost frightening in their implication'. While this seems, to outsiders, a somewhat exaggerated and alarmist view of an entertaining exchange of invective (on the subject of whether Welsh should be compulsorily taught in local schools), there is no doubt at all that this is a field where angels—whether Welsh-speaking or not[24] fear to tread.

WHO ARE THE WELSH?

According to Wynford Vaughan Thomas: 'Cardiff is the official capital of Wales. Swansea is the unofficial capital of the Welsh,' adding, since there are possibly other views on this in distant corners of the Principality, that he writes 'as someone who is completely prejudiced'.

The visitor to Swansea from the world outside would, however, see few visible signs of Swansea's Welshness, apart from the odd street sign or the polysyllabic place-names on bus indicators. If he travelled up the Tawe Valley, he might notice the increasing frequency of gloomy chapels with their proud Hebraic names (Seion, Tabernacle, Carmel, Ebenezer, Bethel, Hermon, Caersalem, Bethlehem, Bethesda, Horeb, Bethany, Libanus, Salem, Nazareth, Babel, Soar, Calfaria) and their notice-boards in Welsh. But in the Town Centre he would notice little that is distinctively Welsh—apart from the Corporation's 'Croeso i Abertawe' spelt out in electric bulbs overlooking the Castle Gardens, alongside its English equivalent, 'Welcome to Swansea'. He would more likely observe the dominant signs of Swansea's Englishness in, for example, the universal shop-names of British 'High Streets'—Woolworths, Boots, Lilley and Skinner, Kardomah, Richard Shops, Radio Rentals, Crown Wallpapers, Littlewoods, Marks and Spencer, C. & A., MacFisheries, W. H. Smith and Son, Home and Colonial, Dolcis, John Collier, Montague Burton, British Home Stores, Scotch Wool Shop, Singer Sewing Machine Co., Scholl Foot Comfort Service—and so on down the roll-call of

---

[24] It may well be that *all* angels are Welsh-speaking—by definition. This is quite likely the case if in fact Welsh is the language of Heaven—as we are informed on good local authority.

names familiar all over Britain. He would hear little, if any, Welsh spoken in public places—but plenty of Welsh accents. He might buy a box of England's Glory matches with the joke on the back in Welsh.

According to the 1961 census, 86 per cent of the people living in Swansea at that date had been born within Wales (see Table 2.1 p. 46), though no doubt many of these were born of immigrant parents—of parents from various parts of England, and from Scotland and Ireland, who had come into Swansea in previous decades. It is likely that some at least of the 13 per cent born outside Wales were the children of Welsh parents. Place of birth (whatever its significance in determining 'nationality'—and there are a multitude of complications here as the recurrent dilemma of 'dual qualifications' in the selection of International Rugby teams in Britain—a matter of vital concern in Wales—annually testifies) is of little use in determining an individual's cultural allegiance. We are not here concerned with Welsh as a nationality (*pace* Plaid Cymru, 'the party of The Welsh Nation') but with Welsh as a distinctive regional culture within Britain.

The surest guide to the degree of Welshness—in this cultural sense —of any population in Wales is provided by the percentage of that population able to speak Welsh. *The Report on Welsh-Speaking Population* of the 1961 census shows that 17·5 per cent of the population of Swansea returned themselves as able to speak Welsh (17·2 per cent bilingually with English). The comparable figure for the population of Wales as a whole at the same census was 26·0 per cent able to speak Welsh. By this test, Swansea is clearly the most Welsh of the three major towns of Wales—Cardiff, the capital, had only 4·7 per cent speaking Welsh, and Newport only 2·1 per cent—but even so, less than a fifth of the Swansea population in 1961 said that they could speak Welsh, and as can be seen from the percentages at successive censuses over the last fifty years, the proportion of Welsh-speakers is steadily declining. In 1901 the proportion of Welsh-speakers in Wales as a whole was 49·9 per cent; by 1911 this had declined to 43·5 per cent, by 1921 to 37·1 per cent, by 1931 to 36·8 per cent, by 1951 to 28·9 per cent and by 1961 to 26 per cent. Similarly, the proportion of Welsh speakers in Swansea had declined over the same half-century from 32·4 per cent in 1901 to 17·5 per cent in 1961.

Our own survey in 1960 in Swansea included a question on ability to speak Welsh (and various other questions about cultural attitudes to Welsh-speaking) but is not strictly comparable with the census data: the census return simply asked the persons enumerated to state whether they were 'able to speak' Welsh (or Welsh and English)—we asked 'Can you speak Welsh—fluently, partly, or not at all?' Sixteen per cent of our random sample said that they could speak Welsh fluently, 12·5 per cent that they could speak some Welsh, and 71·5 per cent that they knew no Welsh whatsoever.

These were the total figures for the sample of the County Borough as a whole: the range of variation by neighbourhood within the Borough by this factor of Welsh-speaking was very great as the following examples show:

Table 3.5: Welsh-speaking by Selected Localities

Subjects Speaking Welsh	Morriston %	Landore %	Sketty %	Townhill %	St Thomas %	Mumbles %
Fluently	46	27	12	3	3	2
Partly	29	27	9	9	5	2
Not	25	46	79	88	92	96
Total %	100	100	100	100	100	100
Total Numbers	167	77	136	187	143	87

Not only was there this variation by neighbourhood (which we will be returning to presently) with the areas in the extreme west, around the Town Centre, and the new housing estates, showing the lowest proportion of Welsh-speakers (about one person in ten with any knowledge of Welsh) and the old industrial communities of the Tawe Valley the highest proportion (about three-quarters of the population of Morriston had some familiarity with Welsh, just under a half speaking it fluently) but also there was a clear variation by age, the older age groups showing a much higher percentage of Welsh-speakers than the younger—a reflection of the decline of Welsh-speaking revealed by the successive censuses. We asked each of our informants whether their parents could speak Welsh, and the results again reflected this decline from the previous to the present genera-tions (31 per cent said that their parents spoke Welsh fluently, 4 per cent partly, and 65 per cent not at all—the figures for fathers and mothers separately being almost identical). That is, the proportion of fluent Welsh-speakers had declined from 31 per cent in the parental generations to 16 per cent in our subjects' generations, with the proportions of those knowing some Welsh increasing from 4 to 12·5 per cent.

It would of course have been possible to solve our problem of cultural classification within our sample of Swansea families by simply using these replies on Welsh-speaking to group our subjects into two categories—those who said they could speak Welsh either fluently or partly on the one hand (558 or 28·5 per cent of our sample) and those who said that they could not speak any Welsh on the other (1,404 or 71·5 per cent of our sample). This would have given us two categories—Welsh and non-Welsh by the factor of the subject's own ability to speak Welsh—to use in the analysis of the information we have collected on various aspects of family behaviour. We, however, decided on reflection not to do this. We felt this to be unsatisfactory on the grounds that the 'non-Welsh' category would contain too many people who, though they now spoke no Welsh themselves, would have grown up in homes which were culturally Welsh by the criterion of their parents' ability to speak Welsh.

Since we are not here concerned precisely with Welsh-speaking in itself but with the Welsh language as an index of cultural orientation, we decided (as with social class) to take a two-generational view and to divide our subjects into two categories by taking account both of the subject's own familiarity with the Welsh language and that of either or both of his parents. In short, if both our subject *and* both his parents could not speak any Welsh at all we placed him culturally in our 'non-Welsh' category: the remainder (that is, those who could themselves speak Welsh either fluently or partly *and* who had one or both parents speaking some Welsh) formed our 'Welsh' category. The following diagram explains the method (and the resulting allocation of individuals in our sample).

		Parents Welsh-speaking	
		Some	None
Subjects	Some	457	100
Welsh-			
speaking	None	339	**1,061**

Our non-Welsh cultural category contained 1,061 persons (54 per cent of the total sample) who could not speak any Welsh themselves and neither of whose parents could speak any Welsh. The remainder of the diagram indicates our Welsh category— a total of 896 persons (46 per cent of the sample) 'exposed' to Welsh culture either through their own ability to speak some Welsh or through the fact that they grew up in homes in which one or both parents could speak some Welsh. As the diagram shows, 457 of this category both speak some Welsh themselves and had parents who spoke Welsh; 339 do not speak any Welsh themselves but came from homes where Welsh was spoken; and 100 had parents who knew no Welsh but claim to speak some Welsh themselves (probably having learnt it compulsorily at school, or possibly through marrying a Welsh-speaking spouse). Our Welsh cultural grouping contains therefore three types of persons—the cultural *élite* of fluent Welsh-speakers,[25] those who claim some familiarity with the Welsh language, and those who, though speaking no Welsh themselves, grew up in homes in which one or both parents spoke Welsh either fluently or partly. Our non-Welsh category comprises the remainder of the population—and is a very mixed bag of English, Irish, and Scots immigrants (or their descendants) together with a substantial— and annually increasing—proportion of anglicized Welsh at least 'twice removed' by the test of language from Welsh cultural traditions.

This is of course a rough and arbitrary classification—as are all methods of pigeon-holing human beings—devised specifically for the purposes of the family analyses which are the main subject of this study. By the criteria of cultural orientation used here, the population of Swansea is divided culturally almost in half—with the Non-Welsh slightly outnumbering the Welsh. We believe this to be a reasonable assessment of the contemporary cultural situation in Swansea.

We followed the exposition of our method of classification by social class earlier in this chapter by a demonstration that the method worked when tested against other data to see whether significant class differences were revealed. It is a good deal more difficult to do this with the cultural classification into Welsh and non-Welsh that we have been explaining here; firstly because we included in our interview schedule only a minimum number of questions which might indicate cultural differences, and secondly because such differences as exist occur primarily in the vague intangible area of psychological attitudes and are less easily defined with sufficient precision to permit a statistical description. Nevertheless the following table, covering a group of selected topics, does demonstrate that there are significant differences between the two cultural categories into which we have divided our main survey sample:

[25] The category frequently referred to by the English as 'the very Welsh'.

Table 3.6: Cultural Differences in Swansea. Main Sample—
Percentages only

Topic	Replies by Category	Welsh No. 896 %	Non-Welsh No. 1,061 %	Total Sample Averages No. 1957 %
Should Welsh be taught to all in Swansea's schools?	Yes	82	64	72
	No	13	26	20
	Don't Know	5	10	8
Sunday-opening of pubs	Approve	35	49	42
	Disapprove	58	41	49
	Don't know	7	10	9
Religious denomination	Welsh Non-conformist	30	2	15
	English Non-conformist	26	23	24
	Anglican	38	61	51
	Roman Catholic	4	10	7
	Other	2	4	3
Religious attendance	Last went to Church or Chapel: Within past week	31	17	23
	Week to month ago	11	12	12
	Month to 6 months ago	15	16	16
	More than 6 months ago	43	55	49
Parents belong to Welsh-speaking Church or Chapel	Yes	57	3	28
	No	43	97	72
Where married	In Church	36	52	45
	In Chapel	27	12	19
	In Register Office	26	23	24
	Unmarried	11	13	12
Football	Subject (or husband) follows: Rugby	22	16	18
	Soccer	27	36	32
	Both	16	14	15
	Neither	35	34	35

Table 3.6 (continued): Cultural Differences in Swansea. Main
Sample—Percentages only

Topic	Replies by Category	Welsh No. 896 %	Non-Welsh No. 1061 %	Total Sample averages No. 1957 %
House ownership or tenancy	Owners	56	41	48
	Corporation tenants	22	35	29
	Tenants of other landlords	22	24	23
Where brought up	In Wales	97	79	88
	Outside Wales	3	21	12

We must add here, before we comment on this table, the important fact that these two groups differed by age, the Welsh on the average being older than the non-Welsh. The mean age of our total sample (it must be remembered that the sample included only persons aged 21 or over) was 48·3 years. The mean age of the Welsh was above this average (50·5 years) whereas the mean age of the non-Welsh was below (46·2 years). This difference has been produced by the fact that we have used Welsh-speaking as the principle of classification—and Welsh-speakers tend to be older on average than people who cannot speak Welsh (this of course being connected with the decline of the language). Some of the differences shown in the above table are importantly related to this difference in mean age between these two cultural groupings. This point must be borne in mind in examining these differences.

Much as one would expect, the Welsh as a cultural group have, almost entirely, spent the period of their schooldays within Wales (as have over three-quarters of the non-Welsh in our sample), and are much more strongly in favour of the Welsh language being taught compulsorily to all children in the local schools (as is the present educational practice in Swansea, for all primary schools at least). This by the way was the only significant difference between the two cultures so far as education was concerned, apart from the fact that a smaller proportion of the Welsh had attended a fee-paying school.

Reflecting perhaps their stronger local attachments, but also a long-established cultural goal, a significantly higher percentage of the Welsh owned their own homes, and correspondingly fewer were tenants. This cultural difference accounts for the fact that the proportion of house-ownership in Swansea generally is well above the average for England (see the comparison given in the footnote on page 54 in Chapter II). It would seem that more of the Welsh prefer to buy their house instead of renting Corporation property, since there is no significant difference between the proportion of Welsh and non-Welsh who are private tenants. The figure for the non-Welsh in Swansea is, on the other hand, almost identical with the English national average.

The Welsh, on the evidence of our survey, showed a strong majority opinion against the opening of pubs in Wales on Sundays; whereas the non-Welsh, with less apparent regard for the local cultural tradition, showed a majority in favour of the opposite view. And, as it turned out later, the latter prevailed when the test came. About eighteen months after our survey, a referendum on this subject was held (in October 1961) in Swansea as in all county and county borough areas in Wales to determine local opinion on this matter and to decide whether or not, by local option, the pubs should be opened on the Sabbath, as in England over the border. In the outcome, 61 per cent of the electorate in Swansea voted in favour of Sunday opening, and 39 per cent voted against—though only 45 per cent of the total electorate turned out to vote.

For many Welshmen this result was a further breach in the cultural dyke holding back the flood tide of anglicization. Breached some years earlier by the Sunday opening of cinemas, another subject which aroused fierce local controversy, this dyke has crumbled quickly. The traditional Welsh Sunday, revered by the active Nonconformists as 'a hollow in the windy hillside of the week' (as one of our older Welsh informants in Swansea described it to us with characteristic verbal imagery), is fast becoming a historical curiosity rather than a present reality. The controversy over Sunday opening of pubs contained many complicated currents of argument and attitude: in important respects, however it was for many a wider problem of cultural preservation rather than an argument either about Sunday or about drink.

Under the former dominance of the Nonconformist pulpit, Welsh traditional culture contains a strong Puritanical (and Sabbatarian) and stern moralistic element with the emphasis on teetotalism and on 'temperance' interpreted as total abstinence, and on the Sunday observances familiar to anyone who has lived in a Welsh community, particularly to the older generation since these restrictions (no washing on the line, no children's games, no gardening or car-washing, no noise, no seaside excursions, no work either in the home or outside other than the minimum needed) are fast disappearing. Whilst these Sabbath-keeping observances tended to be generally kept, and much of the restrictive atmosphere at least still survives in the communities of present-day Swansea, the emphasis on teetotalism was never generally popular nor culturally dominant. The pubs flourished even in the strongholds of Welsh Nonconformism: perhaps there most of all. David Jenkins has described this cultural dichotomy between 'the chapel and the tavern as the two poles of society', and between the *pobl y capel* (the people of the chapel) and the *pobl y dafarn* (the people of the pub), in his shrewd and entertaining analysis of the Cardiganshire village of Aber-porth.[26] Much of this analysis is equally applicable to the predominantly Welsh communities in the Tawe Valley. Morriston has as many pubs as there are chapels.

In Minutes of Evidence to the Poor Law Commission of 1909, a Mr Herbert G. Solomon describes the social conditions in Swansea and concludes his statement with the significant juxtaposition of the following two sentences: 'We are well supplied with churches, chapels, etc., and the inhabitants are a G—d-fearing people . . . Public houses for the sale of drink are very numerous, which tends to much drunkenness and thereby increases poverty and pauperism.' The sight of drunken men in public places has almost entirely disappeared from the contemporary scene in Swansea, a symptom of a profound social and economic change on which many of our older informants commented at length, but there are still 246 public houses in Swansea (almost a hundred more than places of worship)—88 of them within a half-mile radius of Woolworths in the High Street, and the vast majority of the remainder in the old industrial communities of the Tawe Valley (Morriston alone has 21, whereas Sketty, only slightly smaller in population, has only 2). Many of the pubs in the Town Centre were destroyed in the blitz and a number have been demolished with road improvements, but seven new public houses and hotels, some more like 'contemporary' coffee-bars than the traditional pub, have been opened in the Town Centre in the last three years, and on Saturday nights they are all desperately overcrowded. They include the new Three Lamps, built on the blitzed site of the old pub favoured by Dylan Thomas—non-Welsh-speaking himself but a Welshman culturally by the classification used in this book—whose drinking habits scarcely reflected the Nonconformist element in Welsh culture.

As a result of the Sunday-opening poll, all Wales was divided into two parts—wet and dry. Swansea as a County Borough became wet on the first Sunday in November 1961 (a historic day in Wales) in common with the three other County Boroughs in the Industrial South (Cardiff, Merthyr and Newport), and the surrounding county

[26] David Jenkins, 'Aber-porth', in *Welsh Rural Communities*, edited by Elwyn Davies and Alwyn D. Rees, 1960, pp. 1–63.

of Glamorgan, and the four Welsh counties bordering wet England (Monmouth, Brecon, Radnor and Flint). The remaining eight counties of Wales stayed dry. The Sunday-opening map of Wales coincided almost exactly with the 1951 census map of Welsh-speaking —the dry areas being the main strongholds of the Welsh language, the wet areas the most anglicized.

It would have been extremely interesting, recalling the internal diversity of Swansea by this factor of Welsh-speaking, to examine the results of this poll for each of the fifteen electoral wards within the Borough. Not surprisingly, since this subject aroused much local emotion, these results by ward were never recorded and it is thus impossible to map the Sunday-opening vote by ward within Swansea. The total result for the Borough is, however, a good indication both of its degree of cultural anglicization and of the declining influence of the chapels in an era of rapid social change. The chapels fought hard and eloquently (as they did ten years earlier over the Sunday opening of cinemas) for the preservation of the traditional Welsh Sunday, but the voice of the pulpit lacked the power it once had. The decline of Welsh-speaking in Swansea and of the force of proud cultural traditions have gone hand in hand with the declining membership of the chapels. Swansea is no longer the cultural capital of the Welsh; it is now on the wrong side of the cultural curtain separating the characteristic Welsh way of life from the English (or Anglo-American).

A VERY RELIGIOUS PEOPLE?

We cannot undertake in this study a detailed examination of the sociology of religion in contemporary Swansea: we did, however, amass a great deal of information on this fascinating subject, and propose to discuss it at length in a later publication. But as Table 3.6 above shows, religious differences form a vital and basic element in the cultural distinction between the Welsh and the non-Welsh in Swansea today, and some brief comments are necessary if we are to present a clear picture of the social environment in which our examination of family behaviour took place.

Most people seem to think of Wales from the point of view of religion, as a stronghold of Nonconformism, with a multitude of chapels swept by periodic waves of religious revivals, with fervent eloquent preachers thundering with *hwyl* from innumerable pulpits at the ranks of deacons and elders and members in the packed pews below, with splendid chapel choirs leading the full-throated and rapturous hymn-singing and providing eternal renderings of the

'Messiah' for the familiar enjoyment of the faithful: a land of anthems, and of a profound religiosity generated by the sense of solidarity in the small and exclusive and tightly-knit fellowship of the particular chapel. An old-time religion, with a strong Old Testament flavour pervading its evangelical fervour. However true this picture may be of other parts of Wales, and it seems everywhere more true of the past than the present, it is not an accurate picture of Swansea as a whole. Significantly, and perhaps surprisingly for many who live in Swansea, the numerically-dominant denomination in the Borough is the Anglican—that is, The Church in Wales, its title since Disestablishment in 1920, but still more commonly known locally as The Church of England.

When asked what religious denomination they belonged to, 97 per cent of our sample gave one or other of the various Christian persuasions, 1 per cent said that they belonged to non-Christian religions (mainly Jews, but including also some Moslems and Buddhists), and under 2 per cent, that is thirty persons, said that they were atheists or agnostics. This latter figure is much lower than that reported in other surveys in Britain: Michael Argyle, for example, gives 9·5 per cent, the average of three surveys, as the proportion in Britain generally not claiming some religious affiliation.[27] The replies by denomination of our informants are given for the County Borough as a whole in the final column of Table 3.6. As can be seen there, the Anglicans formed about half the total population (51 per cent), Nonconformists well over a third (39 per cent) with Roman Catholics and 'Others' making up the remaining fifth.

When, however, we compare the religious denominations of the Welsh with those of the non-Welsh a striking difference emerges. Well over half the Welsh (56 per cent) are Nonconformists, belonging either to Welsh or English Chapels. The non-Welsh on the other hand are predominantly Anglican, with the Nonconformists reduced to a quarter of the total. We are of course dealing here only with statements of religious affiliation, and not with religious activity, and must accept that a considerable number of these informants are little more than nominal Christians, with the Anglican denomination particularly forming a sort of residual category for those who never go to a place of worship (except for weddings or funerals) and who yet feel, in the prevailing atmosphere, that they ought to say something in reply to this question. But even so, this difference between these two cultural groups in Swansea is indicative of substantial differences in general cultural attitudes and outlook.

It is an extremely difficult matter to assess accurately the degree of

[27] Michael Argyle, *Religious Behaviour*, 1958, p. 37.

religious activity in a given community. There is no doubt that people tend readily to exaggerate the frequency with which they attend a place of worship either to impress the interviewer or out of a sense of loyalty to their particular denomination—perhaps even out of a sense of guilt. We asked our informants both how often they went and when they last went, and decided eventually to consider only the latter set of replies as being the more reliable. Even allowing for this exaggeration, the general level of religious activity in Swansea is astonishingly high compared with that reported elsewhere in Britain (the replies in these other studies being equally liable to this exaggeration). Michael Argyle gives the weekly church attendance in Britain about 1950 as being 14.6 per cent of the population (this being the average of three surveys conducted between 1947 and 1957).[28] The comparable figure for Swansea—of those who had attended a place of worship within the past week is 23 per cent. That is, by this estimate, just under a quarter of the population of Swansea as a whole go to church or chapel on a Sunday. This percentage varies by denomination, we will be explaining presently, and also significantly by this twofold cultural division of the population into Welsh and non-Welsh. Table 3.6 gives the comparable percentages, showing that the proportion of the Welsh who had attended a place of worship within the past week is almost double that of the non-Welsh (31 per cent as compared with 17 per cent) and certainly more than double the proportion quoted earlier for Britain in general. Relatively speaking, then, the figures confirm the greater religiosity of the Welsh within Swansea, and of the Welsh and non-Welsh together in Swansea compared with the general level of religious activity in Britain in the period since the War.

If we take a somewhat broader definition of religious 'actives'—namely, those who have attended a place of worship within the past month—and consider Protestants only, who formed 90 per cent of our survey sample,[29] we can note the variations in religious activity by denomination, and by neighbourhood with Swansea. By this measure of active religious performance, the Welsh Nonconformist Chapels headed the list with 55 per cent of their membership active, followed by the English Nonconformists with 41 per cent, and finally the Anglicans with 25 per cent of the denomination total who had

[28] Argyle, op. cit., p. 6.

[29] That is, omitting Roman Catholics and 'others'. Roman Catholics are a special case because of their unique insistence on their adherents hearing Mass every Sunday as a rule of the Church. Of the 139 Catholics in our sample, 45 per cent had attended Mass within the previous week, and (including these) 56 per cent within the past month.

attended church within the past month. Taking Protestants in the Borough as a whole, just under a third of the population, as represented by our sample, said they had been to church or chapel in the last month—the component percentages (of the total population) being 8 per cent active Welsh Nonconformists, 10 per cent active English Nonconformists, and 13 per cent active Anglicans. These figures indicate by this test of religious activity the relative strengths of the three main Protestant denominations within the Borough. They refer of course, as do all the figures derived from our survey, only to the proportion of the total population aged 21 or more.

As we found with most of the facts of social and cultural behaviour within Swansea, there were striking variations from neighbourhood to neighbourhood in the percentages that active religious worshippers formed of the total Protestant population of the neighbourhood concerned. Morriston well out-stripped most of the other neighbourhoods in this respect, with 59 per cent of our sample saying that they had attended a place of worship in the past month. This is a remarkably high figure, almost twice the Borough average, and in extreme contrast to St Thomas, for example, an old anglicized neighbourhood around the docks, which had a comparable percentage of 19 per cent (or Townhill and Mayhill, a second-generation housing estate, with the same percentage of religious actives). The distribution of religious activity in the Borough was in fact closely correlated with the distribution of Welsh-speaking: the higher the percentage of the population speaking Welsh fluently or partly, the higher the proportion of active church and chapel members. Morriston headed the list in both respects, followed by Waunarlwydd, Llansamlet, Birchgrove, Brynhyfryd and Manselton, and the older middle-class areas of Sketty and Uplands and Killay, and the more Welsh of the post-war estates (Clase and Gendros and Penlan). The least Welsh-speaking and the least religious—by this test of religious activity—were the neighbourhoods of the Town Centre area (St Thomas, Hafod, Sandfields), the pre-war estate of Townhill and Mayhill (occupied originally and mainly by families who had moved out of these congested neighbourhoods of the central area) and the neighbourhoods of the extreme west (Mumbles, Langland, Newton, and West Cross).

The industrial changes that have occurred in the Tawe Valley and the substantial westward drift of the population in Swansea, which we discussed in our previous chapter, have had profound effects both on Welsh-speaking and on religious adherence and performance in this former stronghold of Welsh culture in Swansea. As we saw through the eyes of Mr Hughes in Chapter I, the old industrial communities in the Valley displayed and preserved a social and cultural homogeneity in which Welsh-speaking, chapel worship (with Welsh as a sort of liturgical language, the Latin of the Welsh Nonconformists), and stability of residence over the successive generations were essential elements. Brinley Thomas has recently brilliantly argued the vital correlation between the industrial growth of late Victorian Wales, especially in the South Wales coalfield, and the preservation of the Welsh language:

> Industrial development was on such a scale that Wales was able to retain a large proportion of the indigenous stock which was displaced from the countryside. The young men and women who left the farms and flocked into the mining townships carried the Welsh way of life with them and brought up their children to speak the mother tongue. Indeed, many of these closely packed and isolated communities acted as melting-pots; they were so intensely Welsh that a number of English immigrants—not to mention Italian shopkeepers—were quickly assimilated and picked up the language . . . The unrighteous Mammon in opening up the coalfields at such a pace unwittingly gave the Welsh language a new lease of life and Welsh Nonconformity a glorious noon.[30]

This is what happened in the Tawe Valley. It is now well past noon, however, and the writing is on the wall both for the language and for Welsh Nonconformity in Swansea. There are many and varied reasons for the decline of Welsh—despite the desperate efforts, in which the Welsh chapel ministers have played a prominent part, to prevent it. The two most important reasons, about which we will have to say a great deal in this book, are the decline in family size and the recent physical dispersion of Welsh-speakers. Unlike the Roman Catholics, another minority group, the Welsh, both as Welsh-speakers and as Nonconformists, simply do not produce enough to replenish the previous generation (apart altogether from the questions of the cultural transmission of either the language or the faith to this next generation). The figures on the decline in family size generally, and specifically by denomination, are most interesting; we will be discussing them in our next chapter and will therefore leave this subject, not previously examined in relation to the decline either of the Welsh language or of Welsh Nonconformity, for the present.

The predominant characteristic of local Nonconformity, particularly of Welsh Independents or Congregationalists, is that the members belong essentially to a particular chapel (to Tabernacle, or Hermon, or Libanus, or Soar, or whatever) and this 'particularist' element tends to be strongly stressed in the psychological response to

[30] Brinley Thomas, 'Wales and the Atlantic Economy', in *The Welsh Economy*, edited by Brinley Thomas, 1962, pp. 27–29.

membership. Although Anglicans and Roman Catholics have strong ties with particular places of worship, the organizational structure of these denominations, which stresses that each church is part of the whole rather than the whole a federation of the parts, means that they are, in contrast to most Nonconformist faiths, 'filling station religions', in Fogarty's phrase, in that their members can call in easily at any church of the denomination on a Sunday and transfer their attendance easily from one parish to another with physical moves, the chapel member is much more tied by sentiment as well as by the fact of membership to a particular building. This is of course closely related to the strong sense of cohesion and exclusiveness, in practice if not in principle, which chapels exhibit. Strongly embedded in their locality, with a severely localized membership, such chapels tend to flourish in situations of strong residential stability, and to decline directly with the incidence of physical mobility. The older the chapel, the stronger the sense of family continuity over the generations, the greater the feeling of cohesion, the more difficult it is for the stranger to become part of the fellowship. Apart altogether from external migrations, the large-scale movements of people that have occurred within the Borough in the last forty years or so, but particularly since the war with the rapid expansion of the Corporation housing estates, have detached from their particular chapels large numbers who would otherwise have become members, or continued their existing memberships. There are 142 chapels within Swansea, and almost any annual chapel report shows the effects on its membership of this physical dispersion. Not only are there annual losses by removals, but the lists of addresses of members show that considerable numbers now live in distant parts of the Borough, keeping their names on the chapel roll and continuing to pay their subscriptions, perhaps through a continuation of the sentiments of membership (the nostalgic *hiraeth* characteristic of the Welsh) but no longer active members and, with the next generation, lost for ever to the chapel fellowship. We encountered many cases of individuals, particularly older people, making lengthy journeys to attend chapel services in their former home areas on a Sunday, but these were clearly exceptions, and we must add that the chapels in the Town Centre, both Welsh and English, appeared to suffer least from this physical dispersion of members because of their ease of accessibility by bus and car. It is the chapels in the Valley which have suffered most in this respect: of the 142 chapels in the Borough, 84 are located in the old industrial communities on the east, 33 are in the central area, 20 are in the north-west, the area mainly of the great new estates, and only 15 in the residential districts of the west. We have

131

mentioned the instances of elderly people trying to maintain their connections with their chapels after moving away from their former homes, but mainly of course it is the younger generation, with educational advancement leading to jobs elsewhere and with the new opportunities of homes on Corporation estates or on private estates in the west, who have moved away from the old Valley communities. It is this generation which is thinly represented in the chapel congregations which tend to have membership with an age structure distorted, from that normal in the population as a whole, in favour of the old. We discuss later in this study the importance of religion, and of church and chapel membership, in the lives of the elderly; our survey results shows a much greater incidence of active religious performance among the older age groups as compared with the younger, and this itself shows something of the decline in church- and chapel-going which has occurred over the past two generations or so, though it must be added that religious activity usually increases with age, particularly for women.[31]

The physical mobility which we examined in our last chapter has equally had far-reaching effects on the incidence of Welsh-speaking and on the future of the Welsh language within the Borough. Welsh-as any language, is primarily a means of communication; its survival as a living language, whatever artificial steps are taken to ensure its cultural transmission to the next generation (by compulsory teaching in schools, for example), depends essentially on its usefulness as a form of communication between human beings in their daily lives, and on the existence of social situations in which it can be normally and naturally used. If all, or at least a large proportion, of the population of a given community (or neighbourhood or street) speak the language and use it in their daily intercourse with one another—in short, if it is the language of the streets and playgrounds and shops and pubs, as well as of the chapels and schools, the children will acquire it as part of their natural experience of growing up. This is very largely what happened, and to a lesser extent still happens, in places like Morriston—and certainly north of Morriston in the industrial villages of the Swansea Valley stretching away northwards beyond the Borough and hemmed in by the retaining walls of the mountains on either side. But when a Welsh-speaking family packs its bags and

---

[31] Twenty-three per cent of our total sample said that they had attended a place of worship within the past week. Of the persons over pensionable age in the sample (that is, over 60 for women and over 65 for men) 30 per cent had been to church or chapel in the past week. There was, however, a very clear difference by sex: 37 per cent of elderly women had been within the past week, but only 16 per cent of elderly men.

moves away out of this dominant Welsh atmosphere to a house on a Corporation estate, it may well become the only Welsh-speaking family in the street, surrounded by English monoglots with, for the children as much as for the adults, English replacing Welsh as the normal language of social intercourse.

The Corporation in the allocation of its 14,000 Corporation houses took no account of Welsh-speaking in its selection of tenants, nor presumably in a situation of great housing need could it be expected to do so. It was a case of first come, first served—in order of precedence by application date on the housing list. The net result from the point of view of the Welsh-speakers was a sort of random scattering over the fifteen estates, with the inevitable consequences of this dispersion from the point of view of the language. Had, say, one of the fifteen estates been designated primarily for Welsh-speaking tenants a social concentration could have been produced sufficient to ensure the preservation of the language as the natural and dominant means of communication, and sufficient to support Welsh institutional facilities—say Welsh-speaking chapels, a Welsh school, a Welsh-speaking community centre and so forth. The cultural consequences of such a step, however difficult to effect in practice, might well have been profound in relation to the preservation of Welsh culture within Swansea. The fact is of course that the Corporation did not do this—and for all we know may well not have even considered the possibility. But, whatever it may have achieved in the improvement of housing standards within the Borough, there can be little doubt that the Corporation has unwittingly been one of the major agencies in promoting, through this physical dispersion, the decline of Welsh.

Without this recognition that a living language must have the social contexts in which it can be the natural form of social communication, the evident obsession with Welsh in the educational system in the minds of those most actively and emotionally concerned with the preservation of Welsh seems a curious irrelevance. No matter how much Welsh is taught to schoolchildren, there can be little hope of the language surviving as a living tongue if the opportunities, and indeed the necessity, of speaking it in the daily lives of adults are constantly disappearing. 'What use is Welsh?' is a common question in Swansea, and one that needs a convincing and realistic answer, free from sentimentality, if the language is to survive in the open air rather than moving as Latin has done from the church to the classroom, to be equally dead. The sociologist would be more hopeful about the future of the language if there were even faint signs that its pundits and protagonists were turning from their preoccupation with

education to the encouragement of the use of Welsh among adults—
as for example in encouraging shops and offices to display signs that
'Welsh is spoken here': it is not difficult to think of many other
measures that would be quite simple to put into practice, and which
would have a very considerable effect on the general morale of the
Welsh element of the population. For all the highbrow whistling in
the dark, with the Annual Eisteddfod and Telewele and the Cymm-
rodorion and Welsh dining-clubs and isolated Welsh schools, the
present situation, as the census figures and ordinary common sense
show, is deteriorating steadily so far as the language is concerned.[32]
It is clearly going to take an immense and imaginative, and essentially
practical, effort by the Welsh Establishment (a most exclusive cultural
élite) directed at increasing the opportunities for communication in
Welsh among adults in their normal daily lives, to halt and perhaps
even reverse the trend of decline. This will not be achieved without the
support and goodwill of the non-Welsh speaking majority. In this
respect alone, it may well be too late.

It is tempting to continue this digression on the decline of Welsh
with a thoroughgoing sociological analysis of the factors involved
and a more systematic prognostication of likely developments over
the next generation or so, but this must be deferred to another
occasion. (This could well form a useful contribution to the contemporary sociology of Wales by the newly established School of Social
Studies in the University College of Swansea.) Clearly there are a
whole complex array of factors besides the two, the decline
in family size and the social dilution of Welsh-speakers through
physical dispersion, which we have mentioned here. With the
tremendous social changes of the last half-century or so—notably
the developments in transport, in the cinema, in popular newspapers,
in radio and television—the social and cultural horizons of the old
industrial communities have expanded enormously. The walls of the
traditional cohesive society, with its characteristic peasant culture
(with Welsh and Nonconformity as the cement binding the whole
together), have been breached in a hundred places. The traditional
Welsh picture of close family relationships, of family worship, of
strict control, of tightly-knit kinship networks peopled with a
plethora of aunts and cousins living round the corner, with the
father leading the family to chapel and to Sunday school—this picture

---

[32] The 'slowing down' of the rate of decline in Welsh-speaking revealed by
the 1961 census figures was regarded in some quarters as evidence that these
policies were becoming effective. In fact the slower rate of decline of Welsh-
speaking in the past ten years is partly due to the increasing proportion which
the elderly form of the total population.

has faded like an old print, with the passing of the Victorian era (which ended a good deal later in the Tawe Valley than elsewhere in Swansea) with its 'Old Testament' culture and Sabbatarian observances. The old remember it well, but the younger generation have grown up in a very different social world and cultural environment.

The Welsh Chapels have suffered most of all from the effects of this social and cultural change. Since Welsh-speaking is a requirement of admission to membership, they have continually lost potential members with the continual cultural erosion of the Welsh language. The first Welsh Chapel, Nazareth, which had at the end only ten members, closed in Morriston in 1962. Morriston still has twenty chapels and churches (a higher proportion per population size than any other community within Swansea) and exactly half of these, including one Anglican Church, have their services in Welsh. But all of these have shown sharp declines in membership over the last fifty years, the Welsh Chapels most of all. And the ministers of these Welsh Chapels are finding it increasingly difficult to preserve the exclusively Welsh character of their chapels in the face of a declining incidence of Welsh-speaking in the younger generations and in the social environment generally. Most of them are faced with the dilemma of 'The Compromise', as it is known locally, of facing contemporary reality and admitting some English into the life of the chapel—in the Sunday school for the children perhaps, or in one service each Sunday (or perhaps once a month). Some have accepted this compromise reluctantly, as a contemporary necessity; others have dug their toes in and battled on in Welsh exclusively, for the time being at least. More and more of the Welsh Chapels all over the Borough are having to admit defeat and admit English, or to change over to English altogether. We sent out a postal questionnaire to the ministers or secretaries (of the chapels without ministers) of the 142 chapels in the Borough; 72 replied giving various information about their chapel organizations and statistics. Of those that replied, 28 per cent were wholly Welsh Chapels, 58 per cent were wholly English, and 14 per cent described themselves as 'mixed English and Welsh'. But of the 28 per cent who described themselves as wholly Welsh, many included brief qualifying remarks such as '90 per cent Welsh' or 'mainly Welsh', or 'English service once a month' or 'Welsh except for the children's Sunday school'. At the other extreme, a few of the wholly English Chapels mentioned that they held a service in Welsh once a month, or for their Old Age Pensioners' Club occasionally.

As we conducted our research in Swansea, we were constantly on the look out for signs of diversification within families—in income, or occupation, in residence, in various cultural behaviour and attitudes—comparing the parental generations with those of their children and grandchildren. The case of the Hughes Family Morriston which we examined at length in our opening chapter is a good example of the nature of this internal diversification along many social and cultural dimensions and of its effects on family cohesion. The field of religious behaviour which we are now discussing is an important source of differences between the generations. We asked our subjects whether their own religious denomination was the same as that of their parents. Only two-thirds of our total sample belonged to the same denomination as both their parents (almost a quarter differed from both parents). We also asked those who were married and who had children whether the children's denominations were the same as theirs. In a quarter of our cases, they were not—the Borough average of subjects and children belonging to the same denomination was 75 per cent. But the differences by denomination were very considerable; for the active Anglicans this figure was 88 per cent (13 per cent above the Borough average); for the active English Nonconformists it was 73 per cent (or 2 per cent below the average) and for the active Welsh Nonconformists it was only 55 per cent (or 20 per cent below the average for the sample as a whole). For the non-active Welsh Nonconformists, those who had not attended chapel within the past month, this figure of subjects and children belonging to the same denomination was as low as 38 per cent. In the great majority of cases, the children of these non-active Welsh Nonconformists (as well as in almost half of the cases of actives) had ceased to follow the religion of their parents—and this is clearly bound up with the decline of Welsh-speaking and with the physical dispersion to which we have continually referred. If they have remained 'Chapel' many of these children will have changed over to one of the denominations within the group which we have called 'English Nonconformists', and many will have ceased to be Nonconformists altogether and have drifted into the numerically-dominant Anglican fold. There is little doubt that this is the familiar progression—with the Welsh group of denominations very much at the losing end of one extreme and the Anglicans gaining considerably (with the cultural dominance of English) at the other.

We will return briefly to this subject in our next chapter when we consider the effects on religious denominations and on Welsh-speaking of the dramatic decline in family size which has occurred over the last three generations or so. The points we have wished to emphasize here are the high level of religious practice in Swansea generally on the one hand, and the gradual decline of Welsh Nonconformity on the other in a situation of rapid social change.

Class and the Welsh

The Welsh Nonconformists, and fluent Welsh-speakers generally, form the vital core of the Welsh cultural category, as here defined, within the population of modern Swansea. By our method of classification, the Welsh now form 46 per cent of the general population. Since the classification is based on Welsh-speaking (though it does take a two-generation view), it is clear that with each successive generation the Welsh category is likely to become smaller in size as more and more people become 'twice removed' from their Welsh cultural origins and traditions. The cultural trends, clearly visible in the contemporary social scene, point heavily in this direction.

CLASS AND THE WELSH

In this chapter, we have explained the two basic classification schemes, by social class and by the Welsh/non-Welsh cultural division, that we have used in this study. We can now put them together to show the proportion the Welsh and the non-Welsh form of each of the four social classes which we have determined. The diagram below indicates the contemporary class and cultural structure of Swansea, by our methods of classification, with arrows superimposed to indicate the dominant directions of the social and cultural mobility that we have been discussing in this chapter. As can be seen from the diagram, the Welsh as a cultural grouping are distributed evenly over the four social classes, without significant differences from the percentage they form (46 per cent) of the Borough as a whole:

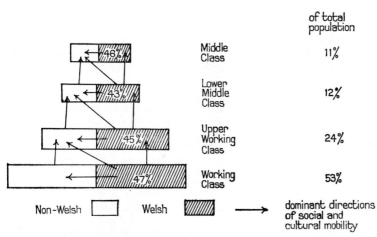

WELSH AND SOCIAL CLASS IN SWANSEA, 1960

The arrows show that cultural mobility (in terms of the Welsh and non-Welsh cultural division) is essentially a one-way process, from Welsh to non-Welsh over the successive generations.[33] This cultural movement, bound up with class mobility, is greater in the working classes than it is in the middle classes who tend both to be more intellectually concerned about cultural roots, and also to benefit more, by admission to the Welsh Cultural 'Establishment', from the emphatic preservation of their cultural traditions, particularly as regards speaking the language (which opens many doors marked 'Private' in Wales, notably in the teaching profession, in the B.B.C. in Wales, and in much of public life generally).

NEIGHBOURHOOD DIFFERENCES

We have continually referred to the striking social and cultural contrasts within Swansea comparing one locality or neighbourhood with another within this extensive County Borough. Our final task in this chapter is to demonstrate these differences by using our two classifications, by class and culture, to show the variations that exist in the social compositions of these component communities.

Tables 3.7 and 3.8 show the distribution by certain selected neighbourhoods, and then by the four major geographical districts, of the four social classes.

West Swansea—the geographical area which is composed of the seven localities of Mumbles, West Cross, Killay, Sketty, Uplands, Brynmill and Mount Pleasant—stands out quite clearly from the other three districts of the Borough in that the traditional and stable working class forms only just over a quarter of the total population (elsewhere this is the dominant social class). The two middle classes form almost half the population of West Swansea; in the other three districts they form well under a fifth of the class structure.

[33] This is a similar conclusion to that reached by Brennan, Cooney, and Pollins who used the simple manual/non-manual occupational dichotomy as an index of social class in South-west Wales (including Swansea County Borough). They discern four social classes without indicating the relative sizes of these classes in the total population. They indicate the relationship between these 'four classes' in the following diagram (of which ours is an elaboration).

Unoriented working class	1		2	Characteristically—Welsh working class
Anglicized middle class	4	←	3	Characteristically—Welsh middle class

T. Brennan, E. W. Cooney, and H. Pollins, *Social Change in South-west Wales*, 1954, p. 183.

Table 3.7: Composition by Social Class—Selected Localities

Social Class	Locality					County Boro' Total
	Sketty Uplands	Brynmill Mt Pleasant	Morriston Ynystawe Glais	St Thomas	Townhill	
Middle Class	34%	21%	6%	1%	4%	11%
Lower Middle Class	24%	21%	10%	5%	6%	12%
Upper Working Class	25%	30%	23%	26%	23%	24%
Working Class	17%	28%	61%	68%	67%	53%
Total %	100%	100%	100%	100%	100%	100%
Total Numbers	180	183	176	143	187	1,958

Table 3.8: Composition by Social Class—Swansea's Districts

Social Class	District				County Borough Total
	West Swansea	Town Centre	Tawe Valley	North-west Swansea	
Middle Class	28%	5%	7%	4%	11%
Lower Middle Class	21%	7%	10%	10%	12%
Upper Working Class	25%	24%	23%	25%	24%
Working Class	26%	64%	60%	61%	53%
Total %	100%	100%	100%	100%	100%
Total Numbers	537	346	553	522	1,958

In Table 3.7 we give the class structure of eight of the total of 23 localities (grouping Sketty with Uplands, Brynmill with Mount Pleasant, and Morriston with Glais) as examples of the variations that exist in the social composition by class of the 'Urban Villages' within Swansea. The middle classes form 58 per cent of Sketty and Uplands, but only 6 per cent of St Thomas at the other extreme. The most working-class area of Swansea is the area immediately surrounding the Town Centre and the docks—the neighbourhoods of Sandfields, Castle, Hafod and St Thomas—an area of rows and rows of small terrace houses and of the highest population densities in the Borough, now being extensively affected by slum-clearance schemes and by spectacular road improvements. This old working-class area is bordered on its western and northern edges (below the Townhill escarpment) by a kind of transitional zone of large, bay-windowed, terrace houses forming the two localities of Brynmill and Mount Pleasant—the class structure of which, given in Table 3.7, reflects this transitional character, with the traditional working class forming only just over a quarter of the population, the traditional middle class about a fifth, and the two mobile classes 'in between' over a half of the total. Apart from West Swansea in general, the dominant social class in the population of Swansea is the traditional working class.

The figures on class structure confirm the popular image of the Borough as being divided basically into two areas—the old, industrial working-class east on the one hand, and the more open and spacious 'residential' and middle-class west on the other—the two areas linked by a common Town Centre, surrounded by old and chiefly working-class neighbourhoods. This dichotomy can be illustrated in many contexts, notably in parliamentary representation and support of the Labour or Conservative Parties. Of the fifteen electoral wards in the Borough, eight are in the Swansea West Constituency and seven are in Swansea East. The Labour Party in Swansea dominates the Borough Council with an overwhelming majority produced from its complete control of ten of the fifteen wards. The ten 'Labour wards' include the whole of the seven Swansea East Constituency, and three of the eight in Swansea West. Significantly in view of what we have been saying about social class, the only wards which Labour does not control are the following: Ffynone Ward (which includes part of Sketty, Uplands and Mount Pleasant), St Helen's Ward (which is almost identical with our Brynmill neighbourhood), Victoria Ward (which includes part of Sandfields, but also substantial parts of Uplands and Mount Pleasant) and Sketty Ward and Mumbles Ward. Politics in Swansea coincides closely with the class structure of the different localities.

At the General Election in 1959, Swansea East continued its tradition, since 1923, of being a safe Labour seat with a vast majority. Swansea West on the other hand, having just been held by Labour at the three previous elections, produced by a small majority a Conservative victory for the first time ever in Swansea (a Liberal stronghold before the rise of the Labour party in Swansea in the twenties). Appropriately enough, in view of the basic dichotomy in the social and cultural composition of the Borough, Swansea sent to Parliament one Labour M.P. from the constituency on the east, and one Conservative M.P. from the constituency on the west. This is the reflection in politics of the substantial contrasts in the class structure and general social attitudes between the east and west within Swansea.[34]

Not only is the central area the most working-class of the four

[34] Swansea West is now (1964) again represented by a Labour M.P., but with a very small majority achieved in a three-cornered fight.

districts of the Borough, it is also the least Welsh,[35] taking the districts in general, as the following table shows:

Table 3.9: *Composition by Welsh and non-Welsh—Swansea Districts*

| Cultural Category | Districts | | | | County Borough Total |
	West Swansea	Town Centre	Tawe Valley	North-west Swansea	
Welsh	36%	31%	69%	41%	46%
Non-Welsh	64%	69%	31%	59%	54%
Total % *Total Numbers*	100% 537	100% 346	100% 553	100% 522	100% 1,958

The only area of the Borough in which the Welsh form the majority of the population is the Tawe Valley, essentially and historically a continuation south into the Borough of the Swansea Valley with its characteristic industrial—Welsh 'valley culture'. Here in the Tawe Valley, and by our method of classification, well over two-thirds of the total population are culturally Welsh—the exact opposite of the 'anglicized' Town Centre.

This is the broad picture of the physical distribution of Swansea's 'two cultures'. The detailed variations by neighbourhood are indicated in the map on pp. 70–1 and by the following table which shows, for selected neighbourhoods, the range of variations by this factor of cultural composition.

Table 3.10: *Cultural Composition of Selected Localities*

| Cultural Category | Locality | | | | | County Borough Total |
	Morriston Glais	Landore Manselton	Sketty Uplands	St Thomas	Mumbles Langland Killay West Cross	
Welsh	84%	67%	41%	30%	25%	46%
Non-Welsh	16%	33%	59%	70%	75%	54%
Total % *Total Number*	100% 176	100% 237	100% 180	100% 143	100% 174	100% 1,958

[35] The difference between the Town Centre and West Swansea is not significant and that between the West and North-west only at the 5 per cent level.

There, in the figures, is the extreme cultural contrast between Morriston at the top of the Tawe Valley (and at the entrance to the Welsh Swansea Valley extending away to the north) and Mumbles, about ten miles away, at the western extreme of Swansea Bay. They are two very different social and cultural worlds.

The evidence on the distribution of Welsh within the Borough shows both the present cultural composition of Swansea's communities and also something of the physical dispersion of the Welsh, as a result of recent population movements to which we have earlier referred. The cultural centre of the Welsh in Swansea is Morriston, followed by old industrial area of Landore and Brynhyfryd immediately to the south of the western flank of the Valley (and including the pre-First World War private estate of Manselton to which many of the skilled workers of the older communities moved to homes of their own). On the opposite side of the Valley, and on the north-western perimeter of the Borough, are the older Welsh villages of Bonymaen and Llansamlet and Fforestfach and Waunarlwydd which have been substantially 'diluted' by the influx of considerable numbers of non-Welsh with the post-war development of housing estates in their immediate vicinities. They still show a majority of Welsh, but the percentage is a good deal lower than that of the Morriston or Landore areas.

Next in degree of Welshness come two very different areas—the one the comparatively long-established middle-class belt of Sketty, Uplands, Brynmill and Mount Pleasant, the other the new post-war housing estates of Clase, Gendros, and Penlan. Both are reception areas for 'displaced persons' from the Tawe Valley. The middle-class movement occurred first in the twenties and thirties when the town was expanding rapidly in the Sketty and Uplands and neighbouring areas, followed by a second wave of removals to the new housing estates in the post-war years. The present incidence of Welshness in these two areas is largely the product of these two waves of movement west out of the Valley.

The historical cosmopolitan character of 'Old Swansea' round the Castle and the docks, indeed its traditional Englishness, is reflected in the fact that under a third of its present population can be classed as Welsh. And this is equally true of the vast Townhill and Mayhill Estate, established on the hills overlooking the Town Centre by the Corporation in the decade before the war and populated mainly by families rehoused from the central area of the town.

The localities which are least Welsh[36] of all are those in the extreme

[36] The difference between Mumbles and St Thomas is not significant.

west, the former fishing village of Mumbles now a jumble of yacht clubs and seaside boarding houses, the select residential districts of Caswell and Langland, and the rapidly growing areas of Killay and West Cross and the Mayals packed with private housing estates. This is the general area of Swansea which has received the main influx of English immigrants, particularly of the managerial class of executives and managers and agents both of the commercial developments in the Town Centre and of the new industries in the West Wales region in general. In this area the Welsh form just a quarter of the total population, and are clearly declining rapidly.

It must be added, to complete this brief sketch of the cultural composition of the Borough, that the dominant patterns of physical movement tend to be away from the Tawe Valley and the east side generally in the direction of the west. And by this we are not just referring to removals. People living on the east and in the Valley travel out to the Town Centre for shopping and entertainments, and to the west side of Swansea to the parks for picnics or to the bays of Gower or to the seaside at Mumbles. Few of those living on the west have any occasion to visit the east (except to visit relatives) and we were constantly struck by the fact that very many of those living in Uplands or Sketty or West Cross or Mumbles appeared to have lived for years in Swansea, perhaps all their lives, without ever having been to Morriston or Bonymaen or whatever, and without knowing anything very much about how the other half of Swansea lives. On the other hand, West Swansea is very familiar to most of those who live on the east. Sketty (to take one example) quite surprisingly has the main bingo hall in Swansea: the Odeon Cinema near Sketty Cross was converted to bingo in February 1962. This bingo club now has over 18,000 members drawn from all over the Borough (and from outside) but mainly from the housing estates and from the old communities of the industrial east. Between 1,500 and 2,000 people arrive every night in Sketty (including Sunday) on crowded buses or by car and motor-bike to attend the bingo sessions. There are five bingo 'palaces' (or whatever the correct noun is) in Swansea—three in the Town Centre, all former cinemas, one on the Townhill Estate, a ballroom used part-time for bingo, and this one in Sketty. It is said that the Sketty bingo club has become the most popular because it is part of a national chain of bingo clubs, and is thus efficiently and professionally stage-managed, with spectacular prizes. The fact remains that few of the middle-class residents of Sketty appear to belong, and that its vast and astonishing membership is drawn mainly from points east. This movement west for entertainment, of which this Sketty bingo is just one example, tends to exaggerate the declining cultural vitality of the communities on the east side of Swansea.

To find Welsh culture in Swansea vigorous and flourishing you have to travel up the Swansea Valley to Morriston. Even here its high noon, as Brinley Thomas puts it, has passed as the rising tide of anglicization washes up the Valley, submerging community after community. But Morriston still has its preponderance of Welsh-speakers, its concentration of Welsh Chapels clustered like an encircled wagon train, and its Orpheus Choir known all over Wales and far beyond the borders of the Principality. This splendid male-voice choir, seven times winner of the National Eisteddfod, has brought fame to Morriston and to Swansea. It is undoubtedly the foremost male-voice choir in Wales. It was formed twenty-six years ago by a local schoolteacher, Ivor Sims, a Morristonian *par excellence*. When he died in April 1961 there was an outburst of community emotion which was both a tribute to this great conductor and a moving example of Morriston's cultural vitality and cohesion. 'Outside the church,' the *South Wales Evening Post* reported,

> 500 people, Morristonians who knew and loved Mr Sims, lined the pavement and the Churchyard railings. Some women were weeping. As the cortège moved slowly down Woodfield Street towards the church gates, it was headed by 100 members of the Morriston Orpheus Choir, hatless and with heads bowed. With them were the members of three other choirs—Treorchy, Manselton, and Pendyrus [the most famous choirs in Wales] . . . Extra police were on duty in Woodfield Street to control the traffic and crowds in one of the biggest demonstrations of affection Morriston has ever seen.

The report of the funeral, with pictures of the choir singing over the grave at the packed Morriston Cemetery, took almost a full page in the local newspaper. The Editor himself, Froom Tyler, described with moving eloquence 'the moment of farewell':

> Our leave taking of Mr Sims in the Parish Church of the place he had made famous through his choir was as he would have liked it to be. It was like the character of the man, and his manner, and his way of conducting—simple, sincere, eloquent more in feeling than in word.
>
> There were two hymns . . . a psalm . . . the prayers, and the death-defiant passage in the First Epistle to the Corinthians—read with resonant assurance.
>
> Then, a little silence, and through the thronged Church, the hushed harmonies of the Morriston Orpheus Choir, Ivor Sims's Choir, singing the spiritual:

Class and the Welsh

Steal away to Jesus . . .
Steal away home

We had heard them sing it so many times before, and it was the familiar unique Orpheus tone, beautifully blended and controlled. It brought memories of innumerable Orpheus nights, of crowded eisteddfodau, of the vast range of their repertoire from their hushed 'God Save the Queen' (they are the only choir to have sung the anthem like a prayer, which it is) to their last triumphant test-piece under Ivor, 'Song of the Spirits Over the Waters'.

'Steal away . . .' There was not a man among them who was not deeply moved, yet they sang it with the old discipline and, in the one *fortissimo* passage, the old dynamic, of which Ivor had told them the secret. They stood at the west end of the church so to most of us they were unseen. It was as though Ivor Sims was conducting in his quiet coaxing way. But he was not. For he had joined the Choir Invisible.[37]

Ivor Sims was buried like the culture hero he was, and all Morriston mourned his passing. In no other community in Swansea would the death of the conductor of a male-voice choir have mattered so much.

In these last two chapters we have briefly surveyed the contemporary scene in Swansea, with a glance at its recent historical foundations, in an effort to bring this modern community to life in the pages of this book. We have concentrated on precise statistical description where possible, rather than on a more general and possibly more entertaining account of the passing scene, because, apart from being more concise than would otherwise be possible, such a descriptive precision is essential to the kind of understanding that we seek in this sociological analysis. In this particular chapter we have sought indirectly to convey as rounded a picture of current social attitudes in Swansea as is possible within such a comparatively brief compass, but our attentions in the main have been concentrated more directly on a sort of jigging and tooling exercise, in the complicated fields of social class and culture, to prepare the way for our analysis of family composition and family behaviour which form the subject matter of the rest of this book. After struggling with the task of trying to condense into two chapters an account of a complex industrial society we return to our themes of family behaviour with some considerable relief.

[37] Froom Tyler, 'The Moment of Farewell', *The Evening Post*, April, 1961.

IV

THE DOMESTIC GROUP

ONE of the basic and central facts about any kinship system is the characteristic composition of the domestic group—that is, the group of relatives who normally share a common residence. When we read the reports of anthropologists and sociologists on tribes and communities scattered all over the globe, it is often this fact more than any other which immediately establishes the difference between particular kinship systems. Whatever the fascinating variations in normal household composition described by anthropologists for communities in Africa and Asia and Oceania, there is clearly a widespread assumption that the characteristic and 'natural' domestic group in Western society is the elementary family of husband, wife and dependent children. This is evident in the size and shape of houses built both by public authorities and by private builders, and also in the welter of public statements by priests and politicians and judges on the perennial theme of 'the home as the foundation of society'. It emerges also in the contemporary usage of the term 'family'. People are of course familiar with other household forms— with elderly people living alone, for example, or with young married couples without children, or with a married child and spouse living with one or other set of parents after marriage—but there is no doubt that they would expect to find in any community in Britain the vast majority of homes containing the basic biological unit of parents and offspring. This is the expected household composition.

There are just under 50,000 domestic dwellings in Swansea (90 per cent of these containing a single household, and 10 per cent of them shared by two or more households). Whatever the expected household composition, the evidence of our survey shows that only about half of this total number of households contain the elementary family of parents and unmarried children alone. As we can see from other surveys in Britain, there is nothing unusual or abnormal about this—

146

though, insufficient attention is sometimes paid to this important fact by those concerned with housing provision.

In this study we are less concerned with the organization of the domestic group but rather with the relationships that extend outwards from this primary group to relatives living apart—to parents (in the case of married adults) and grandparents, to uncles and aunts and cousins, married brothers and sisters and their children, and to the wide variety of relatives through marriage. These two aspects of kinship, the one internal to the domestic group and the other external, cannot, however, be easily and simply separated. Household composition is not a constant. If we recall for the moment the case of Mr Griffith Hughes of Morriston which we discussed at length in our first chapter, it will be remembered that one of the themes which emerged as we listened to this elderly Welshman describing his family relationships was the number of different forms of household composition within a single family network. Mr Hughes and his wife lived alone, though until recently their daughter, Peggy and her husband and children had lived with them while they were waiting for a Corporation house. The other daughter, Mair, is living with her mother-in-law over in Fforestfach, though she and her husband, as yet without children, 'are thinking of buying one of those new bungalows in Cockett, just near to Fforestfach there'. Two of Mr Hughes's three sons are living separately with their own elementary families, but the third has his wife's invalid mother living with him. Mr Hughes's only surviving brother, eighty-year-old Sam, is a widower living with one of his married daughters—whereas his widowed sister, Sarah, lives on her own. Both Mrs Hughes's sisters are widows with married children living away from Swansea: 'they linked up after the second husband died and now live together in the youngest sister's house'. There are yet other variations in the composition of the domestic group mentioned casually in Mr Hughes's account—for example, nieces being brought up, after their mother's death and their father's remarriage, by an aunt, the mother's sister, and uncle. And it is clear from common experience that there is nothing particularly unusual about this 'Hughes Family Morriston'. An examination of most family networks would produce a similar variety of household compositions, though to establish the frequency of particular forms we obviously need to examine and analyse a large number of cases. This briefly is what we do in this chapter, first considering Swansea in general, and then the various social groupings within Swansea to see if there are noticeable differences by social class or cultural grouping or neighbourhood in the ways people live together.

It is clear that household composition both affects external relationships, and is itself a consequence of kinship obligation. Raymond Firth has emphasized the basic importance of the household group within the field of external kinship in Britain—and essentially this is true of any kinship system. He argues that 'the kinship information in the possession of an individual is not a static quantity. It is not normally exercised by and for him alone, but tends to be drawn from and contributed to a household pool. This pooling is a very important aspect of actual kin behaviour. It is the kin of the household then, not of the individual, that are socially most significant.'[1] To this we must add the extra and obvious fact that the household itself is not static—its composition changes and fluctuates with the age of the individual members and with the process of family development over time. We will be discussing this process later in this chapter: first we must examine the domestic groups into which the population of Swansea was divided at the time of our survey.

HOUSEHOLD COMPOSITION IN SWANSEA

In our analysis of the 1,962 households which fell within our random sample, we used the same categories as those used in the study of Bethnal Green by Young and Willmott and therefore, with the reservations emphasized earlier, a direct comparison can be made here. The table below shows the picture of household composition for the Borough as a whole, with the Bethnal Green figures[2] for comparison:

Table 4.1: Household and Dwelling Composition

Household Type	% Households of Each Type		% Dwellings of Each Type	
	Swansea	Bethnal Green	Swansea	Bethnal Green
Person living alone	5	10	5	8
Married couples alone	21	23	19	18
Siblings alone	2	2	2	2
Parents and unmarried children	51	54	49	46
Parent(s) and married son	4	3	5	6
Parent(s) and married daughter	13	5	15	12
Other (Married couples with other relatives other than own children; Other relatives living together; Unrelated persons living together)	4	3	5	8
Totals %	100%	100%	100%	100%
Numbers	1,962	933	1,962	933

[1] Raymond Firth, op. cit., p. 27.
[2] Young and Willmott, op. cit., p. 209.

In a sense this is one of the basic tables of this study. This is how the people of Swansea were living in 1960 when we visited a random and representative cross-section of the population during our survey. The comparison with Bethnal Green suggests some interesting observations, and we will deal briefly with these first. Broadly speaking the picture of household composition in these two very different urban areas follows the same pattern—with two major and significant variations in the figures for 'Person living alone' and 'Parent(s) and married daughter'. In the former case the percentage for Swansea is half that for Bethnal Green, and in the latter it appears about two and a half times more common to find households containing parent and married daughter in Swansea than it is in Bethnal Green. A good deal has been written in recent sociological reports about the major importance of the mother–married daughter tie in family behaviour in Britain—the Bethnal Green study emphasized this as its major theme, and we will be considering this key relationship in Swansea in a later chapter. It is worth noting here, in connection with this, that in Bethnal Green the percentage difference between composite *households* containing a married son and those containing a married daughter is very slight (2 per cent) and is not significant in indicating a preference in favour of living with the married daughter (as compared with the daughter-in-law, the son's wife). In Swansea, the difference is clear and striking (9 per cent) and the preference, so far as living together is concerned, quite evident. It must be remembered that the percentage, as with the other percentages in the table, given for households containing parents and married daughter (13 per cent) is the *average* for the Borough as a whole; when calculated for each of the local communities within Swansea the range for this household type varies from 12 to 20 per cent. It is interesting to note that the percentage of this household type for each single community in Swansea, including the middle-class residential districts, is at least twice that for Bethnal Green, and in one case as much as four times the Bethnal Green figure. This is a substantial regional difference in family behaviour, with the likelihood of a married daughter living with one or both of her parents (or they living with her) being a good deal greater in Swansea than in the East End of London.

In terms of dwelling composition the differences between Bethnal Green and Swansea are, as shown in the table, less marked. We must emphasize that the distinction between household composition and dwelling composition is based on the manner of living—a household being defined as a group of persons who normally eat together (that is, are catered for by the same person, usually the housewife); a dwelling is simply a structurally separate building, or separate part of a building such as in the case of a flat, which may contain more than one household in the sense given above. There are much wider differences in all the categories of household as compared with dwelling composition in Bethnal Green than in Swansea. This arises because 39 per cent of the dwellings in the Bethnal Green sample were shared by separate households, as compared with only 10 per cent in Swansea. This can partly be explained by the differences in the class structure of the two areas. The important point to note here is that *of these shared dwellings*, 85 per cent in Bethnal Green, but only 43 per cent in Swansea (that is 89 dwellings), contained *related* households. This is a complicated point, but an important one in relation to regional differences in family behaviour. In Swansea when relatives live together in a single dwelling they tend to form a composite household ('living through and through' is the local expression) rather than dividing off the house into separate compartments, or using the kitchen separately. It seems that, taking the category of parents and married daughter as an example, when a daughter and her husband live in the same dwelling as the daughter's parents they prefer, or at least it is the local custom, in Swansea 'to live through and through', whereas in Bethnal Green in a similar situation there is a strong tendency to maintain a separate household. We shall refer again to this characteristic of extended households in Swansea.

Of the seven household types that we have distinguished (the final one being a residual category containing a variety of household arrangements not covered by the other six), the elementary family of parents and unmarried children is clearly the most common, followed in order of frequency by married couples living alone (a mixture of newly-married couples without children as yet, childless couples beyond the period of procreation, and middle-aged or elderly couples whose children have married and left home, or whose single children are living away). One in five of all adults in Swansea live in households of this type, and two out of five live in households in which the elementary family is the domestic group.

Ninety-eight persons of the 1,962 we visited were living alone—that is, 5 per cent of the total sample. To the extent that this is a representative sample of the total population of Swansea over the age of 21, we can therefore say that just under 6,000 persons were living alone in Swansea at the time of our survey in 1960. Well over half of the persons living alone in our sample were elderly people over pensionable age (60 out of the 98), and by this reckoning there must be about 3,700 elderly people living alone in Swansea—about 3,000 elderly women and about 700 elderly men, by the proportions in our sample. We will be examining the social condition of the old later in this study. Of the 98 people living alone in our sample, including the elderly, 72 were women (50 widows, 18 single, 1 divorced, and 3 separated) and only 26 were men (8 widowers, 15 single, 2 divorced, and 1 separated). Much of this sex difference is attributable to the fact that women live longer, and the greater proportion of these persons living alone are certainly 'getting on', but it is also a fact that men generally are far less willing and able to look after themselves satisfactorily and to cope with domestic chores on their own. In our society men need women to look after them—and that's a fact.

Close on one adult out of every five lives in one of the two major forms of composite household—households containing three or more married persons—with the strains and stresses particularly character-istic of this form of household produced mainly by the housing shortage on the one hand and by the need to look after elderly relatives on the other. The fact that such composite households are three times more likely to contain parent(s) and married daughter rather than parent(s) and married son is significantly related to the closeness of the mother–daughter tie, to the differences in the roles of sons and daughters in the care of elderly parents, and to the fact that the tensions of 'doubling-up' are less when it is a case of mother and married daughter sharing one kitchen rather than mother-in-law and daughter-in-law.

This assemblage of household types is based on the assumption that a person can live in only one place at a time, that he or she belongs exclusively to one particular household at any particular time—his or her normal place of residence. This seems a quite reasonable assumption, satisfactory in the vast majority of cases. Most people, indeed all except the floating minority 'with no fixed abode' who were in any case excluded from our study by our method of sampling, can give their address when asked. But in practice we found a number of instances, often splendidly complicated, of people spreading themselves as it were over more than one household. The most common instances were when a married daughter and her family lived next door or across the road from her parents. Here the comings and goings, and continual daily interaction, seemed often to make nonsense of the best-laid schemes of definitions of household types. Our notebooks contained numerous examples, particularly from the older working-class neighbourhoods, of this household clustering and interlocking through constant interaction, and not only between the mother in one household and the married daughter in another and not only when the households concerned were within a step or two of one another (though these were both the most common cases).

The following few examples are illustrations of this daily, or at least regular, extension of living over more than one household:

Mrs Mary Matthews and her husband, Dai (a weighing machine operator, aged 64) live in rooms in Sebastopol Terrace, St Thomas, in their son's house, sharing the scullery with the son's wife but living separately and paying the son rent. Downstairs in the same house live the son, John, his wife, Sally, and their two sons, aged 15 and 12. The two families in the house eat separately and live on different floors and thus form separate households. So far so good. But across the road lives Mrs Matthews's husband's sister, Blodwen, aged 58 and a widow, who lives with her unmarried brother, Tudor, aged 61. Dai and his brother Tudor go out to work every day, and so does the son, John; the two children go to school and eat there. Mary Matthews and her daughter-in-law, Sally, have their dinner every day over in Blodwen's house across the road. Blodwen and Tudor come over every evening to watch television with John's family, and the parents come down from upstairs— 'the men more often than not go out together to the pub down the road'. The two boys, grandsons of Mary and Dai, sleep across the road in Blodwen's house 'because there's more room there'. It takes quite a bit of doing to sort this lot out into separate household types.

Another common complication is produced by the practice of living in one household but staying regularly in another for short periods. This quite frequently happens in the case of people working away from Swansea during the week but coming back every week-end. Martha Lewis, aged 81, lives alone throughout the week in Fforestfach. She is the widow of a tinplate worker, and has four children—two boys and two girls. Both the girls are married and both live in other districts of Swansea (Townhill and West Cross) and visit their mother regularly on week days. The two sons, aged 42 and 48, are unmarried and both work away in Ebbw Vale in Monmouthshire. They live in digs there during the week and come home to their mother's house in Fforestfach every week-end. One is a clerk and the other a head packer (which sounds a most interesting occupation).

Gomer Evans, aged 70 and a widower, lives alone in a small flat above his tobacconist's shop in Llansamlet. He has looked after himself since his wife died six years ago. One of his married daughters has bought a new house, with his financial help, on a private estate at West Cross. She goes over to Llansamlet every Wednesday to look after her father ('to give the place a good clean and to see to his shopping for the week'). And every Saturday at one o'clock when he closes the shop for the week-end, Mr Evans gets the bus over to West Cross to stay the week-end with his daughter and her family. 'His room is all ready for him here; he furnished it himself with some of the furniture from the home in Llansamlet. He stays here every holiday, and every week-end'. He goes back to Llansamlet every Monday morning to open the shop, 'and to be independent'.

In addition there are the many intricacies of daily visiting, amounting almost in some cases to common residence. Mrs Ruth Anstey, aged 76, of Waun Wen Terrace in Greenhill has one of her two married daughters living next door. 'I see my daughter next door about a dozen times a day. I just knock on the wall if I want to call her, and she does the same if she wants me. I help her to get the children off to bed every night. I don't know what I'd do without her. She does all the rough work here, then I keep the rest going. I am in next door watching the telly most nights—I can't afford to buy one of my own on my pension'. There are numerous cases of this type, which very often involves leaving young children in the care of grandmothers all day whilst the mothers concerned go out to work.

Another variation which we noticed frequently (and which we will be commenting on later) was that of married sons calling in regularly at their mothers' homes for meals. 'George comes in here every morning at a quarter past eight for breakfast on his way to work' says Mrs Barry, aged 63, of Little Gam Street near the Town Centre, 'he lives out on the Portmead Estate and works in a gents' outfitters in the Kingsway near here. He doesn't start till nine, but his wife has to get to her job at the Trading Estate in Fforestfach by eight. And of course I get his dinner for him here every day too.'

Mr Alun Thomas, a railway clerk, aged 58, of Cwmrhydy-ceirw and working in Swansea High Street Station, told us that, apart from holidays, he had had his dinner every day for more than thirty years, *since* he was married, at his mother's house in the Hafod about five minutes' walk away from his work. His mother died three years ago 'and I can say, with hardly any exceptions, that I saw her every day of my life until she died. Two other married brothers besides myself used to go there for dinner every day.'

Where elderly people were involved, quite often the daily contact concerned grandchildren (and not only for baby-sitting for the children of working mothers). Where the grandmother was close at hand, the grandchildren frequently seemed to be constantly in and out, in some cases staying overnight because of overcrowding in their own homes. We have mentioned the many instances of elderly people dropping in nightly to watch T.V. in near-by married children's homes: this happened the other way about also. Mrs Agnes Charles, aged 47, of Waun Wen Terrace, has five children all of school age. Her mother-in-law, a widow, lives alone five minutes away in Lamb Street. 'The children go every day after school to their Gran's to watch T.V. She has tea ready for them, and the older ones stay till all hours. I don't think it would be nice for me to get a T.V. The children wouldn't go to their Gran's then. She wouldn't like that.'

The social ingenuity of human beings seems endless, and defies rigid classification. Our table of household composition ignores the many complications of which we have given examples above and deals with the broad facts of residence at the time of our survey. We should perhaps add that we also encountered a number of cases of 'irregular households' produced by unmarried people (or at least not married to one another) living together as husband and wife, or by single women with an illegitimate child or children. In the former case, we classified the couple concerned as 'married' (even though they might have mentioned to us that they were not) where it seemed reasonable to do this: in the cases where the persons concerned gave themselves as 'Widow and Lodger' or 'Single man and Landlady' or whatever (and whatever the neighbours may have said, or we thought from the available clues), we classed them under the heading of 'Unrelated persons living together' ('Other' in the table). Such cases were of course rare. And so indeed were cases of overtly-stated illegitimacy. The case, for example, of Miss (or Mrs to the neighbours) Alice Jones, aged 39, of one of the neighbourhoods of the Town Centre area, was a total exception. She said she was single, and her household consisted of herself and five children aged between 2 and 16. She told us that all the children were illegitimate, hinted that several fathers were involved, called herself 'the black sheep of the family', and said that 'her life story would knock spots off ——' (mentioning the name of a well-known film actress which, in the circumstances, we had best omit). She owned the house. We did not inquire into her means of support.

Before we consider the factors involved in household composition there are two other facts about households which are relevant in understanding the characteristics of the domestic groups into which the population of Swansea was divided at the time of our study. These are household size and generation depth. The average household size for our sample as a whole was 3·6 persons per household: the 1951 census figure for Swansea gave the average household size as 3·3, and for England and Wales as a whole as 3·1 persons per household. Our method of interval sampling using the Electoral Register tended to favour larger households, and our figures on household size are therefore exaggerated slightly for this reason. The following table gives the size of the households in which the subjects in our sample lived. We show in the table this information analysed by social class:

Table 4.2: Household Size by Social Class—Percentages only

Household Size	Social Class				
	Middle Class	Lower Middle Class	Upper Working Class	Working Class	Total Sample
Subject living in household containing:					
1 person	8	7	5	5	6
2 persons	29	27	23	21	23
3 or 4 persons	47	47	47	45	46
5 or 6 persons	14	16	19	22	20
7 or more persons	2	3	6	7	5
Total %	100%	100%	100%	100%	100%
Numbers	225	239	473	1021	1958
Average Household Size	3·3	3·3	3·6	3·7	3·6

We can follow this at once with a table showing the generation depth of these households similarly analysed:

Table 4.3: Generation Depth of Households according to Social Class—Percentages only.

Generation Depth	Middle Class	Lower Middle Class	Upper Working Class	Working Class	Total Sample
Subject living in households containing:					
1 Generation	34	32	26	25	27
2 Generations	53	61	58	57	57
3 Generations	13	7	16	17	15
4 Generations	—	—	—	1	1
Total %	100%	100%	100%	100%	100%

The variations by social class in both these tables are slight but significant. The middle class have a noticeably smaller household size, and more persons living in one-generation households compared with the working class at the other extreme (with the two mobile classes displaying their characteristic intermediate behaviour). The vast majority of households in Swansea of all social classes contain less than five persons—the proportion larger than this is less than a fifth for the two middle classes but over a quarter for the two working classes. There are many factors involved in household size, the main one being the number of children per union. As we shall be discussing in our next chapter, there are important differences between the social classes in family size, working class families being on the average larger than those of the middle classes. This is the major reason for this class difference in household size.

Of the 1,962 subjects we interviewed, only 5 per cent (or 103 persons) lived in households containing seven or more persons and only 0·4 per cent (or eleven persons) in households with ten or more. This is a very substantial change from the situation in the early decades of this century, and clearly closely related to the great and recent decline in family size. In 1911 for example, according to the census of that year, 20 per cent of the population of Swansea lived in households with seven or more persons (that is, four times the present figure—not allowing for the slight overestimation of household size in our survey) and almost 4 per cent in households containing ten or more (or about ten times the present figure). Within the space of well under two generations, the size of households has declined dramatically, related of course both to the improvements in housing which we described in our last chapter and also, and mainly, to the sharp reduction which has occurred in the size of the elementary family. The domestic group in Swansea is on the average a good deal smaller than it has been for many generations, certainly much smaller than it was during the childhoods of elderly people still alive today.

Of the eleven households in our sample containing ten or more persons, one belonged by our classification to the lower middle class, one to the upper working class, and the remaining nine all to the working class. Six of these eleven were composite households containing parents, unmarried children, and a married child with spouse, and grandchildren in the one household. The remaining five were simple elementary families (though one of these contained also the illegitimate infant son of the eldest, but unmarried, daughter).

> The distinction of being the largest household in our sample fell to that of Mrs Dorothy Jones, aged 41, wife of a labourer unemployed for many years through chronic asthma. They live in a Corporation house on the Portmead estate, having been rehoused eight years ago from St Thomas, with their eleven unmarried children, ranging in ages from twenty to one month. The four eldest children, two sons and two daughters, are working full-time—the sons both as tug deckhands and the daughters both as shop

assistants. By religious denomination they are a family of English Baptists. Like all the large households we visited they clearly experience considerable difficulties through overcrowding. It is obviously a tight squeeze getting this unusually large family into a Corporation house—but it must be added that, unlike some other families we saw in a somewhat similar situation, this family seemed to us remarkably cheerful and contented. Mrs Jones said brightly: 'My husband and I have astonished both our families by having so many children. They don't think it's quite nice. It's been a struggle sometimes but we've been a very happy family—even if I have felt at times like that old woman who lived in a shoe.' If we had to make a list from our sample of Happy Families in Swansea, this one would certainly be included.

If overcrowding in the above case did not appear associated with misery, it often was in other cases. Marion Jackson, for example, aged 22, wife of a milk roundsman, lives with her husband and two infant children in her parents' home (father a fitter's mate) in a rented terrace house in St Thomas. Apart from Marion's elementary family of four, the household consists of her father and mother and her two unmarried sisters, aged 24 and 21, and three brothers, aged 19, 16, and 15—a total of eleven people (only two of them small children) in a house of two rooms downstairs and three bedrooms—two very small. The landlady had expressly forbidden the front parlour downstairs to be used as a bedroom. Hence Marion and her husband and two children sleep in the middle bedroom, her two adult sisters in the minute back bedroom, and her mother and father *plus* the three grown brothers in the front bedroom. The father is 49 and the mother 43. Marion and her husband have been on the Corporation housing list for the three years since they were married, but have little immediate hope of getting a house. Her parents are apparently not on the housing list. In this case the obvious overcrowding was a source of great stress to the occupants of this small house. Bitter family arguments clearly exacerbated the situation. Marion was in tears about this when we interviewed her.

Ronald Morgan, aged 27, lives with his wife, Moira, and three small children in the Corporation house on Townhill tenanted by his wife's parents. In addition to Ronald's elementary family of five, there are his parents-in-law, both aged 69, a single brother-in-law, aged 44, and the mother-in-law's unmarried sister, aged 70. A total of nine persons, including six adults—in a three-bedroomed house. The situation is made more difficult by the fact that the front room downstairs is monopolized by the father-in-law who has been confined to bed there with illness for a very lengthy period. Ronald and his wife and three children live and sleep in one small bedroom in very considerable difficulty—a sad example of cramped living. He works for the Steel Company of Wales as a wagon repairer. He and his wife have had their name down on the Corporation housing list for over six years.

If the largest households we encountered were of working-class families, this was equally true of the households with the greatest generational span. The seven cases which occurred in our sample of four-generation households (extending from great-grandparent to great-grandchild) were all cases in which the subject we interviewed in these households belonged to the working class. For all four social classes, the domestic group in over eight cases out of ten consists either of one generation alone or, in over half the total number, of two generations. We encountered 297 cases (15 per cent of our total sample) in which the domestic group spanned three generations, with, as the table shows, a higher incidence of these, slight but significant, among the working classes rather than the middle classes.

VARIATIONS IN HOUSEHOLD COMPOSITION

In Table 4.1, on page 148, we compared Swansea with Bethnal Green in terms of household composition. We must now ask whether there are differences within Swansea. So far as household composition is concerned, do the social classes differ from one another, are the Welsh different from the non-Welsh in important respects, are there noticeable differences by neighbourhood? In the next table we examine the first two questions:

Table 4.4: Household Composition by Social Class and Culture—Percentages

Household Type	Social Class				Culture		Total Sample
	Middle Class	Lower Middle Class	Upper Working Class	Working Class	Welsh	Non-Welsh	
Person living alone	8	7	3	4	5	5	5
Married Couples alone	23	23	19	18	22	17	19
Parent(s) and unmarried children	48	48	50	50	44	54	49
Parent(s) and married son	4	6	5	5	5	5	5
Parent(s) and married daughter	12	10	16	16	14	15	15
Other (Category as in Table 4.1, plus 'Siblings alone')	5	6	7	7	10	4	7
Totals %	100%	100%	100%	100%	100%	100%	100%
Numbers	225	239	473	1,021	896	1,061	1,962

The Domestic Group

Taking the question of social class first, the most obvious comment that can be made from the evidence given in this table is that the four social classes do not differ to any very striking extent in terms of household composition. There are slight differences, but the general pattern is very much the same for all four social classes. There are sharp social and cultural contrasts between West Swansea and the Tawe Valley on the east, for example, but if we examine a random sample of homes in each area we would find that in terms of household composition the people of either area live in more or less the same way. It is not possible from the facts of household composition to infer the social class of a given area in Swansea. This obvious and general similarity across the class divisions is the major conclusion that can be drawn from this table. This is a useful finding, even if a somewhat negative one. During our analyses of family behaviour we were constantly impressed by the fact that the middle classes and the working classes appeared to follow very much the same basic patterns of family behaviour, even if, as we have shown in our previous chapter, they differed sharply from one another in other respects. We will have more to say on this point later. For the moment it is clear that no matter how they differ from one another in income or occupation or house-ownership or in material possessions or in cultural attitude, the four social classes in Swansea are more or less identical so far as the structure of the domestic group is concerned. The slight differences that exist do not invalidate the major conclusion that social class is not a dominant factor in determining the social composition of the domestic household.

Within this basic similaritity, however, there are indeed fine distinctions by class which need comment. The variations that occur in the various categories of household type may be slight but they are indicative of an important class difference which will emerge more clearly later when we consider other data. As we will be remarking then, the middle classes seem noticeably less gregarious and cohesive in their general family behaviour than are the working classes. A suggestion of this occurs in this table of household composition. The differences between the social classes in household type appear mainly and significantly in the categories for persons living alone, married couples alone, and in the two forms of composite household formed by parents and married children.

More of the middle classes live alone (or alone with their husband or wife), being either without children altogether or having married children living away. Thirdly and consequently, a smaller percentage of the middle classes live in composite households containing parents and married children (16 per cent compared with the 21 per cent of

159

the working classes, the main difference occurring in the category parent(s) and married daughter). The differences between the classes shown in this table are barely significant, but these slight variations by class in household composition are consistent with our earlier comments that middle-class households had a smaller average size in the number of persons in the group, and might have on average a smaller generational span, than was the case with the working-class households in our sample. The domestic group is smallest among the middle class, and largest among the working class at the other extreme. This conclusion confirms a popular assumption to this effect, though perhaps the most interesting aspect of this evidence is that, whatever popular opinion is about contrasts in family gregariousness comparing the middle with the working class, differences in household composition between the four social classes can barely be discerned.

At first sight there are greater apparent differences between the Welsh and the non-Welsh by this factor of household composition. As the table shows, these differences are concentrated at three points in the range of household types—10 per cent more of the non-Welsh live in households containing parents and unmarried children, 5 per cent more of the Welsh on the other hand fall in the category 'married couples alone', and 6 per cent more of the Welsh live in households belonging to our residual category, 'other'. The first of these three is the major difference. There appear to be two main reasons for the lower incidence of elementary families as domestic groups among the Welsh. First, as we have observed earlier, the Welsh as a whole tend to be older than the English as a whole—the mean age of the Welsh in our sample being 50·5 years as compared with the mean age of 46·2 years for the English. The older the group concerned, the more likely it is that their children will have married and left home. This is the effect of the family cycle on household composition, to which we will be coming in a moment. This to a large extent explains this difference between the Welsh and the non-Welsh in Swansea, and also accounts for the fact that more of the Welsh are married couples living alone. But it is not the whole explanation. We have to add, as the second reason, that the Welsh tend to have smaller families on the average than their non-Welsh counterparts, and they appear to have a larger proportion of childless couples.

In our total sample, there were 297 married subjects without children; 189 (64 per cent) of these were Welsh by our cultural classification, and 108 (36 per cent) were non-Welsh. But the proportions of Welsh and non-Welsh in our total sample were 46 per cent and 54 per cent respectively. There appears therefore to be a definite, if somewhat surprising, relation between being Welsh and, if married, childless. Less than a fifth of all the married couples we visited were childless but, as the above figures show, the great majority of these were Welsh (even though the Welsh were in the minority in our total sample). This is consistent with other evidence on family size, comparing the Welsh with the non-Welsh, and we will be examining this complicated problem of vital statistics in the chapter which follows.

We noted too that there were marked variations in household composition by neighbourhood in Swansea, although the broad pattern was the same for all, the most common household type consisting of parents and married children. Some of these variations were related to the different class composition of our localities. We have suggested that more of the middle classes lived alone, and in fact the percentage of persons living alone in Sketty and Uplands was well over 8 per cent.

As we have observed earlier in this section, social class is clearly a factor in the incidence of what we have called composite households; that is households produced by 'doubling up'. The proportion of this type of household was lowest (14 per cent) in Sketty and Uplands and highest (26 per cent) in working-class Sandfields and Castle. The more middle-class the neighbourhood in Swansea the lower the proportion of composite households; almost all the working-class neighbourhoods were above the Borough average here.

Class is, however, only one of many factors affecting household composition and bearing in mind the smallness of the differences between the classes it would be surprising if differences between localities could be explained in class terms alone. That they could not was borne out by the fact that in spite of the extent to which our expectations of fluctuations in household composition between neighbourhoods, based on our knowledge of their class composition, were fulfilled, other variations could not be explained in this way.

The Brynmill and Mount Pleasant areas, for example, are dominated by the two mobile classes—lower middle and upper working, yet their percentage of persons living alone exceeded that of Sketty and Uplands. They contained the highest proportion of elderly people of all the twenty-three neighbourhoods in the Borough. These two neighbourhoods also had on the one hand the lowest incidence of elementary families as domestic groups (33 per cent, compared with the average of 49 per cent for Swansea as a whole), and on the other the highest percentage of the composite household in which a married daughter and her husband live with one or both of her parents, or the parent(s) live with the married daughter. The percentage of this household type in Brynmill and Mount Pleasant is the maximum for the Borough—20 per cent, or 5 per cent above the average for Swansea.

It is clear that these two neighbourhoods forming a sort of outer semi-circle on the western edge of the Town Centre diverge sharply in household composition from the general pattern of the Borough. They are well above the average in persons living alone, in married couples alone, in parents and married daughters, in siblings living together (say two elderly spinsters, or two widowed sisters); and well below average in the most common household type, parents and un-married children. These divergences from the 'normal' distribution of household composition are not easy to explain: they emphasize the complexity of the factors involved in household composition.

The most obvious facts about these two similar neighbourhoods are their convenient location bordering the shopping centre, the preponderance of large, roomy, three-story terrace-houses with double-bay windows (the sort of houses frequently used as 'digs' by students or let off into 'rooms' for young married couples—'prefer-ably (and often essentially) without children'), and finally their evidently respectable 'lower middle-class' character. As Swansea expanded westward these two localities were initially the residential areas of the comfortable *bourgeoisie*—small shopkeepers and businessmen and commercial travellers and clerks of various grades. With increasing prosperity, many of these have 'moved up' into Sketty and Uplands and later to the newer areas farther west. Many of the large family houses have now been divided off into flats or rooms occupied by elderly widows on small incomes or by young married couples waiting for a house of their own. We encountered numerous cases in this area of an elderly couple (or an elderly widow) living alone on the ground floor, or in the basement in some cases, with the rest of their home let off as rooms for students or boarders or to young married couples ('No children, please')—and with their own married children scattered far and wide.

> Mrs Gwyneth Morgan, aged 72, widow of a Local Government official, lives in Brynmill Terrace in a large three-story house over-looking the Bay, and very 'convenient' for the shops and buses and the near-by University. Mrs Morgan lives alone on the ground floor. The first floor is let off to a young married couple—two large rooms, a small kitchenette, plus use of bath. Two students at the College each have a room on the second floor, and share another kitchenette, and the bath. Mrs Morgan has three children, two married sons and one spinster daughter, a schoolteacher in Bir-mingham who comes home to Swansea every school holiday. One of the sons is a sanitary inspector with the Devon County Council,

and the other a chemical engineer with an Oil Company out in Kuwait in the Persian Gulf. They both spend regular holidays with their wives and children in their mother's home in Swansea, the former every August and the latter for three months every other year when he gets home leave. Mrs Morgan has a widowed sister living quite near at hand in Brynmill who has also let off part of her house as 'digs' for students, though she has a married daughter and her family sharing the rest of the house with her. Mrs Morgan says: 'I wouldn't like to live completely on my own in this big old house. And in any case I couldn't live here on my pension alone. I need the money I get from letting to keep me independent.'

Not all the houses in Brynmill and Mount Pleasant are as large as this, but a substantial number of them are. It seems that a combination of house-type, convenient location, financial necessity, and general 'respectability' of neighbourhood encourage the sharing of dwellings and the formation of composite households. For many recently-married couples this area is a sort of favoured 'staging-post' while they save up the deposit to get a home of their own, or while they wait for their names to come up on the Corporation housing list.

It is here that they come immediately after marriage, whether to live in rooms or, if Brynmill or Mount Pleasant born, to share the home of their parents—usually those of the wife.

The new post-war housing estates, both Corporation and private, show in contrast a quite different breakdown of household composition. All these estates have well above the average proportion of households composed only of parents and young children (61 per cent of their households are in this category, compared with the Borough average of 49 per cent), and consequently many fewer married couples alone, or persons living alone. This is not surprising since the new estates tend initially to be peopled mainly by families with young children—and as one moves about one of these estates one certainly gets the impression that the place is swarming with youngsters. Equally then, certain of the older communities from which these young families have moved to the new estates tend to become relatively denuded of this household type. We have seen already that this was particularly true of Brynmill and Mount Pleasant, and we noticed that it was so also with the old neighbourhoods of the Town Centre, Sandfields and Castle. The new estates also differ from other older working-class areas in having a lower number of composite households (largely because of the policy of house allocation and of course because they are essentially 'first-generation' estates). Apart from this exception and that of

Brynmill and Mount Pleasant, the variation in the number of composite households with class held good for all the neighbourhoods we examined. The linking factor appeared to be income more than anything else. Quite simply the middle classes tend to be better off than the working classes. If you cannot afford to make other arrangement, 'doubling up' in a composite household may well be the only solution in certain circumstances either of housing difficulties immediately after marriage or of the necessity to provide care for an elderly parent. But there is also a noticeable difference of social attitude and expectation between the social classes over this question of living with parents after marriage.

THE FOUR AGES OF THE FAMILY

So far we have been examining the composition of the households in which our subjects lived at the time of our survey. For purposes of analysis and exposition, we have classified these into a series of 'household types', following the categories used by Young and Willmott in their study of Bethnal Green. The result is an essentially static, 'snap-shot' view of Swansea at a particular point in time. We must now emphasize the somewhat obvious, but neglected, point that from the point of view of individual families these are not separate 'household types' but phases in a continuous cycle of development. Domestic groups are 'born' at marriage, expand with births, reach a sort of climax as the period of procreation is passed and as the children grow to maturity, and decline as the children marry and 'leave the nest' to found elementary families (and separate domestic groups) of their own. The original domestic group finally disintegrates with the death of one or both of the original partners. This is the normal and universal familial process. With each phase of the cycle, the composition of the domestic group alters—as children are born, or as they leave home on marriage (or bring in their spouses to form composite households). This natural and continuous rhythm of the successive generations must obviously underly any discussion either of household composition or of family relationships external to the individual household. Here in this endless process are the essential dynamics of family life. It is of course a continuous process within each individual family, though it can without great difficulty be divided into a series of arbitrary but recognizable phases, much as can the life-span of a particular individual. As there are 'seven ages of man', so there seem to be four ages of the family. In the table below, we show the phases into which we have divided this continuous and repetitive cycle of growth and decline, together with the numbers and proportions of the persons in our Swansea sample who fell by our definitions into each phase (taking married persons only of course, since marriage is the starting-point of the cycle):

Table 4.5: The Family Cycle

Family Phase	Definition	Numbers in our sample	Percentage of Total
PHASE I: Home-Making	From marriage to the birth of the first child.	297	17%
PHASE II: Procreation	From the birth of first child to the marriage of the first child	808	47%
PHASE III: Dispersion	From the marriage of the first child to the marriage of the last child	262	16%
PHASE IV: Final	From marriage of last child to death of original partners	358	20%
Total		1,725	100%

We have taken these particular beginning and ending points for the four phases because they can be easily identified for the persons in our sample, and because of course they do represent clear and distinct milestones in the progress of an individual family through this typical cycle. In the average case, with marriage about the age of 23, the first phase lasts about two years, the second about twenty-three years (since it is from the birth to marriage of the first child). The length of the final two phases depends on the number of children born and on the facts of longevity. As we will be explaining in the chapter which follows, there have been dramatic changes in this average and normal family cycle over the last half-century or so with the striking decline in family size and the marked improvement in life-expectancies. And as we will be pointing out then, it is useful in order to clarify and emphasize these changes, particularly those in family size, to divide Phase II which we have called the Phase of Procreation into two sub-phases—'child-bearing' during which births are actually occurring, and 'child-rearing' in which the children born are growing to maturity. It is the very great shortening of the actual period of child-bearing, comparing say the present generation of women with that of their grandmothers, which has produced the most marked change in this family cycle—but we will be coming to this point later.

Each age or phase has its characteristic pattern of household composition, of family behaviour, and of social participation in the life of the community of which the family concerned is a component. The dominant social characteristic of the first phase, as we will be seeing in Chapter VII when we consider the position of newly-weds, is that it is a period of very considerable adjustments and re-arrangements in relationships, particularly with the sudden arrival on the scene of a new set of relatives—the in-laws. Our survey revealed that the majority of marriages begin with the newly-married couple living temporarily with relatives, more often than not in the home of the bride's parents. Hence characteristically this first phase of the family cycle is often spent wholly or partly in a composite household. In the second phase of the cycle, the characteristic domestic group for the larger part of this period consists of parents and dependent children, though towards the end of this phase it is not uncommon for a composite household covering three generations to be again formed with an elderly parent or parents from either the wife's or the husband's side (more usually the former) coming to live with the family.

The Phase of Dispersion begins with the marriage of the first child and continues until all the children are married. As the children marry and leave home, the domestic group goes through a period of declining size, though commonly the size of the group may expand temporarily as one or other of the married children starts off marriage by bringing the spouse into the parental household. The partial rupture of relationships characteristic of this phase may thus be softened by the formation of a temporary composite household. We will be considering examples of the changes in relationships typical of this phase in a later chapter. When all the children have in fact married, even if they have not all left home, the family concerned has entered the last phase of the cycle—and in most cases the original couple find themselves on their own once more.

This, briefly expressed, is of course a *model* of the life-cycle covering the normal or typical case. We will be using it to consider variations in family behaviour, and in particular in our next chapter to consider changes in family behaviour over the generations. There are, it scarcely needs to be emphasized, numerous variations in practice on this general model of the four ages of the family. Some persons never marry and thus never enter on this cycle. Others marry but never have any children and are thus permanently halted as it were in the first phase. In other cases the cycle is abnormal through the death of one or both partners early in the marriage, or through 'broken homes' produced by separations or divorces (though these latter accounted for only 1·5 per cent of the cases in our sample). In yet others, one or more of the children may never marry and remain permanently in the parental home—the case for example of the spinster daughter living with and caring for her elderly father or mother, or of the bachelor son maintaining the home for his widowed mother. In some cases the couple concerned may have well above the 'normal' number of children which will affect in their case the length of the two final phases. These many variations are, however, minority instances. In the vast majority of cases the process that we have outlined above does in fact represent the pattern of family development over the succeeding generations.

We began this chapter by discussing the composition of the domestic group in Swansea, and we have introduced here this notion of the family cycle to emphasize that these two are closely related. We have suggested that the composition of the domestic group characteristically alters according to family phase, and this can now be demonstrated in the following table giving this correlation (we have omitted from Phase I the childless married couples beyond the natural period of procreation—11 per cent of our married subjects: they will never have any children and form a special case best separated from this analysis of household composition by family phase):

Table 4.6: Household Composition by Family Phase

Household Composition	Family Phase			
	Phase I Home-Making	Phase II Procreation	Phase III Dispersion	Phase IV Final
Person living alone	—	—	1%	10%
Married couples alone	57%	2%	5%	48%
Siblings alone	—	—	1%	1%
Parents and unmarried children	—	81%	71%	2%
Parents and married children	40%	17%	21%	28%
Other	3%	—	1%	11%
Totals %	100%	100%	100%	100%
Numbers	97	808	262	358

The figures in heavy type show the forms of household composition characteristic of each of these four phases. Over half of our married subjects who were in Phase I of the cycle (between marriage and the birth of the first child) lived with their spouses on their own, and a little less than a half in a composite household with either their own parents or this spouse's parents. These two household forms accounted for almost the whole of our sample in this Phase. Phase II and Phase III are clearly dominated by the household form of parents and unmarried children. And the final phase (in which all the children are married) is characterized mainly by the two household forms of married couples alone and parents and married children forming a composite household—though, in this phase, substantial numbers of our subjects lived either alone or in households in our residual category (unrelated persons living together, or other relatives living together, for example).

The composite household which includes three or more married persons—a young married couple living with one or other set of parents, or an elderly parent or parents living with a married daughter or son—occurs substantially and significantly in all four phases of the cycle, but particularly in Phase I, because of the high proportion of newly-weds who begin marriage in the parental home on one side or the other. The proportion of these composite households declines sharply in the second phase, and begins to increase again in the latter stages of the cycle (with the problem both of providing accommodation initially for married children and of taking in elderly relatives). We did not ask all the persons we interviewed whether or not they had spent any part of their lives *as children* in households which included other relatives besides their own parents and their brothers and sisters, but it seems clear from our detailed interviewing and from the family case histories that we compiled, that a substantial proportion of them did. Though we do not have statistical evidence on this point about our subjects' experience of composite households as children, we believe that it conforms fairly closely with that reported by James Bossard in an American study. Bossard writes:

> In spite of the shrinkage of living facilities which result from present-day housing arrangements, perhaps a minority of families, especially those with children, pass through the entire child-rearing period without the living-in of persons other than parents and children. A study of four hundred and ten students in a large urban university, made by the author, revealed that only one hundred of the four hundred and ten had grown to college age in families which consisted of parents and children only.[3]

[3] James H. S. Bossard, *The Large Family System*, 1956, p. 43.

To a large extent this situation seems to arise not 'in spite of' but because of 'the shrinkage of living facilities' in modern urban areas. Bossard's conclusion emphasizes the extent to which composite households, wider than the elementary family, are a common feature of the social experience of children as well as of the married lives of adults at one or other stage of the family cycle. For most people at some time or other in their lives the household itself is the scene of kinship relationships and activities wider than those that occur within the elementary family of parents and offspring—a centre not only of casual visiting by relatives living apart, but also, for varying periods in individual lives, of a wider group of relatives actually living together. This relatively-common experience of composite or extended households must be borne in mind in any discussion of the degree of isolation of elementary families in contemporary urban society.

In this chapter we have emphasized the point that, though we are primarily interested in the external kin relationships of the domestic group, the composition of the latter is not a constant—either taking the 'snap-shot' picture of the community as a whole at any one point in time or over the life-cycle of the individual. We have indicated the main variations in household composition and considered these briefly in relation to social class and culture and the 'age' and characteristics of neighbourhoods—and essentially in relation to the process of expansion and decline that the individual and typical domestic group goes through from its founding at the marriage of the husband and wife to their death in old age. Interwoven with this basic and universal cycle, as the major determinant, are a multiplicity of other factors affecting the size and shape of the domestic group— the demographic facts of family size and longevity, the availability of housing and the type of house, the existence and 'availability' of other relatives in the particular case, and not least the attitudes and expectations of the individuals concerned towards kinship obligations outside the immediate, primary family of parents and unmarried children.

We have been considering the physical grouping of relatives in separate households. Before we come to consider the nature and content of wider relationships, we need to examine more closely some basic facts of demography. We have mentioned the fact that households in present-day Swansea are on the average very much smaller than they were before the First World War—smaller indeed than they have been for many generations. This is one of the demographic facts that is fundamentally related to the major changes which have occurred, well within recent memory, in the structure of the family. We cannot proceed with our discussion of family behaviour without taking account of these recent and far-reaching changes in the vital statistics of family life. This is the subject of our next chapter.

V

SOME VITAL STATISTICS

WITHIN the space almost of a single generation there have been revolutionary changes in the roles and attitudes of women. To a large extent these changes have been the product of more than fifty years of radical change in the vital statistics of birth, marriage and death. Time and again our investigations of family behaviour in contemporary Swansea have returned to this basic point of the recent liberation of women from the wheel of prolonged child-bearing—an emancipation which is only just beginning, with the present 'daughters of the revolution', to exert its full effect. A familiar theme of our interviews was that of a growing and deep-seated conflict between the generations over expectations about the roles of women, and over attitudes to family responsibility outside the immediate domestic circle of the elementary family. Much of this conflict, expressed commonly in relation to the care of elderly relatives, appears to centre around the sudden and recent emergence of women from traditional and compulsory and conditioned domesticity into the world outside the home. We have said that present-day Swansea is a radically different place from the Victorian or Edwardian Swansea, that elderly men and women still alive today remember so well from their youth. Of all the many and varied changes that have contributed to this transformation, none has been more telling in its impact on the whole atmosphere and character of family life than this quiet revolution in the social position of women.

There can be few people who find the desiccated figures of the decennial census volumes exciting reading. And yet the series of census volumes over the last century contain a most dramatic story of demographic change. The elements of this story—the plunge in family size, the change in family-building habits, the declining age at marriage and the increased popularity of marriage, the sharp disturbances in the age balance of the population, the increases in life expectancies—are too well known from numerous commentaries as well as from widespread personal experience to require a lengthy description on our part. They have been presented at length in the 1949 Report of the Royal Commission on Population—without question the most important document on the natural history of the family to have appeared in recent decades. More recently still, Richard Titmuss[1] has provided a fascinating summary of the particular changes in the vital statistics of birth, marriage, and death which have affected the social position of women. In this chapter, we draw attention to the effects of these changes on the wider circle of family relationships with which we are particularly concerned in this Swansea study.

FEWER CHILDREN, FEWER RELATIVES

'The fall in the birth-rate in Western societies is one of the dominating biological facts of the twentieth century,' writes Titmuss.[2] The average completed family size of the Mid-Victorian family was 6·16 children. Nowadays (for women married in 1930) the average is 2·09 children. The great majority (63 per cent) of Victorian couples had five or more children; nowadays the great majority (81 per cent) of couples have three or less. The proportion with five children or more has fallen to 12 per cent; that is, one family in eight has this number as compared with two out of every three Victorian families.

'The proportion of childless couples has about doubled; the proportion having only one child has risen fivefold since the nineteenth century and the proportion having two children fourfold. At the other end of the scale the proportion of couples having ten children or more has been reduced from 16 per cent to less than 1 per cent.'[3] The contrast is remarkable. And this decline in family size occurred within less than two generations. As Titmuss has pointed out 'it is the rapidity of this fall which is as remarkable as the extent of the fall over the last fifty years.'

The natural history of the family as a unit of reproduction is a matter for demographers and social historians. However, such a recent and dramatic change has important sociological consequences —and is a vital fact in the analysis of the family relationships and attitudes of the persons who fell within our random sample of the contemporary population of Swansea. In the broad sense of being

[1] Richard M. Titmuss, 'The Position of Women', in *Essays on 'the Welfare State'*, 1958, Chapter 5.

[2] op. cit., p. 89.

[3] Report of the Royal Commission on Population, 1949, Cmd 7695, p. 26.

co-residents of the Borough at a particular point in time, all of the 1,962 people we interviewed were 'contemporaries'. But they belonged of course to a number of different generations, taking their dates of birth, with marked contrasts in their social experience. Five hundred and ten of these men and women were born before the turn of the century: that is, a quarter of our sample were 'Victorians', by birth at least. A further 538 were born in the period between 1900 and the outbreak of the First World War in 1914. That is, over half the total sample were born before the First World War. A further 651 (33 per cent) were born in the period between 1914 and 1930 when the average family size was falling rapidly to just over two children per family. And finally 263 of our sample, or 14 per cent, were born between 1930 and the outbreak of the Second World War when the average completed family size had reached the lowest point of this half-century of rapid decline. Apart from the immense social and economic changes that have occurred over this period covered by the maximum life-span of our sample of the people now alive in Swansea, the physical shape of the family itself has altered tremendously. It is no exaggeration to say that this story of reduction in family size and the consequent contraction in the number of relatives, from the earlier generations to the later *within our sample*, is written across every single family genealogy.

The oldest generation, born in the latter decades of the Victorian century, grew up in a social environment in which large families were the common and expected occurrence. Their familial attitudes were formed in this normal situation—with a large number of brothers and sisters and cousins in their own generation and a large collection of uncles and aunts in the generation of their parents. This point was a recurrent theme of our interviews with elderly people. The variations in individual cases in the numbers of brothers and sisters was of course great, but the average was high (more than four) and the general social experience of large families and of a large number of relatives was extremely common. Trevor Jones, to take one of many examples from our survey, was 69 and was thus born in 1891. He was the last but one of thirteen children (two of whom died in infancy), covering an age span of twenty-two years. His wife, Maud, whom he married in 1917, was one of eleven children covering a span of nineteen years. Two very large families: Trevor was the son of a blacksmith, and his wife the daughter of a collier. Trevor and Maud had just two daughters (now in their thirties) and have three grandchildren. Not one of the twenty uncles and aunts of these two daughters (that is, the brothers and sisters of Trevor and Maud) had more than three children. Five of them remained unmarried into old age, and four more had just one child each. The familial experience of these three generations—that of Trevor Jones's own generation, and of his children and nephews and nieces, and that of his grandchildren—within a single Swansea family is markedly different. His own generation was thickly peopled with relatives; his grandchildren in comparison have remarkably few. Though the actual numbers will vary in other families, this general demographic trend affected the vast majority of families in our sample.

A simple calculation can be made to illustrate the effects of this fall in the size of the elementary family on the numbers of relatives in the immediate kinship network of a particular individual. Suppose we take a fictitious individual, married, with an 'average' number of four children. If we take only this individual's close relatives (brothers and sisters, and his wife's brothers and sisters, parents, uncles and aunts both of himself and his wife, and first cousins on both sides) and give each of this network of closely linked elementary families this average of four children each, the total number of relatives, both immediate kin and in-laws, would come to 358. If we repeat this performance, using an average of three children per family the total number of relatives falls by well over half to 165. With the present-day average of just over two children per union, the total number of relatives—if all families in the network were 'average'—would come to 56. No single grouping of families is neatly average in this way of course but this illustration is not entirely meaningless. The sharp contraction in the *number* of relatives, consequent on the decline in family size over the last fifty years, is a social fact—and a fact which is only now becoming fully apparent as the earlier generations, with their plethora of kin, gradually disappear from the scene.

It is not simply a question of the number of relatives: more importantly it is a question of a change in characteristic familial attitudes as a result of this basic demographic alteration in the *shape* of the family and of the wider kinship system. Much of the vague conflict between the older and younger generations about the performance of family obligations and about the recognition of kinship responsibilities—the tensions for example that can arise in connection with the care of the elderly—seem to be related to this change in attitude resulting from the fundamental fact of decline of family size. It is easier to be aware of this change of attitude than to be able to describe it precisely. In a most interesting American study (quoted earlier)[4] James Bossard, attempts to establish some of the effects that family size has on the family system. The large family he points, out, is exceptionally vulnerable because it is more frequently subject to

[4] James Bossard, op. cit., Ch. 14.

economic pressure, and more likely (because of the greater length of the period of child bearing) to be affected by the loss of one of the parents while there are still young children to be reared. We would add here that the existence of large numbers of young children needing care combined with frequent pregnancies on the part of the mother creates a situation of *recurrent* domestic crisis. It is inevitable that in a large family (whatever may be the part played by kin outside the household) older siblings (especially daughters) will have to assume in times of crisis some of the parents' responsibility for younger children. Bossard notes that in the large families he studied 'sticking together' and co-operation on the part of the children 'is a common device in the large family crisis'. Increase in the size of the family group often but not always meant the assumption of authoritarian roles on the part of the parent but it did tend to result in the formulation of rules of conduct which everyone had to obey. The larger the family, he notes, the greater is the extent to which roles are specialized. The 'large family system' therefore appeared characterized by a strong group and familial awareness, continual personal adjustments, solidarity and sacrifice in major family crises, emphasis on the group rather than the individual, extensive specialization roles associated—in the Durkheimian manner—with a strong sense of *interdependence*, firm parental authority and filial respect, with the basic and dominant theme that of reciprocal help and co-operation.

This characterization has certain important implications. The specialization of roles and necessity for co-operation in domestic crises means that in the large family daughters are extremely likely to learn and be forced to play a female role which is predominantly domestic at a very early age. This will undoubtedly affect their own attitude to domesticity in their adult lives. Secondly the need for the family to achieve a high degree of co-operation if it is to live together, let alone weather recurrent crises, is likely to establish extremely strong ties between its members. Hence in the next generation the attitudes which characterize a large elementary family are likely to be extended over a wider family group. If the family size in the next generation is still large the importance of these ties will be maintained by the continued need of the members of the original elementary family for help and support in recurrent crises.

Conversely the small family is less vulnerable, less subject to recurrent crises; it exhibits less role specialization, less co-operation between siblings, less subordination of the individual to family rules or parental demand. Relationships will be more personal and therefore less stable. Ties between family members (as opposed to those between individuals) will be weaker, and the emphasis placed on the individual rather than the group. Consequently there will be 'little attention to kinsfolk unless they fit into and contribute to, the planned goals of the small family'. In his brief discussion of the *small* family Bossard tends, in our view, not to distinguish sufficiently clearly those characteristics of small American families which derive from their size and those which are due to other factors. But his study nevertheless enables us to appreciate that some of the changes in structure which the family has undergone in the lifetime of our older informants in Swansea are partly attributable to the fall in family size. The contrast between the large and small family is implicit in the words of Mr Hughes of Morriston with which we began this study. Large families have not quite died out in Swansea—eleven households out of the 1,962 in our sample contained ten or more persons, as we pointed out in the discussion of household size in Chapter IV—but there is no question that present-day Swansea, like any other large urban area in Britain, is fully characteristic of what the Report of the Royal Commission on Population called 'the spread of the modern small family system'.[5]

CLASS AND CULTURAL DIFFERENCES IN FAMILY SIZE

Though there has been a general demographic trend over the life-span of our most elderly informants, it has not been uniform for all the social groups within the community as a whole. Family size varies importantly by both social class and by religion. The Report of the Royal Commission on Population divides the fall in the size of the family over the last seventy or eighty years into two distinct phases—the first occurring in the latter half of the nineteenth century in which the heaviest fall was amongst the professional and managerial classes—the Victorian middle classes. During this first thirty years or so the fall was least among the working classes 'which had the largest families at the beginning. The result of these differences in trend was that the variation in family size (by social class) became much more marked'.[6] The middle classes seem to have set the pattern for smaller families, and in the second phase, after 1900, the working classes rapidly followed suit as the gospel of family limitation and family planning (with its obvious social and economic advantages) percolated down the social scale with, in Titmuss's words, 'nothing less

---

[5] Only 12·6 per cent of the married women over 40 in our Swansea sample had had five or more children: a hundred years ago, before the big decline in family size began, 63 per cent of marriages produced five or more children.

[6] op. cit., p. 28.

than a revolutionary enlargement of freedom for women brought about by the power to control their own fertility'.[7]

The fact that the major fall in family size among the working classes followed that in the middle classes by almost a generation suggests that the former copied the latter, that the process of social imitation was the major factor involved, that the middle classes were the standard-setters, and that 'the middle-class ideal' gradually became the accepted ideal for the working classes also. Were this so one could speak of the working classes 'becoming middle class' by having smaller families. This kind of judgement has much currency nowadays—in fields other than family size, in the spread of washing machines, and other household gadgetry, or as regards house-ownership or the possession of cars or the taking of holidays abroad. Clearly social imitation is a ubiquitous feature of any society, and there is some measure of truth in these arguments about the role of the middle classes as the setters of social standards and perhaps even about 'the embourgeoisement of the workers'. But the argument is easily carried too far (usually by middle-class observers of the social scene). The facts suggest a much simpler explanation. The middle classes were first in the field—with smaller families because of their privileged access to education and because of their special concern with preserving their privileged economic status; with better living conditions because they were better off. With the spread of education and, more recently, hard-won improvements in their economic conditions, the working classes have discovered that they can set their sights a good deal higher than they were formerly accustomed to. It seems more accurate to emphasize, with the limitation of family size as with the contemporary improvement in living conditions, that it is less a case of 'middle-class' ideals and values and behaviour being accepted and copied by the 'imitative' working classes than the simple and natural recognition by the community as a whole that these are universal and *attainable* social goals, with obvious advantages. The Report of the Royal Commission discusses the complex of causes of the family limitation and concludes that 'this gradual permeation of the small family system through nearly all classes has to be regarded as a fundamental adjustment to modern conditions'.[8]

[7] Titmuss, op. cit., p. 91.

[8] op. cit., Chapter 5: 'The Causes of Family Limitation'. The causes discussed are population pressure, birth control propaganda and improved birth control methods, decline of the economic importance of the family as a productive unit, economic insecurity and increased opportunities for 'getting on', higher standards of parental care, the improved status of women—and social example.

Though in the contemporary situation the difference that formerly existed in family size between the middle classes and the working classes has been greatly reduced, the working classes continue to produce on average more children than do the middle classes. The class differences in fertility are shown in the following table which includes both the most recent figures on fertility from the 1951 census for the country as a whole and also the analysis of the married women over 40 in our Swansea sample giving their average fertility according to our fourfold classification by social class. The average (2·3 children) for the Swansea sample is higher than the national average (2·01) largely because whilst the census deals only with women aged 45 to 49, our analysis included all women over 40, since the size of our sample made it impossible to deal only with the very small number of women aged 45–49.

Table 5.1: Class Differences in Family Size

Registrar-General's Occupational Class	England & Wales 1951 Census Married Women aged 45–49	Swansea 1960 Sample MarriedWomen aged over 40	Social Class
	Number of live births per woman		
Class I: Professional, etc.	1·5		
Class II: Intermediate	1·6	1·7	Middle Class
Class III: Skilled	1·9	1·8	Lower Middle Class
Class IV: Partly Skilled	2·4	2·1	Upper Working Class
Class V: Unskilled	2·6	2·7	Working Class
All Classes	2·01	2·3	All Classes

The calculation of Net Reproduction Rates and of the Replacement Index (the number of children that must be born year by year in order to 'replace' the generation to which their parents belonged) is a task that can thankfully be left to demographers. It can be seen immediately from the above table that the reproduction rates vary substantially between the social classes, and that indeed only the working classes produce enough children to replace the previous generation. The 'replacement' figure must obviously be at least two children: the Report of the Royal Commission on Population estimates that the adequate family size for the replacement of the population is 'of the order of' 2·8 children per married woman on average. Whatever the varying views on this, the two important points for the sociologist are first that working-class families remain on average significantly larger than the middle-class families, family size decreasing up the social scale. And secondly, that since the reproduction rates differ by social class in this manner, substantial numbers of people must move upwards in the social scale in each generation in order to preserve the existing class structure. Without this substantial social mobility, the existing shape of the class structure, as we have described it, for example for Swansea in Chapter III, would inevitably alter *for demographic reasons alone*. On the basis of the differences in net reproduction rates between the classes, it is of course possible to calculate the percentages of the people who must move upwards in order to maintain the *status quo*. Our sample is too small for a satisfactory analysis here. The point, however, is an important one and could well be borne in mind in studies of the class system.

Besides these differences in family size by class, there are also differences, so far as Swansea is concerned, both by religion and by the cultural dichotomy into Welsh and non-Welsh. In the latter respect particularly these differences are surprising and perplexing.

The following table shows the distribution of family size according to the number of children born to all married women over 40 in our sample. Only a small proportion of these women are aged between 40 and 45 and thus within the age when it is still possible to have children—and only a minute fraction of these will in fact have more children. We can thus take the following figures with confidence as the completed family size of the women concerned. The first column gives the percentage distribution for the sample as a whole, and the other columns for the categories given in the heading—non-Welsh, Welsh, and Welsh-speakers—to enable comparison to be made.

Table 5.2: Distribution over Family by Size of Different Social Groups. (Married women over 40 only.)

Number of Children Born	Swansea Total Sample	Non-Welsh	Welsh	Welsh-speakers only
	Percentages			
None	16	14	19	21
1 or 2 Children	48	43	52	57
3 to 5 Children	26	30	22	16
6 or more	10	13	7	6
Totals	100%	100%	100%	100%
Number of married women	595	312	283	203
Average completed family size	2·3	2·6	2·1	1·9

N 179

The distribution in the column on the left—for our total sample of married women over 40—does not differ greatly from that given for Great Britain as a whole (for marriages of 1925) in the Report of the Royal Commission on Population.[9] The curious fact, shown in the middle two columns, is that the Welsh in Swansea have a much smaller average family size than the non-Welsh and also show marked differences in their distribution over the various family sizes.[10] A surprisingly large number of the married persons in our sample who were childless were Welsh by our cultural classification. This fact can be seen again in this table dealing with married women over 40 alone. Three-quarters of the Welsh have had two or less children, whereas rather over half of the non-Welsh fell in this category. At the other end of the scale the proportion of large Welsh families (with six or more children) is only just over a half that of the non-Welsh.

When we first came to Swansea we thought it likely that we might encounter with the Welsh a high incidence of large families. We were wrong about this. As these figures show, Welsh families in Swansea are on average a good deal smaller than either the national average or the families of the non-Welsh section of the population. The final column, giving this analysis of family size for the Welsh-speakers alone (the cultural *élite* within our broader Welsh classification), shows that 'the more Welsh'—by this test of language—families are, the smaller they are likely to be. And the higher the incidence of childless marriages.

We further noted, though our figures are here dangerously small to draw any firm conclusions, a relationship between smallness of family and Welsh Nonconformism—particularly 'active' Welsh Nonconformists. This group had the smallest family size compared with the other religious denominations—the Roman Catholics having the largest, much as one would expect, followed by the Anglicans and then the English Nonconformists.

We have said that family size varied by social class. Our two middle classes were too small in size for us to examine with any confidence the family building habits of the Welsh middle classes as compared with the non-Welsh middle classes in Swansea. We had large enough groups to be able to do this for the working classes, and here again it was clear that the Welsh working classes have an average family size well below that of their non-Welsh counterparts in the population.

The conclusion that we must draw from these figures is that the Welsh as a cultural category in Swansea, and perhaps the Welsh-

[9] op. cit., p. 26, Table XVII.

[10] The difference between the Welsh and the Welsh-*speakers* is not significant.

speakers and the active Welsh Nonconformists in particular, are simply not producing enough children to hold their own—to replace the parental generation—and, all other factors apart, to maintain their numerical position in relation to other elements in the population. If this is so, these social categories (and the Welsh language) must decline in Swansea *for demographic reasons alone.*

We must say at once that it is extremely difficult to explain these puzzling differences in family size so far as the Welsh in Swansea are concerned. The Fertility Report of the 1951 census does in fact show that the mean family size of Wales II (the predominantly agricultural region of North and Central Wales—and the main stronghold of Welsh-speaking and Nonconformity) and of Wales I (the predominantly industrialized South) exceeds that of all the English census regions, except Merseyside and Tyneside and the rural counties of the North. The Report concludes 'the fertility of Wales entire is clearly greater than that of England'.[11] We are not, however, dealing here with 'Wales entire' but with the urban Welsh in the Borough of Swansea. Our figures do suggest that the family size of the Welsh in Swansea has not always been lower than that of the non-Welsh (this certainly seems so in the average number of births to women now over 60). The fall in family size which affected both groups in the second and third decades of this century seems, however, to have been more rapid and sudden for the Welsh than for other social groupings within the town.

There are likely to be many factors involved here. Two stand out as possible and partial explanations. This plunge in family size occurred mainly just after the First World War in a period of great local economic uncertainty and in a period of industrial contraction and depression (though in the twenties Swansea was less affected by this depression than other areas in South Wales). The close association of the Welsh with heavy industry, particularly steel and tinplate, may well have meant that this section of the population reacted more sharply to the economic uncertainties than did other elements of the Swansea population and had a greater incentive therefore to limit the size of their families for economic reasons. The cultural emphasis on respectability (and the fact that they hovered on the borderline of poverty rather than were plunged quickly into degradation as were other areas in South Wales) may well have reinforced these economic incentives to family limitation.

Secondly and relatedly, it seems likely that an additional incentive to small families, among the Welsh in particular, lay in the fact that the precarious economic condition of the working population made

[11] Census, 1951. Fertility Report, p. 1, iii.

advancement by the traditional Welsh means of education an urgent and pressing necessity. The procreation of small families was one obvious way of ensuring that the children born could be given better educational opportunities than was possible in large families in which the older children were forced into employment as early as possible to help the family in its desperate struggle to make ends meet and keep its collective head above the water of misery and destitution. By limiting their families sharply, the Welsh particularly in the Swansea population seem to have facilitated their own and their children's upward mobility—a traditional and culturally emphasized goal. Whatever the advantages to individual families of this severe restriction of family size, the evidence seems to suggest that the Welsh as a whole *in Swansea* are declining in relation to other elements in the population because their reproduction rate had dropped below that of these other groups, and below 'replacement level'.

MARRIAGE

This fall in the birth-rate, for all sections of the community, has clearly not resulted from any reduction in the amount of marriage. On the contrary, marriage appears to be becoming increasingly popular as more people than ever have taken this particular plunge—and on the average at increasingly younger ages. Titmuss has noted that 'for about forty years before 1911 marriage rates among women were declining' with a smaller proportion of women entering into matrimony with each successive decade.

> But somewhere around this time a change occurred; the amount of marriage began to increase. It has been increasing ever since, and in a striking fashion since the mid-1930's. An increase of nearly one-third between 1911 and 1954 in the proportion of women aged twenty to forty represents, as the Registrar-General has said, 'a truly remarkable rise'. Never before in the history of English vital statistics, has there been such a high proportion of married women in the female population under the age of forty and, even more so, under the age of thirty. Since 1911 the proportion at age fifteen to nineteen has risen nearly fourfold; at age twenty to twenty-four it has more than doubled. . . . There are now fewer unmarried women aged fifteen to thirty-five in the country than at any time since 1881 when the total population was only 60 per cent of its present size.[12]

Maiden aunts have in fact almost gone out of business, and fewer unmarried daughters than ever before survive into middle age, with

[12] Titmuss, op. cit., p. 99.

their spinsterhoods intact, to support elderly parents. In the light of these figures on marriage, the fall in the birth-rates is even more remarkable.

The fact that people nowadays tend to get married younger on the one hand and to live longer on the other means of course that there has been a very considerable increase in the years of married life that married couples can expect. This is particularly true for working-class couples. Early marriage is a good deal less common among the managerial and professional classes than it is among manual workers; it has been estimated that the brides of the former tend to be about two years older than are the brides of the latter (with the husbands concerned on average about two years older than their wives). The range of variation around these statistical averages in individual cases is of course great but, allowing for this difference by social class, the most recent figures point to the conclusion drawn by McGregor and Rowntree that 'over the past two decades of relative prosperity the age [at marriage] has dropped to low levels which are without precedent'.[13]

The details for Swansea need not bother us here:[14] it is clear from the census reports and from the evidence of our own survey that the pattern of marriage statistics for Swansea corresponds closely with that outlined briefly above, and that the following four conclusions of Titmuss are accurate for Swansea as much as for any other community in Britain: 'first, a remarkable increase in the amount of marriage in the community, second, more and more youthful marriage—especially among women, third, a concentration of family building habits in the earlier years of married life and, fourth a substantial extension in the years of exposure to the strains and stresses of married life'. And as Titmuss emphasizes, 'all these changes have taken place during a period of increasing emancipation for women'.[15]

More important than this increased incidence of marriage is the profound change that has taken place, and is taking place, in the character of the marital relationship itself, the crucial relationship within the elementary family. Michael Young and Peter Willmott began their book on the extended family in Bethnal Green with a

[13] O. R. McGregor and Griselda Rowntree, 'The Family', in *Society: Problems and Methods of Study*, edited by A. T. Welford, Michael Argyle, D. V. Glass, and J. N. Morris, 1962, p. 399. This chapter by McGregor and Rowntree is an admirably succinct summary of the 'fundamental changes in family life in England in the twentieth century'.

[14] It will be recalled that in our discussion of housing in Swansea in Chapter II we pointed out that the proportion of married persons in the total population of the Borough has risen from 38 per cent in 1921 to 50 per cent in 1951.

[15] Titmuss, op. cit., p. 101.

memorable chapter entitled: 'Husbands and Wives, Past and Present'. They contrast the old stereotypes of the working-class 'absentee' husband, an authoritarian figure with his life centred on his work-place and the pub, and of his wife trapped in the home and harassed with a succession of pregnancies, with the present emerging pattern of 'a new kind of companionship between man and woman, reflecting the rise in status of the young wife and children which is one of the great transformations of our time'. This is a transformation which is well recognized by the older generations living in the working-class neighbourhoods of Swansea, as in any similar environment anywhere in Britain. The older patterns persist with tenacity in some pockets, of course, but there can be little disagreement with Young and Willmott when they conclude that 'in place of the traditional working-class husband, as mean with his money as he was callous in sex, forcing a trail of unwanted babies upon his wife, has come the man who wheels the pram on Saturday mornings'.

We followed up our main survey in Swansea with detailed inter-viewing of several selected categories of persons within our random sample—subjects of pensionable age, subjects living in households containing at least one elderly person, and subjects who had been married within the last four years. In the latter case we interviewed just under fifty young couples in homes scattered all over the Borough —in the old working-class areas of the Town Centre and Tawe Valley, in the middle-class areas of West Swansea, and in the new and old housing estates. Our interview reports recording these detailed case studies of the elderly on the one hand and of recently-married young couples on the other were packed with familiar comment which echoed this theme of the profound change in the husband–wife relationship which is a product of a variety of causes and of the fundamental trends of social and economic change which we outlined for Swansea in earlier chapters. Working hours have become shorter, work-places separated from residence, work less arduous and physic-ally exhausting, most young wives go on working after marriage, at least until the first baby is imminent, and expect the pooling of in-comes to pay for the 'contemporary' furniture, the television set (which seems to have largely replaced the cinema and the pub as the main avenue of escape from the daily round) and the washing machine and the wide variety of mass-advertised household equipment— perhaps even for the car. The husband is expected to help with the household chores, to stay at home or go out for the evening with his wife, to help with the children, to push the pram, to be something of a Do-It-Yourself enthusiast, to drive the family about at week-ends (if they have a car), to share the major family decisions—over children's education or careers, or over finances and purchases—with his wife and partner. Our case studies of young couples, and of middle-aged couples, confirmed this marked change in the conjugal relationship, and the marked contrast (particularly of course in working-class families) within the recent past. There was of course plenty of variation from family to family—and still cases among young couples of a sharp separation of male and female roles, with the wife following the older pattern of conditioned domesticity and the husband frequently 'out with his mates for a night on the beer', but these cases seemed exceptional considering the vast majority of what have been called 'home-centred couples' among those we visited. And with this pooling of interests within the home, there has been more pooling of kin between husbands and wives—but we will be coming to this point in a later chapter.

It might be added in parentheses that this particular social change is particularly visible in the architecture, culture, and customers of the new pubs that have recently been built in the centre of Swansea to replace or re-establish those destroyed in the blitz of 1941. These new pubs clearly have a strong emphasis on the new concept of the pub as a comfortable, bright, modern place of entertainment for *both* husbands and wives, or young men and their girl friends, enjoying an evening out together. Consequently they look more like coffee-bars than the traditional pub (of which Swansea still has plenty, of course), designed with slide-rule precision by market-researchers to fit what might be called 'the contemporary housing-estate culture' of the modern working classes. The old dingy sparsely-furnished pubs of the docks and valley, with their 'men only' bars, traditional attitudes, and boisterous hard-drinking Saturday nights, are already beginning to seem something of an anachronism. There are those who will not think this a change for the better—though the crowding of the new 'coffee-bar' pubs leaves no doubt as to their popularity, or to the accurate assessment of the brewers' market-researchers.

THE AGE BALANCE

Increased longevity—especially for women—with the sharp reductions in mortality rates through advances in medical knowledge, improved standards of sanitation and hygiene, rising standards of living, and the development of extensive social welfare services, has combined with the fall in the birth-rate to produce a substantial change in the age distribution of the population. This is the third of the major demographic changes which have characterized this century: and it is of course an equally familiar theme of current discussion. The population as a whole has 'aged' at an increasing rate. Since 1871 the number of people over 65 in the nation has increased more than fourfold. The proportion of young people has fallen heavily: the average age of the population has risen by about ten years: and, as in all Western industrial societies, 'the social problem of the old' is causing growing concern. The new sciences of geriatrics and gerontology have been born, and there has been an increasing spate of sociological literature (to which we will contribute later in this study, and in another publication) on 'the social situation of the elderly'.

The two important demographic facts which are relevant here are that the proportion of the elderly has increased relative to other age categories of the population, and that the general increase in longevity has affected women more markedly than it has men.

Just fifty years ago, in 1911, old people over 65 years of age formed 3·9 per cent of the total population of the County Borough of Swansea as it was then constituted. According to the more recent figures from the 1961 census, this proportion has now risen to 11·7 per cent: it has, that is to say, trebled since 1911. The shape of the population pyramid—or 'beehive'—has changed, with the older generations better stocked than ever before, and the younger generations increasingly under-stocked with kin to support them should the need arise. In 1911, if we can put it this way, the ratio of elderly people over 65 to those in the filial generation aged 40–65 was one to five: by 1961 in Swansea this ratio had dropped to one to three—a very considerable decrease of some 40 per cent in this ratio of the elderly to the immediate supporting generation. From the point of view of the family system of care of the elderly, it is clear that this demographic change has very considerably increased the stress and 'burden of dependency' which arises. Titmuss sums up this situation by saying that in terms of demography

> we are half-way—or perhaps more than half-way—in a long-term shift from an 'abnormally' youthful population in the nineteenth century to a more 'normal' age structure in a relatively 'stable' population in the 1970's. Given the expected increase in the working population, this shift does not appear to raise acute economic problems. But it does involve far-reaching adjustments in goods and services. Inevitably, this is a painful process.[16]

Whatever the adjustments needed in society at large—in pensions, and welfare services for the elderly—adjustments of ideas and expectations as regards obligations within the extended family are inevitable

[16] Titmuss, op. cit., p. 60.

if this increased stress is to be accommodated. It is obviously a painful process within the family. Moreover, it is clear that in terms of demography, and availability of kin in the filial supporting generation (apart altogether from the change of attitude resulting mainly from the changed social position of women) the situation is likely to get worse rather than better. The proportion of the elderly can be expected to go on increasing substantially for the next fifteen years, to be 'supported' if need arises by the generation now aged between twenty and forty which, with the decline in family size, is particularly thin on the ground. We shall be considering the role of the extended family in the care of the elderly in a later chapter and will thus defer until then consideration of the implications of the demographic change which we briefly record here.

Of our total sample of 1,962 subjects (over the age of 21), 435 or 22·5 per cent were persons of pensionable age—that is, over 60 in the case of women and over 65 in the case of men. And of all the households we visited, 36·5 per cent contained at least one elderly person. This proportion is only slightly smaller than the proportion of households containing children of school age (45 per cent of our sample). The majority of these elderly persons were women. Taking only the elderly over 65 in our sample, the percentage of men was 45, and that of women 55; and as age increases into the seventies and eighties so does the preponderance of women.

It is becoming increasingly clear, as Titmuss has pointed out, that 'the problem of social policies for old age today and tomorrow is thus mainly a problem of elderly women', and that this situation has arisen because death-rates among women have been declining much more quickly than have the death-rates for men. The average expectation of life for women is now considerably in excess of that for men: according to the estimates of the Registrar-General on the basis of mortality in 1953–55, 22 per cent of males would reach the age of eighty as compared with 40 per cent of women. The dramatic improvements in the life expectancies of women over the last two generations or so are particularly noticeable in the case of *married* women, and are obviously related to the decline in child-bearing as well as to advances in medicine and hygiene.

> Not only have the hazards of child-birth and the frequency of confinements been greatly diminished, but the number and proportion of mothers worn out by excessive child-bearing and dying from such diseases as tuberculosis, pneumonia and so forth are but a fraction of what they were fifty years ago. Above all, the decline in the size of the family has meant, in terms of family economics, a rise in the standard of living of women which has probably been

of more importance, by itself, than any change since 1900 in real earnings by manual workers.[17]

The simple and obvious conclusion, of great importance to the structure of the extended family, is that a middle-aged couple are nowadays more likely than ever before to have their parents alive on both sides of the family (and their children their grandparents), with widowed mothers (and grandmothers) on both sides more likely to outlast their spouses. The three-generation extended family is more likely to occur, and to last for a longer period over the life-spans of those involved, than ever in the past history of the family—even though, with fewer births per union than was the case in the recent past, it is likely to be a good deal smaller in size.

THE POSITION OF WOMEN

We began this brief background review of changes in the basic vital statistics which have altered the shape of the family (and the shape of the population as a whole) with a stress on the revolution which has taken place in the position and roles of women. We return now to reiterate this fundamental theme which is so clearly vital to the understanding of the structure of the contemporary family. There has been little in this chapter which is a new and original contribution to the sociology of the family—except perhaps for the addition of some relevant facts from our survey in Swansea: the trends described and the points made are familiar to any student of sociology. No apology is needed for this. It is impossible to understand the contemporary family system, as we encountered it during our study in Swansea, without a strong sense of the nature and importance of these basic and dramatic—if familiar—demographic changes which have occurred well within living memory.

In summarizing these changes we have leaned heavily on the Report of the Royal Commission on Population, and particularly on the succinct, interpretative essays of Professor Titmuss. One further quotation from the work of this distinguished authority will serve to emphasize the essential point which has been the burden of this chapter:

> At the beginning of this century, the expectation of life of a woman aged twenty was forty-six years. Approximately one third of this life expectancy (or fifteen years) was to be devoted to the physiological and emotional experiences of child-bearing and maternal care in infancy. Today, the expectation of life of a

[17] Titmuss, op. cit., p. 96.

188

woman aged twenty is fifty-five years. Of this longer expectation only about 7 per cent (or four years) will be concerned with child-bearing and maternal care in infancy . . . Most mothers have largely concluded their maternal role by the age of forty. At this age, a woman can now expect to live thirty-six years. And if we accept the verdict of Parsons and Bales, Margaret Mead and others, she has also been largely divested of her role as a grandmother by the professional experts in child care.[18]

Titmuss adds in a footnote that whilst this 'verdict' of American sociologists 'may be true of middle-class white populations in the United States, there are no systematic studies in Britain to support such a conclusion. On the contrary, Young and Willmott have shown that in Bethnal Green, for instance, the mother, whatever her age, rarely ceases to play an important part in the lives of her children and grandchildren.' We shall be discussing our own conclusions on this point with regard to Swansea in the chapter which follows. There can, however, be no dispute over Titmuss's main point in the above quotation, that changes in vital statistics have produced a radical alteration in the maternal, procreative role of women—and thus an equivalent change in the life-cycle of the family. Compared with the situation at the turn of the century, the four phases of the cycle (which we distinguished in Chapter IV) have now taken on a different shape: Phase I (Home-making) begins earlier in the life-spans of the marriage partners with earlier marriage, Phase II (Procreation and Child-rearing) is much shorter with fewer children, Phase III (Dispersion) is shorter for the same reasons, and thus Phase IV (the final phase from the marriage of the last child to the death of the original partners) is very much longer both because of the shortening of the earlier phases and also because of increased longevity. Titmuss has recalled that sixty years ago *about half* of all working-class wives of over 40 had borne between seven and fifteen children. This single fact not only establishes the extent of the change in the shape of the family and in the roles of women which has occurred so suddenly, but also indicates the important conclusion that this is a change which has affected working-class families and working-class wives more recently and to a far greater extent than it has the middle classes.

The changes in vital statistics to which we have referred in this chapter have given rise, particularly in the post-war period, to eloquent and passionate pleas from a variety of sources 'for a re-definition of woman's role in society'. A recent book[19] by Alva

[18] Titmuss, op. cit., p. 91.

[19] Alva Myrdal and Viola Klein, *Women's Two Roles*, 1956.

189

Myrdal and Viola Klein has argued the case for such a 're-definition' in a scholarly, if militant and persuasive, manner. It is a book which is notable for a number of significant omissions. Significant, that is, from the point of view of the student of the organization and functions of the extended family in contemporary society. Take the following extracts, representative of the basic view of the family—and of the role of women—taken by Myrdal and Klein:

> The changed attitude towards ageing, the increase in longevity, the social need of stemming the relative decline of the working population, combine to make it absurd that the youthful grand-mother of 45 today should, *in perpetuation of an out-of-date pattern*, feel that she is entitled to rest on her laurels for the rest of her life like her grandmother who, at that age, had brought up at least half a dozen children and was prepared to settle down to old age. (p. 24, our italics.)

> Modern mothers who make no plans outside the family for their future will not only play havoc with their own lives but will make nervous wrecks of their over-protected children and of their husbands (p. 24.)

> Running a home is an occupation incidental rather than essential to the state of being married. After all it is done also by many unmarried women as well as by and for [*sic*] bachelors. Having small children certainly is a full-time job but . . . this takes up a relatively short and transient phase in a woman's life. (p. 25.)

The American verdict on the grandmother, cited by Titmuss in the quotation given earlier, is clearly accepted by these authors. But are grandmothers redundant? The grandmother of the older generation, after bringing up 'at least half a dozen children' did not settle down to old age: she settled down more precisely to a full-time and active career of 'grandmotherhood' in relation to the extended family. Is this an out-of-date pattern? Have younger married women no accepted roles and obligations in relation to the care and support of relatives, particularly elderly relatives? Has kinship within the extended family of linked households ceased to form 'the first line of defence in sickness, emergency, and old age' (as Hilda Jennings puts it[20])?

Myrdal and Klein apparently think so. Women's roles within the wider family are apparently written off. Their chapter on 'Contemporary Feminine Dilemmas' (Dilemma of Vocational Choice, of Married Women with Careers, of the Housewife—'financial depend-

---

[20] Hilda Jennings, *Societies in the Making*, 1962, p. 108.

ence and low esteem of domestic work') makes no mention whatsoever of what seems to us at least the familiar dilemma of wider familial responsibilities—of the wife, for example, torn between the needs of her own elementary family, or of her own employment outside the home, and the need to support and help an elderly parent or husband's parent. Similarly the following chapter on 'The Next Steps' to help the working mother deals with such things as day nurseries, home helps, increased provision of school meals, rationalizing housework, more convenient houses, extended maternity leave, and increased part-time work without any reference to the common role of 'grandmothers' in supporting the working mother.

In Chapter II, we stated that 14 per cent of the married women that we visited during our survey were working full-time. If we take only married women with mothers alive, and compare those working and those who did not work, it turns out that 36 per cent *more* of those at work lived in the same part of Swansea *as their mothers* than those married women who did not work. And wherever the mothers were living, 11 per cent more of married women working had seen their mothers within the past week at least than did married women who did not. These are facts which merely confirm a common experience —the importance and usefulness of 'grandmothers' in caring for grandchildren, cooking meals, helping with the housework, while the mother—and her daughter—go out to work. The geographical dispersal of related households over separate neighbourhoods, and farther, has limited the more extensive development of this grandmotherly role just at the time when the incidence of married women working is increasing substantially—as more and more women come to adopt the point of view advocated by Myrdal and Klein. That grandmothers are not more readily available to help is one of the strains of the contemporary system, though the help given is by no means insignificant. We shall be looking at this mother–married daughter relationship in our next chapter.

There is no question, however, that Myrdal and Klein are right in their arguments that social change and in particular the changes in the facts of demography have called for a recognition of the transformation that has taken place in the role of women—even if their viewpoint of the family system seems to neglect the importance of wider familial responsibilities, and even if their perspective seems biased towards patterns of behaviour and attitude which are characteristically 'middle-class'. Their basic point is 'that the structure as well as the size of the family has considerably changed during the last few generations. There are no longer maiden aunts and grandmothers living within the close circle of the family, and the separation of the generations has become a generally accepted pattern'. Against this background of demographic change, we consider in the chapter which follows the accuracy of this statement so far as the extended family in Swansea is concerned.

VI

THE EXTENDED FAMILY

IT is immediately clear from popular usage of the term 'family'—
certainly an elastic term which can be stretched to fit a variety of
concepts—that the contemporary emphasis is predominantly on the
domestic unit of husband, wife, and children. In relation to current
social attitudes, it is a significant emphasis. Consider the following
common usages: family allowances, family planning, a family man,
in the family way, starting a family, family doctor, family car, family
size (of tomato sauce bottles or soap packets), problem families,
homeless families—and so on. Here the reference is to the elementary
family—or the nuclear or conjugal or immediate or primary family,
as it is variously called in sociological studies. It is an ubiquitous social
group which is easily identified and described, in spite of its many
variations and complexities. With extremely rare exceptions, each of
these elementary families is set in a context of relationships extending
outwards from the domestic household to parents and grandparents
(or perhaps to married sons and daughters and grandchildren) and
variously to uncles and aunts and cousins, married brothers and
sisters and nieces and nephews, and a mixed collection of 'in-laws'.
In this chapter, and the two which follow, we are concerned to
describe these wider relationships external to the elementary family
and to estimate their social significance. This is the field of 'extra-
familial' kinship in Britain 'pervasive, intangible, still largely un-
studied, with its significance either not appreciated or in danger of
being over-estimated', in the words of Professor Firth.[1]

We noted in our opening chapter the enthusiastic interest that is a
common feature of Welsh households, particularly for the women, in
details of marriages and relationships. The simplest anecdotes about

---

[1] Raymond Firth, 'Family and Kin Ties in Britain and their Social Implications; Introduction', *British Journal of Sociology*, Vol. XII, No. 4, December
1961.

persons or incidents tend often to become impossibly long and complicated as time is taken to 'place' each character mentioned in a kinship context: 'You know who I mean, her father's brother married the youngest sister of Tom Jones, the headmaster of Pentrepoeth School. No wait now, it wasn't his youngest sister—it was his mother's sister's youngest daughter. You remember, Olwen: they lived in the corner house on Cwmbath Road. Her father was one of the Hafod Thomases . . .'. It is one thing, however, to point to the interest in, and extensive circulation of, this kinship information, through these gossip streams and through the Birth, Marriage and Death columns of the local papers, among other channels, and quite another to identify this knowledge with recognition of personal relationship. It is certainly true, as Firth points out, that one frequently encounters instances of a wife being able to give more detailed information about her husband's kin than the husband himself. But equally the woman next door or six streets away, though herself totally unrelated, may have the family of the husband concerned at her finger-tips, particularly if the husband's family is one of the older families of the district. This is a common experience in Swansea in the older, and 'more clannish' as they are often called, communities like Morriston or Treboeth or St. Thomas.

The following case illustrates this distinction between kinship *knowledge* and the *recognition* of personal relationship, in an instance where the parents concerned could conceivably be recorded in a single genealogical chart:

Mrs Murphy, aged 57, a Roman Catholic of Greenhill, a former tough and predominantly Roman Catholic enclave on the east side of the Borough, is a widow of a railwayman, and has two married daughters living away. Her son, Gerald, recently married Dilys from nearby Treboeth, a 'Chapel' area with an above-average incidence of Welsh-speaking. Dilys was pregnant and they 'had' to get married. Gerald and Dilys moved in with her six months ago and they now have twins, aged three months. There is fierce daughter-in-law–mother-in-law antagonism—'she even complains because I smoke' says Mrs Murphy. 'Tells everybody I waste my pension on cigarettes. Proper Chapel she is!' Mrs. Murphy has moved into the front room to be on her own.

Talking about Dilys's 'hordes' of Welsh relatives in Treboeth, Morriston, Landore, etc. she says 'You have to be very careful what you say about them to anybody—they have branches everywhere like Woolworths! I haven't seen any of them since the wedding and don't intend to . . . But a funny thing, talking to Dilys a few days ago, I found out that she and Gerald are *related*! Now isn't that a coincidence for you! Dilys's mother's sister married a grandson of my grandmother's sister—a cousin of mine that is—not a first cousin, mind you—not as close as that. My grandfather came over from Ireland and married a Swansea girl, and of course all the children were brought up as Catholics here in Greenhill. We never had much to do with my grandmother's side of the family. They were all Chapel, you see, and there used to be bitter feelings years ago between the Chapel and the R.C.'s. Her family more or less cut her off when she married an R.C. A wonderful woman she was too, so everybody says—had eleven children but only reared six. I'd no idea—nor did Dilys's mother—that we had a connection. Isn't it odd how these things happen? And I'd never have known if it hadn't been for a chance remark of Dilys's about her uncle having a wooden leg from an accident in the Duffryn Works in Morriston'.

There are several points about this example that we will refer to briefly later (notably the effect of cultural differences on the maintenance of relationship): the important point for the moment is to understand that we are dealing in the later remarks—albeit in an unusual and entertaining instance—with kinship information in its own right, and for its intrinsic interest in relation to social identification, and not with the recognition of personal relationships as an actual, or even potential, basis for social action. A man or woman may know the exact genealogical relationships including names, ages, and many further details of the kin of a brother's wife (and this is quite likely if they live in the same community, and quite possible under other circumstances) without recognizing any personal relationship to them. This fact, easily demonstrated from numerous cases amongst our informants in Swansea, leads us to question altogether the use of the genealogical method *for determining recognized and nominated kin*, a distinction introduced by Firth and his colleagues in their study[2] in 'South Borough' in London, which as the first empirical examination of urban kinship in Britain has become a kind of essential source book of stimulating ideas and concepts for all later studies.

In the first of the two studies reported in their book, Firth and Djamour discuss the problem of the differentiation of kin and distinguish between 'recognized' and 'nominated' kin. 'The former category is made up of all persons who are recognized by the informant as related to him by consanguinity or affinity (that is, through marriages), whether known by name or not'. The latter category includes only those known specifically by name, and is therefore smaller than the first.

[2] Raymond Firth, *Two Studies of Kinship in London*, 1956, p. 42.

Using this distinction they compute the average figure (146) and the range (37 to 246) for the recognized kin of the twelve households they were studying. They say that they were surprised by the numbers of kin recognized and point out that neither investigators nor informants 'expected them to be so high'. Similarly in her study, which follows this approach of Firth and his colleagues, Bott discusses the family relationships of three of her families and gives their 'total recognized kin' respectively as 156, 79 and 124. We must say that we find it extremely difficult to understand what these figures mean, given the characteristically arbitrary quality of this 'recognition' which here simply means knowledge of the existence of genealogically related persons.

If one had time enough to spend on this exercise, it would be possible to sit down with an informant, better still with a household group, particularly if this contains an elderly woman, and record the family tree thoroughly section by section to its farthest limits, in the memory of the informant or household group, including remote relatives through marriages. To a large extent, the 'fullness' of the chart would depend on the skill of the anthropologist concerned in prompting and concentrating his informant's attention on one section at a time. The problem is to know where to stop. Should the kin of a brother's wife be included, or the kin of a mother's brother's wife's sister's husband? They could be put on the family tree, but should they be? They would certainly increase the total number of 'recognized' kin (taken merely on grounds of knowledge) but what is the *social* significance of this exercise? And one can never be certain that relatives, in this vague sense, are not being omitted simply through a lack of concentration or temporary lapse of memory ('the name's on the tip of my tongue but I just can't get it now. It'll come back to me the moment you've gone, I know') or more likely, simply because the investigator is uncertain whether or not to continue the exploration of a particular sector of the genealogy. Further, one cannot be sure that 'the black sheep of the family', if any, or relatives with whom contact has lapsed or been deliberately severed for one reason or another, are not being conveniently forgotten. Given this approach, however, it is not astonishing that both the investigator and the informant would be surprised to find the numbers of 'recognized' kin so high.

At one of our early meetings to discuss our study in Swansea with colleagues in 'neighbouring' departments of the University College (history, economics, politics, geography) this question of genealogies in Swansea was discussed and some time was spent considering the use of information which could be obtained for specific families by exploring the records of births, marriages and deaths maintained by the Registrar-General at Somerset House, or by exploring parish registers to build up accurate family trees to compare with those produced through questioning particular informants. At this stage we were expecting to spend a good deal of time on genealogical explorations, not an unusual expectation for an anthropologist familiar with the use of the genealogical method in primitive society, where kinship is a major and basic element in the total social structure and where it is impossible to understand the social system without knowing the rules of relationship and how the actual lines of relationship are used as the basis for social action—whether in economic co-operation, factional alignments, succession to office, property transmission, and so forth. Such a use of the genealogical method may well be possible, and indeed essential, in the study of small rural communities in Britain.[3] It was neither practicable nor indeed necessary in Swansea as a whole, or within its local communities which in each case have inhabitants numbered in thousands. But the basic point is not one of practicability but of significance, and this essentially has to do with one's grasp of the minor importance of kinship in the structure of the total social system.

In a modern urban society such as Swansea, the system of kinship is fundamentally not a 'genealogical system'. Certainly individuals operate with a vague concept of 'near' (or more commonly in Swansea, 'close') and 'distant' relatives, with reference to genealogical connection but, and this is clearly visible both in the paucity and usage of kinship terms, outside certain immediate relationships the exact genealogical links of a relative to a particular individual are *irrelevant*. The only two contexts that we have been able to discover in which there is anything like a translation into action of genealogical relationships extending beyond 'the inner circle' are in the seating arrangements at a wedding reception, where in the lay-out of the tables the proximity of guests to the bride and groom appears to be determined by their degree of proximity in genealogical connection, and at funerals where similar considerations govern precedence in the cars that follow the hearse to the cemetery.

For these reasons we spent little time on the collection of family trees, though our questionnaire was constructed in such a way that a limited genealogy for 'close relatives' at least could be constructed

---

[3] As Loudon has recently demonstrated in his detailed account of a farmer's funeral in the Vale of Glamorgan: see J. B. Loudon, 'Kinship and Crisis in South Wales', *British Journal of Sociology*, Vol. XII, No. 4, 1961, p. 341. See also the excellent study of a West-country Village by W. M. Williams: *Ashworthy: Family, Kinship and Land*, 1963, Chapter Six, which includes a novel method of drawing a kinship diagram (Fig. 17) which is most instructive.

for each of the 1,962 families we visited. We did not follow the Firth method of calculating the numbers and proportions of 'recognized' and 'nominated' kin. The following quotation from Garigue's study of Italian families in London, included in Firth's report, seems to us to illustrate the problem in the use of the genealogical method that we have been discussing here, and the necessity of distinguishing between kinship information on the one hand and the sociological recognition of relationship on the other:

> The members of Household 3, for instance, included the head of the household's father's brother's daughter's husband's kin (thirty persons altogether) as affines. In this instance, however, not only did these affines live in the same village of origin as Ego, but they also had the same surname as the members of the household without, however, any known consanguinal link.[4]

These thirty persons are included by Garigue in the total *recognized* kin of 'Household 3' without any evidence apart from the knowledge above that any relationship whatsoever is in fact recognized between the household and this remote group of in-laws away in Italy. In our view this is an unsatisfactory use of the genealogical method in the study of urban kinship.

The fieldwork problem is further complicated by the notable absence of normative statements concerning who should or should not be definitely included as a recognized relative by blood or marriage beyond a very close range from a particular individual. For example, there is no rule determining whether a man should attend his brother's wife's father's funeral, though in practice we noted frequent instances of this happening. And what indeed is the nature of the direct relationship between the two sets of parents of a husband and wife, the two sets of grandparents with grandchildren in common? They have a strong 'connection' through their children's marriage and through their common grandchildren, but we noted immense variation in this direct relationship—from almost complete absence of contact to close friendship—in individual cases. With this extreme individual variation, depending on a variety of factors, it is difficult to discover what behaviour is socially *expected* towards any relatives other than those normally described as 'close', and even with these latter the exact description of roles in terms of expectations is difficult. A second complication arises from the perplexing and characteristic vagueness in the language of kinship, particularly with regard to the two most common terms for acts of kin—'relatives' (or 'my family') and 'in-laws' (or 'my wife's family', or 'the wife's people', or

[4] Firth, 1956, op. cit., p. 75.

'my brother's wife's family', etc.), the former of course being used in some contexts—'all my relatives come from Morriston'—to include some or all of the latter. It seems that the most satisfactory method of dealing with this situation is to build up as many cases as possible of actual behaviour in definite situations, and from an examination of the actual relationships of the actors involved to infer the regularities both in recognition and in role expectations, using techniques of quantification, wherever possible. This is the method that we have tried to follow in this study in Swansea.

Before taking up our analysis of the contemporary extended family in Swansea which we present later in this chapter and in the two which follow, we make some general comments about kinship. We must emphasize that we do not attempt in this book to study the kinship system as a whole from the intimate circle of the elementary family to its widest periphery. Our concern is with the immediate relationships outside the elementary family. And we will reserve our more technical anthropological examination of bilateral or cognatic kinship, as we observed it in Swansea, for a technical anthropological journal. It would be out of place here in a study intended for a wider audience. But, in the interests of clarity, it is necessary to present, if briefly, a coherent view of the kinship system and to indicate the main lines of the approach which we have found useful.

THE KINSHIP STRUCTURE

Raymond Firth, in a lengthy and characteristically searching account of the significant differences that seem to exist, from the point of view of the anthropologist familiar with the study of kinship, between kinship in primitive societies and that in Western society, adopts the suggestion of W. H. R. Rivers and describes the English kinship system as a *familial system* 'bearing in mind, *inter alia*, the lack of descent groups in depth'.[5] This is clearly correct. Our two basic terms—the elementary family and the extended family— refer to the two basic and socially-recognized groupings which characterize this familial system: the first a two-generation arrangement of spouses and offspring, the second an extension of this to cover normally three generations and as many elementary families as there are married children of the founding parents. It may of course include additional relatives from the circle of kinship immediately surrounding this core.

What might be called the dynamics of extended families arise from two sources: first and simply, because there are two sets of families

[5] Raymond Firth, 1956, op. cit., p. 18.

involved in every marriage, two sets of previously unrelated grand-parents linked equally to common grandchildren; and secondly because kinship is essentially a *process*, roles and relationships changing as the family passes through its cycle of development from its founding at marriage, through the phases of procreation and child-rearing, and through the phase of dispersion as the children marry and move out of the parental home, to its end with the death of the founding parents. We have referred earlier to this development-al cycle which underlies family behaviour and relationships. The characteristic balances and rivalries within the extended family arise because of the involvement of a number of separate families linked through marriages at various stages of this cycle.

The marriage relationship, linking previously unrelated family groups, is of central importance in our system. As we saw from Mr Hughes's account in our first chapter, the question of whom the children marry has a vital bearing on subsequent relationships. Yet this fact, as we pointed out in a recent paper[6] based on our research in Swansea, is curiously ignored in most existing discussions of kinship in Western society. The most common approach is one which em-phasizes consanguinity to the nearly complete exclusion of relation-ships through marriage. Recognizing the obvious fact, characteristic of the kinship process in all kinship systems, that a man's in-laws become the consanguinal kin of his children, most observers appear to think that the kinship system can be depicted adequately by con-centrating almost exclusively on blood relationships. Alwyn Rees, for example, in his study of Llanfihangel[7] discusses kinship in consider-able detail without any reference whatsoever to relationships through marriage or, surprisingly in his case, to the geography of marriage. Williams, in his book on Gosforth,[8] makes the following brief reference to in-laws, without further evidence or discussion, in his chapter on kinship: 'Relationship by marriage is also recognized in Gosforth but most people distinguish between kin and "in-laws". When informants listed their relatives they invariably left out their "in-laws" . . . Nevertheless ties by marriage are the basis for social relationships and in some cases these ties are closer than those existing between individuals and their remote kindred.' This latter point is very much in accord with the data collected in Swansea: so much so in fact that we have been compelled to make it occupy a central posi-tion in our analysis of family behaviour.

[6] Colin Rosser and C. C. Harris, 'Relationships through Marriage in a Welsh Urban Area', *Sociological Review*, Vol. 9, No. 3, 1961.

[7] Alwyn D. Rees, *Life in a Welsh Countryside*, 1950, Chapter VI.

[8] W. M. Williams, *Gosforth: The Sociology of an English Village*, 1956, p. 74.

The Extended Family

This almost exclusive emphasis on consanguinity has led to an approach which depicts any particular individual as standing at the centre of a series of concentric circles of kinship: the inner circle containing father, mother, brothers, sisters, sons, daughters; the second circle containing grandparents, uncles and aunts, cousins, nieces and nephews; the outer circle a variety of second and third cousins. Alwyn Rees in his Llanfihangel study gives a diagram showing precisely this concentric arrangement of kin according to 'degrees of kinship'. Talcott Parsons produces[9] a similar, though naturally more complicated, diagram depicting his view that the American kinship system is 'structured like an onion' and is made up *exclusively* of interlocking conjugal families. We agree with Parsons that the system is made up of interlocking families but would argue that this approach through consanguinity is an inadequate reflection of the social reality we are trying to describe. The arrangement is not one of concentric circles of the 'onion structure' type: it is a good deal more complicated than this. The kinship structure is essentially made up of families interlocked through a succession of marriages over the generations, each marriage forming a new link and bringing into effect a new set of relationships, and providing a point of balance between the two sides of the family.

We express this view of the system in the diagram on p. 203 showing over a five-generation span the interlocking of three-generation 'cores' through marriage. The diagram is built up with a series of these core-families, each with its characteristic T-shape in the grandparental generation with the two sets of grandparents linked through a marriage of a son or daughter to a common set of grandchildren. It is of course a generalized view of the system of relationships expressing a paradigm rather than any actual instance—though to emphasize the involvement through marriages of different families we use actual, if fictitious, names rather than the more conventional anthropological symbols. We have taken a five-generation view (though recognizing that it is rare in practice for more than three generations to be contemporaneous) so as to inject into an essentially static diagram some sense of the process of kinship and of changing roles and relationships over time as the earlier generations disappear from the scene through deaths, and later generations arise through birth. In this way we see the transition in role and relationship of 'David Jones' in the middle generation, our selected Ego—the anthropologist's Everyman—from son and grandchild to father and grandfather. We see also that the kinship network of any married

[9] Talcott Parsons, 'The Kinship System of the Contemporary United States', *American Anthropologist*, 1943, p. 10.

person contains not only his own consanguinal kin but also essentially sets of relatives through marriage, both through his own marriage and through the marriages of his immediate kin. The diagram emphasizes also that each married person 'may have his own range of relationships which coincides exactly with no other in society.[10]

We must emphasize that the diagram on p. 203 is not intended to be a representation of extended families; it is simply an attempt to reproduce graphically, given the inadequacies and limitations of any diagrammatic representation of the fluid, complex, dynamic process of kinship, the basic view of inter-relationships that we have used in this study. It shows schematically the reservoir or background of kin from which, under certain circumstances of physical availability and proximity of residence (among other factors), 'persistent groupings wider than the elementary family' emerge. These groupings can overlap in membership, and an individual may belong to more than one. It is these wider groupings which we refer to as extended families, adding that they characteristically, but not necessarily, cover a three-generation span from grandparents to grandchildren. To emphasize the importance of this link from grandparent to grandchild—which it may be recalled Mr Hughes in our first chapter described as 'the real tie'—we drew the diagram in such a way that it stressed the complex interlocking of these three-generation cores.

The variations in the composition of extended families can be immense, depending on the existence and availability of relatives in the kinship positions outside the elementary family. From the point of view of an elderly couple their effective extended family could be limited to their married children with their spouses and offspring—this perhaps is the 'classic' extended family in its various forms (according to whether the kinship system stresses a differentiation between sons and daughters, or treats them equally as in our system). A middle-aged, or younger, married couple may well belong to at least two extended families—one on the husband's side including his parents and his married brothers and sisters and their spouses and children; one on the wife's side including her parents and the elementary families of her married siblings. A variety of other relatives may be involved at all levels depending on individual circumstances.

Of the 1,962 persons we visited in Swansea 1,300 (or 66 per cent) were part, in one of a number of possible kinship positions—grandparent, parent, child or grandchild—of a three-generation core-family as depicted in our diagram. And of this 1,300 persons, 852 (or 67 per

[10] Lorraine Lancaster, 'Kinship in Anglo-Saxon Society', *British Journal of Sociology*, Vol. IX, 1958.

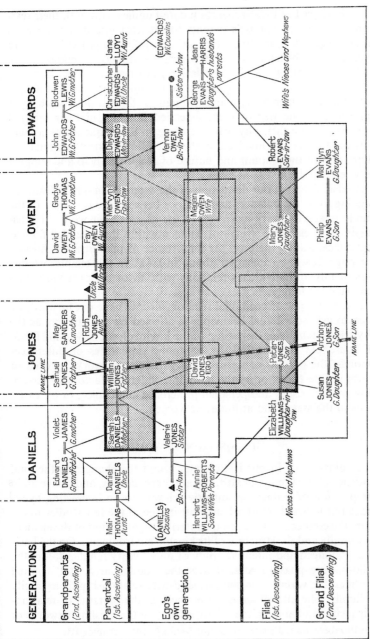

THE KINSHIP PROCESS IN SWANSEA—Interlocking, Three-generation Core Families

cent) were part of three-generation core-families with both their own parents and their spouse's parents (or at least one parent on each side) alive. We must stress that *all* our informants (with the rare exceptions of the handful of elderly persons with no descendants alive and with apparently no living relatives) belonged in some degree or other to extended families—at least in the minimum sense of simple recognition of membership and belonging—though there were great variations in the size of these extended families, in their internal organization, in their physical scattering, in the frequency of contact between the persons involved, in the psychological stress on relationships, and in the amount and nature of reciprocal help and support between members.

A basic theme in our discussion of the extended family in Swansea is going to be the balances and rivalries between the two sides of the family linked by every marriage. In the next chapter we will be discussing this essential structural balance within the extended family, and concentrating there on the importance of relationships through marriage. It will be a chapter about 'in-laws'. In this chapter we discuss mainly an individual's relations with his or her own kin within the extended family.

Using the view of positional relationships we have put forward, we need to ask how actual behaviour is affected by such factors as the physical proximity or dispersion of the kin involved, by varying forms of household composition, by economic similarities or differences amongst the persons concerned in a particular network, by class or cultural differences, or by the more imponderable factors of personality characteristics and personal preference and choice, or by variations in the status and attitudes of women.

THE POSITION OF WOMEN

The points made in our last chapter about the changes in the vital statistics of the family, in attitudes and expectations, and above all in the position of women are directly relevant to an interesting hypothesis put forward by Elizabeth Bott in one of the few studies to explore the connection between the internal organization of the elementary family and the structure of its kinship environment. On the basis of a prolonged and intensive study of only twenty families (all in the child-rearing phase) scattered over the London area, Bott[11] noted considerable variation in the husband-wife relationship from family to family. She also observed differences in the patterns of relationships with, and among, the relatives forming the kinship networks of

[11] Elizabeth Bott, *Family and Social Network*, 1957, chapter III.

the husbands and wives studied. She argues a definite correlation between these two phenomena. We agree, but for different reasons.

Where the husband–wife relationship was based mainly on a sharp division of labour and interests within and outside the home, Bott describes the relationship as *segregated*. At the other extreme were those marriages in which the husband and wife shared many of the household tasks, pooled their finances, shared the main decisions about the upbringing of the children or the furnishing of the home, had friends in common, entertained together and spent much of their leisure together in or out of the home. Bott describes this relationship as *joint*. The distinction is not unfamiliar in common experience. Clearly of course there is much variation (as Bott points out) from family to family between these two extremes, but, whatever the judgement of a particular case, there is no difficulty in agreeing with Bott that these two broad patterns of husband–wife relationship can easily be distinguished, among our Swansea families as much as within the small sample of London families described by her. Indeed it was this distinction that we had very much in mind in our previous chapter when we referred to the striking change that has occurred—comparing the past with the present—in the marital relationship and in the attitudes and expectations of the partners to the marriage itself, to the home and family, and to each other. Given a continuous range of behaviour between the extremes of 'segregation' and 'partnership', it seems clear that there is a strong tendency in modern, contemporary marriages to the latter extreme. We recall that it is this change that Young and Willmott describe as 'one of the great transformations of our time', reflecting the improvements in standards of living and the rising status of women.

As regards the external relationships of these elementary families, Bott observed again a range of behaviour between two extremes. Each family was linked in a network of relationships to relatives, friends, neighbours, workmates and acquaintances. In the case of some of the families she studied, Bott noted that these outside persons, associated with the family, knew one another and met and inter-acted with each other independently. In her terms they formed a *close-knit or connected* network. In other cases the outside persons linked as relatives or friends to a particular family were either strangers to one another or hardly ever met. They were linked separately to the husband and wife, but not to each other. They formed a *loose-knit* network. Clearly again one would expect to find great variation from family to family in the degree of 'connectedness' of their external networks.

In Bott's hypothesis, a segregation of roles in the marital relationship is related to close-knit networks in external relationships. On the other hand, a husband and wife with a joint relationship conjugally are likely to have a loose-knit network externally. 'The degree of segregation in the role-relationship of husband and wife varies directly with the connectedness of the family's social network.[12] Bott implies that this correlation occurs because where a husband and wife come to marriage from social backgrounds in which each belonged to families of origin with close-knit networks (in the sense above), they will each continue to be drawn apart into separate activities and interests. Their 'marriage will be super-imposed on these pre-existing relationships'; each spouse will be linked separately with people outside; they will be likely to 'demand correspondingly less' of each other; hence a high degree of segregation is likely in their relationship. Group pressures from the close-knit networks, group demands on the individual to participate in the network, group expectations about the husband–wife division of role and interest, draw the marriage partners apart into separate well-defined roles. Conversely, where the spouses come from loose-knit networks where the persons involved do not know one another or hardly ever meet, 'social control and mutual assistance' from outside 'will be more fragmented and less consistent'. Since the partners get little help or emotional satisfaction from belonging to a sort of collective network of kin and friends, they are thrown more together, help each other more with familial tasks, rely more on one another as companions. Hence the joint marital relationship which 'becomes more necessary for the success of the family as an enterprise'.

We have summarized this hypothesis at some length, if with little justice to the skill and sensitivity of Bott's analysis, because it is one of the very few original contributions to the discussion of extra-familial relationships in Western society, and has attracted a good deal of attention, and some shrewd criticism.[13] Our own methods of inquiry in Swansea were not designed, or suitable, for the detailed investigation of this correlation between the nature of the husband–wife relationship inside the elementary family and the degree of interaction between the relatives, friends and neighbours in the external social networks. This would require an intensive examination

[12] Bott, op. cit., p. 60.

[13] See Henry Fallding's 'The Family and the Idea of a Cardinal Role', in *Human Relations*, Vol. 14, No. 4, 1961, p. 341. Fallding stresses the point that role segregation within the elementary family is accompanied by a separation of male and female roles throughout a close-knit network, and that it is this fact which maintains the high degree of connectedness of the network.

of activities within households and a pursuit of all the individuals identified in the external network to see how well they knew one another, how often they met, and so forth—and how external demands and pressures were exercised. We did not do this for our Swansea families, nor—externally—did Bott in her London study. However, our extensive contact with a large number of families in Swansea did enable us to reach tentative conclusions on this interesting observation of Elizabeth Bott which has an important bearing on the understanding of the extended family.

We think that the situation and the explanation of her observations are a good deal simpler in practice than she makes out. Allowing for considerable variation in both cases, it seems perfectly satisfactory to distinguish two main types of marital relationship and two broad types of external network. There are families in which the husbands and wives appear to live very separate lives—in terms of expectations of how they should behave at home, or in their interests and activities outside the home. It is not difficult to cite examples of this type of marriage, if indeed it appears to have been much more common in the past with the wife tied down at home with frequent pregnancies and a prolonged involvement in child-rearing whilst the husband went off to long, arduous hours at work and thence with his workmates to the club or pub. Equally there are hosts of marriages, increasingly frequent, in which husband and wife have a good deal more than their marriage in common, with the husband helping with the washing up, pushing the pram, the wife going out to work—and both having common friends and going out together frequently in the evenings. Similarly there are those individuals and couples with scattered relatives and friends with little or no contact independently with one another, and those who belong to a 'circle' of relatives or friends in frequent independent contact. But are these two patterns —the one internal to the family as a domestic group and the other external—related, and if so how?

We see no reason why a couple whose marital relationship is joint, in Bott's terms, should not also be embedded in a close-knit social network of common *friends*, and could easily cite examples of this— though common experience surely makes this unnecessary—from our observations in Swansea. It is less likely that they would belong to a close-knit network of *relatives*. And this is a comment which is relevant to our discussion of the extended family. As Fallding has pointed out it is a question of the kinship solidarity of women in circumstances where women appear to have special roles and responsibilities and interests in maintaining contact with relatives, and in assisting and helping one another in a wide range of domestic tasks.

This stress on the extra-familial roles of women, and on links through women, which knits the extended family together under certain conditions, emerged quite clearly in our presentation of the case of the Hughes Family Morriston in the opening chapter of this study. The critical factor *both* in the nature of the marital relationship and in the internal organization of the elementary family, and also in the 'connectedness' of the external kinship networks is the degree of *domesticity* of the women involved. In our view, it is the social position and attitudes of women which most determine the structure both of the elementary family and of the extended family. The more domesticated the women, the more involved they are in domestic affairs, the more 'homely', the greater the likelihood of a sharp division of roles between husband and wife inside the home and the greater the chance of their involvement externally in frequent contacts with the relatives in their kinship network and in mutual help and interests. Given this level of female domestication, the extended family takes on the aspect of a sort of 'mothers' union' with the men concerned only marginally involved, and fitted in as it were through their relationships to the women.

Since for a variety of reasons, working-class wives are likely to have a higher degree of domesticity than middle-class wives, segregated marital relationships and close-knit networks are more likely to be found in working-class families. Within her small sample, Bott noted

> that the husbands who had the most segregated role-relationships with their wives had manual occupations, and the husbands who had the most joint role-relationships were professional or semi-professional people, but there were several working-class families that had relatively little segregation and there were professional families in which segregation was considerable. Having a working-class occupation is a necessary but not sufficient cause of the most marked degree of conjugal segregation.[14]

To find the necessary and sufficient cause of these observed differences within families and external networks attention has to be directed to the status and attitudes of women—bundled together in our use of the work 'domesticity'—and it is here that class differences are apparent. We will be returning to this point to discuss the behaviour we observed in Swansea later in this chapter.

It would no doubt be possible to construct a battery of sociological and psychological tests to arrange women, or men for that matter, on a scale of domestication. We did not do this, nor perhaps would it

---

[14] Bott, op. cit., p. 56.

contribute significantly to the understanding of the extended family (though it is a common failing of sociology to confuse quantitative precision with significant understanding). It is enough to agree that this range of domesticity exists—with domesticity being defined as the degree of involvement and interest in domestic affairs and household skills. There are clearly a multiplicity of factors (including personality factors) involved here. The vital statistics which we surveyed briefly in our previous chapter are vital in more senses than one: the working-class mother at the turn of the century who by the age of forty had borne somewhere between seven and fifteen children had little option as regards domesticity. Whatever be the precise causes and effects of particular demographic changes, and whatever the complex concatenation of social and economic factors involved, their cumulative effect—and this was the main point of our previous chapter—has been to produce a relatively sudden and revolutionary change in the social position of women. Many women of all classes, perhaps most women, simply no longer see themselves as unpaid domestic servants, confined to their 'women's place' in the home, fetching and carrying for the menfolk and offspring. Though older patterns of behaviour and attitude clearly survive tenaciously, whether in traditional working-class pockets in Swansea due to 'cultural lag', or in individual cases by reason of the personalities concerned, they have an anachronistic flavour. The trend of familial change is away from the former compulsive domesticity of women, and thus away from 'segregated' marital relationships and 'close-knit' networks in the direction of 'joint' marital roles and 'loose-knit' networks. The nature of this trend and its effects on the structure of the extended family form the basic theme of this discussion.

WHERE RELATIVES LIVE

The population of Swansea can be divided into two simple categories: those born and brought up within the Borough or in its immediate surrounding region in South-west Wales, and those born and brought up elsewhere who have moved into the Borough to live and work. It will be remembered that we discussed the present-day composition of Swansea's population from this point of view in Chapter II. According to the 1951 census, 81 per cent of the population were born locally in Swansea or Glamorgan, and a further 6 per cent in other parts of Wales; only 13 per cent were complete 'foreigners' by birth at least (though of course some of these may have been born in 'exile' and have since returned to the land of their fathers). As can be seen from Table 2.1, p. 46, the proportion of immigrants in the population has steadily declined since the censuses of 1881 and 1901—and, as we pointed out then, this follows from the increasing population stability which Swansea has shown in recent decades after more than a century of surging and rapid population growth. This fact, the decline in the proportion of immigrants (judged by place of birth) and the relative stability of the population, must be borne in mind in any discussion of the geography of kinship. There seems a tendency nowadays for people to speak as if we were going through an unparalleled period of population upheaval and movement with 'everybody on the move' much more commonly than was formerly the case. If we take the evidence from the censuses on the population of Swansea as a whole, this view seems quite wrong. It will also be recalled from Tables 2.2 and 2.3 (see pp. 47 and 48), that of the subjects we interviewed (and therefore now living in Swansea) 80 per cent had been brought up locally in Swansea or within twelve miles, and 88 per cent had spent most of their lives in this local region (54 per cent of them in the locality in which they are now living).

On the other hand we have to balance this picture of physical stability and strong local attachments at the gross level of the Borough and region as a whole with the evidence which we gave at some length in Chapter II of the substantial westward drift of population *within* Swansea and of the dramatic changes that have taken place in the distribution of population within the Borough with the spectacular growth of vast new housing estates, public and private, and the related decline of the old Valley communities. These are changes that have happened almost overnight, and it is these local changes—more than far-flung movements—which have most contributed to the firm conclusion in the minds of most of the elderly persons we talked to that relatives are much more scattered now than was the case in their youth. Let Mr Hughes of Morriston speak for them again: 'They don't cling like we did. Once they're married, they're off. We all lived close in the old days. The children are all over the place now, and you never know where they are going next. The Mam holds them together somehow but I don't know what it's going to be like when she's gone.'

We can also recall that an examination of our 1,962 interview schedules to consider the whereabouts of existing relatives by the rough test of the farthest-living relative mentioned in each case (see Table 2.4, p. 51), showed that only a quarter of our total sample of Swansea families had *all* their kin and in-laws mentioned on the questionnaire living locally in Swansea and the region around. Exactly half of all the families had at least one 'close' relative living outside Wales in some other part of Britain, and one family in five had at least one relative living overseas. This is a consequence of the steady annual stream of migration from Swansea (as well as reflecting the fact that immigrants often have ancestral homes and kin in distant parts). Important as these instances are of far-flung relatives in supporting the common view of widely-scattered kinship networks, it is, however, for most families the finer detail of movement and location *within Swansea* which counts most in the organization of the extended family. It seems clear that *relatives within Swansea* tend nowadays to live farther apart and to be more scattered over separate and different neighbourhoods than appears to have been the case in the recent past.

The town has grown and changed rapidly in residential area, and is more spread out: extended families tend in consequence to be more dispersed within the town. This increased physical dispersion is significant in its effects on the psychological cohesion of the extended family—particularly when contrasted with the former recollected situation, incised in the memory of the old, of the compact clustering of relatives in *a single homogeneous locality* such as Morriston or St Thomas, at least in a group of similar and neighbouring localities, say Sketty, Uplands and Brynmill, or the densely-populated localities of the Town Centre or in the Tawe Valley. We have to add of course that the wider distribution of related households in the Borough and outside must be balanced against a very substantial improvement in transport and communications: we will be referring to this in a moment. We must first establish the facts of the physical distribution of close relatives outside the elementary family.

Take first the question of how near married children live to their parents. This fundamental question formed one of the major topics discussed in the Bethnal Green studies of Young and Willmott and their colleagues in the Institute of Community Studies. Young and Willmott stressed the fact that their study revealed that 'more than two out of every three people, whatever their sex, have their parents living within two or three miles—either in Bethnal Green or one of the adjoining boroughs of Hackney or Poplar, Stepney or Shoreditch'[15] And it was apparent that not only did they live as near together as this, but they *wanted* to—for a multiplicity of psychological and practical reasons in relation to mutual help and support (particularly between married daughters and their Mums).

The following table shows how close to each other parents and married children were living at the time of our survey in Swansea. We give the figures separately for married sons and daughters as there are important differences here:

[15] Young and Willmott, 1957, p. 36.

Table 6.1: Proximity of Married Subjects to Parents (791 married people with at least one parent alive)—Percentages

Parents' Residence	Married Sons	Married Daughters
Same locality of Swansea	26%	42%
Other locality in Swansea	45%	38%
Region around up to 12 miles	9%	5%
Elsewhere	20%	15%
Total	100%	100%
Numbers	383	408

The clear conclusion here is that over two-thirds of the married men and over three-quarters of the married women we visited (and who had at least one parent alive) were at least living sufficiently close to have their parents living within the confines of the County Borough. At first sight these figures appear almost identical with those given by Young and Willmott for Bethnal Green, but this similarity is greatly reduced when we remember the sharp differences in the urban geography of Swansea as compared with that of Bethnal Green. Swansea has an area of 41 square miles as against the 1½ square miles of Bethnal Green. Most of our localities *within* Swansea are at least as large in area as Bethnal Green. The more accurate comparison is between our category 'same locality in Swansea' and the figures for Bethnal Green as a whole. Young and Willmott report that 50 per cent of married sons and 59 per cent of married daughters had at least one parent living in Bethnal Green: our figures for Swansea show that 26 per cent of married sons and 42 per cent of married daughters had at least one parent living in the same locality of Swansea. And our figures varied considerably in this respect by locality with the 'age' of the locality and its social composition, much as one would expect: the older neighbourhoods like Morriston, and the Hafod, and Sketty showing the highest incidence of proximity to parents (following closely the Bethnal Green pattern) and the new estates, both public and private, like Penlan and West Cross and Killay, showing the lowest incidence. We also asked those of our subjects who had brothers or sisters how near to them they lived. The proportions having a brother or sister in the same district are very similar to those referring to the residence of parents. Twenty-eight per cent of the men and 35 per cent of the women had a sibling within the same district, and approximately 40 per cent in another part of Swansea. It is not possible to make a comparison with Bethnal Green here since no figures for Bethnal Green alone are given.

Comparing Swansea with Bethnal Green and Greenleigh combined we find that the proportion having a brother or sister in their own neighbourhood in Swansea is 10 per cent higher. This was in direct contrast to the position with regard to parents and children.

We must stress, taking our Swansea sample as a whole, that there is no question that in general married children lived a good deal farther away from their parents after marriage and after they had left the parental home than was the general rule in Bethnal Green where the great majority had their parents 'living within two or three miles'. It may only be a matter of a few miles, but—as we pointed out in our discussion of the lay-out and social composition of Swansea's neighbourhoods in Chapters II and III—these extra few miles provide very important contrasts in social and cultural environment. It may only be ten miles or so from the Valley communities of the north-east of the Borough to Killay or West Cross (and less than five miles from St Thomas or Sandfields in the Town Centre to the vast new housing estates at Penlan and Portmead) but the cultural distance is great. The more dispersed a family is over different neighbourhoods—even within Swansea—according to their social and cultural character, the more likely it is that the kinship solidarity of the family will be affected. And in this respect the figures which are important in our table are those which indicate that three-quarters of the married sons and well over half the married daughters live *away* from the localities in which their parents are living.

There were slight but important differences between the social classes in Swansea indicating, much as one would expect from common experience, the greater physical mobility of the middle classes. The following table shows the differences that emerged in this respect:

Table 6.2: Proximity to Parents by Social Class of Subject (791 married people with at least one parent alive)—Percentages

Parents' Residence	Middle Classes		Working Classes	
	Married Sons	Married Daughters	Married Sons	Married Daughters
Same locality of Swansea	34	30	24	46
Other locality in Swansea	26	33	51	39
Region around	12	5	8	5
Elsewhere	28	32	17	10
Total %	100%	100%	100%	100%
Numbers	**94**	97	289	311

It is clear from this table that middle-class extended families tend to be much more widely scattered (particularly in the substantial differences in the percentages for parents living 'elsewhere') than are their working-class counterparts. The middle-class pattern is particularly affected by immigration into the Borough: it must be remembered here that we are dealing with the responses of married subjects to a question about where their parents were living. Many of the new arrivals in the Borough are persons of a professional or managerial status (doctors at the hospitals, teachers at the University College or Technical College, managers of new light industries and supermarkets, representatives of oil and tobacco and insurance firms, and so forth) and more often than not they have no other relatives within the Borough, or in South-west Wales for that matter. Their parental homes are 'elsewhere'—in London or Leeds or Lancaster. We interviewed a substantial number of these immigrants within our random sample, and they appear in this table to inflate particularly the percentages of the middle classes with parents outside the Borough and its surrounding region. Equally they influenced the patterns of proximity comparing our two cultural categories, the Welsh and English, which otherwise showed no significant variation by this cultural classification from the general pattern for the sample as a whole (shown in Table 6.1). If we examine class differences in the nearness of residence to brothers and sisters a similar pattern emerges. The middle classes are more widely dispersed, the really substantial differences being in the percentages of those whose nearest brother or sister lives 'elsewhere'.

There is obviously a whole long list of factors involved in the choosing or getting of a place to live. In the current situation of an extreme housing shortage in Swansea, which we described in Chapter II, most couples are only too glad to take anything they are lucky enough to be offered, within reason of rent or price, and condition and location in relation to the husband's job. But it is also apparent that kinship considerations play an important part, perhaps even more so because of the extreme difficulties in finding a place of one's own (and because of the extreme delays on the Borough's housing list). We have mentioned the sort of bush-telegraph service that relatives all over the Borough seem to operate on behalf of house-hunting engaged couples or newly-weds. There is also a strong tendency, particularly but not exclusively in working-class families, for a married daughter to try to get a house close to her mother's home: 'the boys usually follow their girls off to where they come from . . . a girl doesn't want to be far from her mother'. (We will be discussing this particular tie later in this chapter.) We did encounter plenty of examples (some given in our description of the household in Chapter IV), of married sons and daughters living remarkably and conveniently close to their parental homes—in what in some cases appeared quite astonishing proximity given the present difficulties over housing. In one street of small terrace houses in Sandfields, for example, Mr and Mrs Lewis—both in their sixties—had *four* of their five married children and their families all living within a distance of fifty yards: two daughters separately a few doors away on the same side of the street, and a daughter and son with their families almost immediately opposite. 'We were lucky', said Mrs Lewis 'the houses became empty all within a year or two as some old people passed on. And I got in first with the landlord. He'd always promised that he'd give me first chance for my kids when the time came, and I damn well saw that he did. After all, I've paid him enough in all the years that I've been here—him and his father. I was born in one of his houses round the corner. He won't do any bloody repairs, but I suppose I can't complain.'

Every year, according to our information from the Housing Department, there are something like a hundred applications from the 14,000-odd Corporation tenants to exchange their present Corporation house or flat for another on another estate in some other part of the Borough. The reasons given in the applications vary but the most common (in this order) seem to be: desire to live closer to an elderly and infirm parent needing regular help, increase in size of the family (perhaps through taking in a relative) leading to over-crowding in the present accommodation, change in the husband's job and need to move nearer to his place of work, and need to be nearer a special school for the education of a physically-handicapped child. The sympathetic Housing Welfare Officer helps to arrange these moves when they become possible as tenancies fall vacant in the place desired. And as in Bethnal Green and doubtless in any Housing Department of any local authority in the country, there are countless and continued applications at the Housing Department counter in Swansea by mothers earnestly requesting help in getting a council house for a married daughter. But, unless there are special circumstances, they have little hope of finding a short-cut through the housing list (on which the waiting time was at the time of our survey approximately ten years).

The business of finding a place for the family to live, within the limitations of income and convenience in relation to the husband's job, seems to be accepted mainly as the responsibility of the house-wife (aided by her female friends and relatives)—at least it seems agreed in practice that her voice will carry most weight in the final decision, 'I got this house through Mum's sister' said Mrs Brown of Manselton.

> She lives along the road here and is very friendly with the estate manager. I used to pass here every day on my way to school from my own home in the Hafod, and I used to imagine one day living in one of these houses with a nice bay-window. We started off with my mother in Neath Road, and then I heard through a girl at work of rooms going vacant in Mount Pleasant. I went round as soon as the shop closed and saw the landlady. We were there for six years —both the children were born there—but I wanted to get back over this way. My husband couldn't care less really, except he'd rather have got out Mumbles way because of his fishing. We've been here five years now and have properly settled. It's only a few minutes away from my mother's and she's a wonderful help with the children, especially if Tom and I want to get out for the evening. I tell Tom we'll get a nice little house over at Mumbles or Newton when he retires.

These comments and attitudes were echoed in interviews with a wide variety of informants—'after all', as one husband put it, 'I'm out all day. The wife has to spend a hell of a lot more time in the house than I do. It doesn't much matter to me where we are as long as she's satisfied. Personally I'd rather be back in Morriston where most of my mates live—but the wife comes from Townhill and won't hear of finding somewhere in Morriston. So that's that.'

The two relevant conclusions from our discussion of the housing situation in Chapter II were that the current housing shortage more or less compelled people to accept a house wherever they could find one, regardless of preferences for particular neighbourhoods or proximity to kin, and thus favoured the dispersal rather than the clustering of families; secondly, that it encouraged the formation of composite households, or 'doubling up', especially in the case of newly-weds living with one or other set of parents for a period immediately after marriage.

The widening range of marriage (which we consider in our next chapter), the diversification of occupations and income among the menfolk of an extended family and the great variation in the location and directions of work-places, together with this housing shortage, have conspired to undermine the solidarity of the extended family— particularly in the working classes where the present situation is a great contrast with that just over a generation ago—as a severely-localized social grouping. There is also a fundamental change of attitude to living 'close', and a difference of expectations. People not only live farther apart whether by choice or of necessity, they have

come to *expect* that they will live farther apart than did the generations of their parents or grandparents. And they want better living
conditions for themselves and their children than those which are
characteristic of the old Valley communities and the antique neighbourhoods of the Town Centre which are rapidly declining and indeed
disappearing with extensive slum-clearance programmes.[16] Recognizing the realities of the present social and economic situation,
parents as well as their married children have come to expect and
accept a wider scattering of the family particularly *within* Swansea—
and there are clear adjustments in the organizations and attitudes of
the extended family to accommodate this change. Though it is easy
to cite examples of a remarkable concentration of relatives in odd
cases in particular neighbourhoods, the fact is nowadays that such
cases are increasingly rare and are commented on as surprising. The
much more common situation, in all social classes, is that described
by Mr Hughes of Morriston with regard to the present distribution
of his married children scattered throughout Swansea, with only one
of his married sons in the next street, and one of his daughters about
'ten minutes away' on a neighbouring housing estate. There may be
regular and frequent contact back to the parental home, presided over
by 'the Mam', but, except at this central meeting-place, married
siblings are likely to have less intimate contact with one another
than they would if they all lived in the same neighbourhood. And
given the diversification that is likely within the family for a multiplicity of reasons, it is now *expected* that this will be so.

We will be examining the position of newly-married couples in our
next chapter, and looking at what we believe to be an important
change in the composition and incidence of composite or extended
households. It will be recalled (see Table 4.1 in Chapter IV) that at
the time of our survey close on one adult out of every five was living
in one or other of the forms of composite household—households
containing three or more married persons and thus 'extra' relatives
beyond those of a single elementary family. Households containing
a parent or parents and a married daughter were three times more
likely than those containing a parent and a married son. This is
evidence of the difference in roles and attitudes of sons as compared
with daughters, and particularly of the stress on the mother–married
daughter tie. In the case of living with and of living near, married
daughters tend to be drawn much more closely to the parental home

[16] See Chapter II, pp. 58–59, for a discussion of replies to the questions 'Do
you want to move from here?' and 'If so, where would you like to live?'—and
also for our examination of the preferences given on the applications for a
Corporation house of a sample of the 6,000 or so on the housing list.

(and consequently their husbands away from their parental homes) than are married sons. We have emphasized the position and roles of women throughout this study in relation to the organization of the extended family: the evidence on proximity indicates that though there has been a marked loosening of the patterns of propinquity this has occurred to a lesser degree with married daughters than it has with sons. The balance of the system is as it were tilted in favour of relationships on the wife's side of the family. This stress is particularly marked in the patterns of contact.

FREQUENCY OF CONTACT

When did you last see your father? Or mother? Or other relatives? We asked our informants a series of questions of this type, and found a good deal of difficulty in interpreting the replies we received. There is an obvious relationship between how near relatives live to one another and how often they see one another. But the patterns of visiting—and the whole perplexing question of 'contact' or nature of internal interaction and communication within the extended family—is a good deal more complicated than this. A social group by definition must have some degree of interaction and communication as an essential requisite of its existence but recognition of belonging cannot simply be related to a particular frequency of interaction on the part of an individual member. An individual can indeed have a strong emotive sense of belonging to the group, and be fully recognized as a member by other participants, under circumstances which limit his participation to a minimum level.

It will be remembered that we rejected the definitions of the extended family used in Bethnal Green which involved a high frequency of face-to-face contact, in that only those relatives were included who lived locally *and who saw one another every day*, or *nearly every day*, or who belonged in some sense to the same domestic unit. In rejecting these definitions we do not wish to imply that frequency of contact (widely interpreted) is not an important—and variable—characteristic of extended families: it is rather that we do not accept an arbitrary, if precise, frequency of face-to-face contact, nor the sharing of domestic functions, as *defining* characteristics. On the contrary it is essential, in the interests of accuracy let alone of common sense, to understand that extended families as recognizable and enduring social entities can be perceived to exist—and are certainly thus perceived by participants—at much lower levels of interaction. By either definition there would not be very many extended families in Swansea, and from those that exist many close relatives, say married children and their families living in another part of the Borough let alone those away in some other part of Britain, would be arbitrarily excluded. In our view, the vast majority of people (indeed all, with rare exceptions) 'belong' to extended families in the sense of having at least some minimum participation in relationships to kin beyond the intimate circle of their elementary families. The question is not one of membership but of discerning and explaining the variations in the levels of participation, and in the maintenance of relationship, and in the recognition of rights and obligations. The structure of the extended family depends on the nature of participation, both practical and psychological, on the part of its individual members. The range of variation is great, and is particularly observable in the patterns of contact which we are here considering. And here again there are notable differences in the behaviour of men and women.

Though the families we visited were a good deal more spread out than those described by Young and Willmott for Bethnal Green, the patterns of visiting appeared remarkably similar, as can be seen from the following table—which gives the information we obtained separately for seeing mothers and fathers in the case of both married sons and married daughters:

Table 6.3: Frequency of Contact with Parents (Married persons only with parent concerned alive)—Percentages

	Mothers		Fathers	
Last Seen	Married Sons	Married Daughters	Married Sons	Married Daughters
Within last 24 hours	31	54	29	47
Within last week	40	27	41	30
Week–month ago	14	7	15	9
Less frequently	15	12	15	14
Total %	100	100	100	100
Numbers	345	348	237	254

The differences in the behaviour of married sons and married daughters is clearly shown in this table—even though approximately 15 per cent of both see their parents less frequently than monthly. We must add that we are of course dealing in this table, as in most of the tables in this book, with what people *say* they do when asked: whether the responses include an element of exaggeration or not, they are an interesting indication both of behaviour itself and of the *expectations* with regard to these relationships. And there is no doubt that a married daughter is expected to be 'closer' to her mother than is a married son.

Over *half* the married daughters had seen their mothers within the past twenty-four hours and 82 per cent had seen them within the previous week. These are quite remarkably high figures of contact given the spacious geography of the County Borough, and are almost an exact reproduction of the figures given[17] by Young and Willmott for the compact, tightly-knit, 'familial' world of working-class Bethnal Green. The figures for married sons and for contact with fathers are equally similar to those given for Bethnal Green. It seems that we are here dealing with a regularity of behaviour which is a common feature of urban kinship in Britain. Married daughters see their parents more frequently than do married sons. Common experience—and our interview reports in Swansea—can produce a variety of cases which are exceptions to this statement, but its general accuracy is not in doubt. The figures suggest that married daughters may also see their mothers more frequently than their fathers, but the difference is not significant.

We found that there were variations in this pattern of contact between the classes in Swansea. The table below compares them:

Table 6.4: Frequency of Contact with Parents, by Social Class of Subject (Married Subjects only)—Percentages

	MOTHERS				FATHERS			
Frequency of Contact	Middle Classes		Working Classes		Middle Classes		Working Classes	
	Sons	Daughters	Sons	Daughters	Sons	Daughters	Sons	Daughters
Within 24 hours	39	44	27	56	37	39	26	48
24 hours–1 week	35	32	43	27	26	28	45	31
Total % within 1 week	74	76	70	83	63	67	71	79
Numbers	97	91	248	256	57	64	180	190

At first sight it appears that there are differences between the classes in the proportions of married children of each sex seeing parents *within a week*. However, none of the differences between the patterns of contact of the two classes which can be discerned are statistically significant. Significant differences only exist between the proportions of subjects having contact *within twenty-four hours*. This is of more than statistical significance. If these proportions are examined several points of importance emerge. First there is no significant difference between any of the figures referring to the middle classes. The middle-

[7] Young and Willmott, 1957, op. cit., p. 46.

class family shows a very even balance in the strength of relationships between parents and sons and daughters. Secondly the figures for the working classes show a marked stress on the relationship between parent and married daughters. Thirdly it is only the figures which refer to contact between *mothers* and daughters, which show a statistical difference between the classes.[18] These variations, though not large, show an interesting and important variation in family behaviour between the classes. It is concerned once again with the position of women.

In working-class families the roles and interests of men and women tend to be sharply differentiated—though, as we have argued at some length, the marital relationship has been undergoing a profound transformation in the direction of the 'joint' relationship (in Elizabeth Bott's terms) which was formerly more characteristic of the educated middle classes of the Edwardian era. The more domesticated women are, the more their mothers have in common and the greater will be the importance of the tie between mother and daughter compared with that between mother and son. Because for a number of reasons working-class women are likely to be more domesticated than their middle-class counterparts we should expect to find a greater stress on the mother–daughter relationship in that class. The figures presented in Table 6.4 show this to be the case. An emphasis on this relationship is shown only by the figures referring to the working class and it is the only significant difference the table does show. Only the rate of contact between working-class daughters and their *mothers* is higher than that of their middle-class counterparts: in fact the rate of contact between middle-class sons and *their* mothers is higher than that for working-class sons.[19] Only the figures relating to daily contact show these differences and this is consistent with the mother–daughter relationship being related to an exchange of domestic functions made possible by proximity of residence. This is a point to which we shall be returning shortly.

We have been dealing so far only with face-to-face contact between parents and married children. We asked also about contact with brothers and sisters living apart and with uncles and aunts and cousins and a mixture of in-laws (we discuss these later in our next chapter). Taking the whole range of blood relatives, 81 per cent of our total sample of 1,962 subjects said that they had seen a relative outside their own domestic group *within the past week*, and a further 11 per cent had seen a relative within the past month. Only forty-three persons (just 2 per cent of our total sample) claimed to have no living

[18] Significant at the 5 per cent level only.
[19] The differences are significant at the 5 per cent level.

relatives or to have lost all contact with those that existed. One in five of both men and women said they had seen an uncle or aunt on their father's side in the past week, and a quarter of the men and a third of the women had seen an uncle or aunt on the mother's side in a similar period, showing again the stress on relationships through women. Just over half the men we interviewed, and two-thirds of the women had seen a brother or sister living apart during the past week —and in all these cases the *frequencies* of contact were slightly lower for the middle classes than for the working classes though the *patterns* of contact were similar for both classes. The frequency of contact with brothers and sisters as well as with other relatives was of course more likely to be higher when the relatives concerned lived near at hand—and also and importantly when the subject's parents were alive (or at least one, particularly the mother). The parental home has a vital function as a central family meeting-place—as we saw quite clearly in the case of the Hughes Family Morriston in Chapter I. Over two-thirds of our subjects with at least one parent alive had last seen their mothers or fathers (or possibly both) and over a third a brother or sister in the parental home.

The fact that these high frequencies of face-to-face contact within the extended family, closely resembling the situation in Bethnal Green, were maintained in the prevailing situation of relatively wide geographical dispersal within the County Borough, is connected not only with what might be called the level of 'kinship sentiment' but also with ease of transport. We gave the figures for car ownership in Table 3.4, pp. 106–7. More than one household in four of our total sample had the use of a car: 59 per cent of middle-class households, 44 per cent of lower middle-class, 30 per cent of upper working-class, and 18 per cent of working-class households. There can be few extended families in which some of the related households do not possess a car—and car ownership is increasing at a considerable rate.

There were times when we felt we ought to describe the contemporary extended family as 'the motorized family' so often did references to the use of cars for maintaining contact crop up in our interview reports:

> 'I've got two married boys living in Swansea,' said Mrs Wright, a widow of 69 living alone in Brynmill, 'and another over in Port Talbot working in the oxygen works. My daughter has a nice little house in Mumbles. All of them have got cars—I wonder what my husband would think about it all if he was alive now. He was a fitter with the Gas Board and walked to work all his life. And the bus had to do us for outings. My daughter often comes over on the bus during the week with her little girl. And the three boys and

the daughter turn up here sometime over the week-end. Sometimes there are four cars parked together in the road out there: and one of them always comes over to take me out for a run on a Bank Holiday—they take it in turns. It's very convenient, and helps me to get about a bit.'

'My daughter's just taken her driving test—passed first time!' said Mrs Lewis, wife of a grocer at Bonymaen. 'She's the only one I've got and I missed her terribly when she and her husband moved over to Penlan. They come over every Saturday of course in the car. "But you just wait Mam" she said, "as soon as I've done my test, I'll be nipping over every spare minute for a cup of tea and a chat!" The buses are so awkward here to get to and fro from Penlan. My husband helped them with the deposit on the car so as to make things easier.'

'My daughter's husband, Jack, and my husband both work over in the steelworks at Margam,' said Mrs Charles of St Thomas. 'Jack calls in here every day on his way from West Cross to pick him up —and two or three times a week Gwen comes over for the day, and goes back with Jack in the evening. I get his meal ready for him then of course.'

'Both my wife and I come from Gloucester,' said Mr Rawlinson, aged 32, a pharmaceutical chemist employed in the Swansea branch of a national firm. 'I often say "Thank God for that"—it saves a lot of mileage! We often trot up to Gloucester for the week-end. We can be there by ten on a Saturday night after the shop closes. We take it in turns to stay one week-end with the wife's parents and one with mine.'

It's not so easy by bus, though Swansea is reasonably well served internally by bus services. But, given the distances involved, the bus services can be inconvenient, slow, and costly.

The middle classes not only have more cars, they have more telephones, write more letters, go away more for holidays (and stay more with relatives, and more of them have relatives to stay for holidays in Swansea (see Table 3.4, pp. 106–7). We must of course add that contact between relatives covers a good deal more than just face-to-face contact. Take the following brief extracts from interviews:

Mrs Turner, 64, wife of shoe-maker in Sandfields, with two married daughters in Swansea, one living with her: 'My boy and his wife are out in Canada. They emigrated about four years ago. He's doing well for himself—a foreman with some builders in Montreal. His wife's from the Sandfields here. They went to school together. She writes regular every two weeks and sends heaps of photos of the kids. I get my daughter to write back—I'm no hand at letter-writing, though I do add a few lines always. They never forget a single birthday in the family and have sent me some wonderful presents I can tell you. There's no sign of them coming back here —they seem properly settled now. But we keep in touch regular, and that's the main thing.'

Mr Rees, 38, a grammar schoolmaster of Sketty: 'No, we haven't a phone now. We used to, but the bills were fantastic. My wife's mother lives with my sister-in-law in Birmingham and they have a phone. Janet was on the phone to them twice a week—*trunk* calls, mind you. After all, we go up there in the car at least half a dozen times a year. So "that's that", I said when the phone bill came "if you've got anything to say write them a letter or save it till we see them". We had the phone taken out in the end—had to, or we'd have been bankrupt!'

Mrs Rhys Davies, 31, just married, wife of a solicitor in Langland: 'I ring Mummy [in Uplands] at least twice a day. Nothing urgent of course. I just make a cup of coffee and settle down by the phone. I don't know what I'd do without it. This house is so *empty* all day, and I hardly see a soul.'

Mrs Chappell, 70, widow of a railwayman, and living alone in Landore: 'Only one son I've got and he's an accountant for a firm out in Singapore. He's been out there twelve years now, both his boys were born out there. I've hardly seen anything of them. They come home for about five months every two years, but then they have to spend half that at least with his wife's mother in Eastbourne. They always come here for a month or so, but I don't think his wife is very keen on Landore. You can't blame her for that—she's used to something different I suppose. But I couldn't live anywhere else after all these years. I get an air-letter from them every month and of course birthday cards and Christmas cards. I've put all the photos they send me in a nice album I got from Boots. When my husband died four years ago, John couldn't come to the funeral of course but he wrote me some wonderful letters that I'll keep for the rest of my days. And he took over the paying of the rent at once through the bank. That was good of him, wasn't it?'

The extended family thrives on face-to-face contact, but it does not depend on it. It can exist as a recognized social entity for its participants even when contact drops to a barely-perceived minimum—the occasional letter or Christmas card, the unexpected visit after a long interval—and when relationships appear dormant or in a state of suspended animation. Witness, we might say, the return of 'exiles' for holidays, and, often after long absences, to attend a wedding or a funeral, more particularly the latter. Weddings or funerals, or other situations of crisis, can bring together and renew relationships between relatives estranged through some quarrel or who have simply drifted apart:

'My father died about six months ago out in Australia,' said Mr Floyd, 61, a storekeeper. 'He was 91 and I hadn't seen him or my mother, who passed on about ten years ago, since he emigrated in 1930 with the Mam and two of my sisters. My oldest brother, George,—he's retired now—lives up in Clydach. I think it must be about twenty years or more since I last saw him—and we were only a fivepenny bus-ride away. But his wife and mine hated each other's guts—God knows why, but there you are. George is a widower now —we didn't even go to his wife's funeral. I thought about it, mind you—but I was working shifts at the time and we were short-handed at the works. I've felt bad about it ever since—after all he is my own brother and we are the only two left here now. Still George turned up at the door about six months ago saying that he'd had a letter from the sister out there saying the Dad had died. Came down to tell me. Well since then we've seen a lot of George. His two boys are married and away in England. He comes down here three or four times a week, and the wife gets him something to eat and, like as not, we go round the pub for a pint. We were never very close even as boys but we've certainly got on well to-gether now. The wife is very pleased to have him down here.'

We of course encountered plenty of cases of quarrels, estrangements, bitterness, hostility, and antagonism between relatives within the extended families we examined in Swansea. But we got a strong impression, confirmed by the statistics on proximity of residence and of frequency of contact and illustrated briefly by the few cases that we have cited from the very large number that might have been included, of the vitality and meaningfulness of these sentiments of kinship. The extended family may be a good deal smaller than it was formerly and more scattered but the psychological responses to relationships beyond the limited circle of the domestic group seemed strong and important in the lives of the people we interviewed though equally there was much idiosyncratic variation here from person to person. Most people, however, and particularly women, seemed interested in describing their relationships with kin and in-laws as if they mattered, and clearly had a sense of belonging to a 'family' wider than that made up of their spouse and children. Proximity of residence is of course an important factor in 'boosting' this sense of relationship: but it is not the only factor. These sentiments of kinship can of course be deceptive: they can easily suggest that these external relationships have a reality, a significance, a social importance which may not be supported when we turn to examine the translation of sentiment into action. Given the relationships we have been describing, what is the practical importance, what are the functions, of the extended family in a contemporary urban society?

THE FUNCTIONS OF THE EXTENDED FAMILY

'Is it my *duty* to visit my relatives regularly?' asked the Personal Posers column of *The Church Times* in the week we began writing this report. Perhaps the most significant point about questions of this type, and we heard many similar questions in Swansea about responsibility and duty regarding kinship ties outside the elementary family, is that they are asked at all. Vagueness and uncertainty about the rules of behaviour so far as these extra-familial relationships are concerned, and the personal dilemmas that arise in this connection, seem a widespread feature of present-day Britain. Compare elderly Mr Hughes's comment, speaking about the kin-infested world of common adversity and mutual dependence in which he grew up in Morriston: 'You could count on your relatives and you didn't have to ask. We knew our duty and we did it'. Have things changed? In the age of the Welfare State and of comparative affluence, is the extended family still the 'first line of defence' in domestic crisis?

We have already cited, in brief 'capsule' form, a considerable number of 'cases' for one reason or another in this and previous chapters, beginning with extracts from our many conversations with Mr Griffith Hughes of Morriston. Though they were included as illustrations of particular points in our discussion, even a quick re-examination of them reveals a wide variety of situations in which extra-familial obligations are being recognized and met. We now come to discuss this subject directly. There have been many points in this book when we have felt a strong temptation to dam the flow of sociological verbiage and speculative comment, and to concentrate rather on the production of 'cases' out of the voluminous hat of our notebooks. It is a strong temptation now. The raw material of people's lives, suitably selected, is often a good deal more interesting—and certainly more readable—than the prosaic gloss of the sociologist.

There seems little point in our giving space and time to an extended discussion of the paired and reciprocal roles that form the consanguinal building blocks of the extended family: mother/married daughter, mother/married son, father/married daughter, father/married son, grandparent/grandchild, married brother/married sister, and so on. We accept that the 'key' relationships here are those between the mother and her married children, particularly that between a mother and her married daughter. The evidence from Swansea only confirms that the familial system is 'matri-centred', as it has been described and elaborated at very considerable length, in a number of other studies in urban areas in Britain, notably of course in the Bethnal Green studies. It seems sufficient to say that the vivid descriptions of Young and Willmott of the close and enduring tie, expressed both in terms of practical domestic organization and in emotional responses, between mother and married daughter in Bethnal Green could easily have been written about Swansea, particularly for the 'traditional' working-class districts but also, if diluted slightly, for the other social classes. We have already discussed this relationship briefly, and given illustrations, in previous chapters and earlier in this chapter. Further elaboration would add little further for Swansea, and little to what is already now well accepted from other studies. And we will in any case be returning to this subject of roles when we consider relationships through marriage, and the balances between 'the two sides of the family', in our next chapter. It seems more useful here to concentrate our attention on the functions of the extended family in contemporary Swansea as they appeared from our observations and analysis—and this is what we now do.

The term 'functions' has of course many complex meanings in sociological theory: here we simply use it to mean 'purposes served'. Our examination of a variety of extended families in Swansea suggests that this vague, variable, amorphous, but recognizable (both by the participants and the social observer) form of extra-familial kinship grouping serves two main and identifiable functions both of considerable social importance. We call these the function of social identification, and the function of social support in crisis—and discuss each briefly and in turn below. They are closely related and 'operate simultaneously or merge into one another in particular instances'.[20] If we take the word 'practical' to mean here concerned with social action, we can say—rather in the style of the radio parlour game—that the former function is mainly psychological with practical connections whereas the latter is mainly practical with psychological connections.

The kinship universe surrounding the elementary family in its

[20] Loudon in his fascinating account of kinship in the Vale of Glamorgan discerns 'three main kinds of function of extra-familial kin ties', namely—ceremonial, evaluative, and supportive. By 'evaluative' he appears to mean the way in which the community uses kinship ties to ascribe status to a particular individual and evaluate his behaviour. This function we include in our wider term 'social identification'. The ceremonial function—assembly at weddings and funerals for example—appears to us not to be separate, but rather an *aspect* of the other two functions described above. See J. B. Loudon, loc. cit., 1961, p. 339.

separate household is not a vague and blurred world of kinship ties extending outwards to an increasingly-remote and unorganized collection of relatives by blood and marriage. It was clear that our informants do not think of it in this undifferentiated way—or even with just the simple distinction between 'near' and 'distant' relatives. They think of their kin in terms of *families*, dividing the kinship universe into sectors as it were, 'wholes', on both sides of the family through their parents, with other familial sectors through their spouse. And they identify themselves, or are identified by others, through these external relationships to these familial sets of kin and in-laws. This identification is an important factor in the finer assessments of social status within a community, and involved in it are important if diffuse elements of social control and restraint and standard. We have referred on several occasions to the keen local interest in 'placing' people in this wider context of kin relationships: 'he's one of the Greenhill Murphys [or the Cwmrhydyceirw Morrises]' or 'I must say I'm surprised to hear that he's in trouble with the police. After all he comes from a very good family in Morriston, deacons on both sides and never a word said against them anywhere.' The individual ceases at once to be anonymous, or the elementary family isolated and 'strange to all others' (in Ruth Benedict's phrase about the family: 'genus Americanum') once these links can be established and the wider families discerned and identified.

It is of course a noticeable fact that the older people get—and the more their own generation of friends and neighbours and workmates gets thinned out with deaths—the greater the interest they take in kinship relationships both within their own families and in the surrounding community. In an important way this interest seems a defence against isolation, against sense of loneliness or confusion in the face of rapid change. Kinship networks extend backwards to previous generations, sideways to one's own generation, downwards to the new and the young. They give a sense of stability and belonging. This psychological reaction is strengthened of course if the related households live close at hand, within easy reach. These extended family relationships are a most important ingredient in that sense of 'community' which characterizes the older neighbourhoods of the town where families have been linked through successive marriages over the generations in a complex web of relationship—vague perhaps, rarely traced in detail, but *known*. Here lies the basis of community solidarity and 'belonging': and the basis of the great contrast with the new housing estates and new middle-class residential areas.

But as we have seen proximity of residence is not an essential

228

element in the structure of the contemporary extended family, nor is a high frequency of face-to-face contact. Relationships can lie dormant for long periods in terms of social interaction and be revived suddenly and even spectacularly in a situation of need or crisis.

'There was a knock on the door one Sunday evening,' said Mrs Price of Cwmbwrla, 'and the chap standing there said "I'm Donald from Bolton. Hullo, Auntie Rhoda. Dad said to come and look you up. I've been sent down here for four months by McAlpine's. Can you put me up?" "Good God!" I said "come in, boy!" I hadn't seen him since he was about six, more than thirty years ago I suppose. My brother moved up to Lancashire in the Depression and made his home there—never came back this way. I could hardly understand Donald's accent with all that funny Lancashire twang. But of course he stayed with us, and went round to see all the family down here. He even turned up my cousins over in Llanelly and I haven't seen them for years. He just walked in the British Legion Club one Sunday and said to one of the older chaps "Are there any Loosemores here tonight? I'm Dick Loosemore's boy from Bolton." They turned out half a dozen relatives (that he'd never seen) for him in no time, and many of Dick's friends from the old days.'

Donald probably never looked back during the whole of his four months in Swansea. He made good use of his extended-family identity card. There were many instances of this type, of individuals using wider familial relationships to provide themselves with a social identification (and help where needed) in situations where they would otherwise be isolated and anonymous.

As in all aspects of familial behaviour that we examined, individual variation within families and from family to family was very great. There were plenty of instances of individuals, particularly those who seemed to have risen far and fast, avoiding mention of family connections in precise terms, or perhaps appearing to stress, in conversation with us, only those links to well-placed, well-set-up, and status-giving relatives in their extended family networks. We noticed that this more often happened with persons in this situation whose relatives live locally rather than with those who hailed from more distant places who perhaps felt much freer to take a 'rosy' view of their family backgrounds making appropriate adjustments in the occupations and social standing of the kin they mentioned. It is a common human foible to 'scorn the base degrees by which we did ascend', in the words of Cassius. And we have to remember that, for whatever reason, 115 persons (of the 2,272 originally selected from the Electoral Register) refused altogether to answer our questions on family relationships, the refusal rate being a good deal higher in the middle-class than in the working-class areas. However, 1,962 did, and from their replies, as from our wider observations in Swansea, we got a strong sense of the function of the extended family as a mechanism of social identification. It is an important function in tempering the tendency to impersonal, faceless anonymity which seems an inherent characteristic of life in crowded urban areas.

Recognition of relationship, awareness of belonging, a sense of identification and reciprocal interest with relatives beyond the elementary family—the stronger these sentiments of kinship are the more effective is the extended family in its complex function of support in need or crisis. But strong sentiment does not necessarily imply a willingness to bear the heavier burden of kinship. As we shall see, much depends on the attitudes and expectations of women.

Need can take a variety of forms from knitting or baby-sitting,[21] help with confinements, assistance with cleaning or shopping, companionship in loneliness, providing hospitality during holidays, help in finding a job or advice with careers, to sustained financial help or the provision of housing accommodation for lengthy periods (or of loans for house purchase) and crisis can be acute as in cases of sudden illness or accident or at times of death, or it can be chronic as in the care of an aged and infirm parent needing constant nursing and attention. Here we must emphasize that in the vast majority of cases of all kinds which we recorded, the need or crisis concerned domestic affairs of one type or another and the actual help given (apart from the particular instance of financial help—though women often had a hand in this somewhere) was given by women. That is, by mothers or aunts or married daughters or daughters-in-law, or by sisters or nieces. Men are certainly 'involved', but in nine cases out of ten the tasks concerned are performed by women—and this of course is not surprising since we are dealing with such things as domestic nursing, child-rearing, house-cleaning, washing, shopping, and the whole gamut of household affairs and skills. It is the world of the mothers' union. We stress this obvious point because here we must return to our argument as to the relationship between the degree of domesticity of the women involved and the effective functioning of the extended family as the first line of defence in domestic crisis.

We have given enough illustrations already of the various types of assistance given to one another by relatives within the extended

[21] Of our sample 332 said that they had had someone in recently to look after the children while they went out for the evening. In 87 per cent of the cases, the baby-sitter was a relative (in over 50 per cent a parent of either spouse).

family; it would not be difficult to include here a long list of further examples of kinship support in times of need and crisis of the kinds mentioned in the first sentence of the above paragraph. For most readers this will be a familiar theme from their own personal experience. And we are in any case going to deal separately in another chapter with the special problems that can arise in the chronic crisis of old age. We accordingly stress in the few examples below cases which illustrate the changing attitudes of women and the personal dilemmas which, in the view at least of many of our older informants with whom we have discussed this question at length, seem increasingly common with the widening interests and activities of most younger women compared with the situation in the days of their mothers and grandmothers.[22]

> 'My mother and I get on quite well,' said Mrs Doreen Fry, 33, wife of an insurance agent living in Cockett, 'but she just doesn't understand that people's ideas have changed. Whenever she comes over here, she complains that the house is untidy, that the children should be in bed by this time, or not out on the street playing on a Sunday, and so on. We just have our differences, that's all. Harold and I go over to visit them regularly in Manselton (and to his mother in Brynmill) and that should be enough, I say. When the youngest child was born I had a job to stop her coming over and taking over the house while I went in the nursing home. She didn't like it at all when I said that Harold could manage perfectly well on his own *and* look after Peter [aged 3]. The woman next door looked after Peter while Harold was out at work—they're a young couple just like us—and we had a woman in twice a week for about a month to do the cleaning. We just preferred it that way.'

> 'Since I've got myself a job on the Trading Estate up at Fforest-fach' said Mrs Lilian Roberts, 'I just don't get time to go over and see my mother [in Llansamlet] I've been worried stiff about her— she lives all on her own there in that old house and is always ill. After all she is over 70 now. But what am I to do? I just couldn't have her here—we haven't enough room for that. Bill [her husband] uses the spare bedroom for his photography and I couldn't ask him to clear it all out. After all it's his home as much as mine. And I couldn't give up my job now—I like the independence for one thing

[22] There are constant references to this change in newspaper reports of speeches and incidences—and sometimes sensational examples of familial neglect. *The Western Mail* of 4 July 1963 reports the Chairman of the County Children's Committee as saying that working wives and the continuing bingo craze are two of the reasons why it is difficult to find enough homes for Glamorgan children deprived of home life. The report is headed 'bingo followers are shunning orphans'.

and the extra money is putting us on our feet nicely. We saved up enough to go to take the children up to Butlin's at Pwllheli last August, and we had a really wonderful time.'

'Yes, my Dad lives with my sister and her husband in our old house at Gorseinon [just outside the County Borough]' said Mr Bernard Harding, 38, a draughtsman living in the Uplands, 'We go over occasionally in the car for an evening. He's been retired for about seven years now—worked all his life in the steelworks in Llanelly. He's taken to coming over to stay with us every so often "for a change". The wife gets really furious but it's very awkward. We can't ask him to stay away—or to go after a week. We haven't any children of our own and we like to get about in the evenings, and we often have friends in for the evening. And of course Mary's out at work all day, and doesn't look forward I can tell you to cooking and cleaning up after Dad when she gets home at night. We've got things nicely organized when we're on our own. You can't blame Mary—she's quite fond of him—but not *living* with us.'

'I don't interfere,' said Mrs Maggie Thomas, 62, wife of a brick-layer living on the Corporation estate at Townhill, 'that's my golden rule. I've got two daughters married and both in Swansea [Brynmill and Penlan] and a married son away in Penarth—and they've all got very nice families. They come here when they feel like it: they always know the door's open. But I've learnt to keep my tongue to myself. I mean, well, young people nowadays are quite different to what we were in our day. They like to be independent for one thing, and they seem to go gadding about much more than we ever did. And as soon as a thing is old they think they can just throw it away and get another. When I remember the darning and patching I had to do! Still I let them get on with it. They know they can always come here for help if they want it, but apart from a couple of weeks when the babies are due, they seem to manage very well on their own. I think they try to have their cake and eat it, myself—but then perhaps I'm old-fashioned. Mind we've got five lovely grandchildren—I will say that. It's a pleasure to see them looking so bonny.'

These illustrations will suffice: the experience is not unfamiliar. People are rarely outspoken to a stranger, however sympathetic, on these delicate inter-personal conflicts within the essentially 'private' world of an individual's extended family. For the most part we deal less with direct and frank statements here (which offend the traditional expected ideals of how relatives should behave to one another) but with the subtleties and nuances of comment, with half-spoken criticism and half-expressed bitterness. But, below the surface, the

232

conflicts and dilemmas are real none the less. Beneath the sentimental façade of kinship feelings—constantly reiterated—lie these practical difficulties of explicit burdens. We can only record our impression that these difficulties are increasing and that these conflicts over expectations between the generations are becoming more common, particularly in 'modern' working-class families recently emancipated from an older family tradition. We will be looking again at this question in our chapter on the elderly.

We might just add that we of course distinguish the kind of veiled conflict which is a consequence of the change in the attitudes of women to domestic roles from the bantering, jocular criticism which seems a common ingredient of many social relations between young and old, and of which the following is an example that we must include somehow:

> 'He sits there all damn day, complaining about everything he lays eyes on,' said Mrs Olwen Morgan, an exceptionally robust and cheerful middle-aged woman whose doddering, elderly father lives with her and her family in Landore. 'It's like having another child about the place. I tell him to shut up forty bloody times a day but he don't take no notice. I'm always telling him I'll have him put away. There's no end to his "do this, and fetch that". Why, he even makes me warm his collar-stud for him!'

The old man clearly doesn't know when he's well off: a *warmed* collar stud on a cold winter's morning seems the height of luxury to us.

In the following chapter we turn to consideration of relationships through marriage, and of the internal balances between the two sides of the family. Some of the ground covered in this chapter will now be re-traversed from another point of view so as to extend and develop the picture we are presenting of roles and relationships within the extended family. But first let us summarize briefly the main points of the argument so far.

We have dealt here mainly with two measurements—proximity of residence and frequency of contact—and concentrated our attention largely on the relationships between parents and married children. We have observed that, in physical scattering as well as in attitude, the tight bonds of the wider family appear to have been loosened considerably. But although the extended family in Swansea is un-doubtedly more dispersed—over a spacious County Borough—than that described by Young and Willmott for 'traditional' working-class

Bethnal Green in the East End of London, the frequencies of face-to-face contact in the two areas are almost identical. We have explained this by arguing that the level of kinship sentiment does not depend essentially on close physical proximity and that the good internal communications of Swansea—and particularly the high and increasing ownership of cars in the contemporary 'motorized family'—make high frequencies of personal contact possible over much wider distances than was formerly the case. Personal face-to-face contact is not, however, an *essential* characteristic of effective membership of the extended family as a recognized and recognizable social entity. Close relatives living far away, even overseas, can be fully involved in the extended family through letters and cards and photographs, or by the use of the telephone in some instances. Relationships can lie dormant for long periods to be suddenly re-activated in need or under special circumstances. In this respect, we have emphasized (though this is essentially a hazardous matter of judgement on the part of the observer) that *expectations* have changed regarding proximity of residence, and that a greater degree of physical mobility, especially in the working classes, is now accepted as normal and natural by both parents and children.

In the tables given and in the cases cited, the importance of the parent/married child/grandchild nexus, which formed the basis of our diagrammatic view of the kinship structure, has been stressed. The data has confirmed for Swansea the well-accepted view of sociological studies of urban kinship of the significance of the mother/married daughter bond—and the general and characteristic emphasis on the roles of women and on relationships through women. We have argued that the profound and recent changes in the social position of women, correlated with changes in the vital statistics of the family, are now just beginning to exert their effort on the whole atmosphere and character of family life. This effect is more noticeable in working-class families than in middle-class families because in the former the change has been more recent and more sudden. Otherwise the general patterns of behaviour—if not the culture—in the family life of the middle classes and that of the working classes appear very similar. There are slight and subtle differences and they have mainly to do with the greater physical mobility of the middle classes. In the two measurements—proximity and contact—we found no significant differences between the Welsh and the non-Welsh in Swansea (we will be discussing this further in our next chapter.).

The picture that emerges, then, is of a vigorous kinship grouping wider than the elementary family similar to that described in the Bethnal Green studies but whose structure has been modified by recent social changes outside the sphere of family life itself. The 'loosening' of the structure which has been described as coming about through the dispersal of the extended family has already been carried a considerable way. Over half of our respondents who had both a parent and a brother or sister living, lived in the same district as neither of them. In 46 per cent of these cases of dispersed families the subject had nevertheless seen *both* a parent and brother or sister within the week. In a further 20 per cent of the cases *one* of these relatives had been seen. In a third of the cases, however, neither relative had been seen for over a week and in a fifth for over a month. This latter group was largely composed of people whose relatives lived so far away that frequent contact was not possible. Even in this category the elementary families still seem to be in touch with other members of the extended family in many ways. In general elementary families in Swansea appear not to be isolated but rather 'involved' in varying degrees in extended families which have a dual function—that of social identification on the one hand and that of practical support in need or crisis on the other. The effectiveness of this wider family in performing these functions is impaired but not destroyed by its dispersal, though this must, if great, make impossible the interchange of *domestic* functions between households which were so characteristic a feature of the extended family in Bethnal Green, and which still constitute in Swansea the chief type of help given in times of crisis. But the continued existence of the extended family does not appear to depend on its ability to give such help. It is a resilient and flexible social institution, which is capable of considerable adaptation.

We now come to the other side of the family, and to an examination of the degree of diversification—in which the range of marriage plays an important part—*within* extended families producing a situation of internal heterogeneity which has vital consequences for the structure of the extended family and for its psychological cohesion.

VII

BALANCES AND DIVERSITIES

THERE are two sets of families involved in every marriage. As they are joined in matrimony, each partner acquires automatically a whole new batch of instant relatives. Through the marriage, two previously unrelated (at least, in the vast majority of instances) family groups become 'connected'—as Swansea people commonly put it. And eventually, if the union is productive, two sets of grandparents—with perhaps otherwise little in common—will be linked through common grandchildren; and two sets of uncles and aunts and cousins will be linked, if vaguely and indirectly, through common nephews and nieces and cousins. Each marriage is a kind of frontier between two families. Along this frontier there is often considerable tension and rivalry and opposition. To put it another way, the relationship between the families on either side not uncommonly reminds one of a tug-o'-war, with the wife's mother giving the main tug on one end of the rope and the husband's mother at the other end, with various family members joining in from time to time. The husband and wife, in this image, are of course the two white handkerchiefs tied to the rope. Neither side is pulling to win, rather to hold their own.

It seems to be one of the basic, traditional ideals of extended family behaviour that there should be a proper balance between 'the two sides of the family'—with the pull from either side, whether fierce or so gentle as to be hardly felt, equally matched. This notion of balance was one of the most persistent themes of our interviews in Swansea. It appeared particularly in informants' assertions about how people *should* behave. It was easily recognizable in accounts of how people *did* behave in a variety of family situations, and indeed it was often easily observable in practice.

At the wedding itself, for example, ushers are commonly instructed to fill up both sides of the aisle equally. The bride's kin are of course put on 'her side' of the church and the bridegroom's kin on the other.

236

But should there be an obvious inequality in numbers, other guests such as friends and neighbours (of whatever 'side') are allocated in such a way as to achieve an approximate—and visible—balance between the two sides. One of us was present just after a wedding when the bride's mother gave a teenage son, who had been an usher, a sharp ticking-off because he had 'made a mess of things' in showing guests to their seats in the church. What had happened was that the bride, being a local girl, was well supported by relatives and friends and neighbours who had filled up her side of the church—whereas for the bridegroom, an Air Force corporal from Kent stationed locally, only a handful of close relatives had travelled down to Wales for the wedding. 'It didn't look right,' said the bride's mother, 'of course, the family have got to go on the *right* side, but the others should have been sorted out equally . . . well, for appearance's sake, isn't it?'

The traditional seating arrangements at the wedding ceremony express visibly and symbolically the ideal of an equable balance between the two families concerned in their mutual support of, and demands on, the newly-married couple. Similarly at the wedding reception, convention requires that there should be more or less an equal number from either side. The bride's mother knows only too well that if care is not taken here (or with the subsequent distribution of pieces of the wedding cake) to be 'fair', there is sure to be 'friction'. Young couples are given advice from all sides to start out on their own—that is, in accommodation of their own separated from either parental household. 'Give yourselves a fair start'—'fair' here, one suspects, has a dual meaning in relation both to the interests of the young couple themselves, and equally and perhaps emphatically to the interests of each set of parents. (Such a 'fair start' is not possible for the majority of newly-weds, as we will be seeing later in the chapter.)

This notion of a fair balance of kinship interests and activities in the relationships extending outwards from the elementary family to both sides of the extended family is constant and pervasive. It is encountered in a wide variety of familial contexts—holidays, excursions, regular visiting, letter-writing, gift-giving at Christmas and on birthdays, often in the performance of familial obligations in sickness or old age. The extended family tradition, as we encountered it in our interviews in Swansea, emphasizes that in the joint relations of a married couple with their parents on either side, and especially in the reciprocal relations between children and their grandparents on either side, there should be a fair and reasonable equality of interaction and sentiment—without an obvious and undue favouritism for one particular side.

In practice a certain tilting of this balance in favour of the wife's side of the family appears to be accepted as normal. A married daughter and her mother are expected to be 'close'. It is considered 'natural' and expected that a married daughter should turn first to her own mother, rather than to her mother-in-law, for all kinds of domestic help—and equally that a mother should seek assistance and support, when needed, from her own married daughter first rather than from her daughter-in-law. We discussed this relationship and this expectation in our previous chapter when we compared the behaviour of married daughters and married sons as regards how close they lived to their parental home and how frequently they saw their mothers and fathers. It is clear that married sons tend to be pulled (in the familial tug-o'-war) closer to their in-laws than is the case with married daughters. For a variety of reasons, both practical and emotional, the balance between the two sides of the family tends to be weighted towards the wife's kin. The point that requires emphasis here is that this conforms with a generally accepted social expectation that this will be inevitably the case. The fair and proper balance is not necessarily an even balance.

However, too marked a disturbance of this equilibrium in favour of either side, most often that of the wife, can lead to sharp inter-family and inter-personal rivalry and friction. Young and Willmott argue that 'in Bethnal Green the great triangle of adult life is Mum-wife-husband' and maintain that the structure and dynamics of the extended family revolve around this key relationship.[1] We have taken a slightly different approach. We see the structure of the extended family as depending essentially and primarily on the four-cornered relationship of husband's mother/husband/wife/wife's mother. The emphasis throughout the kinship system is on the roles of women and on the special concern of women in the maintenance of relationship: women as mothers and sisters and daughters—and women as mothers-in-law and wives and daughters-in-law.

In this chapter, we are concerned with certain aspects of these latter relationships through marriage. From the evidence of our main survey in Swansea relating to 1,250 marriages we consider three points particularly—the choice of marriage partners, where the newly-married couples lived immediately after marriage (in relation, that is, to their respective parental homes), and thirdly, the type of household in which these couples began their married lives. These 1,250 marriages have been completed over a span of close on fifty years. We have divided them into two categories by the date of marriage, taking the beginning of the Second World War as the dividing

[1] Young and Willmott, op. cit., p. 46.

line, so as to observe whether there have been any noticeable changes between the two periods in the behaviour we are describing. In fact, we suggest that the evidence given in this chapter does indeed indicate that important changes have taken place in the arrangement of marriage and in the 'home-making' phase of the family cycle immediately after marriage. It is in this first phase immediately after the marriage that each partner is called on to adjust and modify his existing family relationships to take account both of a change in personal status and of the arrival on the scene of newly-acquired 'in-laws'. We argue that these discernible changes in these patterns of behaviour have had a fundamental effect in disturbing the traditional balances between the two sides of the extended family, and have thus produced a marked increase of tension and uneasiness in family relationships—and a marked decline in the family cohesion that characterized the extended families remembered now by old people in Swansea from their youth fifty years or more ago.

FINDING A PARTNER

As we have seen in previous chapters, Swansea has changed rapidly and radically 'within living memory'. Better education (both in schools and colleges, and in industry and commerce for juniors and apprentices) has greatly extended the opportunities of young people for occupational advancement. The changes in transport and communications have expanded the physical horizons within which they live out their lives. They inhabit more physical space: the local neighbourhood, formerly in the old working-class districts a community of work and residence and worship and recreation, which their parents and grandparents cherished seems to them cramped and confined—and, above all, small. Young people in Swansea today—that is, particularly and increasingly within the last twenty-five years or so—have much more varied opportunities of employment, improved working conditions, a wider variety of recreational activities. The world, and certainly that portion which is contained within the County Borough boundary, has altered rapidly and radically. As its physical and economic and social environment has changed so the wider family has undergone a structural transformation. The tightly-knit, homogeneous, cohesive family characteristic for example of the Morriston of Mr Hughes's youth has been modernized and modified. The contemporary extended family is, as we have seen in the previous chapter, looser in structure, more relaxed in familial attitudes, more widely dispersed, less controlled and disciplined by parental authority, more heterogeneous and diversified in occupation and culture, more mobile. One of the major factors in this emergence of a modified extended family adapted to a changed environment has been the widening range of marriage. Just as it is increasingly less common to find a young man following his father down the mine (or into the steelworks or on to the railways or buses, or even into the family business) so it seems increasingly less likely to find him marrying the girl next door (or in the chapel, or even from the neighbourhood).

'There's a change from the old days, I can tell you,' said Mr Hughes in our first chapter. 'I was one of sixteen in a Sunday school class at the Chapel, and I think there was about ten of them married girls from the Chapel. I could give you their names . . . whole families, all together in the Chapel, that's how it was. All *linked* in the Chapel.' Of his five married children, only one 'married in the Chapel'—and locally in Morriston. Two chose partners from other parts of Swansea, and two from outside Swansea altogether (one, indeed, even married an English girl). Essentially, if not of course in detail, this general pattern seems characteristic of contemporary behaviour in Swansea. The distance—physical, economic, and perhaps even cultural—between the natal homes of the bride and groom is greater now than was formerly the case, particularly in the working-class districts of the Tawe Valley. Education and ambition and opportunity have combined to produce differential occupational and geographical mobility with possible marked differences of income and status—as between father and children, and between brothers and sisters (and uncles and aunts and cousins) within a single kinship network. The greater this internal diversification in practice the more difficult it is to achieve a strong psychological sense of family unity and solidarity. It is even more difficult when the husbands and wives of one's close kin are themselves a mixed bunch in that they come from a variety of social and cultural backgrounds, from geographically dispersed areas, and have obvious differences of occupational status and income. 'It's a matter of luck who they marry', said Mr Hughes. He is clearly right in his obvious realization that who the children marry is a matter of basic importance for the subsequent organization of the extended family (though doubtless most 'children' have other thoughts in mind when making or accepting a marriage proposal). We have said that two families of origin are involved in each marriage. The greater the gap between them—in distance, status, or cultural attitude—the harder it is to achieve and maintain the desired proper balance between the two sides of the family.

Before the First World War and to some extent before the Second it was customary for young people to meet in the chapel or church, or by joining one or other of the neighbourhood 'parades' up and down certain roads in the town.

> 'There was a street near Landore where all the young people used to parade after Chapel. Once the boys brought water-pistols and squirted them all over the girls. I was determined to get my own back, so I brought a water-pistol too and this is the one I caught. He was soaked.'

> 'I met her in the "Bunny Run". That's Woodfield Street in Morriston. We all used to go there 6.30 p.m. every Sunday night. You had to be dressed perfect. It was a disgrace if you wasn't. Then nine o'clock we was in the ice cream shop. I met her there.'

This custom, already on the wane before 1939, seems to have been completely destroyed by World War Two. The improvements in public transport and the re-development of the bombed Town Centre, have greatly increased the extent to which people of all ages, but especially the young, seek entertainment and companionship in the heart of Swansea rather than in their own localities. There has as a consequence been a decline in the social life formerly restricted to neighbourhoods like Morriston and Mumbles, and the other urban villages of Swansea. The decline of the chapels and the church and chapel Guilds and Youth Clubs, and Bands of Hope, has greatly reduced their importance as a neighbourhood source of potential wives and husbands. A recent national survey[2] has shown that the dance hall, youth club and work place as well as private homes form the setting for many 'first meetings' of contemporary married couples and our information from Swansea, based on detailed interviews of a small number of recently-married couples taken from our main sample, confirms this pattern. At the same time several of our recently-married subjects met or were introduced by relations a fact not mentioned by the national survey.

> 'The funny thing was his mother's sister is married to my brother so his aunt's husband is also his brother-in-law!'

> 'I met her at my brother's house. She used to live quite near him and they went to the same Chapel.'

> 'I worked with her sister and we got introduced through that.'

> 'He was a driver for my brother, who was the foreman.'

> 'It was at my father's funeral actually. His mother was a friend of mine though I'd not met *him*, she came to represent his father who was seriously ill at the time.'

[2] Griselda Rowntree, 'New Facts on Teenage Marriage', *New Society*, 4 October, 1962.

Relatives are clearly used to extend the individual's social group, and thus provide a wider range of choice. They also help to avoid the 'dangers' inherent in the casual meeting in a public place such as the dance hall, holiday camp, or the street—of which the following seems a somewhat odd example:

> 'I was walking in Oxford Street see, and my friend and I were looking in the window of a chemists' shop, and he came up and he asked me if I would like him to buy me a hair brush. I think a lot met like that.'

It probably always was 'a matter of luck who they married', but it was not always a matter of chance whether they married a local girl or boy. There was a strong presumption that children would marry within the local community, and this was true even where the work place was an important source of future marriage partners. With the increased separation of work place and residence to which we refer in Chapter II, and the considerable widening of the geographical area of interaction, this presumption is no longer valid.

The amount of migration from and into the County Borough which occurred between and during the wars, and which has been perpetuated by the rapid changes in industrial structure and location since 1945, has meant that a significant proportion of men, more especially in the higher occupational grades, move away from their parental homes before they marry. These people may subsequently find partners whose home, though in areas not far removed from those in which they themselves are living, are considerable distances from those of their parents. Mr Hughes's own son Gwyn who married a girl from London is a case in point. Not only does this tend to increase the cultural range of marriage, it also causes the two sets of parents of the couple to be more widely separated than they otherwise would.

Table 7.1 shows the extent of this geographical widening of marriage range. These figures refer to marriages of subjects who were actually living in the County Borough at the time only. They have been adjusted to allow for the fact that some subjects had parents who were not resident in Swansea at the time and all these cases are included in the figures for the 'region around' and 'elsewhere' as appropriate.[3] There is unfortunately another more serious difficulty

---

[3] 5.7 per cent of our sample, 8.5 per cent of the men and 3 per cent of the women, were not living with their parents at marriage. They formed approximately the same percentage of each marriage group. 9 per cent of the middle class and 5 per cent of the working class were not living with parents at marriage.

involved in the use of these figures. The fact that the middle classes are more geographically mobile than the population as a whole means that they are under-represented in the group of subjects married in Swansea to which our figures refer. Whereas our middle class form 24 per cent of the total population it constitutes only 20 per cent of the group we consider here, simply because 36 per cent of the middle class were married outside the County Borough while only 25 per cent of the working class were not married within the boundary.[4] This means that the middle class married in the Borough (to whom our figures refer) are slightly atypical in that none of them has moved out of the Borough since marriage. This is partly due to their youth: ten per cent fewer of the middle class were married before 1939 than of the working class. The net effect of the differences between this group and the rest of the sample will be to diminish the contrast between the classes in terms of geographical mobility, and this must be borne in mind throughout our discussion of the figures contained in the following tables based on this particular sub-group within our main sample.

Table 7.1: Residence of Marriage Partner immediately before Marriage.
(Marriages of Subjects then resident in the County Borough only)

Date of Marriage	1914–1939	1940–1960	Total
	%	%	%
Residence:			
Same district as subject's parents	32	27	30
Other part of Swansea	49	56	52
Region around up to twelve miles	6	6	6
Elsewhere	13	11	12
Total Number	630	620	1,250

As we anticipated the amount of marriage across the County Boundary though considerable has varied little between the two periods we have taken. On the other hand there has been a decline in the number of subjects marrying within their own locality. Our figures for smaller marriage cohorts suggest that marriages followed this trend throughout the '40–60' period and had become towards the end of it more marked. Is this trend equally marked for both our social classes, however? Table 7.2, an expanded version of 7.1, enables us to compare them. (In this, and other tables in this chapter, we have grouped

[4] Significant at the 5 per cent level only.

our four social classes into two to give large enough groups for statistical analysis.)

Table 7.2: *Residence of Marriage Partner immediately before
Marriage, by Social Class.*
(*Marriages of Subjects then resident in the County Borough only*)

Date of Marriage	1914–1939		1940–1960		Total
Classes	Middle	Working	Middle	Working	
	%	%	%	%	%
Residence:					
Same district as Subject's parents	31	33	28	27	30
Other district of Swansea	41	50	41	58	52
Region around	12	5	12	5	6
Elsewhere	16	12	19	10	12
Total Number	119	511	118	502	1,250

The most immediately striking fact about this table is the very considerable difference between the classes in the extent to which their members marry outside the County Borough. Twenty-eight per cent of the middle class chose partners from outside Swansea in the first period and 31 per cent in the second, compared with 17 and 15 per cent respectively for the working class. This is due partly to the adjustments made to allow for subjects living apart from parents at time of marriage but these do not greatly alter the picture, and the differences remain striking. These differences are an important factor in differentiating the family structure of each class—a point to which we shall return shortly. In the first period there is little difference between the classes in the proportion of those (marrying within the Borough) who chose partners from their own district. If, however, we look at the figures for the second period we see that this proportion has declined noticeably for the working class. In the middle class the decline is smaller. In fact 9 per cent more of the middle class who married within the Borough married within their own district than did the class next to them. This means that while the middle-class range of marriage is wider outside Swansea, within it is narrower than that of the working class. 65 per cent of the middle class, it will be recalled from Chapter III, is concentrated in only seven of Swansea's twenty-four localities.

There are important differences in marriage range between Swansea's various localities. It is necessary to point out that the following figures refer to the populations of the localities as they were at the time of our main survey and not to our subject's residence at the time of their marriage. The figures do, however, give some indication of the very considerable differences between local areas. The proportion of those now living in Morriston for example who found their partners within the district in which they were living at marriage was 48 per cent, while in Townhill (a 'second-generation' housing estate it will be remembered) it was only 26 per cent; in Sketty the percentage was 40 per cent while in West Cross it was only 17 per cent. These figures represent substantial departures from the average for the Borough (30 per cent) and reflect considerable differences between these communities both in their social structure as a whole and in family structure in particular. The communities which are most clearly 'going concerns' in terms both of institutional associations and in the psychological response by individuals to community belonging (but not necessarily the 'oldest' communities), come at the top of the scale as regards the proportion of marriages inside the local community. The housing estates all come, much as one would expect, towards the bottom of this scale. The more you feel you *belong* locally the more likely you are to marry someone within your local group who feels the same sense of belonging. With expanding communications the concept of 'locality' has expanded to cover nowadays a wider physical area.

The evidence clearly indicates that young people nowadays tend on average to find their marriage partners from farther afield than did their parents and, particularly, their grandparents. Are they also marrying more widely in terms of social class? Unfortunately this is not a question which we can answer directly from our survey data in Swansea. It will be remembered that we classified our subjects into four social classes: the method of classification, however, since it took account of a person's self-estimate of his class position, could only be used for persons we interviewed directly. We could classify our *subjects* by class, but not also, from our questionnaires, their parents and spouses' parents. It will be recalled, however, that in Chapter III we do discuss inter-generational mobility in occupations, comparing fathers' jobs with those of their sons. And in the course of this discussion[5] we emphasized the extent to which mobility *through marriage* is a major characteristic of contemporary society. Our conclusion was that a very considerable proportion of Swansea homes are the product of 'mixed marriages' in occupational or social class terms.

[5] See Chapter III, p. 98, for the data on the proportions of inter-marriage between the three basic occupational classes into which we grouped our informants, their parents, and spouses' parents.

We cannot say whether this proportion has in general changed significantly over the last fifty years or so: indeed our analysis in terms of a three-fold grouping by occupation shows no significant variation comparing the data for marriages during the period 1914–1939 with that for those completed between 1940 and 1960. But it is likely that this is much too crude an analysis to discern important but subtle changes in these patterns of behaviour—particularly within the traditional working class. There have been profound shifts in the industrial structure of Swansea and the surrounding region of South-west Wales. Comparison from one census to another, as given in Chapter II, reveals radical alterations in the occupational structure of the population consequent upon the decline of the old 'traditional' industries of the Swansea Valley and the rise of a wide variety of new industrial and commercial enterprises. Education has also had its effect. It is likely that Mr Hughes of Morriston is nearer the truth when he contrasts the situation in his youth as regards homogeneity of occupation and social class ('then we was all in the works you see, sisters' husbands and all—*and* in the Chapel') with the contemporary diversity within the family, and the consequent lower level of family cohesion ('Once they marry, they're off'). In any case, what distressed Mr Hughes was not so much the mingling of different occupations but the marrying of different national cultures within the family. To what extent is his experience typical in this respect? We have reason to suppose that the widening area of marriage must have produced an increase in marriages across these cultural as well as class lines; 19 per cent of our married subjects differed from their partners in their ability to speak Welsh. Table 7.3 shows the changing proportion of cross-cultural marriages for Welsh and non-Welsh speakers in both marriage periods.

Table 7.3: Changing proportion of cross-cultural Marriages.
(Married Couples, with partner living, who were resident in
County Borough at marriage.)

Date of Marriage	1914–1939		1940–1960		Total
Language	Welsh	Non-Welsh	Welsh	Non-Welsh	
	%	%	%	%	%
Of Men	26	12	43	15	19
Of Women	23	15	48	13	19
Total Number	231	382	202	523	1,122

The sharp increase in marriages of Welsh men and women with

monoglot English shows that Mr Hughes's experience of a widening cultural range of marriage is not atypical. (There can be little doubt that this increase of marriage with 'foreigners' has been a major factor in accelerating the dispersal and dilution of the Welsh, and consequently in the decline of the Welsh language.) The English paradoxically show no statistical differences between periods simply because the number of Welsh have declined over the period while the number of English have increased. In a very important sense this table is an understatement of the amount of change that has occurred. As we noted in Chapter III the Welsh *cultural* group is wider than that of Welsh-speaking and we have no doubt that had we been able to compile figures on the basis of culture instead merely of language the change would have been even more striking.

Apart from certain middle-class areas, the localities which have an above-average proportion of internal inter-marriage are those which are predominantly Welsh. Is this because there is a tradition of inter-marriage within these particular localities or because the Welsh themselves are markedly different in their range of marriage from the English? Table 7.4 gives the figures showing the residence of marriage partners at marriage for each of the two cultural groups.

Table 7.4: Residence of Partner immediately before Marriage, by Cultural Group.
(Married subjects resident in County Borough at marriage only.)

Date of Marriage	1914–1939		1940–1960		Total	
Cultural Group	Welsh	English	Welsh	English	Welsh	English
	%	%	%	%	%	%
Residence						
Same district of County Borough as Subject's parents	40	30	34	26	38	28
Other District	45	56	49	63	46	59
Region around up to 12 miles	6	3	8	2	7	3
Elsewhere	9	11	9	9	9	10
Total Number	335	295	263	357	598	652

The figures to the extreme right of the table show that while the Welsh tend to marry, if anything, slightly more outside the Borough than the English 10 per cent more of them marry within their own district. Their slightly 'wider' range outside the Borough is probably a simple result of their geographical distribution within it: the fact that a majority of Welsh-speakers live near the boundary usually at points contiguous to other Welsh areas will naturally mean that more of them will marry across it than will other groups in the population. (The 'region around', particularly the Upper Swansea Valley north of Morriston and Cwmrhydyceirw and Glais is, moreover, predominantly Welsh: the County Borough boundary is simply an administrative convenience, without of course any cultural significance.) It does not mean therefore that the range of marriage of the Welsh is in fact wider. The higher number of Welsh marrying within their own locality does, however, indicate that their narrow marriage range is an important factor in determining the high degree of inter-marriage in the old Welsh working-class communities of the Tawe Valley.

The walls of the old cohesive society have, however, been breached in a hundred places. The old sense of control, discipline, identity, exclusiveness has all but evaporated. 'Things are all mixed up nowadays' . . . 'They come and go so quickly I hardly seem to know anybody round here any longer' . . . 'I don't know what things are coming to—and to tell you the truth I don't much care any longer' . . . these are typical attitudes of the elderly (and perhaps to some degree it has been ever thus). Over three-quarters of our recently-married subjects told us that their own and their partner's families had never met until the engagement. It is probably correct to say that, in the contemporary more tolerant and less restrictive social atmosphere generally, there is a greater sense of *individual* choice—free of familial pressure and influence and, perhaps, opposition—in the selection of a marriage partner. Whether the parents, particularly the mothers, feel 'strongly' or not, the current expectation seems to be that the young people concerned must make up their own minds: their parents, it is assumed, will 'soon get over it'. Longstanding breaches of relationship because of an undesirable marriage now appear rare. In a previous chapter we cited an example of an inter-marriage between a Roman Catholic family and a Chapel family.[6] We pointed out that there was fierce antagonism between Mrs Murphy and her daughter-in-law, but they lived together, and it seems likely that they will establish some sort of *modus vivendi* once things have settled down (the marriage, after all, was only about six months old) and once the son and daughter-in-law can find a home of their own. But if we look farther into the same example we see that Mrs Murphy's grandfather 'came over from Ireland and married a Swansea girl . . . we never had much to do with my grandmother's side of the family. They were all Chapel, you see, and there used to be bitter feelings years ago between

[6] See p. 194, Chapter VI.

248

the Chapel and the R.C.'s. Her family more or less cut her off when she married an R.C.' This strong social control on individual action, supported by sternly-applied sanctions based on a group determination to maintain its exclusiveness, has faded nowadays to the point where it is barely distinguishable in attitude or action. There's an Indian proverb (from the Punjab Hills) which says: '*Just as a log is split by many wedges, so the joint family is split by many wives*' (in the Indian case, this means wives brought home to the joint household by the sons). It is a proverb that one is reminded of when looking at the data in Swansea on these changes in the selection of mates, particularly in those cases where there are marked differences in status or community background or cultural attitude and tradition between the parental homes of the partners to the marriage, or a marked geographical separation of these homes of origin.

FINDING A HOME

We began this chapter with the traditional concept of a proper bilateral balance in the external relationships of a married couple, and of their elementary family, with kin on either side. We have stressed the common expectation that this balance will be weighted towards the wife's side of the family—but noted that too marked a disturbance of this balance can lead to trouble and strife. It is over visiting (whether the visits be regular or intermittent, short or prolonged as holidays, frequent or after lengthy intervals) that dissension most frequently arises. The factor which affects this aspect of behaviour most sharply is the distance between the homes of the parties involved—primarily the couple concerned and the parents on either side. The widening range of marriage can serve to decrease the amount of contact between the married couple and their parents in the period immediately after marriage, by increasing the amount of travelling involved in visiting. Whether this will affect one side more than another will depend on where in relation to the two sets of parents the married couple live. It is therefore to the situation of the newly married couple that we must now turn if we are to arrive at a proper understanding of the factors which in fact determine the pattern of relationships between the couple and their two families. It is in the period immediately after marriage that new relationships are worked out and this 'home-making phase' is therefore decisive in determining the patterns of behaviour that will be subsequently followed.

How many newly-weds in Swansea do get 'a fair start' in the sense of starting out on their own in a home separate from that of either of their parents? How does the housing situation which we discussed in Chapter II affect their chances of a 'place of their own'? Table 7.5 shows how those married in each of the two marriage periods started their married life.

Table 7.5: Type of Household Composition immediately after Marriage, by Social Class and date of Marriage.

Date of Marriage	1914–1939		1940–1960		Total
Classes	Middle	Working	Middle	Working	
	%	%	%	%	%
Type of Household:					
With husband's parents	11	12	20	22	16
With wife's parents	20	28	31	42	34
With other relative	2	11	7	7	8
On own	67	49	42	29	42
Total Number	119	511	118	502	1,250
	% of those living with either parents				
With husband's parents	36	30	39	34	32
With wife's parents	64	70	61	66	68
Total Number	37	205	60	323	625

The most striking change shown by the table is the decline in the number of couples who started their married life *on their own*. This decline has affected both social classes, and especially the middle class. There is no doubt that this is not in itself indicative of a change of preference between the two periods but is largely the consequence of changes in the housing situation. The increased demand for housing has been met in part at any rate by an increase in Corporation building. Since only married people are eligible as applicants and the waiting list was ten years long at the time of our survey, most people's chances of obtaining separate accommodation immediately after marriage had decreased and not increased in the previous thirty years.

Housing pressure forces young couples to look to relatives for temporary accommodation (until they find a home of their own). Because family size has declined sharply in the last few generations young people today tend to come from small families with few brothers and sisters. This means that there is likely to be more room in parental households. As a result well over half the middle class and almost three-quarters of the working class nowadays begin their married lives in composite households—'living through and through' (in the Swansea idiom) with relatives on one side or the other. And this tendency to form a composite household at marriage has substantially increased over the last fifty years or so, as is shown by the evidence given in the above table.

Both social classes in both periods show a marked preference for residence with the wife's as opposed to the husband's parents, though the middle-class preference for the wife's parents is slightly weaker. (The husband's parents seem to be a slightly more popular choice in the later period and this is doubtless connected with the increased demand upon relatives for accommodation resulting from a worsened housing situation.) There is nothing very remarkable about this. As we pointed out when discussing household composition in Chapter IV, the most common type of household arrangement for two related families in the same dwelling is for them to live together as one unit. This means that two women must share the same kitchen and tensions between them are, in general, less likely to arise if those two women are mother and daughter.

The increasing amount of residence with parents after marriage and the marked preference for the wife's people does not by itself necessarily mean that the young couple will be drawn more into the wife's family and away from the husband's. Should the two sides of the family be widely separated a more difficult situation would arise. We have already shown that, since it is becoming more common for husband and wife to come from different localities, this is increasingly likely to be the case. Table 7.6 shows the extent to which the two sides of the family are in fact separated.

It will be seen that for both classes the proportion of couples who started their married life in the district of either parent but not of both is increasing[7] and has resulted in a decline of equal proportion in those living in 'other district' and 'district of both' in each class.[8] The lower section of the table shows a definite bias to residence near the wife's as opposed to the husband's parents. This bias is greater for the working class than the middle class and has increased in both

[7] The difference between the periods for the middle class is significant only at the 5 per cent level.

[8] Bearing in mind their smaller increase in geographical range of marriage, the figures for the middle class are somewhat surprising for it would have been reasonable to suppose that the major loser would be 'other district'. It seems possible therefore that changes in the housing situation have affected those couples who live away from both sets of parents after marriage less than it has those who reside in 'district of both', or that the increased *range* of marriage has resulted in those who can afford to start off on their own, living to a greater extent in parts of the Borough in which neither parents reside.

251

Table 7.6: Area of Residence of newly married couples by date of
Marriage and Social Class
(Couples resident in County Borough at marriage only.)[9]

Date of Marriage	1914–1939		1940–1960		Total
Class	*Middle*	*Working*	*Middle*	*Working*	
	%	%	%	%	%
Residence immediately after marriage:					
District of either parents	57	66	70	74	68
District of both	21	20	14	16	18
Other part of Swansea	22	14	16	10	14
Total Number	104	485	109	487	1,185
	% of those living in district of either parents but not both				
In husband's parents' district	46	40	39	36	38
In wife's parents' district	54	60	61	64	62
Total Number	55	307	71	356	789

classes between the two periods.[10] This increase is in marked contrast
to the decline in the bias towards living with the wife's parents which
we noted in Table 7.5. Both the lower numbers living in the district of
either parents, and the pronounced preference for those of the wife is
due in part to the increase in the number of couples who live with
either parents after marriage. Table 7.7 gives the figures for those who
did not live with their parents after marriage, and enables us to see to

[9] The number of those marrying within the Borough who moved outside it
immediately afterwards has declined between the two periods. This may be
due partly to the fact that the younger group has had less time to move back
into the Borough again and are therefore under-represented in our sample.
These people, who form 5 per cent of the sample, are excluded from this table
and Tables 7.7 and 7.8.

[10] The higher proportion in the second period of working class who live
with their parents and their larger family size mean that the likelihood of
couples being able to live with the wife's mother will be smaller than that in the
middle classes. Hence the preference for living with wife's parents shown by
the figures in Table 7.6 is probably an underestimate, which will affect the
figures in Table 7.7. At the same time the fact that more middle-class people
are found to start married life with relatives and that this is easier to achieve
when those relations are the wife's, mean that the extent of the preference for
the wife's kin shown by the residence pattern of the middle class, will probably
be an overestimate.

Table 7.7: Area of Residence of Newly Married Couples.
(Couples resident in County Borough at marriage only; those
living with parents after marriage excluded.)

Date of Marriage	1914–1939		1940–1960		Total
Classes	Middle	Working	Middle	Working	
	%	%	%	%	%
Residence immediately after marriage:					
District of either parents	46	55	52	50	52
District of both	21	22	11	23	21
Other part of Swansea	33	23	37	27	27
Total Number	72	285	56	163	576
	% of those living in district of either parents but not both				
In husband's parents' district	55	48	38	39	46
In wife's parents' district	45	52	62	61	54
Total Number	33	155	29	82	299

what extent the changes shown in Table 7.6 are independent of these changes in household composition. This table shows no significant difference between periods in either class in the number living in the district of either parents. The increase in Table 7.6 is therefore entirely attributable to the increase of residence with parents after marriage. There may also be a quite independently increasing preference for living near the wife's parents.[11] This explains the discrepancy between the increasing bias to the wife's parent shown by proximity of residence in spite of the decreasing preference for living with them. Hence it seems that because *in the past* the necessity for residence with parents has favoured those of the wife, this weighting has been accepted and appears even where co-residence is not involved.

Because of the lower proportion of the middle class favouring the wife's parents and living with or near either but not both parents in the earlier period, recent social change has had a more profound effect on middle-class patterns of residence than on those of the working class. At the same time the faster rate of change shown by the middle class has resulted in the two classes becoming more alike over the past fifty years. What is the position of our two cultural groups in this respect? Tables 7.8 and 7.9 present the figures

[11] The differences here are not significant.

concerning 'living with' and 'living near' parents after marriage for the English and Welsh.

Table 7.8: Household Composition of Newly-married Couples,
by Cultural Group
(Subjects resident in County Borough at marriage only.)

Date of Marriage	1914–1939		1940–1960		Total
Cultural Group	Welsh	English	Welsh	English	
	%	%	%	%	%
Household type immediately after marriage:					
With husband's parents	11	12	21	22	16
With wife's parents	29	25	42	40	34
With other relatives	11	6	5	8	8
On own	49	57	32	30	42
Total Number	335	295	263	357	1,250
	% of those living with parents				
With husband's parents	28	32	34	35	32
With wife's parents	72	68	66	65	68
Total Number	132	109	165	220	626

Table 7.9: Residence of Newly-married Couples by Cultural
Group.
(Subjects resident in County Borough at marriage only.)

Date of Marriage	1914–1939		1940–1960		Total
Cultural Group	Welsh	English	Welsh	English	
	%	%	%	%	%
Residence immediately after marriage:					
District of either	63	66	72	74	68
District of both	24	16	19	12	18
Other part of Swansea	13	18	9	14	14
Total Number	313	277	247	350	1,187
	% of those living in district of either parents but not both				
In husband's parents' district	42	43	37	39	38
In wife's parents' district	58	57	63	61	62
Total Number	191	171	174	253	789

The Welsh do not differ from the English either in the number who live with parents after marriage or in the proportion of those who live near one set of parents but not the other. In the first period they do show a higher preference for residence with the wife's parents but this difference is not significant and almost disappears in the latter. Like the middle class they are drawing close to the rest of the population. They do show a greater tendency to live in the district of both parents.[12] This is not surprising, if we remember the greater extent to which the Welsh as a group married within their own locality.

It has been necessary to trace the patterns of residence after marriage in some detail if we are to understand their effect on the two sides of the family and the way in which they affect the newly-married couple. If the couple live near to both sets of parents or far enough away from either of them to rule out frequent visiting then the young couple will be able to some extent to control the amount of contact they have with each side—to be fair in fact. If, however, they live with or near either set of parents it is likely that as a *couple* they will be drawn into more frequent association with those parents than with the other 'side'. We have seen that a considerable and increasing percentage of all groups are placed in this position, that to an increasing extent the parents they are likely to be living near are those of the wife. That this is so—even when those actually living with parents are excluded—indicates that the closer association of the newly-weds with the wife's family has come to be accepted and expected.

It is not difficult to see why this should be so. In times of difficulty it is only natural that the children should turn to their parents for help and support. While men turn to their fathers for advice or financial assistance, the help they require does not so frequently involve co-operation over long periods as does house furnishing, child-bearing and rearing and assistance during sickness, which constitute the main spheres of co-operation between mother and daughter. While marriage increases a woman's need for support and advice: it does not to the same extent enlarge that of a man. Whereas the services rendered by fathers to sons are not facilitated by proximity of residence, those performed by mothers for daughters are. For all these reasons is the balance likely to be weighted in favour of the wife's parents.

Because the need for support and assistance is related both to the availability of alternative means of help which can be paid for and to education, the dependence of the daughter upon the mother declines the higher in the social scale the family is situated, and the greater independence of the middle-class daughter is an important factor in

[12] The difference is significant at the 5 per cent level.

255

diminishing the amount of weight attached to the wife's side of the family. At the same time the assistance that men in middle-class occupations are able to give to their sons is likely to be greater and more continuous than in the working class. These factors tend to stress the relationship between fathers and sons, and thus add a balancing weight in favour of the husband's family. The middle classes' greater geographical mobility increases the proportion of middle-class families who live near neither set of parents. Geographical mobility *before* marriage has the opposite effect. Such mobility increases the likelihood of middle-class men finding wives in areas in which they are working but in which their parents do not live, thus increasing the number of men who live after marriage nearer to their wife's parents than to their own. This factor together with the housing shortage has tilted the balance of the middle-class family in favour of the wife's side.

RE-ORIENTATION AT MARRIAGE

The degree to which changes in the balance between the two sides of the family can occur without causing tension and friction will depend on a number of factors. If the balance is disturbed by the necessity for the couple to live with the parents of either partner this will often be accepted by those with whom they do not live on the grounds of expediency. The flexibility of the system, the fact that there are no clearly defined expectations as to the amount of time that ought to be spent by the couple on each side makes small changes, or larger changes over several generations, possible without placing a stress on the whole family. The looser the system is—the less frequently people interact—the more possible will it be to maintain an even balance. The higher the expectations of the parents as to contact with the couple the greater will be the effect on the relationship of changes occurring in residence patterns and other similar factors. The level of these expectations will be associated not only with the class and cultural group to which the parents belong but also with degree of 'closeness' of the tie between the parent and child. Personality factors will be important in individual cases here, but the circumstance most likely to affect closeness is family size. The smaller the number of children, the greater is the emotional investment in any one of them, and the more fierce the parental 'pull' after marriage.

We believe that the tables given in this chapter regarding the range of marriage and the area of residence and type of household of newly-married couples immediately after marriage, reveal when considered together a most important social change which has taken place in our society within recent decades. Contemporary family life occurs in a radically altered social and economic environment. A variety of factors have combined to make it more difficult to maintain the traditional, customary, bilateral balance within the circle of the extended family. In doing so they have influenced the basic structure of these wider relationships outside the elementary family nucleus.

The 1,250 marriages dealt with in the tables in this chapter cover a considerable span of time—close on fifty years—and this itself makes analysis of the information extremely complicated. It is inadvisable, for example, to assume that these figures necessarily indicate a uniform upward trend in favour of living with the wife's as opposed to the husband's parents. However, the sample totals as a whole, representing as it were the 'accumulated experience' in this field of social behaviour over the period, reveal a number of important facts about the urban kinship of Swansea: the preponderating influence of kinship factors in the choices concerning residence at marriage, the range and relative importance of the alternative choices available to a newly-married couple, out of these alternatives the main emphasis on residence in the wife's home district and with the wife's parents, and finally the fact that this pattern of behaviour is characteristic, with only a slight variation of emphasis, of both the middle classes and the working classes, and of both the English and Welsh cultural groupings, in Swansea. It seems likely that this is one of the basic patterns of urban kinship in Britain.

In recent years, about 60 per cent of all marriages have begun with in-laws in the same household—and this represents a substantial change from pre-war years. In more than two-thirds of these cases the husband starts off his married life living in the same house as his mother-in-law (and, contrary to widespread opinion, the likelihood of this happening appears to be increasing). Fewer couples than ever before are 'getting a fair start' in this respect—a point which should be remembered in the midst of contemporary complacency about rising living standards. Since the natal homes of the husband and wife tend nowadays to be more widely separated, the difficulties of maintaining a fair balance in relationships is obvious. The evidence demonstrates clearly that in the first phase of the family cycle— decisive for establishing the subsequent pattern of relationships— there tends, with the formation of a composite household—to be a very unequal 'pull' from one side or the other. More usually, as the figures show, men are drawn into their wife's families at the expense of existing relationships with kin. 'Once they marry, they're off.' 'A son's a son till he gets him a wife, a daughter's a daughter all her life'—the old saying, ubiquitous in Britain to judge by reports of

257

kinship studies, is not unknown in Swansea. An old retired miner from Landore made a jovial comment on this saying when we raised it in conversation:

> 'Ay, ay, I've heard that before—and there's no doubt about it, it's damn true. I've always thought the wedding ceremony in church was all wrong myself. Don't they say "Who giveth this woman in marriage?" And the father of the bride hops forward and says "I do". But he doesn't at all, at least if he does he's not speaking for the wife, now is he? I say it should be altered. "Who giveth this man in marriage"—that's the proper question, lad. And make the *mother* of the bridegroom say "I do". Most fathers don't give a damn either way in my experience.'

So far we have been considering the situation of the married couple, and we have spoken as if they had become at marriage an indissoluble unit. This is of course quite untrue. As James Thurber has pointed out, 'marriage does not make two people one, it makes two people two. It's sweeter that way and simpler.' In fact both partners visit their parents separately, the wife seeing her parents while the husband is at work, the man visiting his mother and father (and other relations too) on the way. In this fashion it is possible for each to maintain a high level of contact with his or her kin in spite of the fact that the marital home is nearer to one parental home than the other. This leads to a curious paradox. The authors of the Bethnal Green study comment on the increasing extent to which husband and wife share their leisure time and they contrast this situation with the old-fashioned practice of segregation of the roles of men and women.[13] Our own observations make us believe that this is also true in Swansea. Hence at a time when husband and wife act as an entity in other social contexts more than ever before they are to an increasing extent acting individually in kinship situations.

However this may be, the extent to which marriage partners do act individually, especially for the men, is probably still small. With the arrival of the first child the interest and concern of both families increases. As Mr Hughes comments: 'It's the grandchildren that are the real tie,' and it is here that most tensions arise. For the grandchildren are of course related by blood to both sides, and if it is true that their arrival sometimes unites their parents it is equally true that it brings together the two sides of the family. The period between the birth of the first child and the death of the grandparents has, as we have noted in Chapter IV, been increasing and this has meant an extension of the period during which tensions are most likely to arise.

[13] Young and Willmott, op. cit., p. 12.

Nevertheless the period when each side of the family does embrace three generations, must of its very nature occur at a time when the grandparental generation is most frequently in need of support of some kind from the children and children from parents. Hence the mutual dependence of the two adult generations provides an excuse for the actual bias in favour of the wife's kin on the grounds of necessity. This can in fact be accommodated by the parents provided the number of children is large enough and includes at least one daughter thus enabling the parents to be cared for, and preventing their making an emotional investment exclusively in the children of a child drawn into the orbit of the other side of the family. It is in those cases where the number of children is small but the level of contact between the wife's parents and the grandchildren is high both in absolute terms, and relative to the amount of contact between the children and the husband's parents, that the disturbing of the balance is likely to result in the relative disorganization of the family system.

The increasing necessity of living with parents after marriage may certainly produce tension between the marital partners. The husbands who were living with wife's parents frequently complained of the extent to which they had become absorbed by the wife's relations, and many seemed to feel guilty at having to admit that they saw more of their wife's relatives than their own. While many of the wives living with their mothers were content with their residence, a far smaller number of their husbands were, the husbands more frequently considering that it was best to live near enough to relatives to see them occasionally rather than so near as to see them frequently or daily. The men were clearly interested in restoring the balance between the two sides. Both men and women, in spite of the greater preference shown by Swansea people for living in one household with the other married couple with whom the dwelling was shared, or perhaps because of it, were quite certain that young couples should start their married life on their own. Hence, although the greater bias towards the wife's side of the family would appear to have been accepted and be now expected, independence at marriage is still clearly thought to be the ideal in spite of the fact that only a third of the newly-married achieve it. It is, as one would expect, the stresses and strains within the household group rather than the wider family group that are most acutely felt. This is particularly so in those cases where the young people are forced to live with the husband's parents. Here the possessive attitude towards domestic arrangements and the greater time spent by the two women together in the home leads to friction so acute that even those few husbands we interviewed who had experienced life with both sides of the family preferred living with the wife's parents to their own. Living with the husband's parents did seem to work in several cases when the wife's own mother was dead. 'She's been a second mother to me. I don't know what I'd have done without her,' was a typical comment. Clearly the need for someone to fill the gap in these women's own family relationships made by the death of their own mothers made trivial any smaller differences between them and their mothers-in-law, which had their own mothers been alive, would probably have been crucial. One useful function that relations acquired at marriage can perform is clearly to fill the blank spaces in the ranks of one's own family. The following extracts from three interview reports illustrate this practice of substitution in situations of need:

Mary Wood, aged 28, a housewife, lives in a Corporation house on the Townhill estate with her husband, a butcher's assistant, two young children, and her husband's father's mother, aged 91, who holds the tenancy. Mary and her husband moved in here on marriage because there was room and because the grandmother needed help and care. Mary's own mother died ten years ago, before Mary was married. Her father has re-married and lives with her two unmarried siblings a few streets away. Her two elder brothers are married and living near-by. 'We are all very friendly and close—Dad's is of course the centre of the family—we're always dropping in there but especially every Thursday. I get on well with my step-mother but I wouldn't like to ask her for anything. I've got eight uncles and aunts, four on each side, and they all live in Swansea with their families—six of them here on Townhill. I see them all regularly—whenever I'm passing in fact and they do the same.' A familiar picture of close consanguineal relationships. But Mary continues: 'My closest friend is my mother-in-law, closer than any of my own family. She lives over in West Cross [about three miles away] and I go over there each Sunday. We are hoping to get a Corporation house over there later on. My husband's mother has been just like a mother to me. She has done everything possible for me—she came to help when I had the children, and I know I've only got to ask and she'd come at once for anything. I really look forward to seeing her every Sunday. She's been a wonderful friend to me.'

Ivor Rhys, aged 60, owner of a furniture shop, has three married daughters but no sons. The husband of one of his daughters joined Mr Rhys as his assistant in the management of the business just after the marriage and has now taken over completely on Mr Rhys's retirement. The daughter and her husband lived in her parents' home at first on marriage, and her father and her husband became 'like father and son'.

Bill Alexander, 46, a welder, lives in a Corporation house on Mayhill with his wife, two children, and his mother-in-law, aged 73. He and his wife expect to get the tenancy when the wife's mother has 'passed on'. Bill has two married sisters living in Sketty and Mumbles respectively, both his brothers-in-law being 'moneyed' [as he says]—the one the owner of three butchers' shops, the other the captain of a merchant ship. He has 'very little to do' with these two, though he sees his two sisters weekly when he visits his 85-year-old widowed mother who is living with the sister in Sketty. He has no brothers of his own. His wife's brother, George, is married and lives a few streets away on Townhill. Bill and George are the same age, and are 'like brothers'. When George, a train driver, was on strike a couple of years ago, Bill gave him a pound a week out of his wages. When Bill was on strike a few months ago, George did the same for him. In the last year, Bill's mother-in-law has been seriously ill. His wife said 'He's been as good as a son to my mother while she's been ill.'

Examples like this of the use of in-laws to fill gaps in a particular individual's network could easily be multiplied. Indeed the factors that we have been discussing in this chapter—geographical mobility at marriage, formation of composite households, greater proximity of residence after marriage to one side of the family rather than the other—make it probable in appropriate circumstances that these gaps will be filled by in-laws rather than by one's own kin.

Following Lloyd Warner's useful distinction, it has become common in the literature to refer to 'the family of orientation' into which a person is born, and 'the family of procreation' founded at his marriage. Given the essential re-arrangements of a man's relationships that his marriage necessarily entails, particularly with the sudden arrival on the scene of his in-laws, it seems we could well substitute 'family of re-orientation' for Warner's latter term.

In this chapter we have pointed to the importance of the four-cornered relationship of husband's mother/husband/wife/wife's mother, and argued that a basic structural characteristic of the urban kinship system is a notional bilateral balance of activities and interests with a social expectation that the scales will be tipped slightly in favour of the wife's kin. The evidence from our study seems to suggest that it does become, and is becoming, increasingly difficult to maintain a 'fair and proper balance' in terms of what people think ought to happen. In fact, with the widening range of mate selection, increasing physical mobility, with the post-war increase in housing difficulties, the smaller family size making it increasingly possible for a newly-married couple to find room with one or other of their parents—for these reasons at least, there has been a disturbance of the balance and a consequent increase in familial tensions. This has occurred at a period when, for demographic reasons, the extended family is already under considerable stress in the performance of one of its most vital functions—the support of the elderly in need. We examine this aspect of the organization of the extended family in the next chapter.

VIII

THE FINAL PHASE

SO far in this book we have used Mr Griffiths Hughes of Morriston to reflect the changes in the patterns of family life in Swansea. We must now turn to Mr Hughes's generation and consider it in its own right. In an age when the phrase 'social problem' is continually on people's lips and in the columns of the newspapers we have, perhaps for the first time, learnt to think of *old age* in this way. Mr Hughes would doubtless be surprised to be told that he constituted a part of a social problem, and like the teenager whom society approaches in a similar manner, he would as likely as not resent it. Living at the hub of his family held together by his wife—the Mam—active and convivial, a respected member of his own community, a deacon of his chapel, he gives the impression—in spite of his head shaking at the changing world around him—of someone to be envied for his security and the satisfaction he derives from his familial and social life. He is not someone to be patronized or pitied. There are nevertheless good reasons why the elderly of the community, in Swansea as elsewhere, are regarded as constituting 'a problem' especially to those social services most closely concerned with their welfare. Perhaps the most important of these are the recent growth of this age group both in absolute terms and in terms of the proportion that they form of the population as a whole, and the remarkable decline in family size in the last fifty years which we have already discussed in Chapter V. We have pointed also to the increasing popularity of marriage. All these factors taken together show that there is a very real sense in which the elderly have come to constitute a social problem for demographic reasons alone. The increase in the size of this group coinciding as it does with the decline in the number of children available to care for them and the increasing number of those children who marry and whose responsibilities are therefore shared between the two sides of the family, has meant that today when their numbers are largest the chances of the family being able to care for an elderly person is lower than it has ever been.

It is a remarkable fact that in the early stages of the growing concern with the social problem of the old the importance of the role of the family in caring for and maintaining them was largely ignored. That the centrality of the family circumstances of the elderly is now widely accepted is due in no small part to the second of the Bethnal Green trilogy by Peter Townsend,[1] who sought to relate the social position of the old and their problems to the wider understanding of the Bethnal Green family gained by Michael Young and Peter Willmott in their earlier study.

In 1951 the proportion of elderly people in institutional care in England and Wales was as low as 3·6 per cent representing a smaller proportion of the population than would be expected if the 1911 rates of institutionalization still applied in 1951.[2] The proportion of people of pensionable age in care in Swansea was 3·1 per cent. Less than 2 per cent of all the elderly persons who fell within our sample, and who responded to a further survey confined to the problems of the elderly, were assisted in their everyday domestic tasks of cooking, washing, shopping, personal hygiene or housework, by statutory or voluntary social services. Yet a medical and psychiatric survey of those over 65 in our sample carried out by a medical colleague estimated that at least 12·7 per cent of those over 65 were incapable of adequate self-care.[3] Only 10 per cent were cared for in any way by the social services. We do not intend in this chapter to present a comprehensive study of the situation of the elderly based on the special survey mentioned above. This must be reserved for another publication. Nor do we quote these figures here in order to assess the adequacy of the social services provided for the old. Their purpose is to show that the burden of the non-specialized care of the elderly is not in fact carried by the social services but in so far as this care is obtained by old people, it is provided by their friends, their neighbours, and of course their families. It is our purpose here to relate our analysis of family structure to the social situation of the old and by examining families involved in the care of the elderly to extend this analysis itself.

---

[1] Peter Townsend, *The Family Life of Old People*, 1957.

[2] These figures are based on a reworking of the figures presented by Brian Abel Smith and Robert Pinker in a paper, 'Changes in the Care of Institutions in England and Wales between 1911 and 1951.' *Manchester Statistical Society Transactions*, 1959–60.

[3] Parsons, P., 'The Health of Swansea's Old Folk'. Unpublished M.D. Thesis. Cardiff, 1962.

The Final Phase

That 'we live in an age of great and rapid social change' is a platitude that is continually reiterated not the least frequently by those who seek to make a contribution to the understanding of the changed position of the old in modern society. The truth of this statement cannot of course be doubted but as an explanation it fails to account for the unique position of the present generation of the elderly. Mr. Hughes's comments on his own social position centre around the changes that have taken place in his lifetime not only in the family but in the local community. Though Morriston is to some extent in his view still 'a tin of worms' yet he was at pains to point out that not only was his extended family no longer confined to Morriston but that the locality no longer functioned as a community in the same way. And here he seems to be referring less to the measurable changes in the structure of family and neighbourhood—the wider range of mate selection, the social and economic mobility which we have already discussed—than to the effect that these changes have had in altering the social *atmosphere*, the spirit which animates the families and neighbourhood of Morriston.

Mr. Hughes's generation is unique in that in its lifetime it has witnessed the decline of social life based on small local communities and has had to come to terms with a society whose structure is altogether looser. People don't live as close, children don't 'cling', people are not 'all in the same boat together'. It is not surprising therefore that the old tend to cling to the areas of the town associated in the past with close-knit communities in which they were reared and where they feel at home. Eighty-seven per cent of people of pensionable age in Swansea had spent the greater part of their lives in the Borough; 67 per cent of Swansea's old people had spent most of their lives in the neighbourhood where they were then residing. A further 15 per cent had relatives in the areas in which they were living and to which they had recently moved. It is likely that the previous removal of these relations was a factor in causing them to leave the locality in which they had spent most of their lives. Six per cent had moved away from the area in which they had spent most of their lives, to new housing estates, and it is probable that the immediate cause of their change of residence was Corporation housing policy. Hence only 12 per cent of the old moved away for other reasons.

This attachment to a physical place in a period of considerable geographical mobility means that the movement of the population away from the traditional areas of settlement leaves small pockets of the elderly such as Little Gam Street which we described in Chapter

265

II.[4] Although the accommodation which the residents of this neighbourhood occupied was scheduled for demolition as 'unfit for human habitation' only three out of the twelve elderly people we interviewed were willing even to consider moving.

Mrs Smith was a small frail old lady, 75 years of age and in poor health. She lived in a two-bedroomed house with her widowed daughter. Her late husband was a railwayman, himself born in the neighbourhood. The house was spotlessly kept though all the furniture was very old. She was very indignant about the proposal to demolish the street.

> 'They say these houses aren't fit for human occupation just because there isn't a bath. How do they think we have managed for the last seventy years? Nobody bothered about us then! Of course I don't want to go. My family have always lived here, my father and his father and his father. I have lived in this house for fifty-seven years—ever since I was married. I'm a Swansea person. I have been all my life. They came to ask me if I'd like to go to Clase. I'd never heard of it. I just broke down and cried. Some of them are thinking of going on Townhill. But that won't do for me. I couldn't manage the hills. All the old people that have gone up there have died. I love living here, we're a community. When my mother was ill Mrs Grimshaw across the way always brought her over something for her tea. Not that we're in and out of each other's houses. I don't believe in that. But I sit at the door every day and I see everybody. If I'm not there they're soon round to ask what's the matter. And if anything goes wrong we've only to knock on the wall and we know Nellie, that's Mrs Hill next door, will be in in a moment.
>
> Then of course it's so convenient. I see my son every morning half-past eight. He comes in for a cup of tea on his way to work. Then my other daughter comes in when she's in town for shopping. And my husband's cousin's wife (husband's father's brother's son's wife) comes in to see me too. If we went to West Cross I wouldn't see anyone. The bus fares are awful. When you're used to plenty of company you can't do without it. If we moved we'd all be split up. I wouldn't mind going quite as much if we were all kept together.'

'We're a community', says Mrs Smith and indeed the elderly inhabitants of Hoskins Place and Little Gam Street share a lifetime's experience of the neighbourhood and each other. Yet the very fact that they are all elderly means that they are not a community in, at any rate, the town planners' sense of the word. The streets form rather a sanctuary, a retreat where they enjoy informal association with their

[4] See Chapter II, p. 65.

contemporaries without overtly recognizing, as they would have to in an Old People's Club, that they are old; where the presence of younger people, new faces, new fashions and new buildings does not underline the extent to which they have been left behind by 'all that progress outside'.

Similar neighbourhoods in other areas provide a community of language and worship as well as of residence. The elderly Welsh are set apart from the rest of the population by the rate of social change even more than the old in Sandfields. Born and bred in a society predominantly chapel-going and Welsh-speaking they have had to learn to live in a town which, in their lifetime, has become secular and anglicized. The chapels, strongholds of both language and religion, provide a cultural and often physical link with the past as well as the means of association with those raised in the same cultural tradition. The clustering of the Welsh and the chapels in the eastern part of the Borough which we noted in Chapter III makes the move away from areas in which they have spent most of their lives even more of an uprooting for the Welsh than for others.

Religious activity is of course important not only for the Welsh but for all old people. This is shown by the higher proportion (41 per cent compared with 33 per cent) of those of pensionable age in our sample who had been to a place of worship within a month, in spite of the fact that they are, as a group, less mobile than the rest of the population. The importance of religion in the lives of the old, combined with the *particularist* character of much of that religion (43 per cent were Nonconformist) is another important factor in increasing their attachment to and involvement with a particular locality. It should not be supposed, however, that the importance of community life for the old means that they are clustered together in a few large neighbourhoods within the Borough, left high and dry by the movement of the rest of the population towards the west. Little Gam Street and Hoskins Place are typical of many small 'pockets' of the elderly, but these are spread fairly evenly throughout Swansea. Table 8.1 shows the proportion formed by people of pensionable age of each of our localities and the way that old people are distributed over them.

The old, while not clustered together in the older parts of the town, are slightly over-represented in the west and under-represented in the older east. The reasons for this distribution are complex. First while it is true that the old are in the main geographically stable, we have nevertheless noted that 35 per cent have moved from the area in which they have spent most of their lives. Thirteen per cent of this group have come from outside the County Borough and half as many

*Table 8.1: Geographical Distribution of People of Pensionable
Age in Swansea.*[5]

	% of locality adult pop.	% of all of Pensionable Age	% of all under Pensionable Age
Oystermouth, Newton Killay, West Cross	23	9	9
Sketty, Uplands	29	12	8
Brynmill, Mt Pleasant	31	13	8
Total West	28	34	25
Sandfields, Castle, Hafod	23	11	10
St Thomas	21	7	8
Total Centre	22	18	18
Manselton, Landore	22	12	12
Morriston, Ynystawe, Glais	22	9	9
Birchgrove, Llansamlet, Bonymaen	22	7	7
Total 'Tawe Valley'	22	28	28
Townhill	17	7	10
Penlan, Clase	10	4	10
Cadle, Waunarlwydd	23	9	9
Total North-west	17	20	29
County Borough	22	100	100

again as were to be expected settled in the west. Secondly the movement west of the whole population meant that those old people
following relatives would also tend to favour the west. Thirdly, unlike
the older areas in the east, the neighbourhoods of Sketty, Uplands,
Brynmill and Mount Pleasant, because they were settled between
forty and seventy years ago, have a genuinely ageing population
structure. These areas have not yet been diversified by an influx of
younger people which the death of the original inhabitants makes
possible.

If we do not wish to give the impression that the old in Swansea
are concentrated in one area nor do we wish to suggest that the
majority of old people live in communities of the elderly like Hoskins

[5] Unless otherwise stated all the tables in this chapter refer to people of
pensionable age interviewed in our main sample (434).

Place. On the contrary the rapid growth in the numbers of Old People's Clubs in Swansea would seem to be evidence of an attempt artificially to create such communities. To the best of our knowledge the first club was founded in Swansea around 1925. (We shall not commit ourselves as to which club this was as there is some controversy in the matter!) At the time of writing there are no less than fifty-three clubs with a book membership of 4,000 or 16 per cent of the relevant age groups. Fifteen per cent of our respondents of pensionable age said they were members of one of these clubs. While there are clubs in most parts of the Borough, their distribution—unlike that of the elderly themselves—is concentrated more in the east than in the west. The clubs number among their members an above-average number of Welsh and working-class people who are clustered in the eastern and central areas of the town. Since these are the areas where community life is the most strong it seems likely that these clubs are an *expression* of a certain type of community life rather than an attempt to create it. A more detailed investigation into Old People's Clubs and their membership which we cannot describe here tends to confirm this impression. Just as the chapel is the formal means of association of the inhabitants of a locality who are already informally acquainted and connected by reason of their long community of residence, so are many Old People's Clubs. Indeed it is possible to regard some chapels as special instances of Old People's Clubs while the clubs themselves, so important a part does religion play in their proceedings, remind one strongly of the less formal meetings of the members of the chapel.

Neighbourhood, club and chapel all provide for the old a means of interaction with others who share the same social and cultural experience and beliefs (of which religion forms a substantial part) rather than a means of combating isolation and loneliness. It is precisely the lack of such feelings and attitudes common to both married children and their elderly parents that render the old to some extent isolated however attentive their offspring. It is to a consideration of the familial situation of the old that we must now turn.

THE FINAL PHASE OF THE CYCLE

'If you ask me, children don't look after old people nowadays—they just can't be bothered.' This remark was typical of many made to us in the course of our investigation by our elderly subjects, and is symptomatic of the feeling of neglect and rejection which characterizes the psychological state of many old people. To what extent it is literally true and how far it is indicative of a change in the relationship of the old to the rest of society more subtle and less easily described than by a sample investigation of behaviour we shall attempt to discover in the course of this chapter.

One of the circumstances which lead elderly people to contrast their own family and social situation with that of their own parents is the smaller number of children and other relatives available to care for them. Another factor which accentuates the feeling of loneliness and desertion by their family is their arrival at the final family phase. So far we have examined the first three phases of the family cycle, dealing in Chapter VI with the phase of procreation and in Chapter VII with home-making and dispersion. The old have, as Table 8.2 shows, characteristically reached the final phase of this cycle when in many cases they are physically separated from their children, all of whom have married and left home. There are many possible responses to this situation on the part of the old. Age certainly has its problems and difficulties but this does not prevent many people from accepting with a certain amount of relief the easier pace of life after retirement and the freedom from the minute-by-minute involvement in the lives of their children which has characterized their lives since the birth of the first child. Mr Hughes evidently enjoyed 'visiting time at the zoo'—the weekly visit of children and grandchildren which turned Saturday afternoon into Bedlam. Nevertheless some elderly people find the sort of contact involved in having two married daughters with attendant children just round the corner exhausting and wished—sometimes forgetting the extent of their dependence upon the help and support they gave—that they lived farther away. Others on the contrary regretted the loss of day-to-day involvement in the life of a younger person. This was particularly true of women for whom the loss of all their children by marriage, where this involved wide physical separation, created the sort of emptiness in their lives which the men more usually experienced at their retirement. Table 8.2 shows how many of the old had reached this final phase, and compares the differing situation of men and women.

Table 8.2: The Family Phase of the Old
(Single subjects excluded)

Phase		I	II	III	IV		
Old People with:		No children	All Children unmarried	Married and unmarried	All Children married	Tot.	No.
Male	%	12	9	26	52	100	141
Female	%	20	4	17	59	100	250
Both	%	17	5	20	58	100	391

The Final Phase

As might be expected a substantial minority of the old were still in the phase of dispersion (III), there were hardly any, all of whose children were unmarried, and the majority (58 per cent) had reached the final phase. Odd as it may seem this majority was larger in the case of women than of men. This is quite simply because the wives of elderly men in the sample are younger than elderly women and it is of course the age of the woman that determines the point which a couple has reached in the family cycle.[6] Equally striking was the large proportion of old people who had no surviving child (17 per cent). Here again the position of women differs from that of men 8 per cent more women being childless.[7] This is also a result of the fact that the women are older than the wives of their male contemporaries. The wives being younger as a group have been subjected to a lower risk of losing children through infant and child mortality[8] than our women subjects.

That there are more elderly women than men even when the lower age at which women qualify for pensions has been taken into account is due to their higher expectation of life and means that the proportion of women widowed is greater than that for men. In fact while nearly half of the elderly women in our sample were widowed under a quarter of the men were. Table 8.3 relates all these factors: childlessness, and loss of children through marriage and widowhood.

Table 8.3: Availability of Children to Old People.

	Single	Other Childless		Total Childless	At least one child unmarr.		All Children married	
		Widowed	Married		Marr.	Wid.*	Marr.	Wid.
Men %	9	3	8	20	25	7	40	8
Women %	11	9	8	28	9	10	24	29
Both %	10	6	9	25	14	9	30	22

* Including divorced and separated people. The number of male subjects is 154; of female 280.

This table shows the unfavourable position of women compared to men: 65 per cent of the men have both a wife and child as opposed to only 33 per cent of the women. The proportion of men who have an unmarried child is one and a half times as high as that for women. Taking both sexes together, 16 per cent of the old are both childless and widowed, and less than half (44 per cent) have both children and

[6] The difference is not significant here but does contribute to a significant difference between men and women revealed by Table 8.3.

[7] The difference is significant at the 5 per cent level.

[8] Only 1 per cent of the 8 per cent difference is accounted for by greater infertility. The remaining difference is due to greater loss of children through death.

spouse to care for them and as many as 25 per cent have no children at all. We pointed out in Chapter V that the fall in family size must mean that the old are less well provided with children than their parents, and that increased longevity has increased the chances of a child having to care for an elderly parent. In addition the proportion of single old people has risen slightly from 7 per cent in 1911 to 10 per cent in 1961. The rise here has been sharper for women than men however; there has been a rise of 6 per cent in the number of single women and of only 0·2 of one per cent in the number of single men. In contrast the proportion of widowed old people has declined slightly in the past fifty years from 47 per cent in 1911 to 40 per cent in 1961. This decline has, however, been sharper for men than women. The proportion of male widowed has fallen by 15 per cent; the proportion of female widowed by only 6 per cent. Once again the position of elderly women relative to men has worsened.

Because of the increased expectation of life of old people, and also because of the earlier age of marriage, they are now more likely than they were to have all their children married—that is to have reached the final family phase. Here then is a very real sense in which the old are not cared for as their parents were: not through any decline in filial responsibility but because, in contrast to their parents, the old of today are less likely to be surrounded by children, more likely to be single, and more likely to have all their children married.

That the larger number of old people in the final family phase has not led to a greater isolation of the old is due, in part, as we showed in Chapter VII, to the increasing number of children who live with their parents immediately after marriage. Many of these remain to care for their parents in old age. The proportion of old people who have a child living and the proportions of those who, having a living child, actually live in the same household, are set out in Table 8.4. Almost half of the people of pensionable age of each sex who have children live with them, and a third of the women and a fifth of the men who have married children, share a dwelling with one of them.[9] By this means the separation of children and parents which would otherwise occur when the old person reaches the final family phase is avoided. The proportions of those living with any child, and of those living with a married child are higher for the widowed[10] and, since

[9] The difference is significant at the 5 per cent level only.

[10] The difference between married and widowed males is significant at the 5 per cent level only in the case of those living with any child, and not significant for those living with a married child.

Table 8.4: Percentage of the Old having Children in the same Dwelling.

	Males		Total	Females		Total
	Married	Widowed		Married	Widowed	
% possessing a living child	90	85	88	80	81	81
Numbers	112	28	140	119	133	252
% of those possessing a living child with a child in the dwelling	41	67	46	41	61	52
Numbers	100	24	124	95	108	203
% of those possessing an unmarried child living with an unmarried child	78	72	77	90	100	96
Numbers	32	11	43	22	29	51
% of those possessing a married child living with a married child	19	35	22	22	44	33
Numbers	90	23	113	91	101	192

more women are widowed, higher for women than men.[11] Because of this fact the proportion of old people living with children does not vary between the sexes as much as might have been supposed having in mind the difference between the availability of children to men and women, as Table 8.5 shows.

Table 8.5: Dwelling Composition of the Old.

	Males %	Females %	Both Sexes %	Phase IV %	Total Sample %
On own	7	19	15	10	5
Married couple	39	27	31	48	19
Widow or u/m. Bro/sis	1	5	4	1	2
Parent and u/m child	21	18	19	2	49
Parent and marr. child	21	23	22	28	20
Other	11	8	9	11	5
Numbers	154	280	434	358	1,962

As one would expect the pattern of dwelling composition approximates to that characteristic of the fourth and final family phase:

[11] The difference for those living with any child is not significant: for those living with a married child it is significant only at the 5 per cent level.

273

the old live, chiefly, either alone with their spouse, or with married children. Nineteen per cent, however, live with a single child and 15 per cent alone. The most striking differences between the sexes—in the number of married couples living on their own and in the numbers living entirely alone—is due to the larger proportion of widows among the women. Because we used the same categories of dwelling and household composition we can compare our figures for Swansea with those in Bethnal Green. This comparison is made in Table 8.6.

Table 8.6: Household and Dwelling Composition of the Old in Swansea and Bethnal Green.

	Swansea		Bethnal Green	
	Dwelling %	*Household* %	*Dwelling* %	*Household* %
On own	15	16	23	26
Married couple	30	33	23	29
Siblings alone	4	4	7	4
Parents and unmarried children	19	20	24	26
Parents and married children	23	19	19	12
Other	9	8	4	3
Numbers	434	434	203	203

Eight per cent fewer old people lived alone in Swansea than in Bethnal Green, but 7 per cent more were living alone with their spouse. This is simply due to the fact that 7 per cent fewer of the Swansea sample were widowed. The difference between the areas in the proportion widowed is not significant. A more important difference shown here is the smaller number of Swansea people living with unmarried children, although the number living with children whether married or not is similar. We shall return to this topic shortly when we consider the dwelling composition for old people in each of our social classes. The most notable contrast between the two areas shown in this table concerns the way in which dwellings are shared. The London figures show that 11 per cent of the elderly live in the same dwellings as relatives but separately from them: 3 per cent with brothers and sisters and 7 per cent with married children. Only 5 per cent of the Swansea sample lived separately from relatives in the same dwelling: 4 per cent with a married child and 1 per cent with other relatives.[12] These figures illustrate an important difference in attitudes to family relationships which is the more remarkable for the

[12] The difference between the areas is significant at the 5 per cent level only.

fact that, compared with Bethnal Green, Swansea includes many more people who live in accommodation which it is possible to subdivide. Peter Townsend refers to the preference of Bethnal Green people to remain 'independent' both after marriage and in old age. In Swansea in the final phase of the family as in the others, a closer and more intimate living arrangement within the dwelling seems preferred.

So far we have compared Bethnal Green with Swansea *as a whole*, but this, as we have seen, is not to compare like with like in view of the contrasting class structure of the two areas. Table 8.7 therefore compares the dwelling composition of our two social classes with that of Bethnal Green.

Table 8.7: Dwelling Composition and Social Class of the Old.

	Swansea		Bethnal Green %
	Middle Class %	Working Class %	
On own	19	12	23
Married couple	34	29	23
Siblings alone	5	4	7
Parents and unmarried children	17	20	24
Parents and married children	14	25	19
Other	11	10	4
Numbers	107	326	203

Since the proportion widowed in each class are the same this factor can be ignored in making inter-class comparisons. The figures show therefore that more of the middle-class old live alone or alone with their spouse, while fewer live with children.[13] However the middle class live predominantly with unmarried as opposed to married children and in this they follow the Bethnal Green pattern. The difference between the two areas lies therefore in the different behaviour of the working class in Swansea. The difference was due to the greater extent to which the working class lived with married children available to them, there being relatively less difference between the classes in the numbers living with single children. Of those with married children 19 per cent of the middle class compared with 34 per cent of the working class lived with them. The Bethnal Green figure was 24 per cent.[14] It seems that in Swansea working-

[13] The difference is significant at the 5 per cent level.

[14] The difference between the proportion for the working class in Swansea and Bethnal Green is significant at the 5 per cent level only.

class old people are less reluctant to live with married children than in Bethnal Green just as they are less unwilling to live through and through. Moreover, a substantial minority (26 per cent) of the elderly in Swansea who possess both married and unmarried daughters live in fact with the married daughter, in spite of the availability of the other. All this seems to point to a greater willingness on the part of working-class old people in Swansea to be involved intimately with their children and perhaps more importantly grandchildren than was the case in Bethnal Green. In contrast to the desire of the old in London to remain 'independent', there was in Swansea almost an air of pride about the way in which we were informed 'we live through and through'. If elderly people felt that young people should be on their own this was because of the benefits that are to be gained by the married child from this arrangement rather than because the old themselves preferred it.

The middle-class situation was in marked contrast. As we have seen, fewer middle-class old people lived with children and only just over half the working-class percentage lived with married children. Although fewer middle-class people possessed single children it is with these children that they predominantly live and the amount of postponement of marriage as indicated by the proportion living with single children over 35 is as high as that for the working class. There can be little doubt that this stress on care by single children is one of the consequences of the greater inter-personal involvement in middle-class family life which results from the small family system which characterizes it.

The smaller extent to which the middle-class elderly are cared for by children in their own homes and the smaller extent therefore to which they provide accommodation for them means that in many cases they will not only be living alone but living in accommodation too big for them. The situation of the working-class elderly person is quite different. Here the chances of their living with married children are high, but the size of their accommodation is likely to be small. 64 per cent of our elderly working-class subjects were living in small terraced houses or similar accommodation compared with only 35 per cent of the middle class. Hence overcrowding might be thought to be characteristic of working-class conditions and under-occupation of those of middle-class people. In fact we found that both situations occurred among the elderly in each class, 20 per cent of the working class compared with 6 per cent of the middle class occupying accommodation too small for their needs, while 35 per cent of the middle class as opposed to 17 per cent of the working class occupied accommodation that was probably larger than they really needed. That under-occupation of this kind should occur amongst the old of whatever class is an inevitable consequence of the decline in their household size as their children marry and move away and of their desire to remain in familiar surroundings. We have seen how the amount of this loss of close association with children is diminished by the continuance and setting up of composite households composed of married children and parents. We have also seen how, in response to their infirmity and widowhood, women are as well provided for in this respect as men in spite of their having fewer available children. Yet the under-occupied dwellings of the old and the 50 per cent who, though having children were not living with them, bear witness to the inevitable movement away from the old by their children in this final phase of their family cycle.

THE OLD AND THE EXTENDED FAMILY

Our discussion of dwelling composition has thrown some light on the extent to which old people in Swansea have 'lost' their children through marriage and the extent to which they share accommodation with them. Thirty-eight per cent of the old have children but do not live with a child. How have the changes which we have described in the functioning of the extended family affected the position of the old. Do children care for their parents in old age? How has the greater dispersion of children affected this care?

Table 8.8 shows the proximity of those not living with a married child or a single child over sixteen to children living away and compares the differing position of the classes in this respect and the Swansea sample to Bethnal Green.

Table 8.8: Proximity of Old People not living with Children to Children Away.

	Middle Class	Working Class	Bethnal Green	Swansea
	%	%	%	%
Nearest child living:				
Same part of Swansea	32	36	69	35
Other part of Swansea	28	44	16	39
Outside the Borough	40	20	15	26
Numbers	47	116	80	163

This comparison is not exact, 'same part of Swansea' being compared with the Bethnal Green category 'within a mile' and we have contrasted 'other parts of Swansea' with the Eastern Boroughs of the Administrative County of London.[15] They do, however, make a rough comparison possible.

Nearly twice as many of those who though they have children do not live with them have children living in the same district in Bethnal Green as in Swansea. Within Swansea itself there is little difference between the classes in the numbers living in the same district but far more middle-class old people have their nearest child living outside the County Borough.[16] We are now in a position to summarize the differences between the classes within Swansea and between Swansea and Bethnal Green. This is done in Table 8.9.

Table 8.9: Residence of Nearest Child of People of Pensionable Age.

| | Swansea | | Total | Bethnal Green |
	Middle Class	Working Class		
% living with any child	39	54	50	52
Nearest child in same district	20	17	18	33
In other district	17	20	19	8
In Region around	5	1	2	3
Elsewhere	19	8	11	4
Total Numbers	78	249	327	167

The same proportion of working-class people in Swansea live with a child as do the people in Bethnal Green. But for both classes in Swansea the proportion with a child in the same district is much lower. The Swansea and Bethnal Green figures are similar only when we consider the proportions living with a child or having a child at least in another district of Swansea or its Bethnal Green equivalent, though even here the middle-class figures show a marked difference from the rest. In other words it is as true of the elderly as of Swansea in general that, compared with Bethnal Green, the elementary families which make up the extended family are far more widely dispersed. This may be seen as the result of the widening geographical range of marriage, difficulties in obtaining houses and the diversification of the extended family in terms of occupation. The table certainly confirms Mr Hughes's observations as to the extent to which the families of the

[15] cf. Townsend, P., op. cit., p. 32.

[16] The difference between the classes is significant at the 5 per cent level.

old are scattered 'all over the place'. There is much less opportunity in Swansea for the sharing of domestic functions between households which the Bethnal Green studies observed in Bethnal Green.

We have seen that the effect of this dispersal on the structure of the extended family was to disturb the balance between the two sides of the family and weight it in favour of the wife's side. From the point of view of elderly people this means that those who still have a child in the same district are more likely to have a daughter living near than a son. If we take all our subjects *who had a child living in the same district*, and exclude those who have no living daughter, we find that in 75 per cent of the cases that child was a daughter. There was no significant difference between the classes here. Nevertheless, of those *who had a living daughter*, approximately 43 per cent in both classes did *not* have a daughter resident within their own district. Even if those without daughters are excluded, therefore, a large minority of elderly people are separated from their nearest daughter by a sufficient distance to make domestic assistance—should it be needed—and frequent informal visiting impossible without a change of residence on the part of either the daughter or the old person.

This separation of the elderly and their daughters cannot but impose a severe strain on those daughters who attempt to care for elderly people over the distances involved. This dispersion of the extended family places the situation of contemporary old people in marked contrast to that of their parents. This is true even for those who have a daughter or son living with or near them. For today the nearest child is often the only child within easy distance of the old person and this means that the burden of care is not distributed among many children and relatives but falls very often upon one child only. Of those who had a daughter in their neighbourhood, 75 per cent in the working class and 90 per cent in the middle class[17] had no other daughter in the same district.

In spite of the wider dispersal of the extended family we found no difference between the proportion of old people in Swansea who had seen a child within the last twenty-four hours and that recorded in Bethnal Green, nor any significant difference in contact between the classes. Three quarters of those in both classes in Swansea who possessed children had seen them within the last twenty-four hours. We have seen that there was little difference in the proportions in both Boroughs living with children, and that the difference in residence lay in the proportions who had a child living in the same district. If we exclude those living with children from the

[17] The difference is not significant.

analysis there is still no significant difference between Swansea and Bethnal Green in the proportions seeing a child within twenty-four hours. In both cases it was approximately 55 per cent. But only 22 per cent in Swansea compared with 38 per cent in Bethnal Green had seen a child within the week. This suggests that where support and care is needed the greater distance separating parents and children in Swansea will be overcome, and that the chief effect of dispersal on *contact* is to reduce the frequency of *occasional* visiting.

The high rate of contact between children and their parents is maintained chiefly by daughters. This is shown by the higher per-percentages of old people living with married daughters as opposed to married sons (27 per cent compared with 11 per cent), having seen them in the last twenty-four hours (57 per cent compared with 42 per cent), and having been visited by a child who had travelled to see them. Ten per cent of those with married daughters, and a fifth of those who had seen a married daughter the previous day, had been visited by a daughter who had travelled to see them. Only 2 per cent of those with married sons had received a similar visit from a son. The amount of travelling to care for an elderly person seems to be directly related to the availability of other relatives. It is highest where the old person has only a married daughter or married son to care for them and lowest where there is an unmarried child available. Where the old person possesses both a married son and a married daughter, travelling to visit on the part of the married son falls away altogether, while it is as high for the married daughter in spite of the availability of the married son as it is in those cases where the old person has only a married daughter to care for them. This shows quite clearly that it is expected that the responsibility for care of elderly parents will fall upon the daughter, but that where this is not possible the function of care is taken over by the son. There are good reasons why this should be so. They concern not merely the fact that the kind of care an elderly person requires is domestic and therefore appropriately provided by women, but the fact that the maintenance of the extended family is based on a reciprocal exchange of domestic services between the households that compose it. This fundamental point was clearly brought out by the Bethnal Green studies and we have emphasized and elaborated it throughout this book. In Swansea as in Bethnal Green these services are largely concerned with the bearing and rearing of children, and the period during which help in raising a family is required by their children extends well into 'pensionable' old age. If we examine the life cycles of elderly people in our sample we find that less than a third of them married their last child before their sixties. The average period of child-bearing of their children is approximately five years and it is reasonable to suppose that help in child-rearing would be welcome for at least five years after the last child is born. It would be fair to say that two-thirds of those in the sample who had children, will not cease to have a grandchild under five years of age until they are well into their seventies. For the vast majority of old people therefore, the period when they are likely to need (in various degrees) support from their children will over-lap with the period when the children will welcome various forms of help from them. There will be a considerable period in fact when reciprocation of services between parents and children will be possible.

There can be little doubt that elderly people in Swansea frequently play an important part in helping to care for their grandchildren. We have already noted that over half of those of our subjects with young children who had recently had a baby-sitter called upon a parent to perform this service. Over half of those elderly people who were living with one of their married children shared the dwelling with young grandchildren. Moreover, if we examine how it came about that old people come to share dwellings with relatives it is apparent that in a large proportion of the cases this form of living arrangement came about to benefit the relatives they lived with rather than the old people themselves. In 49 per cent of the cases the old person shared a dwelling with a child who had continued to live with his or her parents after getting married. And in nearly all these cases the elderly person was not in need of care at the time of the marriage. In 26 per cent of the cases the relative had moved in to live with the elderly person. About a quarter of this group were cases where the arrangement primarily benefited the old person and a further third benefited both parties. The old in households of this type not only provided accom-modation for married daughters and their daughters' husbands, but cared for grandchildren where the children's parents were unable to accommodate them, provided houses for married grandchildren at their marriage as they had done for their parents before them and in a few cases even opened their doors to newly-wed nieces and nephews. In the remaining 25 per cent of the cases, the elderly person had moved *to* the relative. Here in the majority of cases the move primarily benefited the old person. Of all the cases in which an elderly person shared a dwelling, in only one-third had the arrangement come about to benefit the old person *alone*.

Sharing accommodation makes possible the interchange of services with the least difficulty. But we have seen that in over a third of the cases the old person is separated by some distance from their nearest child. It is extremely difficult for old people to help their children when they are widely separated from them and possibly in poor health themselves. The effect of the separation of the homes of elderly people from those of their married children is to make reciprocation of any help they may receive difficult, if not impossible. And this disturbs the *exchange* of services which, except in old age, characterizes the family system.

We have noted that two-thirds of the old are likely to have young grandchildren until well into their seventies. But one-third is not and there can be little doubt that this proportion has increased and will increase with time. For the effect of the falling age at marriage has been to increase the proportion of old people whose period of dependence no longer coincides with the period in which the children need accommodation and domestic help. As a result an increasing number of elderly people are likely to suffer a complete reversal of roles in old age: no longer capable of any useful function, they are, after a life of giving, reduced to an existence in which they can only take. It is not surprising that some have difficulty in adapting to this situation.

THE BURDEN OF OLD AGE

In this chapter we have shown that demographic changes by altering the shape of the life-cycle of the elderly, have increased their need for, and reduced their chances of being able to obtain, effective care from their children. They are less likely to possess a child who will be able to care for them, more likely to have all their children married, more likely to be widowed. We have seen also that the changes in the structure of the extended family, notably its geographical dispersal, have disturbed the smooth interchange of domestic services between parents and children, and concentrated the responsibility for this provision on one child: the nearest daughter. This dispersal of the family group has not prevented the maintenance of high rates of contact between parents and children even where considerable distances within the County Borough are involved. It has meant an increase in the burden of caring for elderly people, and a decline in contact between children and elderly parents who do not need daily support and help.

This 'burden' is largely a domestic one. Yet we have also seen that because of the shorter period of child bearing, education, and increasing opportunities of employment the younger woman of today is less domesticated than she has ever been. Fortunately, in one sense, the period of need of the elderly overlaps the early phases of the life-cycle of their children, making it possible for the elderly woman, at any rate, to 'repay' the care which she receives from a married-daughter in terms of accommodation or help with grand-children. Where there is this happy conjunction of mutual need, the lesser domestication of the younger woman serves, if anything, to strengthen the tie between parent and child rather than weaken it, pro-vided that the old person lives with or near enough to the daughter to be able to reciprocate the help received. Where mother and daughter are separated, however, and this is so it will be recalled in 43 per cent of the cases, the lesser degree of domestication of the daughter will have the opposite effect. The necessity of performing domestic tasks for an elderly person, or even visiting them frequently to 'keep an eye on' them, and see that they are all right, falls heavily upon the daugh-ter who is, or wants to be, back at work, and who has relegated domestic duties to a relatively minor place in her life. The separation from her own parents already increases the burden of raising a family. The need of the elderly parent for care increases it still further.

In situations of this kind, the provision of the day-to-day support and help which would be given almost unconsciously by the married daughters of an elderly person living near by, becomes a duty—an obligation—to be conscientiously performed by the children, and creates a feeling of dependence and, almost, of *imposition* in the old person. Where parents and children live close together, especially if there is more than one child in the vicinity (and it has been shown that this in Swansea today is rarely the case), the amount of support for the old person can grow imperceptibly over time, as their need increases. It need not necessarily involve, on the part of parent or child, any clear realization of its amount or necessity. Where there is a separation, casual 'popping in' and chance meetings give place to planned visits governed by the times of buses, the husband's shift and the time the children come out of school. And it seems to be to the sense of being tiresome intruders in their children's lives rather than an integral part of them that old people referred, when they said, as they often did, 'children don't look after the old people like they used to'.

Mrs Jones, a widow in her seventies from St Thomas, whose husband was a railwayman, has two children both married, one living in Sandfields and the other in Sketty. Her reaction when we asked her to contrast the situation of the old today with that of her own elderly parents was typical:

'Of course children don't look after the old people like they used to do when we were young. Children just don't care any more.

283

When you are old they don't think you are worth bothering about. I mean you can see that with all these Homes, can't you? Children didn't put their parents in Homes in my young days, I can tell you. Myself I think you should keep your respect, keep independent from your children, if possible. Mark you, my two are very good, I will say that. Mary comes around two or three times a week and Dave and his wife come and take me for a run in the car every Saturday which is very nice but I'd rather they didn't. You know what it is: they come round and take me out and then bring me back here at five and then—they're off. Like they were saying "There we are Mam, we've come and given you your little bit of pleasure, now we're going off to have ours!"''

Although Mrs Jones begins by pointing to old people's homes as evidence of neglect by children, it is clear that she herself is not one of those whose children 'just don't care any more' but one whose own sense of grievance lies in the recognition that her contacts with her children do not arise naturally but are a result of a consciously accepted and discharged obligation on their part. That this should be so stems not merely from physical separation of parents and children but from the diversification of the family in terms of class and culture. The old no longer share with their children an involvement in the same community, the same interests, the same acquaintances. Because of the children's mobility in cultural economic and educational terms they have less to give whether of money, advice or understanding of their children's world or problems.

The dispersion and diversification of the extended family and the lesser domestication of women, have made old age a burden in an increasing number of cases, not only to the children upon whom the responsibility of care falls, but also for the old people themselves by depriving them in old age of many of the functions that their parents were able to exercise. Many of them feel themselves to *be* 'a burden'. We asked all our subjects whom they thought should 'be responsible' for caring for old people. *More* old people than their juniors considered that the State as opposed to relatives should be responsible for the old. It is indeed a far cry from the days of Mr Hughes's youth in Morriston to a society where the old wish to be dependent on the State in order to feel more independent of the family. This attitude on the part of the old heavily underlines that, however important may be the greater dispersal of kin and the consequent difficulty in exchanging services between the households of the extended family, there are other and more subtle and equally important differences between the family circumstances of the old today and those of their parents. They arise from the diversification of the family rather than its dispersal. It is the inability of the elderly to share their children's lives rather than their households that leads to the sense of neglect and isolation which many of them possess. Mr Hughes, echoing we believe the opinion of his contemporaries, has the last word. 'There's a different atmosphere now altogether, I can tell you!'

IX

CONCLUSION

THE dominant conclusion that we have reached, after this most instructive exercise in Swansea, is that it is an extremely difficult task to write intelligently about one's own contemporary urban society. It is a good deal easier, as one of us at least knows well, to write about Kathmandu or Calcutta. This is not just a light-hearted comment: there are good reasons for this difficulty.

Not least among them is the fact that the persons one is writing about can themselves read—perhaps a few of them may actually read the book itself (rather than summaries by journalists). And each of them is likely to have formed very decided and personal views about Swansea, about social class and the Welsh, about the chapels, and about the nature and importance of family life in the nineteen-sixties. After all, it is his society that is being examined, his town—and he does *live* there. The accuracy of statement and comment must be tested against his own experience. This thought—of the 'voters' of Swansea looking over our shoulder as we write—can be very off-putting and restricting. It is an experience which the anthropologist writing about Africa or Central Borneo is happily spared. The sociologist of contemporary Western society works in a spotlight of public attention which is the lot of few other academic disciplines. Perhaps this is why some sociological writers occasionally appear to take refuge in a swirling smokescreen of unresolved statistics, or behind an impenetrable blockade of a bizarre and freshly-minted terminology, where they can at least be commended for their scholarship. Another solution to this dilemma is to avoid 'theory' and deal directly with 'urgent social problems' in a popular style, certain that you will be commended for your humanity. We have tried here—and we are aware how unsuccessfully—to find a middle way between these alternatives.

The one essential quality required by those who venture to study

286

their own society is the quality of *detachment*, the ability to stand apart in imagination from the familiar social situations one is recording and thus to perceive the basic and general patterns that underlie the apparently unique and personal behaviour of individuals. But the more familiar the situation, the more one is involved oneself as a member of the society, the more difficult this detachment is. Referring to the approach of the social anthropologist, Nadel wrote: 'The motions of a roundabout are puzzling only until we lift the trap-door and discover a well-known engine driving the thing'.[1] The trouble is that as members of the society we hardly find the motion of the social roundabout puzzling at all: we just take it for granted that things work this way. And if we are persuaded to lift the trapdoor and look at the engine, it appears so well known that it is hard to see it with fresh eyes and describe its parts and inter-connections with such precision that our understanding is increased. Paradoxically perhaps, the more foreign, alien, unusual, the society a sociologist or anthropologist is examining, the easier it is to perceive its essential structures and the easier it is to describe in a meaningful way.

This problem of detachment is not the only difficulty in studying our own society (indeed this problem can be and is overcome to a considerable extent through an emphasis on precise and 'objective' statistical measurements). There is the much more intractable problem of the great range of individual variation in behaviour, particularly within the field of family and kinship behaviour which we have been discussing in this book. The high incidence of individual variation and the constant intervention of the more imponderable factors of personal preferences, personality characteristics, individual selectivity in relationships, increase the difficulties of orderly, precise description. We must emphasize that this high incidence of individual variation in kinship behaviour in urban areas is itself an important and significant conclusion of our study, and of previous studies. While the *elementary* family is a basic structural unit of the society and is thus controlled by a variety of sanctions both legal and diffuse, in relation to the *total* social system the kinship structure and the organization of *extended families* is not of major and critical importance. Kinship is essentially a minor matter in the structure of urban Swansea, if important in the lives of individuals. The basic structural framework of the total society is closely bound up with the economic system, and its spinal cord, as it were, is the nexus: education-professional or vocational training—occupation-employment-income-status-social class. Kinship and the family are

[1] S. F. Nadel: *The Foundations of Social Anthropology*, 1951, p. 199.

'involved' throughout of course, but marginally. The kinship system itself does not bear any great structural 'weight' from the point of view of society as a whole, and this fact itself opens the door to individual variation, individual preference, in this marginal field of behaviour. It is not an area of social life which is governed by strict control, or firm and precise sanctions—as we have seen in our discussion—and this is fundamentally related to its minor importance in the total system.

We have taken eight fairly long chapters to state our conclusions and have produced only a fragment of the data: the remainder must await other occasions—and it would be tedious to gather in this final chapter a sort of anthology of reiterated conclusions collected chapter by chapter. We will content ourselves with a brief summary of the main points of the central argument.

There are six basic points, and they are all related to the recent and rapid acceleration of the social and economic changes that have taken place within the life-times of elderly people still alive in Swansea and which in sum have made the Swansea of the nineteen-sixties such a radically different place from the Victorian or Edwardian Swansea that the old remember with such nostalgia:

(i) The case of the contemporary structure of the Hughes Family Morriston with which we began this study is reasonably typical of present-day extra-familial behaviour and attitudes in the modern urban society of Swansea. We encountered only rare cases of elementary families entirely isolated from kin, though there was vast variation in the type of external contact and in the psychological importance attached to relationships. We emphasize that in order to understand the extended family in a modern urban environment it is essential to see it as an enduring social *entity*—the elementary family writ large—and not as a precisely-defined social group based on proximity of residence or on an arbitrarily-determined high frequency of face-to-face contact. We have described it rather as a variable, amorphous, vague social grouping within which circulate—often over great distances—strong sentiments of belonging, and which is recognizable as a social entity of some significance by the observer, and certainly by the participants. It is clear that the extended family as a whole is more widely dispersed than seems formerly to have been the case. We refer here not to the separation of individual members from the rest of the family by large distances but to the dispersal of the extended family as a whole within the large area of the County Borough. On the one hand this is balanced by a great improvement in communications, especially as a result of increasing car ownership, and on the other by a general *expectation* that greater physical dispersion of this latter type is natural and normal under modern social conditions. The extended family is a resilient institution and is clearly undergoing a basic adjustment in behaviour and attitude to adapt itself to the contemporary situation of increased physical and social mobility. The wider kinship group is not so much decomposed by current social change, but is rather *modified* to produce a looser, more adaptable structure.

(ii) The key relationship within the extended family is that consisting of wife's mother–wife–husband–husband's mother. The familial structure in practice is built around this central balance between the two sides of the family, linked through the marriage to a common set of grandchildren. There is a socially-accepted weighting of this balance in favour of the wife's side of the family, and this is linked with the dominant stress on the roles of women and relationships through women. Too great a disturbance of this balance—to one side or other of the family—can produce severe internal friction and tension. Disturbances of this balance can be caused by physical separation, composite households, status differences between one side or other, personality factors. There is evidence, particularly in the increased formation of composite households immediately after marriage through housing shortages, that recent social change has operated in such a way as to increase the disturbance of this central balance between the two sides of the family. This we believe to have resulted in increased tension and stress in relationships between children and parents and the two sides of their families.

(iii) Extended family cohesion depends on a variety of factors. Cultural and economic homogeneity among the members of separate but related households, encourages this cohesion. Recent social change, particularly in educational opportunity, in industry and employment generally, and in the range of marriage, has undermined familial solidarity. This diversification within the extended family has reduced family cohesion, substituting often a sentimental façade of relationships for the former virile gregariousness and strong common interests. In many extended families nowadays, married brothers and sisters are scattered over separate and disparate neighbourhoods within Swansea, or farther afield, and sharply diversified by occupation (or husband's occupation), income, culture and attitude. They appear to have little in common, besides a vague sense of relationships—and besides their elderly parents.

(iv) The extended family appears to have two main functions, both

289

of considerable social importance. We describe these respectively as those of social identification and social support in need or crisis. While the Welfare State may deal increasingly with major crises arising from the shortages of housing, unemployment, sickness and to a smaller extent, old age, the role of the extended family is still important and often vital. The provision of aid does not depend precisely on proximity of residence—there are many important kinds of aid which can be given over long distances—but it is of course closely related. Aid can take a wide variety of forms but it is connected in the vast majority of cases with domestic affairs of one kind or another—and is thus mainly the province of women. The effectiveness of the extended family as a mechanism of support in need depends to a large extent on the attitudes of women and the willingness of women to accept the burdens involved.

(v) The greater the level of female domesticity, the stronger the cohesion of the extended family and the more effective its function of support for the individuals or elementary families who 'belong'. The decline in family size, the liberation of women from the rack of prolonged child-bearing, the increased life expectancies (particularly for women), better educational and employment opportunities, more convenient homes and more household gadgets, better incomes, shorter working hours for men, holidays with pay, the 'great trans-formation' in the relationships between husbands and their wives—all these factors at least have conspired to produce a profound social revolution in the status and attitudes and interests of women. So far as the effectiveness of the extended family is concerned, it is a change which is only just, 'with the daughters of the revolution', beginning to exert its effects. This change in the position of women has been more sudden and more recent in working-class families than in the middle classes. There is a relationship between the degree of domesticity of women, the nature of the marital relationship, and the shape of the external kinship network. In Bott's terms, the trend of change is always from the compulsive domesticity of women and thus towards 'joint' marital relationships of the partnership or companionship type, and towards 'loose-knit' external familial networks.

(vi) The differences in the organization of the extended family by social class in Swansea, or by the Welsh/non-Welsh distinction, are slight, and only barely discernible. There appears no single item of kinship behaviour which is immediately recognizable as a char-acteristic of one social class rather than another. Indeed the whole trend of change referred to above is in the direction of a *convergence*[2] in behaviour between the social classes. There are of course cultural differences between the classes, and the middle classes by and large are more affluent and their extended families more dispersed physically. It seems, nevertheless, correct to speak of a single pattern of family behaviour—and a single set of attitudes—which is characteristic of modern Swansea as a whole, recognizing as we have insisted throughout that the variation in behaviour in individual cases can be immense.

Such a description of the changing structure of the extended family necessitates a further consideration of some of the wider themes concerning family structure in an urban industrialized society, to which we devoted some space in the first chapter of this book. We noted there that it has been widely assumed in the past either that *in fact* urbanization isolates the elementary family and decomposes the wider kinship group or that disruption and isolation must *necessarily* occur because the extended family system is in fundamental conflict with a modern industrial economy. Those who criticized such assumptions had done so on three main grounds. It had been asserted, first, that in this country at any rate, disruption is currently brought about by rehousing and migration and may therefore be only a temporary phenomena; secondly that the traditional pattern of working-class family life in urban areas is characterised by a clustering of kin and day-to-day sharing of domestic functions by related and neighbouring households; thirdly that a modified form of the extended family can be and is being maintained in the face of physical and social mobility since the functions vital to its maintenance are not inconsistent with the occupational system and can with the aid of improved transport facilities be discharged over greater distances.

We have argued that in Swansea the traditional working-class family structure is currently undergoing a permanent change, both at the level of behaviour and of expectations as to behaviour, and that whether the extended family is thought to be incompatible with a modern industrial economy depends largely on the way 'extended family' is defined. We have endeavoured to show that in Swansea, at any rate, a high degree of industrialization and social mobility, and a wider dispersal of the family has not prevented the maintenance of

---

[2] We thus are very much in support of the view of converging class behaviour expressed by John H. Goldthorpe and David Lockwood in their excellent articles: 'Not so bourgeois after all,' in *New Society*, Vol. 1, No. 3, of 18 October 1962. Our discussion of class in Chapter II was written before their article appeared but it can be seen that we hold similar views.

high levels of contact and the interchange of services between related households. There *is* a kinship grouping, wider than the elementary family, which, though often dispersed, has the same composition as the classical extended family, whether or not it is called, as we have argued that it should be, an 'extended family'.

We began this book with a direct prescription to compare our findings with those of the Bethnal Green studies, and we have at various points made these comparisons. There is no question that basically the patterns of family relationship described by Young and Willmott are similar or identical with those we encountered in Swansea—so much so that it seems broadly correct to speak of a single form of extended family organization which is probably common to all urban areas in modern Britain. But while they seem to have been more concerned with a static description and an emphasis on the supportive functions of the extended family in a web of 'traditional' close-knit, face-to-face, intimate and personal relationships, we have emphasized the change and adjustment in this pattern in response to the needs and challenges of a rapidly changing environment. The extended family in Bethnal Green is itself a modification of the classical extended family in response to an industrial environment. The extended family in Swansea is a further modification of this kinship grouping. It still performs, in spite of its greater dispersion, most of those primarily domestic functions of help in crisis which was characteristic of the extended family found in Bethnal Green, although because of its greater dispersal and diversification it is currently under some stress which affects both its cohesiveness as a social group and its efficacy in discharging those functions customary to it.

In what light may this further modification of the extended family be seen? As a necessary or occasional concomitant of urbanization or industrialization or both? Only when the *precise* relationships between changes in family structure and other changes in the social or economic structure of society are traced will it be possible to arrive at any useful conclusion as to whether the modification of the extended family which we have described will continue and if so how fast it will occur and what the social consequences of such modification will be. It is not possible to embark upon an elaborate and detailed analysis here. It is possible to indicate certain relevant considerations.

The argument that urbanization necessarily isolates the kinship group, if 'urbanization' is taken to mean merely the growth relatively densely populated large settlements, is quite simply disproved by the data from Bethnal Green and by other studies. If on the other hand it is taken to mean the growth of a particular type of social structure, then as Goode has pointed out, '"urbanization" is not the *cause* of changes; it *is* those changes'.[3] For example Louis Wirth in his famous paper 'Urbanism as a way of life'[4] writes that 'since the city does not reproduce itself it must recruit migrants from other cities, the countryside . . .' This means that by definition an urban population must be highly mobile and *therefore* offer little opportunity for the establishment of extended family relationships over a sufficiently small area to make an exchange of, at any rate, domestic services possible. If urbanization is the spread of social relationships and the development of social structures which characterize such a city then urbanization physically isolates the nuclear family and disrupts the exchange of some services *by definition*. Such characterizations as Wirth's have great value as ideal types. They make it impossible, however, to regard urbanization as a cause of the modification of extended family relationships.

The argument that 'modern industrial economy' is in conflict with the extended family is, however, worth more detailed examination. Changes in the industrial structure of Swansea have affected the family in three ways; through their effect on patterns of residence, occupational mobility, and the degree of domestication of women. Industrialization because it usually means (in the long run) a growth in the size of the productive unit involves either the growth of towns, or an increase in travel to work. Developments in the South Wales area in the last twenty years, and elsewhere, have shown that improved communications have made it possible to assemble quite large work forces not drawn from the immediate neighbourhood. Nevertheless the distance people are willing to travel is limited and the establishment of very large new works has in some cases had the effect of increasing the size of neighbouring settlements. If these new settlements reproduce themselves there is no reason why they should be a cause of *continuing* geographical mobility and therefore of extended family dispersal: unless of course the works themselves grow in size or change their location with every generation. Even if they do increase their size this would mean the dispersal of only a proportion of extended families in each generation. Hence whether industrialization or industrial change will affect the extended family in this way will depend on the extent of re-siting of industry and the rate of growth of the size of the work force relative to the

[3] Goode, W. J. The process of role bargaining in the impact of urbanization and industrialisation on family system. *Current Sociology*, XII, iii. 1963–64, p. 3.

[4] Reprinted in Hatt, P. K., and Reiss, A. J.: *Cities and Society*, 1957.

numbers of potential employees in the area within which people are in fact willing to travel to work.

Industrialization and industrial change can, however, affect the dispersal of the extended family in two other ways. First re-location of industry may seriously diminish employment opportunities in the area, leading to a net loss of population by migration. This occurred in Swansea in the nineteen-hundreds and again between the wars. This, however, did not appear to disrupt family structure but merely made the maintenance of contact with one member difficult. Severe loss of population would of course cause severe disruption in the generation in which it occurred. But there is no reason why the families concerned should not in time re-establish extended family networks in the area to which they had gone. Secondly if industrial activity requires a high degree of specialization of work skill, the amount of individual geographical mobility needed to acquire employment and promotion may be very considerable. Such mobility may well affect all members of the family and result in a very wide dispersal indeed, which is likely severely to interfere with its functioning as a group. It would appear that such mobility is responsible for the higher proportion of middle-class people very widely separated from children or parents. However the figures indicate that even here, where such considerations are most relevant, its disruptive effect on the family has not so far been great.

The extent to which it is necessary to move in order to find employment will depend also on the density and distribution of jobs over the area in which the individual considers to be his universe of employment. One of the reasons for the greater dispersal of American families (if they are indeed more dispersed than in the United Kingdom) probably lies in the differences in the population density of the two countries. These points have been made to show that the effect of the industrial institutions on the dispersal of the family is highly complex. It would be fair to say that in industrial societies, as opposed to pre-industrial societies, the family is likely to be more dispersed and subject to periodic disruption resulting from changes in the size and location of industry. But whether that dispersal will be so great as to prevent even the exchange of domestic help between related households, and whether enough families will be affected by it to result in any material modification of family structure, does not seem inferrable from the process of industrialisation itself.

The consideration of the effect of industrialization on the family through the occupational structure is even more difficult to determine largely because the consequences of industrialization upon the occupational structure are not at all clear. There is some evidence that the proportion of white collar to manual occupations is increasing.[5] This may be seen to be due to an increase in the size of work establishments in some industries and to a decline in the demand for unskilled labour due to increasing mechanization and automation of productive processes. These trends, other things being equal, in so far as they are 'built into' the industrialization process are likely to make for increasing and continuing occupational mobility. The fertility figures for Swansea show that a considerable amount of upward mobility is necessary to maintain the existing class structure. Changes in differential fertility could severely diminish the effects of the upwards re-distribution of occupations on occupational mobility, and it is difficult to see how it could be argued that any particular pattern of fertility among the different occupational groups is a necessary concomitant of industrialization. Once again it would be fair to say that in the industrial society there is likely to be more mobility than in the pre-industrial. But how great that mobility will be depends upon a complex of factors and it is the extent of this mobility, rather than its existence, which will determine just how far the functioning of the extended family is thereby affected. We saw in Chapter III (p. 97) that the amount of inter-generational mobility in Swansea across the manual/non-manual boundary was 27 per cent. We believe that because of changes in the industrial structure this proportion will be found to have been higher for the younger members of the population. But even so such levels of mobility have only modified and not destroyed the extended family as a social group. This may very well be a consequence of the difference between the speed of social and occupational mobility which we discussed in Chapter III and which underlay our system of assigning individuals to social classes. The discrepancy between occupational achievement and social acceptance by another social group, by slowing down the rate of social mobility of individuals, enables the extended family to accommodate large changes in occupational status on the parts of its members because the consequent changes in *social* status are much smaller. In the majority of cases they were sufficient to lead to a reduction of contact and general loosening of the family structure but not great enough to disrupt it. At the same time in some cases the necessity of maintaining some family ties because of the functions the family still performs, may well be a factor in slowing down social, as opposed to occupational mobility. On the other hand, as we pointed out in Chapter II some people may take advantage of the necessity for

[5] See for example Bendix and Lipset: *Social Mobility in Industrial Society*, 1959, for figures illustrating the growth of the rates of white collar to manual worker in manufacturing industries in the first half of this century.

residential mobility to achieve cultural and social mobility in advance of occupational achievement.

Changes in the level of female domestication are not in our view inferrable from the process of industrialization itself. True, industrialization is likely to lead to higher real incomes and, at certain stages in economic growth, to labour shortages which will encourage female employment. Where female employment and high real incomes coincide, mechanization of household tasks and the consequent decline in female domesticity is likely to occur. There is no reason to suppose that this coincidence will *necessarily* take place and even where it does its effect on the domesticity of women may be modified by cultural factors, in particular attitudes to family limitation, and it would be a brave man who would assert that there is any simple relationship between real income and family size. It does not seem therefore that any of the factors which have been effective in producing the modification of the extended family which we have described in Swansea, though operative in industrial societies, will necessarily be of an extent likely to produce further modifications. In other words we do not see any reason to suppose that the high degree of face-to-face contact between members and the exchange of domestic assistance between households which have characterized the extended family in the past will necessarily disappear. Whether or not they will continue to be characteristic of the extended family will depend on the particular combination of factors affecting the family in a particular society. Even where it is not possible for high rates of contact and the exchange of domestic services to be maintained, the material from Swansea suggests that the extended family, however loose its structure, is still likely to show a considerable vitality. This will be so because, as we have tried to show, domestic functions are not the only functions that the extended family performs, though in Swansea, as in Bethnal Green, they predominate.

When we come to consider how likely it is that families *in general* will cease to provide domestic help and assistance for their members we must take into consideration the extent to which it is probable that the domestic functions of the extended family will be undertaken by other institutions. It does not seem possible to us that social services are capable of or suited to the provision of informal domestic help and support at time of crisis for the majority of families. It must be stressed that we refer here not to the exceptional 'crisis' situation but to occasions such as childbirth and rearing, illness and old age which are common to *all* families. This is partly because the scale of organization of such support would be vast and costly; but we believe 'social' provision to be inappropriate for another reason. The importance of family help in time of crisis does not lie only in its ability to provide purely material services. It lies rather in its ability to provide support for its members at times of difficulty and this support is effective because of the strong emotional ties between members. This is an extremely obvious point but one which cannot be sufficiently stressed. It was well recognized by our informants. The provision of this type of care, which might be described as 'affective', is likely to continue to be of importance whatever changes may occur in the domestication of women.

The inability of other institutions to provide care in crisis situations may within certain limits set a term to the extent to which individuals are willing to accept wide separation from other members of the family, and the deprivation of help and support which this entails. This is particularly so in the early part of the family cycle. The provision of *ef*fective care is dependent not only on the degree of female domestication but upon proximity of residence. The provision of *af*fective care is dependent on social and cultural proximity. Mobility, cultural social and geographical, can therefore determine the extent of its provision. It is possible that the existence of the extended family may well serve to limit the mobility of individuals in the early part of their lives. The need for care in old age occurs, however, at a time when the likelihood of the children having been affected by mobility of all kinds is very much greater. On average the child is in the late thirties or early forties when the parent attains the age of seventy. By then the extent of the child's mobility may be sufficiently great to make the provision of both effective and affective care more difficult. We have stressed that the extent to which old people are separated from their children is small and that this is so largely because of the temporal overlap of the periods of need on the part of parents and child. Yet very low ages of marriage could result in a separation of these periods of need, and allow time for the separation of parent and child between the cessation of help by the parent and the parent's need of help from the child. This might result in a fragmentation of the extended family within the developmental cycle of each family group.

It would be rash to suggest therefore that the extended family will undergo no further modification. But this modification is more likely to come about through changes in demographic patterns—not determined by industrial and economic factors—working in conjunction with increases in mobility of all kinds (itself the result of economic and industrial changes), than as a result of economic and industrial change *alone*. While modification of extended family structure is unquestionably associated with economic factors it is by no means clear that they will necessarily operate in an industrial society to an extent and in such combination both with each other and with demographic and cultural factors, as to lead to the *decomposition* of the wider kinship group. Nor do we see any reason to suppose that this is currently happening in Swansea.

If it is not possible to make statements of wide generality about the changes which necessarily occur in the extended family in an industrial society it is equally difficult to make predictions as to the changes it is likely to undergo in our own society, since these will depend on the extent of changes in economic and demographic factors which are extremely difficult to determine. The general considerations which we have already discussed make it seem unlikely, that, in the next quarter of a century or so, though the number of dispersed extended families in Swansea may increase, the extent of their dispersal will itself widen sufficiently to make *impossible* the high levels of contact, and the exchange of domestic services which now exist. A word of warning is none the less appropriate here.

One way in which severe disruption of the extended family can be caused is through the intervention on the part of 'planners' in the processes of adjustment and adaptation to change. This was a consideration the authors of the Bethnal Green studies had very much in mind. They advocate the planned reconstruction of Bethnal Green so as to conserve and encourage the cultural strengths which they perceive embedded in the stable and tenacious family organization of the traditional working classes of the East End. This seems to us a sentimental view of the family. 'Coronation Street' could doubtless be anywhere in Britain, and we can enjoy its documentary realism and accuracy—and admire the cultural virtues of this reality—without failing to recognize its anachronistic flavour in the nineteen-sixties and that the trends of social change are strongly against this traditional close-knit neighbourhood pattern and its related family structure. To expect 'the planners' to hold back the tide of social and economic change (though of course we can expect them to be more humane than they are) is to attempt to hold back the sea by royal decree. Yet, however optimistic one may be about the continued vitality of the extended family, however sanguine about its adaptability, planning policy still has the power to disrupt it by separating related households by impossible distances and preventing its reemergence as a functioning group by taking no account of family circumstances in allocating housing. We have no criticism of the Swansea Local Authority on this particular score, but wish none the less to echo the authors of the Bethnal Green studies in warning that the effect of planning policy on the extended family can be ignored only at our social peril. But we do not argue that planners should deliberately attempt to preserve the traditional working-class community. The cohesive society was stable and enduring and 'people knew where they were', but it seems also to have been the stagnant society. It is simply out of date, for all its old-fashioned cultural virtues—and our informants in Swansea, even though the old characteristically looked back with pride and nostalgia, were certainly not slow to recognize this basic fact.

Yet it must be recognized that the transition from the 'cohesive' to the mobile society has been achieved at a cost which can be gauged more precisely than can the loss of 'atmosphere' and the sense of belonging. With the coming of the Welfare State, the family has been relieved of a great part of the economic burden imposed by the need of its members in times of crisis. But that the present social services can provide other forms of non-specialized care for those in need as adequately as they do, is a measure of the extent to which that care is provided in the majority of cases by the family. As the new modified form of extended family becomes more widespread, its ability to ful-fil the functions of non-specialized care will become increasingly impaired and the demands made upon the social services are likely to increase. Is it possible for social policy to facilitate the support of the extended family for those of its members in need? Or must we resign ourselves to an even vaster expansion of the preventive and non-specialized social services than is already required?

We have noted that if the dispersal of the extended family within Swansea has had little effect on frequencies of visiting, at any rate between parents and married children, this is due to good internal communications and the increase in car ownership. 'Good' is, how-ever, a relative term. Modern bus services are 'good' in the sense that they make possible high rates of contact between the members of a dispersed extended family that would have been impossible fifty years ago. This is not to say that they leave nothing to be desired. The topography of the Borough has been responsible for the growth of mainly radial roads and bus services. The growth of new estates on the periphery has meant that a need has grown up for new roads and services linking these estates to each other rather than with the centre of the town, and these have not yet been provided. The pro-vision of a more adequate road network and more versatile and cheaper—if necessary subsidised—bus services would be a vital aid to the continued successful functioning of the extended family in its more dispersed form. Equally, reduced telephone rentals and charges would be of considerable importance in popularizing the use of this means of communication which at the present is remarkably unpopular in Swansea (only 15 per cent of our subjects possessed telephones) largely because the majority found them too expensive. There seems good reason to regard communications as social services which can play an important role in maintaining the extended family in its dispersed form.

There is one way in which 'social policy' in Swansea is already working so as to assist the maintenance of relationships between the households that compose the extended family. The policy of the local housing authority of not allocating corporation houses on the basis of a points system, but, with a few exceptions, providing housing according to the length of time the applicant has been on the waiting list, has the effect of forcing many young married couples to live with their parents for the first years of their married lives. This of course facilitates the provision of care by the mother for the married daughter, and emphasizes the stress on this particular tie characteristic of the society. It does, however, mean that, for a large part of the period in which the size of the elementary family is at its maximum, accommodation must be shared and that, soon after adequate accommodation is provided, the size of the household declines rendering the house bigger than is required. This policy therefore seems undesirable for at least two reasons: it prevents the provision of housing at the time of the families greatest need, and it may cause wastage of scarce accommodation at a later stage in the family cycle, though in a minority of cases it makes possible the sharing of the dwelling with elderly parents because they happen to need assistance when the space becomes available. To reverse this policy and give priority to parents with young children would, however, separate mother and daughter during or just after the birth of the children and thus render a continued exchange of services more difficult. The choices that housing authorities must make in cases of this kind are extremely difficult. It is probable that there is no general policy answer to problems of this kind. On balance we would suggest that priority should be given to parents with young children, that they should be able to refuse offers of accommodation without prejudice to their future chances and that a social worker should discuss the problem with each family as their turn for housing came up. It was our experience that people accustomed to the support and help a closely-knit extended family can give were sometimes unaware of the importance and extent of that help and consequently found it difficult to make any real choices between alternatives offered to them. Whether a family is happier in a new council house separated from relatives and friends or in uncomfortable and crowded conditions surrounded by friends and relations will depend very largely on the family concerned. The most important point is that families should be given, if humanly possible, the chance to choose between alternatives which are real and meaningful to them and which they *understand*.

Though an intelligent sympathetic and *informed* social policy can do much to assist the extended family to adapt to the new social circumstances in which it finds itself, we believe it must be recognized that, in our society, the modified form of the extended family which is characteristic of Swansea has come to stay, as a result of the demands made upon it largely by economic institutions. It is likely that, as time goes on, more and more of families in Swansea and in other urban areas in Britain will come to exhibit this modified structure, and this will involve the reduction of their effectiveness in providing various types of domestic care for their members. It is as well to recognize now, while the full effects of this modification have still to be felt, the lower level of performance which the extended family is likely to exhibit as a direct consequence of economic changes which are so often applauded on other grounds. It is easy to forget, as we move forward into the seventies, and indeed into the rest of the century, that modernization involves a cost which is social as well as economic. If our society wishes to obtain the material benefits which modernization makes possible, then it must be willing to recognize the effect that such modernization will have upon the family and try to make some provision for the needs thereby created. It is not enough to wait until such time as the need is acute and then indulge in jeremiads about the decline of family responsibility.

We have said that in Swansea, the wide open spaces on the hills to the west enabled what amounted to a new town to be built alongside the ruins and dilapidations of the old valley communities of the industrial valley on the east. Equally a new and more modern society is emerging rapidly out of the abandoned background of an older social tradition. The facts seem to point to the emergence of a modified form of extended family, more widely dispersed, more loosely-knit in contact, with the women involved less sharply segregated in role and less compulsively 'domesticated', and with much lower levels of familial solidarity and a greater internal heterogeneity than was formerly the case in the traditional 'Bethnal Green' pattern. It is a form of family structure in which expectations about roles and attitudes are radically altered—and, in particular, in which physical and social mobility are accepted. It is the form of extended family which is adjusted to the needs of the mobile society.

There is bound to be stress in such a profound change, particularly for the old, but it is not possible to set the clock back by artificial planning techniques. It is a long journey culturally from Landore or Bonymaen or St Thomas to the new estates at Penlan or West Cross or Sketty Park—and the move can be a painful process for the first generation. But their children will not want to go back.

Appendix I

LIST OF REFERENCES

ANDERSON, N., *The Urban Community: a World Perspective*. Routledge and Kegan Paul, 1960.

ARGYLE, M., *Religious Behaviour*. Routledge and Kegan Paul, 1958.

BENDIX, R. and LIPSET, S. M., *Social Mobility in Industrial Society*. Heinemann, 1959.

BELL, N. W. and VOGEL, E. F., *Toward a Framework for Functional Analysis of Family Behaviour, in* BELL, N. W. and VOGEL, E. F. [Eds.], *A Modern Introduction to the Family*. Routledge and Kegan Paul, 1960.

BENEDICT, R., *The Family: Genus Americanum, in* ANSHEN, R. N. [Ed.], *The Family, its Function and Destiny*. 2nd Edition. Harper, 1959.

BOHANNAN, P. J., *Justice and Judgement among the Tiv*. O.U.P., 1955.

BOSSARD, J. H. S., *The Large Family System*. University of Pennsylvania Press, 1956.

BOTT, E., *Family and Social Network*. Tavistock Publications, 1957.

BRENNAN, T., COONEY, E. W. and POLLINS, H., *Social Change in South West Wales*. Watts, 1954.

CARLSSON, G., *Social Mobility and Social Structure*. Lund, 1958.

COUNTY BOROUGH OF SWANSEA, *Development Plan*. 1955.

DONNISON, D. V., COCKBURN, C. and CORLETT, T., *Housing since the Rent Act*. Occasional papers in social administration, *No.* 3.

FIRTH, R. [Ed.], *Two Studies of Kinship in London*. London School of Economics, Monographs on Social Anthropology, 1956.

GLASS, R. [Ed.], *The Social Background of a Plan. A Study of Middlesborough*. Association for Planning and Regional Reconstruction, 1948.

HATT, P. K. and REISS, A. J. *Cities and Society*. Free Pree, 1957.

JACKSON, B. and MARSDEN, D., *Education and the Working Class*. Routledge and Kegan Paul, 1962.

JENKINS, D., *Aberporth in* DAVIES, E. and REES, A. D. [Eds.], *Welsh Rural Communities*. University of Wales Press, 1960.

JENNINGS, H., *Societies in the Making*. Routledge and Kegan Paul, 1962.

LEWIS, J. P., *Population. in* THOMAS, B. [Ed.], *The Welsh Economy: Studies in Expansion*. University of Wales Press, 1962.

LINTON, R., *The Natural History of the Family. in* ANSHEN, R. N. [Ed.], *The Family its Function and Destiny*. 2nd edition. Harper, 1959.

MARRIS, P., *Widows and their Families*. Routledge and Kegan Paul, 1958.

MCGREGOR, O. R. and ROWNTREE, G., *The Family*. in WELFORD, A. T. and ARGYLE, M. *et al. Society: Problems and Methods of Study*. Routledge and Kegan Paul, 1962.

MEAD, M., *The Contemporary American Family as an Anthropologist sees it*. in STEIN, H. D. and CLOWARD, R. A. [Eds.], *Social Perspectives in Behaviour*. Free Press, 1958.

MINCHINTON, W. E., *The British Tinplate Industry*. Oxford, 1957.

MYRDAL, A. and KLEIN, V., *Women's Two Roles*. Routledge and Kegan Paul, 1956.

NADEL, S. F., *A Black Byzantium*. O.U.P. for the International African Institute 1942.

NADEL, S. F., *The Foundations of Social Anthropology*. Cohen & West, 1951.

NOTES AND QUERIES IN SOCIAL ANTHROPOLOGY. 6th edition, Routledge and Kegan Paul, 1951.

NUFFIELD FOUNDATION, *Old People*. 1947.

ORWELL, G., *The Road to Wigan Pier*. Penguin Edition, 1962.

PARSONS, P. L., *The Health of Swansea's Old Folk*. Unpublished M.D. thesis. University of Wales, 1962.

PARSONS, T., *The Social Structure of the Family*. in ANSHEN, R. N. [Ed.], *The Family: its Function and Destiny*. 2nd edition. Harper, 1959.

REES, A. D., *Life in a Welsh Countryside*. University of Wales Press, 1950.

RICE, M. S., *Working Class Wives*. Harmondsworth, 1939.

ROYAL COMMISSION ON POPULATION, Cmd 7695, H.M.S.O., 1949.

THOMAS, B. [Ed.], *Wales and the Atlantic Economy*. in THOMAS, B. [Ed.], *The Welsh Economy; Studies in Expansion*. University of Wales Press, 1962.

TITMUS, R. M., *Essays on the Welfare State*. George Allen and Unwin, 1958.

TOWNSEND, P., *The Family Life of Old People*. Routledge and Kegan Paul, 1957.

WILLIAMS, D. T., *The Economic Development of Swansea and of the Swansea District*. Swansea University College, 1940.

WILLIAMS, R., *The Long Revolution*. Chatto and Windus, 1961.

WILLIAMS, W. M., *The Sociology of an English Village: Gosforth*. Routledge and Kegan Paul, 1956.
    Ashworthy: Family, Kinship and Land. Dartington Hall Studies in Rural Sociology. Routledge and Kegan Paul.

WILLMOTT, P. and YOUNG, M., *Family and Class in a London Suburb*. Routledge and Kegan Paul, 1960.

YOUNG, M. and WILLMOTT, P., *Family and Kinship in East London*. Routledge and Kegan Paul, 1957.

List of References

REFERENCES TO PERIODICALS

ABEL SMITH, B. and PINKER, R., 'Changes in the Use of Institutions in England and Wales between 1911 and 1951'. *Manchester Statistical Society Transactions*, 1959–60.

ABRAMS, M., 'Social Trends in Electoral Behaviour'. *Socialist Commentary. May* 1962.

BLAU, P. M., 'Social Mobility and interpersonal relations'. *American Sociological Review. XXI No.* 3, 1956.

FALLDING, H., 'The Family and the Idea of a Cardinal Role'. *Human Relations*, Vol. 14, No. 4, 1961.

FIRTH, R., 'Family and Kin Ties in Britain and their Social Implications'. Introduction. *British Journal of Sociology*, XII, No. 4, 1961.

GOLDTHORPE, J. H. and LOCKWOOD, D., 'Not so Bourgeoise after all'. *New Society*, October 18th, 1962.

GOODE, W. J., The 'Process of role bargaining', *Current Sociology*, XII No. 3, 1963–4.

HALL, J. and CARADOG JONES, D., 'The Social Grading of Occupations'. *British Journal of Sociology*, I No. 1, 1950.

HOGGART, R., 'The Challenge of the Working Class Scholar'. *The Observer*, February 11th, 1962.

HUMPHRYS, G., 'The Economic Importance of Commuters to their Area of Residence'. *Journal of Town Planning Institute*. March 1962.

LANCASTER, L., 'Kinship in Anglo-Saxon Society'. *British Journal of Sociology*. IX, Nos. 3 & 4, 1958.
 'Some Conceptual Problems in the Study of Family and Kin Ties in the British Isles', *British Journal of Sociology*. XII No. 4, 1961.

LASLETT, P., 'The Solid Middle Class', 'The Social Revolution of our Time', *The Listener*. January 4th and 11th 1962.

LITWAK, E., 'Occupational Mobility and Extended Family Cohesion', 'Geographic Mobility and Extended Family Cohesion', *American Sociological Review*, XXV Nos. 1 & 3 1960.

LOUDON, J. B., 'Kinship and Crisis in South Wales', *British Journal of Sociology*, XII No. 4 1961.

MINCHINTON, W. E., '"New" South Wales', *The National Provincial Bank Review*. No. 54. May 1961.

PARSONS, T., 'The Kinship System of the Contemporary United States', *American Anthropologist*, 1943.

ROSSER, C. and HARRIS, C. C., 'Relationships through Marriage in a Welsh Urban Area', *Sociological Review*, IX No. 3 1961.

ROWNTREE, G., 'New Facts on Teenage Marriage', *New Society*, October 4th 1962.

THOMAS, J. M., 'Eight Hundred Years a Town', *Picture Press, The Journal of the Pressed Steel Company Limited*. I No. 2, 1962.

TYLER, F., 'The Moment of Farewell', *South Wales Evening Post*, April, 1961.

Appendix II

THE INTERVIEWING SCHEDULE

UNIVERSITY COLLEGE OF SWANSEA
DEPARTMENT OF SOCIAL SCIENCE

COUNTY BOROUGH OF SWANSEA · SURVEY OF FAMILY COMPOSITION

INTRODUCTION

I come from a social research section at the University College of Swansea. We are doing a survey of family life in Swansea, and will be visiting some 2,000 households to ask some questions about housing and about how far away people live from their relatives. These households have been chosen quite at random from the List of Voters, and your name has come up. Would you please help us by answering a few questions —it won't take long ? We hope to write a book about Swansea, but of course anything you tell us will be absolutely confidential because no names will be published or used in any way whatsoever.

1	2	3	4	5	6	7		

Appendix II

TABLE I—First of all, can you tell me who lives in your household?

No.	RELATIONSHIP TO SUBJECT	FIRST NAME	SEX M. F. 9	AGE	Same Household as Subject Yes No	MARITAL STATUS M. S. W. D. Sep. 10	WORKING Full Part Not	OCCUPATION (at 60 if retired; husband's occupation for married and widowed women) 11	WELSH SPEAKING Fluent Part Not 12
1	SUBJECT		A B		A B	1 2 3 4 5	6 7 8		A B O
2			A B		A B	1 2 3 4 5	6 7 7		A B O
3			A B		A B	1 2 3 4 5	6 7 8		A B O
4			A B		A B	1 2 3 4 5	6 7 8		A B O
5			A B		A B	1 2 3 4 5	6 7 8		A B O
6			A B		A B	1 2 3 4 5	6 7 8		A B O
7			A B		A B	1 2 3 4 5	6 7 8		A B O
8			A B		A B	1 2 3 4 5	6 7 8		A B O,
9			A B		A B	1 2 3 4 5	6 7 8		A B O
10			A B		A B	1 2 3 4 5	6 7 8		A B O
11			A B		A B	1 2 3 4 5	6 7 8		A B O
12			A B		A B	1 2 3 4 5	6 7 8		A B O

CHECK : Boarders ? So there are .... of you living here altogether?

8

Housewife is (Give No.) ....
Household Head is (Give No.) ....

IF SUBJECT IS WORKING FULL OR PART TIME

2. Can you tell me where you work?

   Same part of Borough ... 1
   Other part of Borough ... 2
   Outside Borough up to 12 miles ... 3
   Outside Borough more than 12 miles ... 4

   (Write In Reply) ....

3. Do you normally work shifts?   Yes 5   No 6

   Does your Spouse work shifts?   Yes 7   No 8

   [12]

4. Are there any other households in this dwelling?   Yes 1   No 2

   IF YES,
   Are any of the people related to you or to your Spouse?   Yes 3   No 4

   IF YES, Who are they?   (Record in Table 1)

   [13]

5. Do you (or any other member of your household) OWN this house/flat?   Yes 5   No 6

   IF NO, Who is it owned by?   Corporation 7
   Relative living away 8
   Other landlord 9

   [13]

6. IF RENTED, who holds the tenancy?   Subject A   (Give relationship
                                          Spouse B   to Subject)

   Other relative in household   O

   Other relative not in household   1

   Other   2

   IF SUBJECT or SPOUSE or OTHER RELATIVE, was the previous tenant related to you?   Yes 3   No 4

   IF YES, Who was it?   (Give relationship to Subject)   No (First tenancy) 5

   Did you take over the tenancy when they died?   Yes 6   No 7

   IF NO, did a relative help you in any way to obtain this tenancy?   Yes 8   No 9

   IF YES, Which relative was this?   (Give relationship)

   [14]

7. How long have you lived at this address?

   Since birth   1

   More than 20 years   2

   Between 10 and 20 years   3

   Between 5 and 10 years   4

   Under 5 years   5

   IF NOT BORN HERE
   Where did you live just before your move here?

   Same part of Swansea   6

   Another part of Swansea   7

   In region around   8

   Elsewhere   9

   Did you already have relatives living in this part of Swansea?   Yes 7   No 8

   [15]

8. Where were you brought up ? (i.e., where was your home mainly during your school days?)

This part of Swansea 0

Elsewhere in Swansea 1

In region around 2

Elsewhere in Wales 3

Elsewhere 4 .... [16]

9. Where have you spent most of your life?

This part of Swansea 5

Elsewhere in Swansea 6

In region around 7

Elsewhere in Wales 8

Elsewhere 9 .... [16]

10. Have you ever had living with you any child under 15 **other than your own** for a year or more?

Yes 1

No 2

IF YES, who was it?

Brother's child 3

Sister's child 4

Daughter's child 5

Son's child 6

Other relative's child 7

Foster child 8

Other 9 .... [17]

11. Have you ever acted as a god-parent to any child other than your own?

Yes 1

No 2

IF YES, who was it?

Brother's child 3

Sister's child 4

Daughter's child 5

Son's child 6

Other relative's child 7

Friend's child 8 .... [18]

12. Can I ask at what age you finished full-time education?

14 or under A

15 B

16 or more O

Did you go to a College or University?

Yes 1

No 2

IF YES, which?

During your school-days from 5 onwards, did your parents send you at any time to a private fee-paying school?

Yes 5

No 6

If you have any children (or if you had any) do you think that they should be taught Welsh in School?

Yes 7

No 8

Don't know 9 .... [19]

13. May I ask you about religion ? Which denomination do you belong to?

(*Write In*) ....

IF MARRIED, what denomination does your spouse belong to?

(*Write In*) ....

IF WITH CHILDREN, what denomination did your children belong to when young?

(*Write In*) .... [20]

14. Do you ever go to Church or Chapel?

Yes A

No B

IF YES, do you still attend the same place of worship that you went to before you were 15?

Yes 0

No 1

How often do you go to any place of worship?

More than once a week 2

Once a week 3

Once a month 4

Only special occasions 5

When did you last go?

Within last week 6

Week to month ago 7

Month to 6 months ago 8

More than 6 months ago 9 [21]

The Interviewing Schedule

OMIT QUESTIONS 15-20 INCLUSIVE IF SUBJECT IS SINGLE

May we ask you some questions about marriage and children? We are trying to find out whether there is a tendency nowadays for married children and relatives by marriage to be much more scattered than they used to be?

Yes A   22
No B

15. Could I ask you first of all whether you have been married more than once? Would you please give me some brief details?

MARRIAGE	DATE	YOUR AGE AT THE TIME (22)	YOUR HOME DISTRICT BEFORE MARRIAGE (Write in)	SPOUSE'S HOME BEFORE MARRIAGE (23)				Write in actual Reply	HOME IMMEDIATELY AFTER MARRIAGE				WHERE WAS THIS HOME?					MARRIAGE ENDED?		
				Same District as you	Other part of Swansea	Region around	Elsewhere		With husband's parents	With wife's parents	With other relatives	On Your own	In husband's home district	In wife's home district	In Other part of Swansea	Other district both	Elsewhere (specify) (24)	Continues	Death of partner	Divorce
FIRST				1	2	3	4		5	6	7	8	1	2	3	4	5	6	7	8
SECOND				1	2	3	4		5	6	7	8	1	2	3	4	5	6	7	8
THIRD				1	2	3	4		5	6	7	8	1	2	3	4	5	6	7	8
FOURTH				1	2	3	4		5	6	7	8	1	2	3	4	5	6	7	8

Taking your **first** marriage only, where were you married?

Church   1
Chapel   2
Registry Office   3

25

IF MARRIED IN CHURCH OR CHAPEL,

Was this particular **place** of worship :

One to which you **both** belonged at the time of the marriage   4
One to which **wife only** belonged at the time of the marriage   5
One to which **husband only** belonged at the time of the marriage   6
One to which **neither** belonged at the time of the marriage   7

313

OMIT IF SINGLE

TABLE 16—Have you any CHILDREN alive who don't live at this address? Yes [26] 1 No 2

How many? ....

SEX M. F.	FIRST NAME	AGE	MARITAL STATUS M. S. W. D.	Children under 15 Yes No	RESIDENCE This part of Swansea	Other part of Swansea	Region around	Else-where (specify)	Write In Reply	WHEN LAST SEEN 24 hrs.	24 hrs. to wk.	Wk. to mth.	Mth. to yr.	Yr. +	WHERE LAST SEEN This home	Child's home	Other relative's home	Else where home	OCCUPATION
3 4			1 2 3 4	1 2	5	6	7	8	[26]	1	2	3	4	5	6	7	8	9	
3 4			1 2 3 4	1 2	5	6	7	8		1	2	3	4	5	6	7	8	9	
3 4			1 2 3 4	1 2	5	6	7	8		1	2	3	4	5	6	7	8	9	
3 4			1 2 3 4	1 2	5	6	7	8		1	2	3	4	5	6	7	8	9	
3 4			1 2 3 4	1 2	5	6	7	8		1	2	3	4	5	6	7	8	9	
3 4			1 2 3 4	1 2	5	6	7	8		1	2	3	4	5	6	7	8	9	
3 4			1 2 3 4	1 2	5	6	7	8		1	2	3	4	5	6	7	8	9	
3 4			1 2 3 4	1 2	5	6	7	8		1	2	3	4	5	6	7	8	9	
3 4			1 2 3 4	1 2	5	6	7	8		1	2	3	4	5	6	7	8	9	
3 4			1 2 3 4	1 2	5	6	7	8		1	2	3	4	5	6	7	8	9	
3 4			1 2 3 4	1 2	5	6	7	8		1	2	3	4	5	6	7	8	9	

(Question boxes: [26] RESIDENCE, [27] WHEN LAST SEEN)

So altogether you have (add in children from Table 1) .... children living now? [28]

314

The Interviewing Schedule

17. Have you had any children that died?   Yes 1   IF YES, how many?............ So you had............children born alive altogether?
   No 2

18. Have you any grandchildren?   Yes 3   IF YES, how many?............
   No 4

| 29 | 30 | 31 |

TABLE 19—May I ask about your in-laws? First, your spouse's parents. (ASK ONLY ABOUT THOSE NOT LIVING IN SAME HOUSE AS SUBJECT)

ONLY IF ALIVE

	A L I V E D	AGE	RESIDENCE					HOW LIVING					WHEN LAST SEEN				WHERE LAST SEEN			OCCUPATION
			This part of Swansea	Other part of Swansea	Region around	Else- where or overseas	Write in Actual Reply	Alone	Alone with spouse	With unmar. child	With married child	In Other or hosp.	24 hrs.	24 hrs. to wk.	Wk. to mth.	Mth. to yr.	Yr. +	Your home	Their home	Spouse's Parents' home	Other
			33					34					35				36			37
SPOUSE'S FATHER	A –	32	1	2	3	4		0	1	2	3	4 A	0	1	2	3	4	1	2	3	
SPOUSE'S MOTHER	B –		5	6	7	8		5	6	7	8	9 B	5	6	7	8	9	4	5	6	

TABLE 20—Now your spouse's brothers and sisters. (ONLY THOSE NOT IN SAME HOUSE AS SUBJECT)

FIRST NAME	SEX M. F.	AGE	RESIDENCE					MARITAL STATUS M. S. W. D.				HOW LIVING		WHEN LAST SEEN				WHERE LAST SEEN			OCCUPATION
			This part of Swansea	Other part of Swansea	Region around	Else- where or overseas	Write in Actual Reply					With one or both parents	Sep. from parents	24 hrs.	Wk. to wk.	Mth. to mth.	Yr. to yr. +	Your home	Their home	Spouse's Parents' home Other	
			38											39							
	1 2		3	4	5	6		1	2	3	4	A	B	1	2	3	4	5	6	7	8 9
	1 2		3	4	5	6		1	2	3	4	A	B	1	2	3	4	5	6	7	8 9
	1 2		3	4	5	6		1	2	3	4	A	B	1	2	3	4	5	6	7	8 9
	1 2		3	4	5	6		1	2	3	4	A	B	1	2	3	4	5	6	7	8 9
	1 2		3	4	5	6		1	2	3	4	A	B	1	2	3	4	5	6	7	8 9
	1 2		3	4	5	6		1	2	3	4	A	B	1	2	3	4	5	6	7	8 9
	1 2		3	4	5	6		1	2	3	4	A	B	1	2	3	4	5	6	7	8 9

TABLE 21—Now i would like to ask you about your own parents and grandparents. (ONLY THOSE NOT LIVING IN SAME HOUSE AS SUBJECT)

	ALIVE / DEAD	AGE (40)	RESIDENCE (41)				HOW LIVING (42)					WHEN LAST SEEN (43)					WHERE LAST SEEN (44)				OCCUPATION (45)	WELSH SPEAKING (46)		
			This part of Swansea	Other part of Region Swansea	Elsewhere and where	Write In Reply	Alone Spouse	Alone with unmar. child	With mar. child	With home	In Other home or hosp.	24 hrs	24 to wk.	Wk. to mth.	Mth. to yr.	Yr. +	Your home	Your Parents' home	Other relatives' home	Other home		Yes	Part	No
FATHER	A –	40	1	2	3	4	0	1	2	3	4 A	0	1	2	3	4	1	2	3	4	45	1	2	3
	B –		5	6	7	8	5	6	7	8	9 B	5	6	7	8	9	5	6	7	8		4	5	6
MOTHER	A –		1	2	3	4	0	1	2	3	4 A	0	1	2	3	4	1	2	3	4		1	2	3
	B –		5	6	7	8	5	6	7	8	9 B	5	6	7	8	9	5	6	7	8		4	5	6
FATHER'S FATHER	A B		1	2	3	4	5	6	7	8	9 0	1	2	3	4	5	6	7	8	9		1	2	3
FATHER'S MOTHER	A B		1	2	3	4	5	6	7	8	9 0	1	2	3	4	5	6	7	8	9		1	2	3
MOTHER'S FATHER	A B		1	2	3	4	5	6	7	8	9 0	1	2	3	4	5	6	7	8	9		1	2	3
MOTHER'S MOTHER	A B		1	2	3	4	5	6	7	8	9 0	1	2	3	4	5	6	7	8	9		1	2	3

21a. Could you tell me what religious denomination your parents belong to (or belonged to, if not now alive)? Mother ....
Father ....   } Write In

Comparing your own religious denomination now with that of your parents, Is it :   the same as both   2
same as father only   3
same as mother only   4
different from both   5

Do (or did) either of your parents belong to a **Welsh-speaking** Church or Chapel?   Yes   6
No   7

IF YES, are you still a member of a **Welsh-speaking** Church or Chapel?   Yes   8
No   9

47

TABLE 22—Can you tell me about your brothers and sisters who are alive now? (ONLY THOSE NOT LIVING IN SAME HOUSE AS SUBJECT)

SEX M. F.	FIRST NAME	AGE	MARITAL STATUS M. S. W. D.	RESIDENCE This part of Swansea / Other part of Swansea / Region around / Else where	Write in Reply	WHEN LAST SEEN 24 hrs / 24 hrs to wk. / Wk. to mth. / Mth. to yr. / Yr. +	WHERE LAST SEEN Your home / Bro. sister's home / At your parents' home / Other relatives' home / Other home	OCCUPATION
1 2			1 2 3 4	3 4 5 6 (48)		0 1 2 3 4 (49)	5 6 7 8 9	
1 2			1 2 3 4	3 4 5 6		0 1 2 3 4	5 6 7 8 9	
1 2			1 2 3 4	3 4 5 6		0 1 2 3 4	5 6 7 8 9	
1 2			1 2 3 4	3 4 5 6		0 1 2 3 4	5 6 7 8 9	
1 2			1 2 3 4	3 4 5 6		0 1 2 3 4	5 6 7 8 9	
1 2			1 2 3 4	3 4 5 6		0 1 2 3 4	5 6 7 8 9	
1 2			1 2 3 4	3 4 5 6		0 1 2 3 4	5 6 7 8 9	
1 2			1 2 3 4	3 4 5 6		0 1 2 3 4	5 6 7 8 9	
1 2			1 2 3 4	3 4 5 6		0 1 2 3 4	5 6 7 8 9	
1 2			1 2 3 4	3 4 5 6		0 1 2 3 4	5 6 7 8 9	

So you have .... brothers and .... sisters alive at present? Including any that may have died, how many brothers and sisters did you have altogether? ....

50

317

TABLE 23—We would now like to ask you some questions about your Uncles and Aunts (if any) who are alive now, and not in your household.

(a) FATHER'S Brothers and Sisters

SEX M. F.	AGE	MARITAL STATUS M. S. W. D.	RESIDENCE This part of Swansea / Other part Swansea / Region around / Elsewhere where	Write in Reply	WHEN LAST SEEN 24 hrs. / 24 hrs to wk. / Wk to mth. / Mth to yr. / Yr. +	WHERE LAST SEEN Your home home / Your Their home home / Your Parent's home / Other relations home / Other	OCCUPATION	Do you have fairly regular contact with this relative Yes / No
A B		6 7 8 9	1 2 3 4 **51**		5 6 7 8 9 **51**	1 2 3 4 5		6 7
A B		6 7 8 9	1 2 3 4		5 6 7 8 9	1 2 3 4 5		6 7
A B		6 7 8 9	1 2 3 4		5 6 7 8 9	1 2 3 4 5		6 7
A B		6 7 8 9	1 2 3 4		5 6 7 8 9	1 2 3 4 5		6 7
A B		6 7 8 9	1 2 3 4		5 6 7 8 9	1 2 3 4 5		6 7
A B		6 7 8 9	1 2 3 4		5 6 7 8 9	1 2 3 4 5		6 7
A B		6 7 8 9	1 2 3 4		5 6 7 8 9	1 2 3 4 5		6 7
A B		6 7 8 9	1 2 3 4		5 6 7 8 9	1 2 3 4 5		6 7

(b) MOTHER'S Brothers and Sisters

SEX M. F.	AGE	MARITAL STATUS M. S. W. D.	RESIDENCE This part of Swansea / Other part Swansea / Region around / Elsewhere where	Write in Reply	WHEN LAST SEEN 24 hrs. / 24 hrs to wk. / Wk to mth. / Mth to yr. / Yr. +	WHERE LAST SEEN Your home home / Your Their home home / Your Parent's home / Other relations home / Other	OCCUPATION	Do you have fairly regular contact with this relative Yes / No
A B		6 7 8 9	1 2 3 4 **52**		5 6 7 8 9 **52**	1 2 3 4 5		6 7
A B		6 7 8 9	1 2 3 4		5 6 7 8 9	1 2 3 4 5		6 7
A B		6 7 8 9	1 2 3 4		5 6 7 8 9	1 2 3 4 5		6 7
A B		6 7 8 9	1 2 3 4		5 6 7 8 9	1 2 3 4 5		6 7
A B		6 7 8 9	1 2 3 4		5 6 7 8 9	1 2 3 4 5		6 7
A B		6 7 8 9	1 2 3 4		5 6 7 8 9	1 2 3 4 5		6 7
A B		6 7 8 9	1 2 3 4		5 6 7 8 9	1 2 3 4 5		6 7
A B		6 7 8 9	1 2 3 4		5 6 7 8 9	1 2 3 4 5		6 7

318

TABLE 24—We have asked you a lot of questions about relatives. Are there any other relatives (cousins for example) we haven't mentioned so far whom you have had contact with **at least twice** in the last three months?

RELATIONSHIP TO SUBJECT	SEX M. F.	AGE	MARITAL STATUS M. S. W. D.	RESIDENCE This part of Swansea / Other part of Swansea / Region around / Elsewhere where	Write in Reply	WHEN LAST CONTACTED 24 hrs. / 24 hrs. to wk. / Wk. to mth. / mth. +	WHERE LAST SEEN Your home home / Their home home / Your parents' home / Other relatives' home / Other	IF NOT SEEN What other contact specify	OCCUPATION If married or widowed	Do you have fairly regular contact with this relative Yes No
53	1 2		1 2 3 4	1 2 3 4		1 2 3 4	1 2 3 4 5			1 2
	1 2		1 2 3 4	1 2 3 4		1 2 3 4	1 2 3 4 5			1 2
	1 2		1 2 3 4	1 2 3 4		1 2 3 4	1 2 3 4 5			1 2
	1 2		1 2 3 4	1 2 3 4		1 2 3 4	1 2 3 4 5			1 2
	1 2		1 2 3 4	1 2 3 4		1 2 3 4	1 2 3 4 5			1 2
	1 2		1 2 3 4	1 2 3 4		1 2 3 4	1 2 3 4 5			1 2
	1 2		1 2 3 4	1 2 3 4		1 2 3 4	1 2 3 4 5			1 2
	1 2		1 2 3 4	1 2 3 4		1 2 3 4	1 2 3 4 5			1 2
	1 2		1 2 3 4	1 2 3 4		1 2 3 4	1 2 3 4 5			1 2
	1 2		1 2 3 4	1 2 3 4		1 2 3 4	1 2 3 4 5			1 2
	1 2		1 2 3 4	1 2 3 4		1 2 3 4	1 2 3 4 5			1 2
	1 2		1 2 3 4	1 2 3 4		1 2 3 4	1 2 3 4 5			1 2
	1 2		1 2 3 4	1 2 3 4		1 2 3 4	1 2 3 4 5			1 2
	1 2		1 2 3 4	1 2 3 4		1 2 3 4	1 2 3 4 5			1 2
	1 2		1 2 3 4	1 2 3 4		1 2 3 4	1 2 3 4 5			1 2
	1 2		1 2 3 4	1 2 3 4		1 2 3 4	1 2 3 4 5			1 2
	1 2		1 2 3 4	1 2 3 4		1 2 3 4	1 2 3 4 5			1 2

25. Of all your relatives who do not live at this address, which particular one do you see most often?

(*Write in Relationship*)

 ──────────── [54]

How often do you see this particular relative?

    Daily   A
    Weekly   B
    Monthly   O
    Yearly   I   [55]

26. When was the last time any friend or neighbour visited you in this house?

    Last 24 hrs.   2
    24 hrs.–Week   3
    Week–Month   4
    Month–Year   5
    Year +   6
    Never   7   [55]

27. Supposing you could move easily from here, would you like to move away from this part of Swansea?

        Yes   A
        No   B

IF YES, what part of Swansea would you most like to live in?

(*Write in reply*) ──────────── [56]

28. IF MARRIED, do you and your spouse ever entertain friends/neighbours **together** in this home?

        Yes   I
        No   2   [57]

IF YES, when was the last occasion?

    Past week   3
    Week–Month ago   4
    Month–6 mths. ago   5
    More than 6 mths. ago 6

29. Have you been away from home for a holiday or visit in the past 12 months?

        Yes   A
        No   –   [58]

IF YES, did you stay with relatives?

        Yes   B
        No   O

Do relatives regularly come to stay with you for holidays?

        Yes   I
        No   2

30. Where did you have tea on Christmas Day last year?

    This home   3
    Own parents' home   4   [58]
    Spouse's parents' home 5
    Married daughter's home 6
    Married son's home   7
    Other relative's home   8
    Other   9

31. Would you approve of public houses in Wales being opened on Sunday?

        Yes   A
        No   B   [59]
        Don't know O

32. May I ask you this? If you were asked what social class you belonged to, what would you say?

    (*Write in*) ────────────

FOR THOSE WITH CHILDREN UNDER 15 AT HOME

33. Does anyone (other than spouse) ever mind the children for you while you go out?

        Yes   A
        No   B   [60]

IF YES, when was the last occasion?

    Past week   0
    Week–2 weeks   I
    2 weeks–month   2
    More than month 3

Who actually minded the child/children on this occasion?

    Husband's parent 4
    Wife's parent   5
    Other relative   6
    Neighbour   7
    Other   8

Does this particular person normally live in your household?

        Yes   –
        No   9

320

34. Are you a member of any social club or organisation **in this particular district**?

Yes 1   **[61]**
No 2

IF YES, when did you last go to a meeting?

Past week 3
Week-month 4
Month + 5
Never 6

Does your spouse also belong to this Club (or to at least one of these Clubs)?

Yes 7
No 8

35. Including organisations both in this district and elsewhere, do you belong to any of the following?

Choir or operatic society A   **[62]**
Church or chapel guild B
Social club or ex-Services Association 0
Sports club 1
Drama club 2
Evening Classes 3
Local branch of Political party 4

36. Can I just ask you a question about football? Do you (or does your husband) follow Rugby or Soccer?

Rugby 5   **[62]**
Soccer 6
Both 7
Neither 8

37. Does your household have a

    Television? Telephone? Car? Piano?   **[63]**
Yes   1   3   5   7
No   2   4   6   8

38. Do you think that nowadays relatives do as much for each other as they used to in the past?

Yes A   **[64]**
No B
Don't know 0

39. Who do you consider should be **mainly** responsible for caring for elderly persons who are unable to look after themselves?

Relatives 1
The State 2
Neighbours 3
Don't know 4

40. Which of the following statements is nearest to your opinion of the people around here? (I mean, of course, **speaking generally**)

I don't notice them very much 5
They are very easy to get on with 6
They are inclined to be difficult to get on with 7
Can't say 8
Refuse 9

41. All these questions are completely confidential of course, and no names will be used at all. With this in mind, would you answer a final and very general question about your/your husband's earnings?

(IF RETIRED, please give weekly earnings **before** retirement)

Under —6 per week A   **[65]**
£6— £8 a week B
£8—£10 a week 0
£10—£15 a week 1
£15—£20 a week 2
£20—£25 a week 3
£25—£30 a week 4
Over £30 a week 5
Refuse 6
Don't know 7

THANK YOU. I hope that I have not taken up too much of your time. We are most grateful for your help with this particular study.

(HAND INFORMANT LETTER OF THANKS)

321

Page 13

TO BE COMPLETED BY INTERVIEWER

Subject's Name ....

Address ....

....

Interviewer's Name ....

Date of Interview ....

Day of Week ....

Time ....

Subject was alone   a

Spouse present   b

Children present   c

Other adults present   d

Type of **Dwelling**

Block of Flats	0
Small Terraced House	1
Large Terraced House	2
Semi-detached House	3
Detached	4
Apartment over Shop	5
Caravan	6
Other	7
Bungalow	8
Pre-fab.	9

Comments on Interview :

....

....

....

....

....

....

....

....

....

....

....

Appendix III

THE REPRESENTATIVENESS OF
THE SAMPLE

METHOD OF SURVEY

THE statistical data presented in this study was derived from a 2 per cent random sample of the population of the County Borough of Swansea drawn in the Spring of 1960. The sampling frame used was the Electoral Register for the Borough, the qualification date for inclusion being November of the previous year. This register includes in theory all residents entitled to vote that is those aged 20·5 years at the qualifying date. The survey was conducted over a period of six weeks commencing during the last week in April. At the time of survey therefore the Register was between five and six months out of date. An investigation into the changes in the completeness of the Electoral Register with time by Gray and Corlett[1] has shown that 3·6 per cent of the population were not registered at the qualifying date and that a further eight months after that date a further 4·2 per cent had moved from the address under which they were registered, a loss of just over $\frac{1}{2}$ per cent per month. Hence it was reasonable to assume that in Swansea at the time of survey successful contact could be made with respondents representing only between 93$\frac{1}{2}$ per cent and 92$\frac{1}{2}$ per cent of the population. Gray found that of the age, sex and income-group distributions only the age distribution of the registrants differed significantly from the non registrants, the latter having a higher percentage under 30. The difference in the age distributions between the registrants was, however, small and amounted to only ·7 per cent. Eight months after the qualifying date the under-representation of the age group 20–30 had increased to 1·8 per cent. It was reasonable to suppose therefore that the Swansea sample would be under-represented in the same way by slightly less than 1·8 per cent.

---

[1] Gray, P. G., Corlett, T. and Frankland, P., 'The Register of Electors as a Sampling Frame', Central Office of Information, November 1960.

Y   323

Table I: Initial Response Rate

	No.	%
Sample drawn	2,272	100
Contacted but refused	169	8
Contacted and schedule completed	1,876	82
Not contacted (moved)	132	6
Not contacted (dead)	42	2
Not contacted—no information	54	2

Table I sets out the response rate of the Swansea survey. It will be seen that the loss through removals was much higher than anticipated. Because we were anxious to diminish this loss and that occurring through death, substitutes were taken where possible, the following procedure being adopted.

1. *Movers.* No attempt was made to follow movers. It was assumed that the person that would have been interviewed, had the electoral register been up to date, would have been one of the present occupants of the dwelling or part of the dwelling in which the original subject had lived. The interviewer obtained a list of the present occupants of the dwelling and by the use of random numbers determined which was to be taken as a substitute.
2. *Deceased Persons.* These were replaced by the ninth name after that of the deceased on the electoral register.

Some of the substitutes were themselves not contacted or refused. Table II shows these figures and the final response figures for the final sample.

Table II: Final Response Rate

	Sample before substitution	Substitutes for movers	Substitutes for dead	Final Sample	%
Completed	1,876	60	26	1,962	87
Refused	168	25	2	195	8
Non contact	—	47	14	61	2
Non contact less those substituted for	54	—	—	54	3
Total	—	132	42		
				2,272	100
Total sample before substitution	2,098	—	—		

Tabulations were made for the substitutes and other respondents and no significant difference found between the two groups. Table III compares the response rate for Swansea and Bethnal Green. While

Table III

	Swansea		Bethnal Green	
Sample size	2,272	100	1,096	100
No. completed	1,962	86	933	85
Non-contacts	115	5	109	10
Refusals	195	9	54	5
Sampling interval	1:50		1:36	
Sample as % of electoral population	1·7%		1·6%	

the response rate was similar for both areas the number of non-contacts is lower for Swansea than Bethnal Green because of the attempt in Swansea to reduce this figure by substitution. The higher refusal rate in Swansea was due to the existence of middle-class areas in Swansea where the rate of refusal was sometimes very high reaching 18 per cent in Ffynone Ward. This might have affected the representativeness of the sample. That it did not do so can be seen from the table in the next section. Although it is not possible to know *who* refused, our interviewers were asked to obtain as much information about them as possible. From their notes it seems likely that it was working-class people in middle-class areas who were responsible for the high refusal rate there, and that the effect of this was cancelled out by the low refusal rate of working-class people in working-class areas. Fforestfach Ward for example had a refusal rate of only 3·9 per cent.

THE REPRESENTATIVENESS OF THE SAMPLE

In order to ensure that it was not skewed the sample was compared with data from the census. This was not a very satisfactory procedure with regard to occupational class since at the time of writing the occupation tables of the 1961 census were regrettably still unavailable. These comparisons are set out below.

The major discrepancy shown here lies in the under-representation of the Swansea sample in the 20–29 group equivalent when both sexes are taken together, to 4·2 per cent. A deficiency of approximately 1·8 per cent was expected. A further loss was, however, sustained by reason of the fact that six months after the compilation of the register it contained the names of no one under 21. This accounts for a further 1 per cent loss, leaving a discrepancy of 1·4 per cent. Moreover, the register does not include people in institutions and common lodging houses nor were these included by Gray in his investigation. A considerable proportion of populations of these places is likely to be in this age group. These

Appendix III

Table IV: Age – Sex distribution

	Survey		Census 1961	
	Men %	Women %	Men %	Women %
20–29	11·9	14·8	18·8	16·4
30–39	20·5	19·0	21·0	18·2
40–49	22·1	20·2	20·2	19·2
50–59	21·6	18·0	19·2	18·8
60–69	14·7	15·7	13·0	15·2
70–79	7·8	8·8	6·3	9·1
80–89	1·3	3·2	1·5	2·9
90 +	·1	·3	·09	·2
% of Men and Women	49	51	48	52

factors also partly explain the under-representation of those in occupational Class V shown in the next table.

Table V: Occupational Class

Registrar-General's Occupational Class	Survey	Census 1951
I	5·2	3·0
II	15·8	12·4
III	52·8	50·4
IV	13·2	13·0
V	12·3	21·2
Not known	·7	—

It is also likely that there was a slight exaggeration of occupational status by our informants [especially by women of their husbands' job]. There is in any case a long-term trend away from unskilled to skilled and semi-skilled employment which has undoubtedly reduced the proportion in Class V between the date of the census and that of the survey.

It should be borne in mind therefore throughout that the sample is slightly under represented in the 20–30 age group and possibly Occupational Class V, but is in all other respects representative of the adult population of Swansea.

Statistical Significance

All statistical differences *referred to in the text* are significant at the 1 per cent level except where otherwise stated in the text or footnotes.

326

INDEX OF SUBJECTS

Three indexes have been compiled: subjects, authors, place-names. Where the place-name is used to refer to a particular study it is not included in the index of place-names but in the index of subjects.

INDEX OF AUTHORS

334

Index of Authors

Reiss, A. J.—293
Rice, M. S.—3.
Rivers, W. H. R.—199
Rowntree, G.—183, 241
Royal Commission on Population
—172, 176–8, 180

Shils, E.—25
Smith, R.—35
Stein, H. D.—20

Thomas, Brinley—50, 130, 144
Thomas, Dylan—40, 85, 125
Thomas, J. M. Mansel—45, 48
Thomas, Wynford Vaughan—81, 117
Titmus, R. M.—25, 32, 172, 176–7, 182–3, 186
Townsend, P.—25, 29–30, 38, 264, 275, 278

Tyler, F.—144–5

Vogel, E. F.—29, 32

Warner, Lloyd—261
Welford, A. T.—183
Williams, D. T.—44–5
Williams, R.—23, 88
Williams, W. M.—197, 200
Willmott, P.—19, 25–6, 29, 37, 60–1, 81, 90–2, 96, 148, 164, 183–4, 189, 205, 211–12, 220, 227, 233, 238, 258, 264, 292
Wirth, L.—293

Young, M.—19, 25–6, 29, 37, 60–1, 81, 90–2, 96, 148, 164, 183–4, 189, 205, 211–12, 220, 227, 233, 238, 258, 264, 292

INDEX OF PLACE NAMES

336